The Disadvantaged Consumer

The Disadvantaged Consumer

Alan R. Andreasen

Foreword by
Mary Gardiner Jones

THE FREE PRESS
A Division of Macmillan Publishing Co., Inc.
NEW YORK
Collier Macmillan Publishers
LONDON

The Free Press
A Division of Macmillan Publishing Co., Inc.
866 Third Avenue, New York, N.Y. 10022

Collier Macmillan Canada, Ltd.

Library of Congress Catalog Card Number: 75-2805

Printed in the United States of America

printing number

1 2 3 4 5 6 7 8 9 10

Library of Congress Cataloging in Publication Data

Andreasen, Alan R
The disadvantaged consumer.

Includes bibliographical references and index.
1. Poor as consumers--United States. 2. Negroes as consumers. 3. Consumer protection--United States. I. Title.
HC110.C6A74 381'.3 75-2805
ISBN 0-02-900690-2

To Margaret and Maia

Contents

List of Tables

Foreword

THE TRAGEDY of the poor and the disadvantaged is that theirs is a true culture of poverty which constantly reinforces itself and makes escape for each succeeding generation more difficult. As neighborhoods deteriorate, education and jobs—the means traditionally observed by Americans as their keys to freedom and uplift—also deteriorate. As money incomes decline, the economy of the neighborhood plummets. Landlords do not or cannot make necessary repairs. Shopkeepers either leave or stay to try to make ends meet by raising their prices and making sales at any cost by fair, but more often by unfair and illegal, means.

Frauds and deceptions—which can be said to be present in varying degrees in all marketplaces—become tragic instances of deprivation and genuine financial and psychological injury when practiced against the disadvantaged and poor who have no other defenses or escape.

Alan Andreasen's book presents a rare and much needed documentation of the systematic nature of the discrimination which confronts the disadvantaged consumer in our society and which renders, from the outset, any piecemeal solution to these problems almost doomed to failure. His book is timely. If the 1970s and 1980s are to witness—as I believe they will—a genuine institutionalization of the goals of the consumer movement in the decision-making processes of both government and business, then it is vitally important that this institutionalization be total and not simply a response to the needs of only one segment of that consuming public.

The Consumer Movement, with all of its supporters and promoters in the halls of the legislatures, in the public interest bar, and in a host of consumer groups and organizations, has for the most part been largely ineffective in taking up the special consumer problems of the poor and disadvantaged. The comprehensive nature of the problems of the poor and the disadvantaged, encompassing as they do every facet of their lives from inadequate housing and ineffective educational facilities to deteriorating neighborhoods and a job market almost entirely out of their reach, make their consumer problems essentially unresponsive to the typical ad hoc remedial type program which the consumer movement has thus far authored. The consumer movement has been highly effective in creating a heightened awareness on the part of the business community of the needs and concerns of the typical consumer in the marketplace. It has produced what I believe is a real shift in the reciprocal obligations of merchants to consumers, in the ethic of product safety, and in the concepts of responsibility for product misuse and product defects. Unfortunately, these important gains have had very little effect on the consumer problems of the poor. Their problems are much more fundamental and go to their very real inability to participate in the marketplace on any terms which are even roughly comparable to those enjoyed by their more affluent compatriots.

Law enforcement officers and regulatory agencies charged with promoting competition and eliminating dishonesty and unfairness in the marketplace are almost as helpless as the victims to take effective steps in the typical ghetto marketplace. Allocating scarce resources to what must essentially be finger-in-the-dike operations when proceeding against ghetto frauds is all too frequently regarded as throwing good money after bad with little hope of tangible effect. The typical cost/benefit approach to resource allocation in the law enforcement field will cause ghetto frauds to come out at the bottom of the list of priorities. Why? Because on any scale of priorities based on the size of the transactions, the number of persons affected, and the size and importance of the defrauding seller, proceedings against national sellers with their vulnerability to public opinion, high visibility to other sellers, and sheer volume of sales will always place these sellers' illegalities much higher on the priority list than the typical ghetto merchant who is not deterred by possible adverse public opinion, nor by what happens to his neighbors down the street, nor even in many instances by the prospect of a cease-and-desist order against him.

Some gap between rich and poor will always exist to some extent in society. But the United States has always prided itself on its melting pot abilities, on the flexibility of its class structures, and on the upward mobility opportunities for all citizens in its society. Although these goals have always been more often honored in the breach, nevertheless they remain important ideals to which we must constantly aspire. In the present period of what I believe is truly dynamic and genuine change being effected in relationships between consumer and business interests and in the responsibilities and accountabilities of government for the impact of their decision on the consumer interest, it would be tragic if in making these changes we ignored once again the poor and the disadvantaged in our country.

Alan Andreasen's book offers us one last opportunity to understand the needs of this important segment of our population whose voices are too little heard in the halls of legislatures, or in the meeting rooms of government and business officials purporting to act in their interests. He points to the solutions which he believes offer some promise of making the American marketplace accomplishments open to the disadvantaged as well as to the affluent. I hope—as he does—that his book will be read by consumer activists, by businessmen, by government officials, and by all individuals concerned to redress the injustices, inadequacies, and failures of our society which still fall too heavily on too large a number of our citizens.

MARY GARDINER JONES

Preface

THIS IS A BOOK about a complex public policy issue, having two major components. First, is there a distinct group of consumers who because of their low and unstable incomes, their minority racial status, their difficulties with the language, or their old age achieve significantly less value for their consumption dollars in the domestic marketplace than does the rest of society? Second, if such a group exists, can anything be done about its market disadvantage? Beginning with David Caplovitz's pioneering study *The Poor Pay More*, published over 10 years ago, there has been a substantial and accelerating outpouring of research and rhetoric tending to support the proposition that there is indeed a group in society that we shall call the disadvantaged consumers. These materials, however, are complex, contradictory, at times incomplete, and extensive. Although several important books and survey articles have appeared in the last five years attempting to pull parts of the material together, there has not heretofore been an attempt to assemble these in their totality and put them into a perspective that would be useful for the determination of public policy. This book is such an attempt.

Objectives

The basic objectives of the volume, then, are to try to understand the consumer problems of the disadvantaged, in particular those who are poor and black, and to understand what is being done and what can be done about these problems. In the main, the approach will tend to be scholarly. I shall attempt to rely on documented evidence whenever it is available about how poor and black consumers cope with the marketplace. However, when the data are weak or absent, reasoned speculations will be offered as to what seems to be the true state of affairs.

As first of all a piece of scholarly reportage, the book carries this traditional caveat: while I have tried to be thorough, my personal idiosyncracies and the exigencies of dealing with a fast-moving field have undoubtedly left gaps. And the reader is forewarned that because the subject in many of its key areas has attracted only a limited number of able scholars, there will be times when we must rely on the work of only a few.

The book, however, is also intended to be more than merely a reporting of what others (and I myself) have said about disadvantaged consumers. It also represents an attempt to integrate the material into a conceptual framework that both organizes the evidence and points to its logical consequences. Thus while the book is directed in the first instance to an academic audience, it is perhaps not overreaching to suggest that it is a book for activists as well as marketing scholars, for the disadvantaged themselves and for those who simply wish to learn something about them, e.g., businessmen, social workers, government functionaries, and government critics. It is not claimed that it is a definitive work, only that it gives some shape to the diverse information (and lack of it) existing in diverse sources in marketing and related journals, in press releases and newspaper accounts, in conference proceedings and in my own and others' personal experiences. It is, I hope, a work that will spur others to reflection, research, and, most importantly, direct action on what is one of the most serious and perplexing socioeconomic problems of the mid-twentieth century.

Acknowledgments

Many friends and colleagues have encouraged me in the present undertaking and over the years have contributed significantly to the development of my thoughts on this complex subject. A particular debt of gratitude is owed to Marcus Alexis, Perry Bliss, David Caplovitz, Naylor Fitzhugh, Marjorie Girth, George Haines, Mary Gardiner Jones, Leonard Simon, Thaddeus Spratlen, and Frederick D. Sturdivant. Students of mine at both the State University of New York at Buffalo and UCLA provided useful comments about earlier versions of my materials. Detailed and extremely helpful reviews of specific chapters were provided by Marjorie Girth, Mary Gardiner Jones, and Thad Spratlen. Fred Sturdivant reviewed the entire manuscript and offered his usual extensive and penetrating commentary. As is conventional, the aforementioned are absolved of responsibility for errors of omission or commission committed here.

Mrs. Nancy Pilon typed the manuscript, and my secretary, Sharon Murawski, assisted in various critical details of final preparation.

Finally, I must express my deepest appreciation to my wife, Margaret, who has put up with my absences, disappointments, and frustrations in this task for too long a period. Truly, without her love and forebearance this book would never have been written.

ALAN R. ANDREASEN

The Disadvantaged Consumer

1. Consumerism and the Disadvantaged

It is ironic that just as the American economy passes the trillion-dollar level and as median family incomes cross the $10,000 mark, the nation faces the most virulent outbreak of consumer dissatisfaction since the Depression years. By objective standards, ours *ought* to be an age of well-satisfied consumers. The American marketing system is presumed to have delivered to Americans the highest standard of living in the world.[1] It is a system that is more progressive, is more efficient, and offers more diverse choice than any other system devised anywhere, anytime. It has contributed immeasurably to the phenomenal growth in the average American household's material well-being through the 1960s and into the 1970s.

Yet, in what seems like a perverse rejection of the system that produced such affluence, a rapidly growing number of consumers are suddenly realizing they have been lulled into a false sense of security. They have come to see that while the system may indeed be huge and efficient, it is certainly not *just*, either in its treatment of most consumers or in the distribution of its vaunted fruits across all segments of the consuming population. As Magnuson and Carper have noted:

> . . . the consumer . . . would be shocked and surprised if he knew how inadequately protected he is, how lax we have been in guaranteeing fair play and justice between buyer and seller. . . . [Our] total approach to consumer problems [has] not been modernized to cope with the recent explosion in consumer buying and credit and the changing conditions in technology and marketing. Most regrettably, that ruthless medieval philosophy "caveat emptor" is in some instances still too much with us.[2]

Partly as a result of the efforts of Senator Magnuson, Ralph Nader, and a growing phalanx of consumer crusaders, consumers are now indeed "shocked and surprised" and, more importantly, are finding strong voices and virulent actions to bring about a basic realignment of power in the marketplace.

This growing struggle of a significant number of consumers outraged with the quality of the marketing system and its practices has come to be known as "the consumerism movement." [3] The movement has hit particularly hard at the distributive justice of the marketing system and thus, in one sense, has provided the stimulus for this book, a systematic analysis of the extreme plight of America's most seriously disadvantaged consumers.

Consumerism: A Historical Perspective

As Hermann and Nadel have shown,[4] consumerism is not a new phenomenon; some form of consumer movement has been with us periodically since 1891. Indeed, the present wave of interest in consumerism is the third in contemporary history. The first took place at the turn of the century. Public concern with the competitive practices of the corporate monopolies and with food and drug safety was nurtured in the growth of a popular political movement, Progressivism, and spurred on by the personal activism of Dr. Harvey Wiley and by Upton Sinclair's vivid description of unsanitary practices in the meat-packing industry in *The Jungle*. This concern led to the founding of the first national consumer's organization and to the passage of the first laws primarily designed for the protection of consumers.[5] In 1898 the National Consumers League was formed; in 1906 both the Federal Food and Drug Act and the Meat Inspection Act were passed; and in 1914 the Clayton Antitrust Act and the Federal Trade Commission (FTC) Act became law.[6] While imperfect instruments often doing more to protect businessmen than consumers, these organizations and laws set the precedent both for consumer self-help and for government regulation of business in the consumer interest.

The second wave of consumerism took place in the late 1920s and early 1930s and was significantly influenced by the Depression and the rise of the New Deal. There was growing public awareness of the failures of the Clayton Act to protect consumers from predatory corporate pricing practices and of the FTC and Food and Drug Acts to protect them from a broad range of corporate deception. This awareness, coupled with a Depression-based need to maximize value for shrinking spending power, led to (1) formation in 1928 of the first consumer product testing organization, (2) the founding of Consumers Union in 1935, (3) a strengthening of the FTC Act in 1938 by the passage of the Wheeler–Lea amendment, and (4) passage of a stronger Pure Food and Drug Act in 1938. The period also saw the establishment of the first consumer councils in government bureaucracies. Again a major figure, Rexford Tugwell, was prominent in securing these advances as was a "shocking" book, Kallent and Schlink's *100,000,000 Guinea Pigs*.[7]

During these first two waves consumer issues constituted one set among many associated with two major political movements, Progressivism and the New Deal. This is partly because consumerism is what Nadel calls "a diffuse issue of low salience." [8] In the first half of the twentieth century it was not a central concern of consumers and only became prominent in the sweep of *other* political-historical events. Because of its secondary status, consumerism died each time a world war brought about a decline in the political movements that supported it.[9]

The present wave of consumerism has its roots in the late 1950s in the perceptive and inflammatory writings of Vance Packard[10] and in the investigations of pricing and product safety in the drug industry by Estes Kefauver's Senate Subcommittee on Antitrust and Monopoly begun in 1957. Mark Nadel argues, however, that the real takeoff point for the movement's present rapid growth came in 1965 and 1966 with the auto safety hearings from which Ralph Nader emerged as a national figure and from which developed the National Motor Vehicle and Safety Act of 1966, the first of many recent pieces of consumer legislation.[11]

As Nadel notes, the current wave has a number of parallels with earlier waves:

LINKAGE TO A POLITICAL MOVEMENT

Nadel argues that support of consumer issues by the Johnson administration in 1964 and 1965 follows from its search for a set of dramatic, broadly based issues to follow on the heels of the "war on poverty" thrusts of 1963 and 1964. Consumerism was particularly appropriate because it would likely involve relatively *low-cost* legislative and administrative initiatives, a strategy which Johnson needed to balance the high costs of his two wars, poverty and Vietnam. (Although President Kennedy was responsible for the first Presidential consumer message sent to Congress in 1962, he adopted a relatively low profile on consumer issues.)

PRESENCE OF MAJOR SCANDALS

The Thalidomide scare (i.e., the realization that except for the persistent efforts of Dr. Frances Kelsey, a medical officer in the Food and Drug Administration, the fetus-deforming drug would have been sold in the U.S. in addition to Germany, where most of the deformities appeared) and General Motors' personal harassment of Ralph Nader brought wide public attention to the whole field of consumerism and to Nader as its principal spokesman.

INTERVENTION OF MAJOR PERSONALITIES

Nadel credits Ralph Nader and Betty Furness with major roles in promoting the present wave of consumerism. While the former's position is well known, Nadel argues that Miss Furness, because of her "star quality" and because of her role as Johnson's Special Assistant for Consumer Affairs, was able both to publicize consumer issues and to force the administration to support proconsumer positions it might not otherwise have supported.[12]

THE PUBLICATION OF A MAJOR JOURNALISTIC EXPOSE

In the present wave this role was played by Nader's *Unsafe at Any Speed.*[13]

Social Factors

Besides these historical circumstances, a number of broad social factors have contributed significantly to consumer support of the consumerism movement at this time:

1. The rapid growth of real spending power in the U.S. has led many consumers to a level of satiation with respect to the "standard package" of middle-class consumption goods. This satiation, it might be argued, is a satiation of *quantity*. Most consuming households have roughly as many *things* as they want and now are turning their attention to the *quality* of those things and, by extension, to the quality of the lives they live.[14]
2. This concern with life's quality finds sources and resonances in other subject areas. The manifest growth in people's concern for preventing war and human destruction, in protecting and enhancing our plant and animal ecology, in developing newer, more open forms of human organization and interaction—all these bespeak a concern for the quality of our human existence that reinforces desires for an improved marketing system.
3. Another cause of the current resurgence of consumerism, as well as growth in other areas of concern, is what seems to be a growing sense that individuals *can* have an effect on their own lives, that they *can* make real changes in the institutions that in large measure control their lives. After a decade of alienation and withdrawal, Americans are finding that actions of "the little people" often, although not uniformly, can bring about needed social improvements. They have seen the "McCarthy kids" bring down a President and persistent reporters reveal a major White House scandal. They have seen riots —for all their negative results—bring about real positive changes in the lives of inner city residents. If action in these areas can yield results, perhaps consumer activism will pay off too.
4. Contributing to this sense that real changes are possible is the fact

> that there is now "a legal and political structure that is much more willing to take action." [15] Congressmen have found that consumerism is a "hot" issue, and many have chosen to invest much of their political ambition in it. Their interest has led to a rapid outpouring of consumer legislation as well as to increased enforcement efforts on the part of federal, state, and in some cases local consumer protection agencies. Fears of even more legislation seem in turn to have led to much more vigilant self-policing by private industry.

The impact of consumerism since 1965 is considerable:

Item: From 1966 to 1970, 19 new pieces of federal consumer legislation were passed, compared to only 3 from 1962 to 1965.[16]

Item: From 1963 to 1965, an average of 6 consumer protection articles appeared annually in popular magazines; in 1970 there were 48 such articles.[17]

Item: Between two Opinion Research Corporation studies in 1967 and 1969 the percent of Americans who felt new consumer protection laws were necessary rose from 55 to 68, and the percent agreeing that there is too much power in the hands of a few large companies rose from 54 to 78.[18]

Item: Complaints to New York City's Commissioner of Consumers Affairs rose from 45,000 in 1968 to 82,000 in 1970.[19]

Item: *Business Week* estimated that over 400 consumer bills were in congressional committees at the end of 1969.[20]

A further indication of the impact of the movement is the virulence of the opposition it has attracted. As might be expected, the business community and its allies are those who feel most threatened. As Nader has pointed out, the labeling of the movement as an "ism" is part of the business counterattack:

> Consumerism is a term given vogue recently by business spokesmen to describe what they believe is a concerted, disruptive ideology concocted by self-appointed bleeding hearts and politicians who find that it pays off to attack corporations. "Consumerism", they say, undermines public confidence in the business system, deprives the consumer of freedom of choice, weakens state and local authority through Federal usurpation, bureaucratizes the marketplace, and stifles innovation.[21]

This kind of attack was exemplified in 1969 by Secretary of Commerce Maurice Stans, then the Washington voice of business, who said that the public had to decide whether we "are going to let the wave of consumerism move too far and destroy the freedom of choice of consumers." [22] However, perhaps the most vitriolic attack and the strongest mark of fear in the ranks of business was a series of articles in the business periodical *Barron's* charging close ties between those in the consumerism movement and international communism![23]

On the other hand, this fear and the need for a vigorous counteroffensive is seen by many as unnecessary, since, as in the past, peoples' basic interest in the consumer problem is neither broad nor deep. According to John S. Coulson, "the new breed of consumerists will, like old soldiers, fade away." [24] There are a great many others, however, who feel that with the continued pressures of inflation and the "dollar crisis," as well as the continued growth of national interest in the quality of life, the consumer movement will in the future greatly expand its scope and influence. Among this cadre is Elizabeth Drew, who feels that particular impetus for this expansion will be given by the fact that problems that have always plagued the poorest consumers have finally been taken up by the middle class. As Ms. Drew notes:

> It is a simple historical fact about the way America works that until the middle class is organized around a significant social change, it doesn't happen. Take any of the important movements of the last decade . . . I don't recall our political leaders talking about the problem until it moved out of the ghetto and into the suburbs.[25]

The Disadvantaged Consumer

The last sentence is the basic departure point for this volume. If the current success of consumerism stems, at least in part, from moving the vocal center of the problem "out of the ghetto," we must ask whether this relocation has substantially benefited those who are left behind, because it is just those who are left behind who, most concede, ought to benefit most from consumerism's growing successes. It is this group that is the focus of this book, the individuals who are particularly handicapped in achieving adequate value for their consumer dollar in the urban marketplace because of their severely restricted incomes, their minority racial status, their old age, and/or their difficulties with the language. This is the group I have chosen to call the disadvantaged consumers. While we are all disadvantaged consumers in some way, it is important to ask whether this group's problems are *qualitatively*, not just quantitatively, different from those faced by the rest of society. Because if they are qualitatively different in significant respects, then we must seriously question whether taking the consumerism issue out of the ghetto is really in the interest of these truly disadvantaged people.

Organization: The Basic Hypotheses

The chapters to follow are organized around three basic hypotheses about the sources of consumer disadvantage for the poor and the racial minorities (see Figure 1-1):

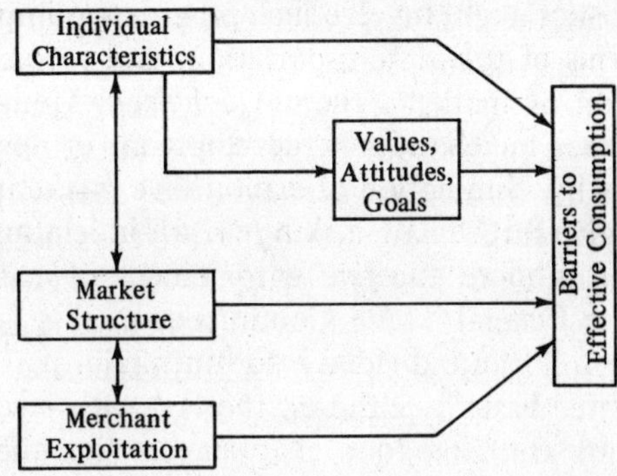

FIGURE 1-1 *Structure of Disadvantaged Consumer Problems*

1. *The disadvantaged consumer hypothesis* argues that the problems of disadvantaged consumers are primarily attributable to their personal characteristics, the kind of people they are. It holds that the real problem is that disadvantaged consumers are just too old, too poor, too uneducated, too unsophisticated, too definitely of the wrong race, etc., to be able to be effective consumers in the urban marketplace.
2. *The market structure hypothesis* argues that the problem is not who the disadvantaged consumers are, but where they must shop. This hypothesis says that the real problems involve a scarcity of convenient low-cost mass merchandisers, a scarcity of specialty stores, higher operating costs, bad management, and higher prices and narrower assortments in outlets existing in areas where disadvantaged consumers live.
3. *The exploitation hypothesis* argues that the problem is not who the disadvantaged are or what the market structure is like where they must shop, but the exploitative practices of merchants with whom they come in contact. This hypothesis holds that the real problem is merchants' use of "bait and switch" ads, unconscionable pricing techniques, fraudulent sales practices, illegal credit contracts, and the like.

The perceptive reader will immediately note that these hypotheses are not mutually exclusive. For example, a person who is poor, black, and uneducated (consumer characteristics) must live and shop in ghettos where low sales volume and high costs of operation have driven out low-cost mass merchandisers (a market structure problem). These factors in turn reduce effective competition, thereby making possible unconscionable pricing practices on the part of some of the remaining merchants (an exploitation problem).

It is also clear that each of these three sources of disadvantage is associated with specific courses of remedial action. Removal of handicapping consumer characteristics might involve such programs as improved consumer education, new forms of urban transportation, and income enhancement programs. Correction of market structure deficiencies might involve subsidies to low-cost mass merchandisers, development of new forms of merchandising, etc. Finally, elimination of exploitative marketing practices presumably would involve further law making (truth in lending, truth in packaging, etc.) as well as more effective enforcement of existing laws (e.g., strengthening of the Federal Trade Commission).

The chapters to follow are divided into four major parts, the first three dealing with the three basic hypotheses, the last with recommended solutions. The first part contains four chapters on the characteristics and problems of the two major disadvantaged groups, the poor and the racial minorities (primarily urban blacks). In each case the group's major socioeconomic characteristics, attitudes, and values are described in an introductory chapter which is followed by a chapter on the group's major problems as consumers. Since the book is primarily about consumer problems and not about poverty or race per se, the descriptive chapters dealing with the poor and the blacks are quite brief.

The second part contains two chapters analyzing the marketplace where most disadvantaged consumers live, looking first at the dynamics of the business structure there and then at the problems and practices of the merchants operating within that structure. The third part turns to the problem of merchant exploitation, looking first at charges of price discrimination against disadvantaged consumers and then at the very broad range of nonprice gimmicks and strategies used by venal merchants to trap the unsuspecting. The final part returns to the three basic hypotheses, presenting chapters describing and evaluating the principal means offered for eliminating, or at least moderating, the problems associated with the three basic causative forces. A final chapter then discusses several of the issues raised in this introduction and reflects upon the implications of the present analysis for the broad area of public policy.

A Cautionary Note

It should be pointed out that the principal focus of our investigation in the chapters to follow will be disadvantaged consumers in *major urban centers.* This primarily reflects the availability of good research data as well as my own interests. The reader is cautioned at the outset that a major finding of the investigation carried out in preparation for this work is that we now know very little about the consumer problems of the rural and migratory poor, the elderly, and other racial minorities besides blacks. The extent to which the patterns and problems discussed here extend beyond the urban context should constitute a major concern of academics and researchers for the coming decade.

Notes

1. Philip Kotler, *Marketing Management: Analysis, Planning and Control,* 2d ed. (Englewood Cliffs, N.J.: Prentice–Hall, Inc., 1972), p. 812.
2. Warren G. Magnuson and Jean Carper, *The Dark Side of the Marketplace* (Englewood Cliffs, N.J.: Prentice–Hall, Inc., 1968), p. ix.
3. David Aaker and George S. Day (eds.), *Consumerism: Search for the Consumer Interest,* 2d ed. (New York: The Free Press, 1974).
4. Robert O. Hermann, "The Consumer Movement in Historical Perspective," *Agricultural Economics and Rural Sociology,* vol. 88, February 1970; Mark V. Nadel, *The Politics of Consumer Protection* (Indianapolis: The Bobbs-Merrill Co., Inc., 1971).
5. Nadel, *op. cit.,* pp. 7–16.
6. Susan Wagner, *The Federal Trade Commission* (New York: Praeger Publishers, Inc., 1971).
7. Arthur Kallent and F. J. Schlink, *100,000,000 Guinea Pigs* (New York: Grossett & Dunlap, 1933).
8. Nadel, *op. cit.,* pp. 235–6.
9. *Ibid.,* pp. 3–30.
10. For example, Vance Packard, *The Hidden Persuaders* (New York: Pocket Books, 1957).
11. Nadel, *op. cit.,* pp. 41–2.
12. *Ibid.,* pp. 52–3.
13. Ralph Nader, *Unsafe at Any Speed* (New York: Grossman Publishers, 1965).
14. Aaron S. Yohalem, "Consumerism's Ultimate Challenge: Is Business Equal to the Task?" Paper delivered to the American Management Association, Nov. 10, 1969.
15. Aaker and Day, *op. cit.,* p. 14.
16. Ralph M. Gaedeke and Warren W. Etcheson, *Consumerism: Viewpoints from Business, Government and the Public Interest* (San Francisco: Canfield Press, 1972), pp. 373–5.
17. Nadel, *op. cit.,* p. 35.
18. Harry W. O'Neill, "The American Consumer: Bothered, Bewildered, Belligerent," paper presented at the 1974 Conference of the American Association of Public Opinion Research, Lake George, N.Y., June 1, 1974, pp. 7 and 10.

19. *Ibid.*
20. Aaker and Day, *op. cit.*, p. 16.
21. Ralph Nader, "The Great American Gyp," *New York Review of Books*, vol. 11, Nov. 21, 1968, p. 27.
22. *Congressional Record*, Sept. 30, 1969, p. H8695.
23. Shirley Scheibla, series of articles on consumerism, *Barron's*, Aug. 17–Sept. 14, 1970.
24. John S. Coulson, " 'New Consumerists' Breed Will Fade Away," *Marketing News*, Mid-June 1971, pp. 5–8.
25. Elizabeth Drew, review of *Citizen Nader*, *New York Times Book Review*, Mar. 19, 1972, p. 10.

PART 1

THE DISADVANTAGED CONSUMER

2. The Poor Consumer

IN 1963, DAVID CAPLOVITZ, a sociologist at Columbia's Bureau of Applied Social Research, published a study of durable goods purchases of residents in four New York City low-income projects that startled the academic community and the popular media with the finding that for given goods and services, the poor pay more than the rest of society.[1] His study dramatically showed that "people with little money, with little competence as consumers, and with little chance of avoiding exploitation in the marketplace: consumers 'poor' in three senses of the word," [2] with astonishing frequency were charged outrageous prices and unconscionable interest rates and sold unneeded, misrepresented, and shoddy merchandise. The poor consumer's involvement in the marketplace not only obtained him less value for his money, it all too frequently led to entanglements in the world of credit and the legal system that often through their effects on his employment caused his income itself to decline. Caplovitz painted a depressing picture of an inevitable cycle of poverty leading to debt in turn leading to deception and brushes with the law, finally leading to repossession, garnishment, unemployment, and reduced income which in turn made the poor consumer even more in need of debt and thus propelled him through the cycle again.

It was the major contribution of Caplovitz's analysis that the consumer problems of poor people were seen to stem not merely from their poverty but also from other characteristics, attitudes, and values associated with that poverty. As will be discussed below, lower income is linked to many other undesirable characteristics such as lower education, lower rates of automobile ownership, and poorer health as well as to minority racial status and old age. These socioeconomic characteristics in turn lead to mediating feelings of alienation and powerlessness as well as to preferences for particular outlets, products, and media. Further, these two sets of factors "create the conditions for the emergence of a deviant market structure and, indirectly, of a set of exploitative practices of merchants who operate within that structure. . . ." [3] All these multiple factors then create barriers to effective consumption or to obtaining what the Kennedy Consumer Advisory Council called the four basic "consumer rights." [4]

Thus the consumer problems of the poor stem from several sources. This and the following chapter seek to isolate the barriers to effective consumption faced by the poor that are principally caused by the characteristic of poverty itself, recognizing that being poor inevitably means *also* that one must shop in a defective market structure and be exposed much more often than is average to exploitative merchants and creditors. The effects of the latter two sources of disadvantage will be discussed in later chapters. This chapter also discusses characteristics, attitudes, and values associated with poverty, postponing consideration of the major consequences of also being a member of a racial minority to later chapters.

The problem here, in short, will be to come to some understanding of the nature, extent, and general consequences of poverty in America in the 1970s before turning attention to the more immediate issues of the effects of poverty on consumption.

Who Are the Poor?

SOME PROBLEMS OF DEFINITION

A first question that confronts an accounting of data on poverty is what in fact is meant by poverty. For a long time, and in isolated cases today, a crude criterion of $3,000 of annual family income was used as the criterion of poverty—a figure that "has its historical roots in two groups of studies begun at the turn of the century, one seeking to establish minimum family budgets in real terms at different levels of living, and the other attempting to measure the cost of living".[5] While "a valuable shorthand figure, roughly separating the poor from the rest of the nation,"[6] the figure has obvious limitations in that it does not account for such characteristics as family size, urban or rural residence, and age of head of household. Thus with the onset of the war on poverty in 1964, it was necessary that a more comprehensive definition of poverty be developed, one taking into account several of the objections raised earlier. This definition was developed by Mollie Orshansky of the Division of Economic and Long Range Studies of the U.S. Department of Health, Education, and Welfare in two 1965 articles.[7] This is the definition on which most federal antipoverty programs are based and in terms of which progress in the fight against poverty is officially measured.

THE ORSHANSKY DEFINITION

Orshansky in fact developed two measures of low income, a lower index which indicates the official upper income limit of those who are poor and a second, higher index adding a group of "near poor." The two groups, poor and near poor, are together generally referred to as "low income" households. The indexes themselves are based primarily on the Department of Agriculture's Economy Food Plan, which specifies a daily market basket of foods needed to provide an adequate, nutritious diet on an "emergency" basis (i.e., when income is very low) for families of various sizes and composition. This set of food requirements is then priced according to the most recent national cost-of-living data and multiplied by 3 to arrive at the total daily family budget for the poverty level. A multiple of 3 is used under the assumption that at the income level in question food expenses represent roughly one-third of all current consumption expenditures. In general the "near poor" levels are about one-third higher than the poverty level.

Since the Orshansky poverty index is used in generating most federal poverty data, it will be used in the discussions to follow. However, the reader should be aware that the index is not without its critics.[8]

WHO IS POOR?

There are three statistics that yield insight into the characteristics of the poor:

1. *Absolute numbers* of individuals or households in poverty in various socio-economic categories. This yields a sense of which groups bulk large or small among the total population of American poor.
2. *Poverty rates,* which report the proportion of all households or individuals in a particular category which is poor. Such figures indicate the probability that a household or an individual is poor given the possession of certain characteristics.
3. *Income deficits,* which report the extent to which the incomes of different groups fall below their respective poverty income thresholds. This yields a sense of *how* poor each group is, a factor which may extend or mitigate the degree of poverty found in (1) and (2).

HOW MANY POOR?

The basic unit for poverty accounting necessarily is the household, since it is the basic economic unit whose income is or is not adequate for its members. Thus to simply report, as many do, that one-half of all poor are children is not an operationally useful statistic (except, perhaps, for portraying more vividly the calamity of poverty), in that children are not usually responsible for their own poverty. Data that imply causes are infinitely more useful. Since income levels are the critical determinant here, a portrait that shows incidence of poverty by *employment status* would yield a better sense of the contribution of certain immediate causes to lower incomes among the poor (granting that these causes themselves may have deeper roots).[9] These data are reported in Table 2-1.

TABLE 2-1. Employment Status of Families and Unrelated Individuals in Poverty, 1970

	Families		Unrelated Individuals	
	No.[a]	*%*	*No.*[a]	*%*
Ill or disabled	857	16.5	1,159	23.1
Family responsibilities				
Female heads not working[b]	819	15.7	1,770	35.3
Female heads working part time	348	6.6	450	9.0
	1,167	22.4	2,220	44.2
Unable to find steady work				
Female heads working full time less than 50 weeks	340	6.5	303	6.0
Male heads not working[b]	560	10.7	368	7.3
Male heads working part time or full time less than 50 weeks	1,105	21.2	510	10.2
	2,005	38.4	1,181	23.6
Inadequate salaries or wages				
Male heads working full time	921	17.7	113	2.3
Female heads working full time	147	2.8	168	3.3
	1,068	20.5	281	5.6
Other				
Students	57	1.1	170	3.4
In Armed Forces	56	1.1	11	0.2
	113	2.2	181	3.6
Total	5,210	100.0	5,022	100.0

[a]In thousands.
[b]Excludes students and ill or disabled.
Source: U.S. Bureau of the Census, *Current Population Reports,* Series P-60, no. 81 "Characteristics of the Low Income Population; 1970" (Washington: Government Printing Office, 1971).

Table 2-1 reports that there were slightly over 10,000,000 poor household units in 1970, approximately one-half of which were unrelated individuals (49%) and one-half families (51%). Unrelated individuals in poverty were primarily the elderly. About 56% of unrelated individuals were 65 years or older and about three-quarters were 55 or older. Consistent with this characteristic is the fact that two out of three unrelated individuals appeared to be poor primarily because of illness or disability or household responsibilities. A further 24% were poor because of the difficulties of getting steady work, although a substantial proportion of this group presumably were elderly and therefore not working full or part time because of age or household responsibilities. Only a small proportion of unrelated individuals appeared to be poor because they were students or because they had full-time jobs and their salaries were too low.

The problems of families were considerably different and in many ways much more serious, in that such households, including all their members, accounted for 80% of all poor individuals in 1970. The problem with families was, first of all, one of getting and holding a job. Almost two in five poor families appeared to be poor primarily because the household head could not find year-round full-time employment.[10] A further 20% were poor because the full-time jobs they *did* have did not pay them enough to bring them over the poverty line. The latter predicament is even more disheartening when one learns that 37% of these families had one or more *additional* earner besides the full-time working head.

The final group of almost 2 in 5 (38.9%) of all poor families was poor either because the head was ill or disabled or because there was no male head of household and the female head chose not to—or was unable to—work full time.

POVERTY RATES: THE IMPACT OF POVERTY

The preceeding discussion only indicates proximate causes of poverty. It does not indicate factors associated with these causes, for example, the extent to which lower educational achievement produces unemployment or lower-than-adequate earnings on steady jobs for poor households.

Insight into these more basic causal factors is provided by an analysis of characteristics associated with high poverty rates, i.e., the percentage of those in a category who are poor. In 1970, 12.6% of all households were officially classified as poor, including 10% of all family households and 32.7% of all households of unrelated individuals. Comparisons with these standards make it clear that old age and racial or ethnic minority status yield a much higher probability of being poor. Poverty rates for those 65 and older, Negro, and of Spanish origin were, respectively, 24.6%, 33.6%, and 24.3% in 1970.[11] In addition to these most widely known correlates the following characteristics—several of which are interrelated and are also related to age and/or minority status—are associated with high poverty rates:[12]

Characteristic	Percent Poor
Female-headed family	38.4
Child under 18 living in female-headed family	53.4
Living on a farm	18.5
Living in the South	14.8
In families of seven or more persons	22.8
In family where head has less than eight years schooling	25.2

That many if not all of these characteristics are associated with long-term poverty status is attested by an extensive longitudinal analysis of flows of families into and out of poverty between 1965 and 1966 by Terence Kelly. Kelly concludes:

> Even after holding constant a large number of relevant social and economc influences, we find an acute persistence of poverty in particular categories: the aged; families and individuals living on farms; the South; households headed by a female, a non-white, or an uneducated person.[13]

Some further comments on changes in the extent of poverty are included below.

INCOME DEFICIT: HOW POOR IS POOR?

Total income for all poor households in 1970 from all sources was approximately $17.043 billion. That is to say, the "poverty market" is a $17 billion market. This total was about 60% of the total needs of poor households of $28.490 billion according to the Orshansky definition. The total income deficit in 1970 thus was $11.45 billion, or 40% of needs. The average (mean) income deficit for unrelated individuals was $806, or about 42% of needs, while for families the mean deficit was $1,419 per family, or 39% of needs. It should be further noted that not all income received by poor households is from their own private endeavors. In 1970 about 43% of the aggregate income of poor families came from payments from social security, public assistance, unemployment and workmen's compensation, and various government pension systems. Thus the task of bringing present poverty households up to the poverty threshold would mean additional public outlays (ignoring administrative costs) of $11.447 billion (the poverty deficit) on top of about $7.3 billion currently spent on various welfare programs.

CHANGES IN POVERTY OVER TIME

There has been a substantial decrease in the pervasiveness of poverty since 1959 in the number of poor, in the aggregate income deficit, and in poverty rates. Partly this is the result of long-term growth in the country's GNP and partly—as the more rapid decline from 1965 onward suggests—the result of programs under the war on poverty. Over the period from 1959 to 1970 there has been a net outflow of about 11 million people from the official poverty rolls, a decline of about 30%. However, since total population has grown during the period, poverty rates have declined even faster, from 22.4% to 12.6% of the population, down about 44%. These reductions, however, have been greater among families than among unrelated individuals, as the following figures on the number of people in poverty show:[14]

	1959	1970	DECREASE
Families	7,974,000	5,214,000	35%
Unrelated individuals	5,894,000	5,023,000	15%

It is perhaps encouraging to note that the rates of decline are substantially in excess of those predicted by Lampman in 1966.[15]

Table 2-2 reports the employment status of the poor in 1959 and 1970. The table indicates clearly that the major beneficiaries of long-term real economic growth and of the various antipoverty programs have been those with the most going for them to begin with, households headed by males in the labor force. Almost 90% of the decline in the number of poor families between 1959 and 1970 is accounted for by reductions in the number of households with male heads working only part time or getting less than adequate wages working full time. Thus it is not surprising that families with female heads grew substantially in their relative importance among the poor, rising from about 22% to 32% of all poor. (Proportions of females among unrelated poor individuals remained largely unchanged at about 72%.) The other group growing in relative importance among the poor between 1959 and 1970 is the ill and disabled. This group is growing in absolute numbers along with total population, yet apparently has not been receiving more public assistance.

Finally, it should be noted that although the poor are becoming relatively fewer in number and their average income is increasing, they are becoming *relatively poorer* than the rest of society. Between 1959 and 1971 there was a 49% increase in poor incomes but an 84% increase in the dollar gap between poor and nonpoor over the same period. The nonpoor were 4½ times better off (in terms of annual income) than the poor in 1959. In 1971, they were 5½ times better off.[16] Herman Miller sees this relative decline as a major neglected characteristic in statistical analyses that show improvements in the incidence of poverty:

> We have surely learned enough about relative incomes and rising expectations during the past decade to know that they cannot safely be ignored. As the income of society grows, the poor expect to share in that growth. In these days of rapid communication, the poor know what is going on about them. They can see how people live in the suburbs and in the more affluent parts of the central cities and they know that they are not sharing the affluence that surrounds them. Any statistical definition that fails to take this fact into account soon loses its validity. Any social policy that ignores this simple truth will eventually run into trouble. If we remove our rose-colored glasses

TABLE 2-2. Employment Status of Poor Families, 1959 and 1970

	1959		1970	
	No.[a]	*%*	*No.*[a]	*%*
Ill or disabled	793	9.5	857	16.5
Female heads not working full time				
Not working[b]	984	11.8	819	15.7
Working part time[c]	614	7.4	688	13.2
	1,598	19.2	1,507	28.9
Male heads not working full time				
Not working[b]	749	9.0	560	10.7
Working part time[c]	2,389	28.7	1,105	21.2
	3,138	37.7	1,665	31.9
Heads working full time				
Male	2,409	28.9	921	17.7
Female	208	2.5	147	2.8
	2,617	31.4	1,068	20.5
Other				
Students	12	0.1	57	1.1
Armed Forces	162	1.9	56	1.1
	174	2.0	113	2.2
Total	8,320	100.0	5,210	100.0

[a]In thousands.
[b]Excludes students and ill or disabled.
[c]Includes those working less than full time and those working 1 to 49 weeks.
Source: U.S. Bureau of the Census, *Current Population Reports,* Series P-60, no. 81 "Characteristics of the Low Income Population, 1970," (Washington: Government Printing Office, 1971).

and correct our misleading statistical indicators, we will see that there is more poverty and inequality in America than we had imagined.[17]

The poor's perception of this great and growing inequality has a major effect on the poor's values, goals, and attitudes, as will be seen in the next section.

The Subculture of Poverty

Poverty is, of course, much more than mere statistics. To be constantly faced with the day-to-day experience of poverty and the prospect that future escape from that role is at best problematic cannot help but force poor households to adopt views of the world and their own place in it that are very different from the rest of society. It is, however, a matter of major concern to social scientists and public policy makers whether the differences in life view between the poor and the nonpoor are essentially *qualitative* or *quantitative* in nature. Some, such as the late anthropologist Oscar Lewis, view the poor as being qualitatively different, holding that poverty should be conceived:

> . . . as a subculture with its own structure and rationale, as a way of life which is passed down from generation to generation along family lines. . . . By the time slum children are age six or seven they have usually absorbed the basic values and attitudes of their subculture and are not psychologically geared to take full advantage of changing conditions or increased opportunities which may occur in their lifetime.[18]

In Lewis's view, if one were to remove the sources of poverty (as through guaranteed income programs), changes in values and behavior would be very slow developing because of the deeply rooted nature of the poverty culture.

Others, such as Valentine and Liebow,[19] reject the culture-of-poverty concept, arguing that the poor in the main share the basic values of the larger society and that their attitudes and behaviors are mainly an *adaptation* to their current poverty. As Liebow in his study of poor streetcorner men expresses it:

> From this perspective, the streetcorner man does not appear as a carrier of an independent cultural tradition. His behavior appears not so much as a way of realizing the distinctive goals and values of his own subculture or of conforming to its models, but rather as his way of trying to achieve many of the goals and values of the larger society, of failing to do this, and of concealing his failure from others and from himself as best he can.[20]

As Sturdivant has pointed out, "Liebow's position would suggest that . . . once the sources of failure were removed the lower class could fulfill their middle-class values." [21]

The issue of the validity of these alternative views about the sources of poor people's unique attitudes and perceptions has profound importance for public policy. Therefore this issue will be central to the evaluation in Chapter 10 of alternative approaches to eliminating consumer disadvantages. However, it is sufficient for the present analysis to note that despite disagreement about sources there is general agreement between the two factions on the *character* of the poor's attitudes and perceptions. The following sections will describe the major dimensions of these attitudes and perceptions. It must be emphasized that these descriptions are necessarily broad and therefore ignore great diversity among the poor. Also, by emphasizing differences between the poverty subculture and the rest of society, the descriptions ignore the many similarities between the groups that stem from their mutual participation in larger cultural groupings (Occidental, urban, American). It is, for example, important to point out that despite their poverty, the poor want pretty much what the rest of America wants—more money, a better education, occupational advancement, better housing, and the like. They are little different in their consumer aspirations:

> Inside their homes, they value the same things as the general run of Americans—comfortable and durable furniture, a television set, an array of electrical appliances, and, to give life grace as well as comfort, a few ornaments and art objects. Tastes in style are definitely American—modern furniture, colored telephones, pole lamps, systematic color schemes.[22]

In important respects these aspirations are carefully nurtured by the marketing community, particularly through advertising on television, with which the poor spend a good deal of time.

SELF-PERCEPTIONS

As many authors have pointed out,[23] the poor see themselves in the following way:

1. RELATIVELY DEPRIVED. The poor are falling farther behind the rest of society in terms of income received, and understandably they feel relatively deprived economically. This is particularly damaging in a society which holds as principal life goals the accumulation and open display of material goods and the upward mobility of families and the self-improvement of individuals. The pervasive American media which portray these symbols of achievement and frequently recount tales of those who have "made it" render it impossible for the poor to escape the feeling that they have failed in ways that most of America has defined as failure.[24]

2. MANIPULATED EXTERNALLY. The poor view their lives fatalistically as being influenced mostly by others and/or by chance. After all, they can see that their poverty itself is often the result of chance: of being born into a poor family that forces children to get out and work early instead of enabling them to get the education needed to escape from poverty, of getting injured or contracting a debilitating disease, of not being given (by "them") a decent-paying job, of being fired arbitrarily or when there (mysteriously) appears something called a recession, or of having a husband or father run out on them.

3. POWERLESS. Since chance and others rule their lives, the poor often feel they can really do little themselves to alter their circumstances.

4. ALIENATED. Since others control their destinies and since often the behavior of these others suggests they don't care, the poor typically feel cut off, alienated, disinherited by their society. This is reinforced by the fact that

their poverty, work life, and residence typically cut them off from much physical contact with the middle class except in superior-subordinate relationships.

It should be pointed out that these self-perceptions are not altogether incorrect. It is unfortunately quite accurate to say that in most urban areas the poor are indeed deprived, manipulated, and powerless and have good reason to be alienated. This is perhaps most true with respect to politics:

> . . . [T]he poor are politically invincible. It is one of the cruelest ironies of social life in advanced countries that the dispossessed at the bottom of society are unable to speak for themselves. The people of the other America do not, by far and large, belong to unions, to fraternal organizations, or to political parties. . . . They have no face; they have no voice. . . . There is not even a cynical political motive for caring about the poor, as in the old days. Because the slums are no longer centers of powerful political organizations, the politicians need not really care about their inhabitants. The slums are no longer visible to the middle class, so much of the idealistic urge to fight for those who need help is gone. Only the social agencies have a really direct involvement with the other America, and they are without any great political power.[25]

These are not the only reasons society has ignored the poor. Many believe the poor ought to be ignored because they will never contribute to, and in fact may disrupt, the normal workings of society. This view fails to distinguish between what some have called the "good" or "respectable" poor and the "bad" or "disreputable" poor. Marx's description of the *lumpenproletariat* captures the view of the latter that is often applied to the former as well:

> Along with ruined rows of questionable means of support and questionable antecedents, along with foul and adventures-seeking dregs of the bourgeoisie, there were vagabonds, dismissed soldiers, discharged convicts, runaway galley slaves . . . in short, the whole undefined, dissolute, kicked about mass that the Frenchmen style "la boheme." [26]

Similar is the view that the poor do not deserve to be brought into the mainstream because they will not help themselves. One-third of those surveyed in a 1964 Gallup Poll believed that a person's lack of effort was more often to blame for his being poor than uncontrollable circumstances.[27]

Another view now somewhat rarely voiced publicly is that poverty is inevitable and "benevolent" to the society as a whole because, as Andrew Carnegie put it, poverty is "bracing . . . the only school capable of producing the supremely great." [28] This view argues that the poor ought not to be helped into the mainstream because poverty is good for them.

Finally, there is a perhaps less conscious feeling that the existence of a lower-class outgroup confers higher status on the higher-class ingroup, the classic rationale for prejudice.

One of the major consequences of these views that the poor needn't or shouldn't be given a share in the mainstream is that the poor too often receive shoddy and unequal treatment from the greater society's major institutions. This is manifest in such relatively mundane affairs as irregular and inefficient garbage collection in poor neighborhoods and in more serious matters such as lower-quality schools and more punitive law enforcement.[29] As will be indicated below, it is also manifest in the market structure and merchant practices faced by the poor.

ATTITUDES

What general attitudes tend to go along with these self-perceptions of the poor?

1. INSECURITY. The employed poor are frequently "last hired, first fired." They are often in jobs subject to cyclical and seasonal layoffs. Financial emergencies can compound problems when the rent isn't met or when clinics cannot be attended. While the health of the poor may be no worse than that of the rest of the population, sickness is something greatly to be feared because when it comes, its effects on sparse resources and savings and on fragile family structures can be disastrous. Similar fears attend encounters with the police or the courts, with a legal system that seems to give excessive vigilance to law enforcement in poor communities while largely ignoring what the poor feel are equally serious or more serious crimes in non-poor communities. Such fears may also attend encounters with merchants, credit agencies, banks, and the like.

2. HELPLESSNESS. Since the poor have no political "muscle," until recently no one took an interest in their plight. Further, because of their limited resources, limited education, and limited life experiences, the poor are ill equipped to help themselves. On the job, at the clinic, at his landlord's (since he rents usually), and perhaps at the hard-selling credit merchant's, a poor man often feels he is subject to the whims of others. This feeling, needless to say, compounds his insecurity.

3. FATALISM. Insecurity, helplessness, limited life experiences, and an inability to achieve society's most prized goals lead understandably to a sense of fatalism. The poor feel they cannot control their own lives. They feel that chance and the actions of others keep them in their abject state and that when they try to move up and out, the odds are usually against them, although they can hope a lucky break will soon come along. This can, of course, be seen in part as a rationalization of failure.

4. PRESENT ORIENTATION. When other factors control one's future and in all likelihood society will make it impossible to achieve anything even if

planned and saved for, then one might as well enjoy life now, spend now, drink now, be reckless, and let the future take its own course. This attitude is often seen as explaining poor people's unwillingness to engage in preventive medical care even when free. And it also may explain why many poor people undertake substantial consumer debts.

ROLE RELATIONSHIPS

How do these attitudes exhibit themselves in the major relationships poor people have with others and with the working and leisure worlds? One apparent result of these attitudes cited in the literature is that there is among the poor a simplification of life experiences. In their work they deal with simplified problems and have little need or opportunity to think creatively or independently. While they may have moved among jobs or among communities, their experiences along the way tend to repeat themselves. Their poverty, their large families, and, often, their broken homes limit the kinds of leisure pursuits they can enjoy. Simply getting by is an almost all-consuming enterprise. This limited experience can prove a major handicap in a complicated, bureaucratic market system.

There is, second, often an inflexibility in role relationships among the poor. This is understandable in that when one cannot count on the future, the rest of society, or even on chance, then the real solidity in one's life *can* come from a relatively stable personal life pattern. Thus it has been found that the poor tend to be rigid and authoritarian in child training in order to minimize child-induced disturbances. They tend to be set and rigid in their marital roles and in their perceptions of their spouses' roles. They tend to routinize their behaviors—for instance, always to visit the same bar on the same day at the same time with the same group. They keep their circle of social contacts small and generally within the family or neighborhood. Media contacts are routinized and nonthreatening and often serve as a vehicle for escape. Such inflexibility can prove a major inhibitor when one is encouraging the disadvantaged to break out of undesirable credit or shopping patterns.

THE FAMILY

Such role relationships show up most strongly in poor people's approaches to marriage and childbearing. First of all, the rigidity of roles in an otherwise insecure world manifests itself in the fact that both husband and wife typically tend not to alter their life-styles much with marriage. Courtship is short, mates are frequently chosen from nearby residents, and marriage itself is "just something one falls into." The partners keep the friends and the routines they had when they were single. There develops a sharp separation of roles within the family: the husband is the money earner and dominant figure in the household; the wife is the housekeeper–mother who is responsible for wisely spending the family's money and for bringing up the children. Husbands have little to do, for example, with helping with children's schoolwork, deciding on insurance, or planning vacations. The husband, while demanding deference to his authority, also demands his freedom to maintain his social ties with "the boys" and perhaps even to "fool around" as he did before marriage.[30]

What results from this maintenance of old roles and separation of duties within the family is considerable emotional isolation between the spouses. This in turn makes it difficult to weather crises and tends to negatively influence the outlook and personality of the children. It also leads to more frequent divorce and separation than in the upper classes and more frequent mention of marital dissatisfaction in interview questions. As Besner puts it:

> . . . the husband regards the home simply as a retreat for the satisfaction of physical needs. . . . A "good wife," for him, is one who prepares the meals for the family, keeps his clothing in order, raises the children, and frees him from everyday worries. . . . This is antithetical to the wife's wish for emphasis on the interpersonal aspects of marriage, the friend–lover role. Her wish for open expression of affection is not met by the husband who does not see this as important. . . . [The] lower class wife must endure emotional deprivation as well as the ever-present fear of physical–economic deprivation.[31]

She puts up with this in part because her husband takes her off her family's hands economically, offers to meet some of her immediate economic needs and to provide some chance for improvement in the future, and provides the legitimization she needs for the children she wants to make her life more complete. Indeed, the mother–child relationship is seen by most observers as the strongest tie in the world of poverty. This tie leads to considerable dependence of children on mothers and a reluctance to confide or otherwise relate intimately to fathers. This lack of intimacy is one explanation for the fact that in poor areas once-married females with children are reluctant to remarry. In many two-parent households, a husband is not only an emotional burden on the wife but also, when he is unemployed, an economic burden. Single women with jobs and children have two of the major advantages of marriage without the cost. And if they take a lover from time to time,[32] their other major need may be met without the enduring complications and heartache of marriage. Thus there are pressures to keep the broken home broken.

But there are costs. The absence of father, even if he is often distant, authoritarian, and unemotional (except when he is angry), can have a serious affect on single-parent children. Bartemeier has suggested that such children have an overattachment to their mothers and have a weak basis for establishing male and female roles. They have poor peer group relations, feel inferior and insecure, and focus on the present more than the future.[33] These are all characteristics that can lead the next generation back into poverty, thereby continuing its debilitating cycle.

Also, older children in such households often prematurely take on adult roles: boys enter the labor force early to replace a missing breadwinner; girls fill in as housekeepers for missing mothers; children more often do the shopping. Conflicts with lovers of the mother can arise in children of both sexes—jealousy in the boy and sexual rivalry in the girl. This foreshortening of childhood and its concomitant interference with education can have long-term consequences in adult adjustment for such children as well as for their siblings; it again reduces the probability such children will ever finally emerge from lives of poverty.

COMMUNITY AND SOCIETY

A final general correlate of the goals and attitudes of the poor has been a lack of community organization by and for poor people.[34] Until the recent formation of welfare rights and black and Mexican–American neighborhood "power" groups, poor communities had been notoriously hard to organize. Given their feelings of alienation and helplessness as well as their understandable preoccupation with mere survival, poor people had little time, money, or motivation for organizing for self-help. While this condition is changing somewhat under external financing and staffing help as in the work of the late Saul Alinsky,[35] the reluctance of the poor to join organizations is a major barrier to improving their welfare—particularly as consumers.

Notes

1. David Caplovitz, *The Poor Pay More* (New York: The Free Press, 1963).
2. *Ibid.*, p. 11.
3. Alan R. Andreasen, "Consumerism in the Inner City," paper presented at Brookings Institution Conference on Consumerism, University of Rochester, June, 1972, pp. 6–7.
4. Executive Office of the President, *Consumer Advisory Council: First Report* (Washington: Government Printing Office, 1963).
5. Robert E. Will and Harold G. Vatter (eds.), *Poverty in Affluence* (New York: Harcourt, Brace & World, Inc., 1965), p. 5.
6. *Ibid.*

7. Mollie Orshansky, "Counting the Poor: Another Look at the Poverty Profile," *Social Security Bulletin,* January 1965, pp. 3–28, and Mollie Orshansky, "Who's Who among the Poor: A Demographic View of Poverty," *Social Security Bulletin,* July 1965, pp. 3–30.
8. Harold W. Watts, "The Iso-Prop Index: An Approach to the Determination of Differential Poverty Income Thresholds," *Journal of Human Resources,* vol. 2, no. 1, Winter 1967, pp. 3–18.
9. Sar A. Levitan, Garth L. Mangum, and Ray Marshall, *Human Resources and Labor Markets* (New York: Harper & Row, Publishers, 1972), pp. 401–48.
10. It should be noted that *under*employment as well as traditional unemployment creates serious problems for the disadvantaged.
11. U.S. Bureau of the Census, *Current Population Reports,* series P-60, no. 81. "Characteristics of the Low Income Population, 1970" (Washington: Government Printing Office, 1971).
12. *Ibid.*
13. Terrence F. Kelly, "Factors Affecting Poverty: A Gross Flow Analysis," in President's Commission on Income Maintenance Programs, *Technical Studies* (Washington: Government Printing Office, 1971), p. 46.
14. U.S. Bureau of the Census, *op. cit.*
15. Robert J. Lampman, "Population Change and Poverty Reduction, 1947–1975," in Leo Fishman (ed.), *Poverty and Affluence* (New Haven, Conn.: Yale University Press, 1966), pp. 18–42.
16. Herman P. Miller, "A New Look at Inequality, Poverty, and Underemployment in the United States without Rose Colored Glasses," *Review of Black Political Economy,* vol. 3, no. 2, Winter 1973, p. 32.
17. *Ibid.*
18. Oscar Lewis, *La Vida: A Puerto-Rican Family in the Culture of Poverty —San Juan and New York* (New York: Random House, Inc., 1965), p. xliii.
19. Charles A. Valentine, *Culture and Poverty: Critique and Counter-Proposals* (Chicago: The University of Chicago Press, 1968); Eliot Liebow, *Tally's Corner* (Boston: Little, Brown and Company, 1967).
20. Liebow, *op. cit.*, p. 222.
21. Frederick D. Sturdivant, "Subculture Theory: Poverty, Minorities, and Marketing," in Scott Ward and Thomas S. Robertson (eds.), *Consumer Behavior: Theoretical Sources* (Englewood Cliffs, N.J.: Prentice–Hall, Inc., 1973), p. 486.
22. Lola M. Irelan and Arthur Besner, "Low-Income Outlook on Life," in Lola M. Irelan (ed.), *Low-Income Life Styles* (Washington: U.S. Department of Health, Education, and Welfare, 1966), p. 6.
23. See, for example, Irelan and Besner, *op. cit.*; Lee Rainwater, Richard P. Coleman, and Gerald Handel, *Workingman's Wife* (New York: McFadden Books, 1962); and Peter H. Rossi and Zahava D. Blum, "Social

Stratification and Poverty," paper presented at Sociological Research Association, San Francisco, August 1967.

24. It is, of course, true that American poverty is much less than that of other countries, and indeed many of the American poor have accomplishments to be proud of relative to their own past and that of their parents. It is in large measure their sense of deprivation relative to what they believe they deserve that gives rise to the goals, attitudes, and values discussed in this chapter.
25. Michael Harrington, *The Other America: Poverty in the United States* (New York: Macmillan Publishing Co., Inc., 1962), p. 6.
26. Karl Marx, *The Eighteenth Brumaire of Louis Bonaparte*, translated by Daniel De Leon (Chicago: Charles H. Kerr and Co., 1914), p. 83.
27. George Gallup, *Gallup Poll Report*, Spring 1964.
28. Andrew Carnegie, "The Advantages of Poverty," in Will and Vatter, *op cit.*, p. 64.
29. Both adult and youthful offenders from lower socioeconomic groups make up a much higher proportion of court cases, prison inmates, individuals with police records, and the like. While this is partly the result of greater criminality, it is also often the result of greater vigilance by the police in poor areas, greater difficulty of the poor in getting legal aid, and greater willingness, conscious or unconscious, of judges to give hard sentences to the poor and to America's minorities.
30. Arthur Besner, "Economic Deprivation and Family Patterns," in Irelan, *op. cit.*, pp. 15–29.
31. *Ibid.*, pp. 19–20.
32. Often, deserted disadvantaged wives have a series of liaisons which may or may not produce children.
33. Leo Bartemeier, "The Contribution of the Father to the Mental Health of the Family," *American Journal of Psychiatry*, vol. 110, October 1953, pp. 277–80.
34. Julian Woodward and Elmo Roper, "The Political Activity of American Citizens," *American Political Science Review*, vol. 44, no. 4, December 1950, pp. 872–85.
35. For a discussion of Alinsky's work see Charles E. Silberman, *Crisis in Black and White* (New York: Vintage Books, 1964).

3. Consumption Problems of the Poor

A MAJOR CONCLUSION to be drawn from the preceding chapter is that the poor are not simply rich people with less money. Being poor means that one possesses specific socioeconomic characteristics and certain values, self-perceptions, and attitudes that are quantitatively *and* qualitatively different from those of the nonpoor. The burden of the present chapter is to see to what extent these subcultural differences are reflected in the *consumption patterns* of the poor. Thus the sections to follow shall ask (1) in what ways are the consumption patterns of the poor different from those of the nonpoor, (2) what accounts for the differences found, and (3) to what extent are the patterns qualitatively rather than just quantitatively different. In a sense, our principal concern will be to ascertain whether there is something distinct that might be called (after Lewis) a "disadvantaged consumer subculture." [1]

In evaluating the consumption patterns of the poor, it seems useful to consider their problems in terms of two major classes of decisions:

1. Decisions to allocate funds across broad consumption categories and between consumption and saving. These will be called *budgeting decisions.*
2. Decisions to select specific products, services, and outlets among alternatives available to meet given consumption needs within the budgeting period. These will be called *purchasing decisions.*

The sections to follow will indicate that with respect to budgeting decisions, a major problem for the poor appears to be that although they have needs in many respects not unlike those of the nonpoor, they simply lack both the level and the stability of incomes to be able to keep within their meager earnings. With respect to purchase decisions, we shall see that their major problems are in accumulating adequate information and having sufficient mobility to achieve lowest costs for given needs. Some of these problems in choice optimization of the poor, however, may be more apparent than real in that they simply reflect the imposition of middle-class value structures on non-middle-class households.

Budgeting Problems and Decisions

LIMITED DISCRETIONARY INCOME

One of the first and most obvious disadvantages of being poor is that one has limited money to spend over and above basic necessities and other nondiscretionary items. Table 3-1 reports 1960–61 Bureau of Labor Statistics (BLS) basic expenditure data for three- and four-person families with before tax incomes just above the 1961 poverty level and for families of average before tax income and similar size (3.7 persons).[2] These figures show that after setting aside money for food, shelter, and clothing and for unavoidable payroll deductions for medical care, social security, and pensions, typical poor families have used up perhaps 70% of their available money receipts after taxes. On the other hand, average nonpoor families are required to allocate only 57% of disposable income to such necessities.

It may be further noted, however, that these crude calculations substantially understate the true differences in discretionary income between poor and nonpoor families for two reasons. First, many of the necessary expenditures of the nonpoor are really discretionary. The nonpoor allocate a substantial portion of their higher incomes toward increasing the *quality* of the food, clothing, and shelter they acquire. To the extent that such choices may be considered discretionary, the necessary expenditures of the nonpoor are overstated at 57%.

Second, not all discretionary expenditures of the poor are truly discretionary. For example, some transportation and personal care expenditures and perhaps some medical expenses may in fact be requirements for holding a steady or part-time job. Thus the true proportion of discretionary income available to the poor is even smaller than the 30% indicated in Table 3-1, perhaps as little as 10% or 15% for families just above the official poverty level. Finally, it should also be noted that this proportion would be even smaller if the free goods noted in Table 3-1 were not available to the poor.

This dramatic difference in ratios of discretionary to total income points up several obvious problems for disadvantaged households as consumers. First, it shows how ill equipped financially they are to deal with emergencies; this explains why many of the poor often do not attend medical clinics even in the event of serious illness and why many choose to avoid legal action when seriously defrauded. Second, it shows how critical the cost of necessities is to the economic well-being of the poor and why so much of the vocal concern they have shown as consumers in recent years[3]

TABLE 3-1. Nondiscretionary Expenditures of Selected Poor and Nonpoor Families, 1960-61

	Poor Families				Average Family	
	3 Persons		*4 Persons*		*3.7 Persons*	
	Amount	*%*	*Amount*	*%*	*Amount*	*%*
Money income after taxes and other money receipts	$3,211	100.0	$3,648	100.0	$6,779	100.0
Expenditures						
Food	941	29.4	1140	31.2	1493	22.1
Shelter	478	14.9	494	13.5	803	11.9
Utilities	202	6.3	224	6.1	292	4.3
Household operation	181	5.6	225	6.2	341	5.0
Clothing	309	9.6	413	11.3	641	9.5
Prepaid medical care	63	2.0	70	1.9	107	1.6
Social security, pensions	49	1.5	92	2.5	219	3.2
Total	$2,223	69.3	$2,658	72.7	$3,895	57.4
Available for discretionary expenditures	$ 988	30.7	$ 990	27.3	$2,883	42.6
Value of Free Items Received						
Food	$ 14		$ 27		$ 12	
Housing	47		47		37	
Clothing	46		53		65	
Transportation	14		11		11	
Medical care	34		40		39	
Other	33		23		48	
Value of home-produced food	30		36		15	
Total	$ 218		$ 237		$ 226	

Source: Adapted from Helen H. Lamale, "How the Poor Spend Their Money," in Herman P. Miller (ed.), *Poverty American Style* (Belmont, Calif.: Wadsworth Publishing Company, Inc., 1966), pp. 150–61.

has been over such things as the cost of food and housing. Third, it points up the hurdles the poor must face in acquiring even a small proportion of the standard American package of discretionary goods and services, hurdles that lead many poor people into dissaving and the use of credit.

DISSAVING

Traditional Puritan American wisdom would suggest that the poor *ought* to adapt to their poorer circumstances and to the fact that necessities take up a higher proportion of their incomes by cutting back on their discretionary spending. Data from the 1960–61 BLS study in Table 3-2 indicate, however, that families in both poor and nonpoor circumstances tend to allocate about the *same proportion* of their total money income to discretionary items no matter what proportion of such money income is taken up by necessities. That is, while poor families do appear to scale down their set of "standard" discretionary needs somewhat in line with their lower incomes, they apparently do not take adequate account of the larger "bite" of nondiscretionary items. The obvious result is that the poor must dissave —either withdraw savings, sell assets, or undertake debt obligations. Thus because their incomes were less than their consumption needs in 1960–61, three- and four-person poor families increased their liabilities over the period (or decreased their savings, if any) $235 and $383 respectively while the average family added to their savings in the amount of $173.[4] In 1960–61 an income of about $5,000 was typically necessary before net savings were undertaken.[5] Up to that point—that is, among the poor—dissaving was required to meet felt consumption needs.

ACCUMULATION OF DEBT

For most of the poor, dissaving does *not* mean drawing down savings. For example, a recent study of liquid asset holdings showed that about one-half of all families with incomes under $3,000 had no liquid assets at all, with median holdings for all such families at $40.[6] For those without liquid assets (and for some with them) the fact that consumption needs are in excess of total money income means that they must acquire some amount of debt, a behavior which is, of course, not peculiar to the poor. Credit usage in the country as a whole has been growing at an astonishing pace, increasing sixfold between 1950 and 1970, a phenomenon that undoubtedly both makes it easier for the poor to get credit and creates some group pressure to do so.[7]

Five basic forms of such financing are possible: direct loans (secured and unsecured) to be paid in installments, single-payment loans, retail sales contracts, revolving credit accounts, and regular charge accounts (including credit card accounts). The range of sources from which such credit can be obtained is broad, including retail outlets, banks, credit unions, finance companies, friends and relatives, and "loan sharks." Direct installment loans and retail sales contracts (together labeled "installment credit") made up by far the bulk of consumer credit obligations outstanding in 1970, a proportion which had been growing steadily since 1950.[8]

Contrary to popular belief, the poor do not use installment credit any more often than nonpoor families, although there is some evidence that they are more likely to use informal credit like that at the corner grocer.

TABLE 3-2. Discretionary Expenditures of Selected Poor and Nonpoor Families, 1960-61

	Poor Families				Average Family	
	3 Persons		*4 Persons*		*3.7 Persons*	
	Amount	*%*	*Amount*	*%*	*Amount*	*%*
Tobacco	$ 83	5.8	$ 95	5.4	$ 117	3.7
Alcoholic beverages	37	2.6	39	2.2	103	3.3
Other real estate	2	0.1	2	0.1	5	0.2
House furnishings and equipment	166	11.6	207	11.8	341	10.8
Personal care	110	7.7	132	7.5	176	5.6
Medical care[a]	177	12.4	250	14.3	291	9.2
Recreation	109	7.6	142	8.1	258	8.2
Reading	25	1.8	29	1.7	56	1.8
Education	22	1.5	39	2.2	59	1.9
Automobile	447	31.3	520	29.7	892	28.3
Other travel and transportation	40	2.8	40	2.3	77	2.4
Other expenditures	44	3.1	79	4.5	125	4.0
Personal insurance[b]	84	5.9	99	5.6	172	5.5
Gifts & contributions	82	5.7	82	4.7	307	9.8
Savings					173	5.5
Total	$1,428	100.0	$1,755	100.0	$3,152	100.0
Total as percent of money income after taxes and other money receipts		44.5%		48.1%		46.5%

[a]Other than prepaid medical care.
[b]Other than social security, etc.
Source: Adapted from Helen H. Lamale, "How the Poor Spend Their Money," in Herman P. Miller (ed.), *Poverty American Style* (Belmont, Calif.: Wadsworth Publishing Company, Inc., 1966), pp. 150–61.

When all households are considered, the poor (i.e., those with incomes under $3,000) are less often installment credit users than the rest of the population.[9] This is in part because, as noted earlier, poor households include substantial numbers of groups of unrelated individuals who are very likely to be old and therefore not likely to be purchasers of debt-producing consumer durables. However, according to Caplovitz, families with incomes under $3,000 comprised about 13% of all families in 1969 and 13% of all credit users (i.e., those making payments on installment contracts).[10]

While poor families may be in debt as often as the nonpoor, the *amount* of their debt is usually less. As reported by Katona and his colleagues, the amount of debt incurred is positively correlated with income.[11] As incomes rise, the average amount spent by households for durables on installment debt over $200 increases substantially. This is in part explained by the fact that average poor households purchase fewer and/or less expensive automobiles, home improvements, and major durables than other households—items which quickly drive up the amount of incurred debt.

Lest the preceding suggest that credit usage is not really a serious problem for the poor, four further facts must be introduced. First, although the poor who have debt have smaller amounts of debt than the nonpoor, this debt usually represents a much higher proportion of their total income. Katona and his colleagues found that of the 29% of families with incomes below $5,000 who had installment debt in 1969, 36%—over one in three—had annual debt payments amounting to 20% or more of their annual incomes. This compares to 23% of those with incomes from $5,000 to $9,999 and 13% of those with incomes of $10,000 and over.[12]

The second important fact is that being in debt, including informal debt for groceries and the like, has important secondary consequences for the poor that it does not so often have for the nonpoor. As shall be demonstrated later, it typically means that the poor are more restricted to shopping in their own communities, where they are known but where prices are higher, assortments smaller, and retail management poorer. This, coupled with the weaker credit ratings of the poor, means that they must pay higher initial cash prices for goods and higher credit charges. These consequences, of course, further shrink the buying power of the poor family's dollar.

Third, the need for credit puts the poor into the hands of those merchants, door-to-door peddlers, and the like who are the most frequent sources of outrageous consumer exploitation. And finally, all these factors lead to higher incidences of default on debt, as reported in Table 3-3.

RATIONALITY AND THE DISADVANTAGED CONSUMER

This finding of extensive credit use by a substantial proportion of the poor brings the discussion to a head-on confrontation with a major—although often unstated—issue in analyses of disadvantaged consumers: do they behave "irrationally" in the marketplace? As noted in the previous chapter, many Americans tend to view the disadvantaged as *disreputable*, as behaving irresponsibly, as having too many babies, not looking for work aggressively enough, "living in sin," drinking excessively, and thus contributing to (if not causing) their own socioeconomic downfall. Without addressing the merits of this view, only contending that it has a substantial popular appeal, it may be asked whether disadvantaged consumers' behavior fits this "expected" pattern.

The charge of irrationality in consumption behavior takes two general forms. The first form alludes to the assumed *self-indulgence* of the poor. It points to the fact that many of the poor are heavily in debt, that many

TABLE 3–3. Distribution of Defaulting Debtors, by Income and Race, 1966

	All Families, %	Credit Users NORC Survey, %[a]	Default Debtors, %
Income			
Under $3,000	13[b]	13	12[c]
$3,000–$3,999	7	7	12
$4,000–$4,999	7	9	15
$5,000–$5,999	8	11	15
$6,000–$7,999	19	23	24
$8,000–$9,999	15	15	12
$10,000 and over	31	22	10
	100	100	100
Race			
Whites	72–64[d]	85	28
Blacks	18–34	15	65
Puerto Ricans	10–2	e	7
	100	100	100

[a]Credit users in the National Opinion Research Center study are those who were making payments on installment debts at the time of the interview.
[b]U.S. Bureau of the Census, *Current Population Report on Consumer Income, 1966,* table 1.
[c]Omits unrelated individuals and those not reporting income.
[d]Range in four cities sampled in Caplovitz's study.
[e]Less than ½%.
Source: David Caplovitz, *Debtors in Default,* vol. I (New York: Bureau of Applied Social Research, Columbia University, 1971), pp. 2–3 and 2–11.

claim to be undernourished yet own color television sets or fancy cars, or that people who can't get jobs wear $40 shoes. To bolster this sort of argument, supporters note many sociologists' conclusions that the lower classes lack extended planning horizons and are very present oriented in their treatment of money. They note Caplovitz's suggestion that the poor may tend to engage in *compensatory consumption*[13] to make up for losses in other areas of life (jobs, affection, respect) and consider it as support for their contentions.

The second, more general form of the irrationality argument alludes to the unwillingness of the poor to act carefully in the marketplace in ways that will overcome their poverty. A spokeswoman for this position is Louis G. Richards, who asks:

> How do consumer practices of the poor compare with the recommended rules of financial management? On almost every count, we have found that the poor fail to use what many would call the rational solution:
>
> 1. Although they spend most of their income on basic needs, those who buy durable goods make serious inroads on their incomes.

2. Most do not use more deliberation, consult more sources, or shop more widely, to get the best buys. Instead, many depend on known merchants or relatives for judgments of what to buy.
3. Few have savings of any size; most do not have life insurance; only about half are covered by medical insurance.
4. It is doubtful whether many carry out home production activities to supplement cash purchases.
5. Many probably do not make full use of the programs established to provide services and goods free or at reduced rates.[14]

These arguments imply that the poor get into debt because they are more irrational than the nonpoor, they are more self-indulgent, and they engage in less planning and careful shopping. And indeed, as Richards has suggested, much of the credit behavior of the disadvantaged (as well as other behavior discussed below) fits this conception of the irrational poor. It is the contention here, however, that this behavior can also be explained —perhaps explained *better*—by a conception of the poor as acting as rationally and carefully as they can *given their disadvantages.*

RATIONALITY AND CREDIT USE

An alternative explanation for the heavy use of credit by many of the poor is based on the fact that the incomes of those who are poor are not only low but also *highly unstable.* As noted in Table 2-1, only *one head in five* of a poor family was employed full time for 50 or more weeks in 1970. This compares to two out of three heads of nonpoor households. As indicated in the previous chapter, this unstable employment pattern apparently has led many poor people to see major parts of their lives as always fated to be unpredictable and at the mercy of the decisions of others —employers, welfare officers, or just "fate." For them, then, a critical piece of information for sound financial planning is simply missing: *they cannot really predict what their future incomes will be.*

Poor families have a number of strategies they might adopt in the face of this uncertainty. Decision theorists suggest at least three possible strategies, (1) minimaxing, (2) maximaxing, and (3) maximizing expected value.[15]

MARKETPLACE STRATEGIES

1. MINIMAX STRATEGY. This strategy is highly conservative. It minimizes the maximum loss that could occur under the worst circumstances. In fear of the future calamity of a substantial loss of income, a minimaxing poor family would behave as Richards would presumably like, spending only

cash, buying only basic necessities, engaging in home production of food, and trying to save what little it could for emergencies.

This is indeed the pattern Rainwater and his colleagues found for working-class wives, a group economically just above the poorest.[16] They found members of this group typically were not confident about their economic futures. They were not sure their husbands' earnings would rise significantly or that economic conditions would improve much. This concern about a potentially chaotic future coupled with a suspicion of merchants led them to express a real desire to pay cash for everything. At least then they would "know where we are" and besides they "suspect a bit of financial treachery is usually involved in 'time payments.' "[17] While this was the desire in most households, many of which set up crude "tin can" accounting systems to budget their cash, about two out of three had some consumer debt at the time of the study.

2. Maximax strategy. The opposite of minimax, this strategy recommends taking the action that would give the best outcome in the most favorable future income circumstances. This strategy could well lead to considerable accumulation of debt by poor families in the expectation (hope) that future income stability and salary increases would permit paying off of any debts incurred. It is entirely possible that many poor families would adopt a maximax strategy merely as a *commitment of hope*. As Irelan and Besner put it in another context:

> A lower-class youngster has more urgent, material reasons for wanting an improved future. His present is painfully unsatisfactory. His urge toward better, stabler occupations is not so much drive for achievement as flight from discomfort and deprivation.[18]

Such behavior could be considered self-indulgent only by the most unfeeling.

3. Maximizing expected value. This strategy requires the household to assume neither the best nor the worst future, but to estimate realistically the likelihood of each possibility and choose the course of action that would lead to the maximum weighted average outcome given all possible circumstances. This strategy could also lead to considerable debt accumulation under the following presumably common conditions:

The likelihood of favorable economic circumstances is considered quite high. This presumably would be more true of those poor who are younger, are better educated, have specific job skills, and the like. It would also be true of those whom Bauer and his colleagues considered "strivers," those whose motivations to achieve upward economic mobility are quite strong.[19] Finally, it may also be true for those who are temporarily reasonably well off and have what Martineau suggests is a short time horizon.[20]

The costs of being caught in unfavorable circumstances are not seen as very high. This might occur in two cases:

1. Where the consumer's limited education and lack of market sophistication means that he or she simply knows less about the unfavorable consequences of being entrapped in an undesirable marketing system or of defaulting on debts—likely repossession, court costs, effects on credit ratings, or effects on future employment opportunities.
2. Where the consumer knows the likely consequences but estimates the potential dollar losses to be relatively small since there will be few possessions to repossess or wages to garnishee. He or she may also believe that in the worst possible circumstances there are no good jobs or careers that preclude skipping out on accumulated debts.

DISCUSSION

In summary, then, while some of the poor may get themselves into debt out of self-indulgence or careless planning, it is at least quite plausible to suggest that many do so as the result of reasonably careful calculations of the consequences of their actions. That their actions often unfortunately do have undesirable consequences can be seen as attributable to their unstable income patterns.

While no comprehensive evaluation of this contention has been undertaken, some support is found in Caplovitz's recent study of why debtors defaulted on consumer loans in four major metropolitan areas.[21] In this study Caplovitz found that the poor were more likely to default on their debts than the nonpoor and that unexpected loss of income and voluntary overextensions of credit were the two most frequently mentioned reasons for defaulting given by both groups. One might expect that if the poor are more often self-indulgent and imprudent planners of their debt, more often accumulating debt in excess of 20% of their incomes, then voluntary overextensions would be reported by them as a much more common reason for default than would be the case for the nonpoor. On the other hand, if the poor really do plan as well as they can but are often caught unexpectedly by a sudden loss of income due to job loss or illness, etc., one would expect *this* reason to show up more often. Relevant data for these hypotheses are presented in Table 3-4.

The table tends to provide good support for the contention that the problem of the defaulting poor is that they more often have sudden income losses. These losses have a strong inverse relationship to income. On the other hand, the poor are much less likely to report overextensions of credit

TABLE 3-4. Reasons for Default, by Income

Reasons[a]	Under $4,000, %	$4,000 to $5,999, %	$6,000 to $7,999, %	$8,000 and Over, %
Loss of income	54[b]	52	44	38
Voluntary overextension				
Low Debt-to-Income (0–9%)[c]	4	14	18	15
Medium Debt-to-Income (10–14%)	10	21	30	33
High Debt-to-Income (20% +)	28	42	54	58
Total	15	27	34	29

[a]Multiple answers permitted.
[b]Percent of individuals.
[c]Percent debts to total income.
Source: David Caploritz, *Debtors in Default,* vol. I (New York: Bureau of Applied Social Research, Columbia University, 1971) pp. 9–4 and 9–12.

than are the nonpoor *even when extent of indebtedness is controlled.* Caplovitz suggests that this finding is related to the fact that a high debt-to-income ratio for the poor is brought on by *one* major purchase whereas for the nonpoor it is the result of several purchases.[22] This again would support the conception of the poor as making careful decisions to buy needed items even though doing so would appear to get them seriously overextended. The nonpoor, on the other hand, become overextended in the manner many have ascribed to the poor, namely by getting further and further into debt through self-indulgence, buying more and more on what the British call "the never-never." These findings, however, should not obscure the critical fact that the poor more often *do* default on their debts. And even for those poor who do not default, entry into debt *doubly* penalizes them, since they must pay more for their goods through legitimate interest charges and higher prices as well as subject themselves more often to the nefarious tactics of unscrupulous merchants and creditors. As Chapter 9 will indicate, credit charges and credit contracts are together the single most frequent source of fraud and illegitimate higher costs foisted upon the disadvantaged by exploitative merchants. While it is possible that this exploitation is anticipated by some of the poor, the analysis in this section suggests that many of them may well subject themselves to it voluntarily assuming, perhaps fatalistically, that it is the best they can do given their disadvantaged circumstances.

Finally, it should be noted with respect to the remarks made in Chapter 1 that to the extent others in the consumer movement share Louise Richards's perspectives, there may well be within the movement a serious misunderstanding of the motives and goals of disadvantaged consumers, a problem of intellect and empathy that may explain some of the movement's lack of impact in this critical area.

Purchasing Decisions: Choosing Alternatives[23]

Given that inner city consumers have established budgeting priorities, how effectively are they able to gather information and make choices about alternative offerings that may meet their specific needs?

Needed information would include:

Information on the range of alternative products and services that might meet these needs.

Information on the characteristics of each alternative:

1. Composition and construction
2. Likely peformance
3. Warranties and guarantees
4. Average market (or suggested list) price

Information on alternative sales outlets:

1. Product availability
2. Product price (relative to market coverage)
3. Availability of credit
4. Cost of credit
5. Other outlet benefits (stamps, games, free delivery, friendly salesmen, etc.)

Such information can be obtained from five basic types of sources varying as to whether the medium is personal or impersonal and whether or not the source is perceived to be an advocate for the product or service in question.[24] The source types are:

1. Personal advocate sources, principally salesmen
2. Impersonal advocate sources—print, radio, and television advertisements, billboards, and the like
3. Personal nonadvocate sources—friends, neighbors, coworkers, and the like
4. Impersonal nonadvocate sources—*Consumer Reports,* Department of Agriculture bulletins, social welfare handouts, and the like
5. Individual investigation or experience, primarily visits to outlets for comparative shopping and/or recollections of past experiences with the product or outlet

Before the information-gathering and choice strategies of the poor can be evaluated, some sense of exactly what it is the poor consumer is attempting to achieve must be developed. Here the answer as reported in the research of Feldman and Star would appear to be that, on the surface at least, he or she is primarily interested in minimizing prices. According to Feldman and Star, almost six in ten shoppers with income under $3,000 (in 1963) can be described as follows:

> These are the shoppers who feel that they ought to keep shopping until they have assured themselves that they are getting the best possible prices, and/or feel obliged to spend as little money as possible by stretching their budget. Their first concerns when making a purchase are: "Can I afford it?" and "Could I get it cheaper somewhere else?" [25]

PRICE REDUCTION STRATEGIES

Thus it may be asked to what extent does the behavior of the poor reflect price reduction strategies. The following shopping strategies may be hypothesized as likely to help minimize prices:

1. Reading newspaper ads
2. Comparison shopping
3. Patronizing supermarkets instead of small local food stores
4. Patronizing discount houses instead of neighborhood durable goods stores
5. Buying unbranded over branded goods in many food categories

As Richards noted,[26] the rather sparse evidence in this area suggests that in *none* of these cases do the poor behave more than the nonpoor in the hypothesized price-reducing fashion (although I shall again point out why such behavior may be quite rational given the characteristics and problems of the poor).

1. Reading newspapers. If a lower-class family wished to reduce the cost of the market basket of goods and services it purchased weekly, an obvious place it would begin would be with the daily newspaper ads. Here may be found the special sale prices for durable goods, the shopping specials at the neighborhood supermarkets, and the special bargain supplements for the discount houses. The consistent finding in the literature, however, is that there is a much lower level of newspaper readership among the poor than among the nonpoor, which would suggest that this sort of price-minimizing behavior is not the typical pattern among the poor.[27] For example, Greenberg and Dervin found that only 17% of their poor sample in Lansing, Michigan, read all of the newspaper regularly, as compared to 39% of the nonpoor.[28] Block and his colleagues did, however, find that

among the poor in St. Louis, reading (presumably of newspapers) was positively associated with interest in price as a food store selection criterion.[29]

2. COMPARISON SHOPPING. If the poor do not use newspapers as extensively as the nonpoor, one might expect them to engage in more personal checking of alternative prices. Yet one of the most frequently quoted findings of Caplovitz's pioneering study of poor New York City consumers is the extent to which the poor have much narrower shopping scope for consumer durables and clothing purchases than do the non-poor.[30] Caplovitz asked his respondents three sets of questions from which he constructed an index of shopping scope. The three questions were:

1. Did the family buy at least one appliance outside what they themselves defined as their neighborhood?
2. Did they *prefer* to shop in neighborhood stores or in big "downtown" stores?
3. Did the wife or mother ordinarily buy her clothes downtown or in the neighborhood?

The proportions indicating intermediate or broad shopping scope by income grouping are as follows:[31]

INCOME	PERCENT INTERMEDIATE OR BROAD SHOPPING SCOPE
Under $2,500	49
$2,500–$3,500	53
$3,500–$4,500	62
$4,500 and over	74

This restricted amount of comparison shopping was also reported by Feldman and Star,[32] who found that poor families:

1. Visited fewer shopping centers each year
2. Made fewer shopping trips
3. Made fewer shopping trips to discount stores
4. Made fewer shopping trips to downtown stores
5. Traveled less time to their shopping location

These early findings with respect to durables are disputed in Day and Brandt's more recent study of California shoppers. In their study, they found that nine out of ten poor credit shoppers traveled "a few miles or more" to purchase a car or household durables. It is, however, strongly possible that this finding is affected by the fact that California cities are very spread out and automobile travel is a major dimension of the state's life-style and by the fact that the authors' definition of low income was higher than that considered in other studies (under $7,500 per year).[33]

Several studies of food-shopping behavior show the poor as much more restricted geographically than the nonpoor in their choice of outlets for major and fill-in purchases.[34] More generally, Block and his colleagues found that only 23% of households in a low-income area of St. Louis had automobiles and 42% said they were limited to shopping within walking distance.[35] These findings support Kelvin Wall's conception of the low-income consumer as "a block dweller, who sees himself as part of his immediate environment and neighborhood . . . and as a consumer . . . is strongly motivated to shop within these confines." [36]

Berry and Solomon and Goodman,[37] on the other hand, have argued that the poor are not so restricted in food shopping as many seem to think, that they will go some considerable distance to shop in food supermarkets. Berry and Soloman found that 65% of poor respondents in their Denver study area would go outside or to the edge of their community to shop at supermarkets. Goodman found that 81% of the low-income families he studied in Philadelphia went outside his study area to shop at chain supermarkets. However, since the study area did not include major shopping thoroughfares within only a few blocks of the sample population, the usefulness of Goodman's findings is questionable.

The weight of evidence, therefore, would seem to be that the poor are less geographically mobile in their shopping behavior than the nonpoor and probably do less comparison shopping before making given purchases.

3. Patronizing supermarkets. Data on the use of supermarkets are also somewhat mixed. Though Goodman and Berry and Solomon found that 81% and 65%, respectively, of their poor respondents shopped in supermarkets for their major food purchases, other studies have indicated that the poor are much less likely than the nonpoor to use such outlets. Typical of these findings are those of Alexis, Simon, and Smith and the work of Kunreuther.[38]

4. Patronizing discount houses instead of local stores. Caplovitz[39] and Feldman and Star[40] provide conflicting data about whether the poor are more likely to patronize higher-cost local outlets and peddlers rather than discount outlets despite their stated greater interest in minimizing prices. For example, Caplovitz compares sources of television sets and washing machines in New York City for his low-income sample with those of a sample of all New York City residents and finds very little use of discount house outlets by the poor.[41] Caplovitz further provides data elsewhere in his study showing that durable goods purchased in outlets other than discount houses were much higher priced for the poor.[42]

The data in Feldman and Star are somewhat more recent (1963) and show that use of discount houses instead of non-discount department stores decreases as incomes rise in Chicago. It is possible that the two studies reflect different market structures in the two cities. The results may also reflect the different phrasing of questions in the two studies. Caplovitz asked where specific appliances were purchased. Feldman and Star asked their respondents which they used *more*, discount houses or department stores, and it may be they use *both* relatively infrequently (the former because they are not available and the latter because they are too high priced and lack credit availability) compared to neighborhood outlets.

Until more data are available, the question of discount house use by the poor must be considered unresolved.

5. PRIVATE BRAND USAGE. The data on private brand usage are inconclusive. An exploratory study by King and DeManche[43] showed greater awareness and usage of private brands by 50 low-income residents in public housing projects in a medium-sized Southern metropolitan area compared with a convenience sample of 25 middle-income families. These data, although suspect because of the lack of sampling controls, do show the poor as minimizing price in this fashion.

More extensive and more carefully controlled studies by several authors,[44] on the other hand, have shown relatively small relationships between demographic characteristics and private brand usage. For example, Myers[45] did not find income significantly related to private brand attitude (although it was in the expected inverse direction), while education was slightly positively related and perceived social class position was negatively related. Frank and Boyd[46] found that family size was positively related to private brand attitude. The pattern of these results seems to support King and DeManche, but it must be remembered that the degree of relationship is very small. For example, *all* the personality and socioeconomic variables in Myers' study only account for 15% of variance among individuals in private brand attitude.

SHOPPING AND RATIONALITY

If the poor are less likely to read newspapers, comparison shop, patronize supermarkets (and perhaps discount houses), or buy lower-priced private brands despite their *greater* interest in saving money, it again must be asked whether this is evidence of irrationality, of some form of self-indulgence, or of a lack of careful planning and execution. The poor say they want to save money, yet they don't seem to *act* in ways that would achieve such a goal. "Irrationality" seems to be the explanation offered by White and Munger when they note that "a [smaller-income] buyer who is willing to go deep into debt for the sake of a grossly uneconomical purchase may also be quite willing to take the most convenient loan rather than worry about a few extra dollars interest."[47] It is, however, more likely, as suggested in the discussion of credit use, that the poor (like the rest of us) try to be as rational as they can but for various reasons end up appearing less rational than the middle class feels they ought to be.

Three sets of hypotheses may be advanced to explain the shopping behavior of the poor as a rational outcome of their goals and circumstances. The first hypothesis, the *ignorance hypothesis,* suggests that the reason the poor do not do a very good job of minimizing prices is that they are unsophisticated in dealing with the marketplace. A second hypothesis, the *constraints hypothesis,* suggests that the poor go about minimizing prices as they do because objective circumstances limit them from being more exhaustive in their search. The final hypothesis, the *preferences hypothesis,* suggests they behave in the marketplace as they do because their goals and preferences in shopping are not really as the middle class would presume. Each of these hypotheses will be taken up in turn.

THE IGNORANCE HYPOTHESIS. There is considerable evidence in the literature that the poor are less knowledgeable than the nonpoor about many aspects of the marketplace. For example, Caplovitz points out that the poor are much less likely to know where to turn for assistance in the event they are defrauded.[48] Monroe and LaPlaca show that in most studies of unit pricing the poor are less likely to use unit-pricing information when it becomes available, although this was not always the case.[49] King and DeManche find them less knowledgeable about the prices of selected food items.[50] Juster and Shay,[51] White and Munger,[52] and Mandel[53] all find the poor less knowledgeable about interest rate alternatives available to them. In a multivariate analysis of credit knowledge (i.e., knowledge of which institutions charge the highest and lowest rates and what interest is typically charged for an auto or home loan or for a department store charge account), Mandel found that lack of income and education were strongly linked to lack of credit knowledge. And the National Commission on Consumer Finance found that recent interest rate disclosure information had less effect in "high risk markets." [54]

In sum, then, it seems reasonable to conclude that the poor are less knowledgeable than the nonpoor. This characteristic may well be related to the poor's lack of education, to their rural or foreign backgrounds, to their age and/or to their lack of facility with the English language. If this is the case, then consumer education programs might prove particularly valuable in improving their circumstances. On the other hand, it is also possible that the poor *appear* ignorant and unsophisticated simply because they don't *need* to know as much about the marketplace as the nonpoor because of the constraints they face in their mobility and local shopping alternatives. Let us now attend to this hypothesis.

THE CONSTRAINTS HYPOTHESIS. It can be argued that the shopping behavior of the poor merely reflects the fact that their physical mobility is limited and the already-noted fact that their incomes are low and unstable. Their physical mobility is restricted in a number of ways:

1. They less often own an automobile. As data from 1970 show, only four out of ten families with incomes under $3,000 own an automobile compared to nine out of ten of those with incomes over $6,000.[55]

2. The public transportation system they might use as an alternative is better designed to bring people to the center of town to work and shop than to transport the poor to suburban shopping areas. While the poor often use the downtown areas for specialty goods shopping, low-cost supermarkets and discount centers are seldom found there. To get to these outlets in outlying shopping centers by public transportation, the poor typically would first have to go to the center of town and then back out to the shopping center. And, of course, there is rarely public transportation between shopping centers. To visit a second center the autoless poor consumer in most cities would have to go back downtown first.

3. While some families without cars could conceivably make such trips, their time is often constrained by the fact that all adult members (e.g., in a single-parent household) are working.

4. The presence of many young children in some families discourages extended shopping trips.[56]

5. For the elderly poor, physical infirmities and general lack of energy make shopping a major chore, especially in areas where stores do not provide ramps, elevators, wide aisles, etc., to aid the more seriously handicapped.

As a result of all of these constraints it is not unusual to see poor shoppers throw away much of the savings they might have achieved in shopping at a distant supermarket by taking a taxi back to their residences!

In addition to these physical constraints to mobility, a factor restricting the poor to neighborhood shopping already noted is their need for credit for food and clothing and for durable goods. As Caplovitz has shown with respect to durable goods, a major reason local retailers and peddlers are preferred to the discount houses is that they are the few places where the poor feel they can get credit.[57] Even for food products, corner outlets are often preferred over supermarkets because the latter do not provide the credit the poor sometimes need to tide them over between paychecks or to keep them provisioned in the frequent eventuality a paycheck is missed.

Day and Brandt, on the other hand, have recently concluded that:

> . . . low income buyers and minorities in particular were not especially constrained in their choice of retailer by (a) a lack of credit availability, at least from other retailers, (b) their willingness to consider unfamiliar retailers (as measured by the likelihood of having an idea where they could obtain credit before starting shopping and their reliance on past relationships), and (c) their need for convenience or proximity to the retailer (as measured by the distance traveled to make the credit purchase).[58]

The possible confounding effects of California's unusually spread-out market structure and the authors' generous definition of low income on their results in this study have already been noted. It should also be noted, in contrast to the above conclusions, that the authors did find that (1) 30 percent of all buyers and 44 percent of all credit buyers "gave some consideration to where they could get credit in their selection of a retailer" and (2) 22 percent of the "poor" and only 7 percent of the "nonpoor" said they "would have bought elsewhere had they been able to pay in cash." [59]

Even for those who don't need credit, instability of incomes presumably has the indirect effect of discouraging the poor from shopping outside their own area or from reading the newspaper ads by making it virtually impossible for them to plan for sales or bargains. If families are uncertain about how much money they will have to spend next week or next month, it is unlikely that they will feel free to allocate much of this week's earnings to take advantage of this week's special sales at discount houses or department stores, to pick up "10 cans of Campbell's tomato soup at the unheard of low price of 89¢," and so on. Further, there is little reason to look ahead to the ads for *next* week's sales if it is entirely possible the family's financial situation may be even worse then.

Finally of course, there are the psychological constraints. Many of the poor, particularly those who are black, often feel timorous about venturing out of their own community. As Rainwater and his colleagues said in *Workingman's Wife:*

> In many ways, then, these women are not optimistically oriented toward spending and buying. In general, they lack confidence in their own buying skills and exhibit a distrust of the business community—which they see as being only too ready to take advantage of their own ineptitude.[60]

An example these authors give of such a householder's approach is the following:

> I try to buy at little places I know—where they will make things good for you and they won't be snotty. I may pay more sometimes by not looking around for bargains, but the stores I know are good and if anything goes wrong they will take it back. I get personal attention and service because they know me. For example, I buy meat from a butcher I know—the meat isn't any cheaper there, but he always gives me choice cuts. He has better meats and I feel that I get a better deal there than if I went scouting around all over.[61]

Caplovitz finds that this timorousness about leaving the area is, in part, a function of urban sophistication. He finds that shopping scope is directly related to income, education, command of English, and length of time in the New York area and youth.[62] With the exception of youth, these desirable characteristics are much less frequently found among the very poorest members of the consuming public.

The net result of these physical, psychological, and financial constraints is to effectively limit many of the poor to shopping in their own area. As Chapter 6 will vividly detail, the retail structure in poor areas is particularly limited in the number of supermarkets, discount houses, and other low-cost mass merchandise outlets available for the poor to patronize if they wanted to. Further, the structure is overpopulated with small, under-capitalized, badly managed outlets with very limited product assortments sold at high prices.

These factors jointly may account for the shopping behavior findings reported earlier. The poor less often read newspaper ads because they are less likely to be able to shop in the supermarkets, discount houses, and department stores that advertise there. Further, they less often read ads because they do not contain what is often the most critical information for the poor, i.e., whether they personally can get credit and what the monthly cost of such credit will be.

Comparison shopping is, of course, physically difficult for the poor and in many cases a waste of time if the choice of outlet and perhaps even the choice of the product itself is determined by where the poor consumer can get credit. (The latter, of course, explains well lack of knowledge among the poor about credit and finance charges.)[63] The lower frequency of patronage of discount houses and supermarkets by the poor in contrast to their admitted price consciousness is explained on the basis of credit needs and the restricted market structure in the areas where they must shop.

Finally, the finding that the poor are not obviously greater purchasers of private brands can also be explained by the fact that the poor more often patronize small local outlets. As indicated, such outlets are undercapitalized and have limited assortments. Under such capital constraints, retailers typically carry only one or two brands in each product line. The criterion usually used for choosing such brands is volume—stock the best sellers. And the best sellers almost always are the national brands. Thus the fact that the poor appear to prefer national brands may largely be a function of product availability, not preference.

THE PREFERENCES HYPOTHESIS. It has already been suggested that some of the apparently irrational shopping behavior of the poor with respect to products and outlets can be explained by the fact that they more often patronize outlets in their own poor neighborhoods. In the previous section it was suggested that they remain in their own neighborhood because they are constrained from going beyond it. While such constraints undoubtedly account for much of such behavior, it is also plausible that many poor people shop in their own neighborhoods because they want to. Two motivations basic to at least some of the poor—the need for flexible credit and the need to socialize—many well account for this phenomenon.

1. *The need for flexible credit.* It is important to note that the poor do

not simply need credit per se; they need what Caplovitz calls flexible credit.[64] Low income drives the poor to lenders and retail outlets that are willing to take poorer-than-average risks. While such credit can often be obtained from many large-scale retail outlets and personal loan companies, albeit at higher-than-average interest rates, a second requirement for those poor people with potentially unstable incomes is that the lender must be flexible enough to forgive an occasional missed payment or to reschedule loan payments in particularly difficult times. It is rare for bureaucratic sources such as personal loan companies to be this flexible. The poor therefore naturally turn for credit purchases to local merchants and to peddlers who come to know them and their family circumstances fairly well and adjust their credit-granting and repayment policies accordingly. As Caplovitz has noted:

> The merchant starts from the premise that most of his customers are honest people who intend to pay but have difficulty managing their money. Missed payments are seen as more often due to poor management and to emergencies than to dishonesty. The merchants anticipate that their customers will miss some payments and they rely on informal controls to insure that payments are eventually made.[65]

There are other benefits for the merchant:

> More importantly, the frequent contact of a weekly-payment system enables the merchant to get to know his customer. He learns when the customer receives his pay check, when his rent is due, who his friends are, when job layoffs, illnesses, and other emergencies occur—in short, all sorts of information which allow him to interpret the reason for a missed payment. Some merchants reported that when they know the customer has missed a payment for a legitimate reason such as illness or a job layoff, they will send a sympathetic note and offer the customer a gift (an inexpensive lamp or wall picture) when payments are resumed. This procedure, they say, frequently brings the customer back with his missed payments.[66]

2. *The need to socialize.* It was suggested earlier that taking on debt may be a way of making concrete the wish to escape the terrible burden of poverty. So, in a sense, may the shopping experience be seen as a way of escaping the drudgery and dullness of life in what is often a crowded, dilapidated flat constantly oppressed by the fear of financial disaster. Lacking income, time, or transportation for many of the conventional diversions, many poor housewives may choose a shopping trip in their local community as a chance to see new things, meet with friends, talk with storekeepers and salesmen, and otherwise develop their social contacts. Martineau first noted this tendency among the poor:

> We have found that the customer generally thinks of shopping as a total experience which runs through a number of departments in a number of

> stores and ends when she (or he) returns home. . . . Curiously, the lowest-income shoppers mentioned the holiday aspects of such a trip more than any other group, probably because their routine lives are closer to humdrum practicality.[67]

Sociologist Gregory Stone was also describing the poor when he spoke of the "personalizing consumer":

> Without access to either formal or informal channels of social participation, because of her lower social status, her very few or very many children, and the fact that she had spent the early years of her married life outside the local area, this type of consumer established quasi-primary relationships with the personnel of local independent retail institutions . . . [which] compensated for her larger social losses. . . .[68]

This relative emphasis on social contact may explain why Collazzo found the poor much more satisfied with stores they patronized and much less frustrated when they were out of stock. Collazzo found the poor much less frustrated by the facts that "clerks [are] slow to serve you," "clerks pounce on you as soon as you enter," and "clerks sell aggressively." [69]

It has already been noted that the poor make extensive use of peddlers. A major reason for patronizing peddlers, besides their convenience and flexible credit policy, is that they provide an important social contact and diversion.

> That dealing with a peddler can be more than business, that it can develop into a personal relationship, is suggested by the more than a third of the ninety-one families who reported spending time in small talk with the peddler. The deepening of a personal relationship is also implied by its extended duration. More than half of those in debt to peddlers had been dealing with the same man for more than a year; about a third, for more than two years; and eleven families, for over five years.
>
> The peddler operates within the social networks of his customers, as shown by the fact that more than 70 per cent of these families know other people who buy from their own peddler. Through these networks of social ties, the peddler can exercise a measure of control over his customers, for when trying to collect from a recalcitrant customer, he can apply pressure to friends, neighbors, and relatives. He can shame the delinquent customer into paying by complaining to his friends or relatives, or he can threaten to withhold service from the friends until they persuade the delinquent customer to make good his debt.[70]

It is clear that the poor realize they pay more when dealing with peddlers ("Charley" or "Mr. Ben") but are apparently willing to do so in return for the flexible credit and the important social interaction it brings.

Finally, it is possible that the need to socialize may also help explain low readership of newspapers by the poor. A number of studies have shown that the poor are likely to rely more on personal than impersonal sources when seeking product information. While such information-seeking behavior may provide important personal gratification to the poor, it is questionable whether it provides the precise price data they say they need. But then such behavior may more accurately reflect their *real* goal hierarchy.

Summary

This chapter has introduced briefly several of the major consumption problems faced by the poor. While, as expected, a major cause of these problems was seen to be low income, it was also seen that characteristics associated with low income—instability of incomes, lower education, large families, lack of transportation, and the like—make their own contributions. Further, it appeared possible that these characteristics in some instances (that is, for some poor households) have their influence, as suggested in Figure 1—1, through attitudes and values—the need for hope, the need to socialize, etc.—which may be the more immediate link to their consumption problems.

The poor's consumption problems were related both to the way in which they allocate funds between spending and saving and the way in which they make product, brand, and outlet choices. With respect to budgeting choices, a great many of the poor do not adopt a conservative strategy of living within their limited means, but instead overspend their income and undertake considerable debt—for some, debt amounting to 20% or more of their incomes. The consequences of entering into such debt are several. First, it increases the probability that the household will become insolvent. Second, the addition of credit costs to overblown retail prices increases the total cost of merchandise purchased. Finally, entrance into credit agreements further restricts the mobility of poor households and subjects them to considerable merchant exploitation.

It was suggested, however, that poor households do not necessarily overspend their incomes and get into debt out of some need for self-indulgence or because they are careless planners, but because they lack a key piece of budget-planning information, namely the likely amount of their future earnings. What appeared as irrational behavior may well simply be the reasonable response of the poor to their own peculiar circumstances.

The latter was suggested also as the principal explanation of poor people's behavior in seeking to minimize the prices they pay for goods and services. It was suggested that while the poor may be more ignorant about available alternatives and less likely to read newspapers, comparison shop, patronize supermarkets or discount houses, or buy private labels than the nonpoor, those characteristics could quite plausibly be explained as a rational outgrowth of the constraints on, and preferences of, the poor—

their physical and psychological immobility, their need for flexible credit, or their need to socialize.

It has also been suggested that the problems of the poor stem not just from their own characteristics, who they are, what they want, but from characteristics of the market they patronize—the absence of mass merchandisers, the poor management that exists in small stores, and the existence of frequent exploitation. This theme of the *interrelatedness* of the causes of disadvantaged consumer problems is one that will continue to be emphasized throughout this volume.

A second theme is that the problems of the disadvantaged are not just quantitatively, but qualitatively different from those of the nondisadvantaged and that those who insist that the poor are behaving irrationally may be seriously misperceiving their true problems. Such misperceptions represent a very dangerous base on which to formulate public policy, a point to be developed further in later chapters.

Notes

1. For an excellent discussion of the concepts of subculture as applied to consumer behavior see Frederick D. Sturdivant, "Subculture Theory: Poverty, Minorities, and Marketing," in Scott Ward and Thomas S. Robertson (eds.), *Consumer Behavior: Theoretical Sources* (Englewood Cliffs, N.J.: Prentice-Hall, Inc., 1973), pp. 470–520.
2. Age of head in the poor and nonpoor groups was essentially the same, but as expected, education of the poor was 1.7 to 2.1 years less than of the nonpoor. In addition, about 41% of the poor owned their own homes and 68% to 77% had their own cars. Of the nonpoor, 67% owned their own homes and 92% owned automobiles. See Helen H. Lamale, "How the Poor Spend Their Money," in Herman P. Miller (ed.), *Poverty American Style* (Belmont, Calif.: Wadsworth Publishing Company, Inc., 1966) pp. 150–61.
3. See, for example, U.S. Congress, House Committee on Government Operations, *Consumer Problems of the Poor: Supermarket Operations in Low-Income Areas and the Federal Response*, Thirty-eighth Report (Washington: Government Printing Office, 1968).
4. The figures in tables 3-1 and 3-2 do not yield these net effects on assets and liabilities because of reporting errors in the original consumer data.
5. Lamale, *op. cit.*
6. George Katona et al., *1969 Survey of Consumer Finances* (Ann Arbor: Survey Research Center, Institute for Social Research, University of Michigan, 1970), p. 25.
7. Board of Governors, Federal Reserve Board, *Federal Reserve Bulletin*, March 1972, p. A-52.

8. *Ibid.*
9. Katona et al., *op. cit.*, p. 23.
10. David Caplovitz, *Consumers in Trouble* (New York: The Free Press, 1974), pp. 2–3.
11. Katona et al., *op. cit.*, p. 77.
12. *Ibid.*, p. 25.
13. David Caplovitz, *The Poor Pay More* (New York: The Free Press, 1967), p. 13.
14. Louise C. Richards, "Consumer Practices of the Poor," in Lola M. Irelan (ed.), *Low–Income Life Styles* (Washington: U.S. Department of Health, Education, and Welfare, 1966), p. 82.
15. David W. Miller and Martin K. Star, *Executive Decisions and Operations Research* (Englewood Cliffs, N.J.: Prentice–Hall, Inc., 1960), pp. 86–94.
16. Lee Rainwater, Richard P. Coleman, and Gerald Handel, *Workingman's Wife* (New York: McFadden Books, 1962), pp. 165 ff.
17. *Ibid.*, p. 166.
18. Lola M. Irelan and Arthur Besner, "Low–Income Outlook on Life," in Irelan, *op. cit.*, p. 5.
19. Raymond Bauer and Scott Cunningham, *Studies in the Negro Market* (Boston: Marketing Science Institute, 1971), pp. 34 ff.
20. Pierre Martineau, "Social Classes and Spending Behavior," *Journal of Marketing*, vol. 23, no. 2, October 1958, pp. 121–30.
21. David Caplovitz, *Consumers in Trouble* (New York: The Free Press, 1974).
22. *Ibid.*, pp. 9–11 ff.
23. Material for this section is drawn from Alan R. Andreasen, "Consumerism in the Inner City," paper presented at Brookings Institution Conference on Consumerism, University of Rochester, June 1972.
24. Alan R. Andreasen, "Attitudes and Consumer Decision," in Lee E. Preston (ed.), *New Research in Marketing* (Berkeley, Institute of Business and Economic Research, University of California, 1966), pp. 1–16.
25. Lawrence P. Feldman and Alvin D. Star, "Racial Factors in Shopping Behavior," in Keith Cox and Ben M. Enis (eds.), *A New Measure of Responsibility for Marketing* (Chicago: American Marketing Association, 1968), p. 222.
26. Richards, *op. cit.*
27. See, for example, Audits and Surveys, Inc., *The Buffalo Metropolitan Market and Its Newspaper Audiences: Size and Characteristics, 1966* (Buffalo: Buffalo Courier-Express, Inc., 1967), and O'Brien–Sherwood Associates, *Profile of the Los Angeles Market, 1963* (Los Angeles: Los Angeles Herald-Examiner, 1964).
28. Bradley Greenberg and Brenda Dervin, "Mass Communication among the Urban Poor," *Public Opinion Quarterly*, vol. 34, no. 2, Summer 1970, p. 231.
29. Carl E. Block, Corrine S. Cope, Joseph T. Kunce, and David Hartson,

The Badge of Poverty (Columbia: Regional Rehabilitation Research Institute, University of Missouri–Columbia, March 1970), p. 60.

30. Caplovitz, *The Poor Pay More*, p. 55.
31. *Ibid.*
32. Feldman and Star, *op. cit.*
33. George S. Day and William K. Brandt, "A Study of Consumer Credit Decisions: Implications for Present and Prospective Legislation," in National Commission on Consumer Finance, *Technical Studies*, vol. 1 (Washington: Government Printing Office, 1973), pp. 88–9. The authors acknowledge the possible effect of "California sprawl" but counter that perhaps half of their respondents had a shopping center *nearer* than where they bought their car on credit. This finding, however, is misleading in that car purchases are evidently included and there are typically few or no car dealers in disadvantaged areas but many shopping centers.
34. Marcus Alexis, Leonard Simon, and Kenneth Smith, "Some Determinants of Food Buying Behavior," in Marcus Alexis, Robert J. Holloway, and Robert S. Hancock (eds.), *Empirical Foundations of Marketing: Research Findings in the Behavioral and Applied Sciences* (Chicago: Markham Publishing Company, 1969).
35. Carl E. Block, "Prepurchase Search Behavior of Low Income Households," working paper, University of Missouri–Columbia, Columbia, September 1970.
36. Quoted in Kevin Wall, "Marketing in Low-Income Neighborhoods: A Systems Approach," in Bernard A. Morin (ed.), *Marketing in a Changing World*, Proceedings of the American Marketing Association Spring Conference, June 1969, p. 25.
37. Leonard L. Berry and Paul J. Solomon, "Generalizing about Low Income Food Shoppers: A Word of Caution," *Journal of Retailing*, Summer 1971, pp. 41–51, 92; Charles S. Goodman, "Do the Poor Pay More?" *Journal of Marketing*, vol. 32, January 1968, pp. 18–24.
38. Alexis, Simon, and Smith, *op. cit.*, and Howard Kunreuther, "Why the Poor May Pay More for Food: Theoretical and Empirical Evidence," *Journal of Business*, July 1973, pp. 368–87.
39. Caplovitz, *The Poor Pay More*.
40. Feldman and Star, *op. cit.*
41. Caplovitz, *The Poor Pay More*, p. 53.
42. *Ibid.*, p. 90.
43. Robert L. King and Earl Robert DeManche, "Comparative Acceptance of Selected Private-branded Food Products by Low-Income Negro and White Families," in Philip R. McDonald (ed.), *Marketing Involvement in Society and the Economy* (Chicago: American Marketing Association, 1969), pp. 63–9.
44. See, for example, John G. Myers, "Determinants of Private Brand Attitude," *Journal of Marketing Research*, vol. 4, February 1967, pp. 73–81;

and T. R. Rao, "Are Some Consumers More Prone to Purchase Private Brands?" *Journal of Marketing Research,* vol. 6, November 1969, pp. 447–50.

45. Myers, *op. cit.*
46. Ronald Frank and Harper W. Boyd, Jr., "Are Private-Brand-Prone Grocery Customers Really Different?" *Journal of Advertising Research,* vol. 5, December 1965, pp. 27–35.
47. James J. White and Frank W. Munger, Jr., "Consumer Sensitivity to Interest Rates: An Empirical Study of New-Car Buyers and Auto Loans," *Michigan Law Review,* vol. 69, no. 7, June 1971, p. 1220.
48. Caplovitz, *The Poor Pay More,* pp. 175 ff.
49. Kent B. Monroe and Peter L. LaPlaca, "What Are the Benefits of Unit Pricing?" *Journal of Marketing,* vol. 36, July 1972, pp. 16–22.
50. King and DeManche, *op. cit.*
51. F. T. Juster and R. Shay, *Consumer Sensitivity to Finance Rates: An Empirical and Analytical Investigation* (New York: National Bureau of Economic Research Occasional Paper H88, 1964).
52. White and Munger, *op. cit.*
53. Lewis Mandel, "Consumer Knowledge and Understanding of Consumer Credit," *Journal of Finance,* vol. 26, December 1971.
54. National Commission on Consumer Finance, *Consumer Credit in the United States* (Washington: Government Printing Office, 1972), p. 177.
55. *Statistical Abstract of the United States,* 92nd annual. ed. (Washington: Government Printing Office, 1972), p. 321.
56. Caplovitz, *The Poor Pay More,* p. 70.
57. *Ibid.,* p. 54.
58. Day and Brandt, *op. cit.,* p. 89.
59. *Ibid.*
60. Rainwater et al., *op. cit.,* p. 171.
61. *Ibid.,* p. 174.
62. Caplovitz, *The Poor Pay More,* pp. 54–7.
63. Mandel, *op. cit.*
64. Caplovitz, *The Poor Pay More,* p. 78.
65. *Ibid.,* p. 23.
66. *Ibid.,* p. 24.
67. Pierre Martineau, "The Personality of the Retail Store," *Harvard Business Review,* vol. 36, no. 1, January–February 1958, p. 55.
68. Gregory P. Stone, "City Shoppers and Urban Identification: Observations on the Social Psychology of City Life," *American Journal of Sociology,* vol. 60, July 1954, p. 42.
69. Charles J. Collazzo, Jr., "Effects of Income upon Shopping Attitudes and Frustrations," *Journal of Retailing,* vol. 42, no. 1, spring 1966, p. 3.
70. Caplovitz, *The Poor Pay More,* p. 79.

4. The Black Consumer

RACE HAS BEEN a source of disadvantage in America almost from the founding of the country. From the first encounters with the Indians through the landing of the first black slaves at Jamestown in 1619 to the continuing subtle practices of housing and job discrimination in the 1960s and 1970s, the color of one's skin has been an inescapable badge of one's class status in the United States.[1] For the blacks and browns of America this has effectively meant that their lives are lived "in the back of the bus" of the American society.

This chapter traces briefly some of the major elements of this racial minority experience, using as point of focus the experience of American blacks, particularly those in Northern urban centers. The discussion proceeds from a model like that proposed in Chapter 2, linking race to consumer problems both directly and as mediated through values and attitudes. As in Chapter 2, a major problem in attributing effects to the factor of race is that race is closely associated with a number of other important social characteristics.[2] To be black, for example, means that one is also likely to be poor or to be young or to live in a racial ghetto. On the other hand, some of these characteristics, such as poverty and ghetto residence, are not merely associated with skin color, but, more accurately, are the *result* of it. Thus, establishing a relationship between race and consumption problems is a difficult matter of disentangling cause and effect, a task not very well handled to date in the marketing or economic literature.

There are some who argue that there is nothing uniquely black in terms of values and culture, that "the Negro is only an American, and nothing else." [3] The position taken here, however, is that two factors—the historical experience of black Americans from slavery onward and white America's continuing imposition of racial discrimination in education, housing, and employment—create within the contemporary black community a set of shared experiences and views of the world that set blacks apart from the rest of society in terms of the basic goals and behavioral patterns they bring to the marketplace. Whether these differences will disappear some day in the absence of racism is a matter of speculation; certainly their effects are amply evident today.

Black Socioeconomic Identity

The nature of blacks' cultural differences is, of course, embedded in who they are. Thus this chapter will first review some fundamental socioeconomic conditions in which blacks differ from whites, beginning with the most central, poverty.

BLACKS IN POVERTY

The strong association between race and poverty was pointed out in Chapter 2. In contemporary America the probabilities of being poor are much greater if one is nonwhite than if one is white. In 1970 there were an estimated 25.1 million nonwhites in 6.5 million households in the U.S., of whom almost 90% (22.7 million) were officially classified as "Negro." In that year slightly over one in three (33.6%) black individuals were poor, compared to one in ten (9.9%) whites.[4] The 8 million black poor in 1970 comprised 30% of all poor, yet blacks comprised only about 11% of the total population.

More importantly, poverty has been much harder to eliminate for nonwhites than whites. Government data indicate that since 1959, when poverty statistics were first collected, the number of whites in poverty has declined 38.7% while the number of nonwhites in poverty has declined only 27%. While poverty rates for both groups have declined substantially, they have declined less rapidly for blacks. As a consequence, nonwhite poverty rates have inched up slightly from 3.1 to 3.2 times white rates.[5]

It is significant to note that these data also suggest strongly that were it not for the war on poverty and the 1964 Civil Rights Act, things might be much worse for blacks. From 1959 to 1965, while the number of whites in poverty was declining 21% the number of poor nonwhites was declining only 3%. As recently as 1965 about one-half of all blacks were officially poor. Since 1965, however, greater nonwhite progress has been made. From 1965 to 1970 the number of nonwhites in poverty declined 24.8%, which is somewhat better than the 22.3% decline for whites.[6]

It is also important to note that the structure of black poverty is considerably different from that of white poverty (Table 4-1). First, black poverty is more a family problem than a problem for unrelated individuals. Blacks comprise 28% of all poor families and only 17% of all poor unrelated individuals. To put the situation another way, while only 37% of all poor

TABLE 4–1. Employment Status of Families and Unrelated Individuals in Poverty, by Race, 1970

	Families				Unrelated Individuals			
	White		Negro		White		Negro	
Employment Status	No.[a]	%	No.[a]	%	No.[a]	%	No.[a]	%
Ill or disabled	578	15.6	273	18.9	b	b	b	b
Family responsibilities								
Female heads not working	529[c]	14.3	283[c]	19.6	2,291[d]	55.5	369[d]	43.9
Female heads working part time	174	4.7	171	11.8	343	8.3	101	12.0
	703	19.0	454	31.4	2,634	63.8	470	55.9
Unable to find steady work								
Female heads working full time less than 50 weeks	195	5.3	144	10.0	263	6.4	38	4.5
Male heads not working	489[c]	13.2	64[c]	4.4	629[d]	15.3	144[d]	17.1
Male heads working part time or full time less than 50 weeks	848	22.9	246	17.0	370	9.0	121	14.4
	1,532	41.4	454	31.4	1,262	30.6	303	36.1
Inadequate salaries								
Male heads working full time	734	19.9	170	11.8	77	1.9	36	4.3
Female heads working full time	72	1.9	72	5.0	137	3.3	30	3.6
	806	21.8	242	16.7	214	5.2	66	7.9
Other								
Students	38	1.0	15	1.0	b	b	b	b
Armed Forces	44	1.2	6	0.4	11	0.3	f	f
	82	2.2	21	1.5	11	0.3	—	—
Total[e]	3,701	100.0	1,445	100.0	4,121	100.0	840	100.0

[a]In thousands.
[b]Not reported separately.
[c]Excludes students and ill or disabled.
[d]Does not exclude students and ill or disabled.
[e]Totals in some cases do not equal column entries due to rounding.
[f]Base less than 75,000.

Source: U.S. Bureau of the Census, *Current Population Reports,* series P-60, no. 81, "Characteristics of the Low Income Population, 1970" (Washington: Government Printing Office, 1971).

black households consist of unrelated individuals, more than one-half of all poor white households are so classified.

These differences are closely associated with age. As noted in Chapter 2, unrelated individuals are mainly people over 65. It is therefore not surprising that 23% of all poor whites are over 65 years of age compared to only 9% of all poor blacks. (Among *all* whites, those 65 and over constitute 10% of the population; and among all blacks, those 65 and over constitute 6%. This difference, in part, reflects differences in longevity between the races.)

The other major differences between blacks and whites are that poor black families are much more likely to be headed by women and that, although unrelated poor individuals of both races are more likely to be women, this is somewhat less likely to be the case for blacks. The following are the percentages of females in each group:

	WHITE	BLACK
Family heads	29	57
Unrelated individuals	74	64

This difference, to a small extent, reflects differences in marital status in the total black and white populations.

In summary, then, in general terms white poverty can be seen as much more often a problem for older unrelated females and families with male heads, whereas for blacks the problem is more often one for female-headed families. More significant, however, is the role employment status plays in black poverty.

The employment status of poverty by race reported in Table 4-1 is very different for blacks and whites. Among unrelated individuals, the problems of blacks are relatively often problems of men not finding work or not being paid enough for full-time work to get them above the poverty threshold. As expected from earlier discussions, among unrelated whites a higher proportion of those in poverty is found to be single females, presumably mostly old, not seeking work, than among blacks. Among families—again as expected—a relatively high proportion of black poor people are found among female-headed families not working or not working full time. Among whites, relatively more poor families are found to be headed by males not working.

It is generally well known that approximately twice as many blacks as whites are usually unemployed at any given time. But it also is true that *employed* blacks are much less likely to work the full year than employed whites. While there is little difference between white and black women, in 1970 only 59% of all working black males worked year round full time compared to 67% of white males.[7] In 1970 only 50.4% of all working blacks worked 50 or more weeks, compared to 58.2% of all working whites. It is undoubtedly true that this instability of job experiences for blacks is in large measure the direct or indirect result of discrimination, of making blacks "last hired, first fired."[8] As discussed below, this job instability appears to have a significant effect on blacks' credit usage.

OCCUPATION

It is well known that blacks are more concentrated in lower-status or unskilled occupations than whites and that much of this is the result of direct or indirect discrimination. In the present context, however, it is important to note the extent to which blacks lag behind whites in white-collar occupations. In 1970 only one in six black males had a white-collar job compared to two in five white males. Also, one in three black women had a white-collar job compared to three in five white women.[9]

Perhaps the most discouraging indicator of black income problems and the discouraging character of continuing income differentials is data on returns to schooling by race. As Welch indicates in a recent article, it was the case in 1966 that for those black males who entered the labor force in the early fifties and before, going on in school was much less valuable to them than it was to whites. For black males with eight or more years of work experience, an extra year of schooling in 1966 was worth only one-half to two-thirds of what it was to whites in terms of direct income returns. Thus as years of schooling increase, blacks in this group fall farther and farther behind whites. Welch's data, however, offer some hope by revealing that in 1966 those recently in the labor force (i.e., those most recently schooled) had *greater* returns to extra years of schooling than whites. This, Welch suggests, may be evidence that recent improvements in black schools are paying off in encouraging blacks who might not have gone on to further schooling in the past to continue their education and thereby narrow the income gap between themselves and whites.[10]

EDUCATION

As the preceding discussion implies, historically there has been a considerable gap in years of schooling between blacks and whites, although this gap has narrowed considerably in very recent years. By 1970 virtually the same proportion of the black population 3 to 34 years old as of the white population in the same age bracket was enrolled in school.[11] However, when this figure is broken down by age classification, it is clear that this is primarily due to the heavier enrollment of blacks in preschool programs and that in all other age groupings blacks are behind whites, with the lag growing beyond the 14-year age group.[12] Even if blacks were to *equal* whites in the proportion of each age cohort in school, this does not mean they would have had about the same number of years of schooling completed. This is the case since by the time they get to high school, less than one in two blacks are in the modal grade for their age compared to two in three whites, and blacks are three times as likely as whites to be two or more years below the mode.[13] Relatively fewer blacks complete high school, the minimum cutoff for many white-collar jobs. Only 54% of black males and 58% of black females aged 24 to 29 in 1970 had completed high school compared to 79% and 67% of white males and females, respectively, in this age group.

It further must be remembered that the increase in years of schooling for blacks has been very recent, and thus older black consumers are at a considerable educational disadvantage compared to their white counterparts. This is shown in the figures for level of schooling completed by those over 25 in 1970;[14] only 31.4% of such blacks had completed high school and 4.4% had completed college, compared to 54.5% and 11.3% for whites. Median years of schooling for blacks in 1970 were still only 9.8 years, compared to 12.1 years for whites.

Of course a reduction in the gap in years of schooling between blacks and whites does not necessarily mean that the *quality* of educational achievement is reduced. Many studies have shown that the performance of blacks in the weaker institutions they attend is uniformly poorer than that of whites.[15] The Coleman Report, for example, estimated that by the time they leave high school, blacks may lag behind whites *in the same grade* as much as 3 to 3½ years in educational achievement.[16] However, it is suspected that this discrepancy may also be lessening. As an article in *The Conference Board Record* noted in August 1972:

> However, it is probable that the [educational] quality lag has also begun to shorten. This assumption is based on the large-scale shifts of the black population from the rural South to the metropolitan North and West whose standards of education are higher; the greater proportion of blacks being educated in desegregated institutions at all levels—elementary, secondary, and universities and colleges; and efforts to improve instruction in ghetto schools.[17]

OTHER CHARACTERISTICS

In addition to income, employment, and educational differences, there are three other major socioeconomic differences between blacks and whites that have significant effects on black consumption problems. These differences are in residential location, age, and family status.

1. RESIDENTIAL LOCATION. With respect to residential location, the critical distinction is the extent to which blacks are segregated into urban ghettos. Over one-half of all blacks are still located in the South and 44%

of these in Southern nonmetropolitan areas. But blacks are increasingly moving North and West and to the metropolitan centers.[18] To a large extent the interregional changes also involve a movement off farms into cities, particularly the central cities of large metropolitan areas. Three out of four blacks now live in metropolitan areas, and about 80% of these live in the central cities of those metropolitan areas (mainly in black ghettos). About one-third of all blacks now live in the central cities of Northern and Western metropolitan areas where they now make up 18.5% of the resident populations. Indeed blacks are now rapidly approaching domination of a great number of major cities. Given that black immigration to cities is now accompanied by massive white out-migration to the suburban fringes, this domination is expected to grow substantially in the next decade.

Where they do live, blacks are much more likely not to own their own homes, to live in housing with inadequate plumbing, and to have a house in overcrowded condition, although all these conditions are improving.[19] Only 42% of black housing units in 1970 were owner occupied compared to 65% of white housing units. Only 83% of black housing had all plumbing facilities compared to 95% of white housing. And finally, 16% of black-owned housing and 23% of black-rented housing had more than one person per room; the comparable figures for white housing in 1970 were 6% and 9% respectively. These features of higher rental occupancy and overcrowding have important consequences for black consumption problems, as has the basic fact of ghettoization itself.

2. Age and family status. It is important to understand that blacks are much younger than whites, have a higher fertility rate, and more often are members of female-headed households, all of which affect their consumption behavior. The median age for blacks is about 22.4 years compared to 29 years for whites. This, of course, implies that there are relatively more black children and, thus, more children per black household. "Central city" black families both above and below the poverty level are about half a person larger than white families, as the following average family sizes for 1970 indicate:[20]

	Blacks	Whites
Below low income level	4.2	3.7
Above low income level	3.9	3.3

This larger family size in turn places added strain on already-smaller black incomes and creates a greater pressure for the use of credit or a reduction in savings to meet current needs.

The younger age of blacks is also associated with a higher rate of population growth. In 1970, in each age bracket between 15 and 54 black women had more children than white women. This of course is in part a function of education and income; fertility declines with increases in both. Thus partly because education and income for both groups is increasing and partly as a consequence of improved birth control techniques, fertility rates have been declining for both groups.[21]

With respect to the status of the family itself, blacks are more likely to be members of female-headed families than whites, a phenomenon which is growing more common. As in the white community the husband-present home is the dominant configuration, but this is much less so than in the white community. Of about 4,928,000 black families in 1970, two-thirds had a husband and wife present, while 27% had a female head only.[22] Comparable figures for whites are eighty-nine and nine percent respectively. The percentage of black female headed households has increased five percentage points (about one-fifth) in the last ten years. Female-headed black families are more likely to reside in urban areas than are black husband-wife families. Black female-headed families are also likely to be younger than white female-headed families in the Northeast and North Central regions. Female-headed black families in urban areas were also more likely to have incomes under $3,000.

Attitudes and Values

As indicated earlier, because of the above differences in socioeconomic characteristics, it is difficult if not impossible to define what is unique about black attitudes, values, and, as shall be indicated in the next chapter, purchase behavior that one can associate only—or at least primarily—with blackness.[23] Many of what appear to Northern middle-class whites as cultural differences, such as language and some dress and housing preferences, are more properly attributable to differences in geographic background and in social class. Thus it is not surprising to find that since blacks are more often poor or more recently poor, they reflect many of the feelings of fatalism, helplessness, insecurity, and the like that were attributed to the poor in Chapter 2.

There is, of course, one feeling that is predominantly black (it is shared by other racial and ethnic minorities), and that is the feeling of being discriminated against. Blacks know that at present they cannot join certain clubs, live in certain areas, take certain jobs, join certain unions, or travel in certain parts of the country without harassment, or get a business loan from certain banks. This knowledge is a burning part of the black psyche no matter what their station in life. It is knowledge that causes many blacks to feel more alienated, insecure, more powerless, and sometimes more fatalistic than whites who are otherwise like them in age, income, and education.

Bullock believes that black insecurity in particular has a major effect on consumption behavior:

> Another need which we observe to be operative in the consumer behavior of Negroes and whites is that of security. Some degree of insecurity seems to grow directly out of their respective social–cultural setting, and additional anxieties are apparently fostered by the goal blockages which they encounter in their pursuit of belongingness.
>
> The Negro's insecurity begins basically at home. It is planted in his personality structure there, and its effects are spread to encompass a great portion of his life in the larger society. Our findings have led us to believe that this is not the case with whites. Instead, serious forms of anxieties seem to develop somewhat later through the compulsion to push ahead and out of those changes in our national and international life which they define as threats to their status position.[24]

Such insecurity manifests itself in greater feelings of alienation and anomie on the part of blacks, as indicated in the work of McClosky and Schaar,[25] and Killian and Grigg.[26] It also may well explain Bauer and Cunningham's finding that middle- and upper-income blacks perceive themselves as having lower social status than do whites even when income and education are matched.[27]

The subject of black self-esteem, which plays an important role in the analysis of black consumption problems, has been the subject of important studies by several authors. The problem blacks must face, as suggested by Grier and Cobbs in *Black Rage*, is that there is "an attitude, shared by black and white alike, that blacks are inferior." [28] The consequences of this attitude in terms of blacks' negative self-concept is well documented in the research of Kenneth Clark[29] and others. Recently some of this work has been challenged by Baughman, who suggests that low self-esteem may not be as pervasive among blacks as suspected, although he suggests that high self-esteem among blacks often requires adoption of a cynical attitude and a feeling of estrangement toward both black and white.[30]

That black feelings about white prejudice are well grounded in fact is reported in a number of studies. For example, Campbell and Schuman, in a recent large-scale study of 15 Northern cities,[31] found discriminatory views held by a substantial proportion of whites:

Statement	% Agreeing
Whites have a right to keep Negroes out of their neighborhood	30
There should be some limit on the Negroes moving into an all white neighborhood	48
I oppose laws to prevent job discriminaton	19
I'd rather our small children had only white friends	33

The researchers, however, conclude:

> We have indeed revealed much evidence of white dislike and resentment of Negroes, much white support of segregated social patterns, much white resistance to equal rights in housing, and much white unwillingness to admit the facts of social discrimination. . . . [But there] is no universal pattern of racial conduct among white people in this country; there is on the contrary a fundamental and perhaps growing schism between those whose basic orientation toward Negroes is positive and those whose attitudes and behavior are negative.[32]

This theme of a growing gap between much of white society and blacks and their supporters is one echoed in the conclusion of the Kerner Commission study of the civil disorders of the mid-1960s.[33]

There is some evidence, on the other hand, that overall racial prejudice may be declining.[34] However, it is likely to be some time before the critical handicaps of job and residential discrimination disappear. Projections by Schwartz in 1967[35] suggested that it will be 1986 before 90% of whites will not move if a black moves next door, and 1982 before 90% will be willing for blacks to go to the same schools. Recent reactions of Northern whites to black school busing suggest that Schwartz's projections are highly optimistic.

Summary

The preceding brief overview sought to point out several principal characteristics of black consumers. It has been shown that they are much more likely to be poor than are whites. This inevitably means that on average they will have less education, poorer jobs, and less income than will whites. But more importantly, it has been suggested that *even with income (poverty status) controlled* there are significant differences between blacks and whites. These differences can be attributed to two factors, racial discrimination and cultural differences between the races. Racial discrimination has its impact in four ways that are very relevant to the present analysis:

First, it has resulted in blacks getting schooling inferior to whites both in numbers of years and in quality of education each year. This, of course, can have significant impact on blacks' market sophistication, especially when dealing with formal bureaucratic relationships such as credit contracts or the courts.

Second, discrimination has undoubtedly resulted in black incomes at a given level being more *unstable* than white's. This, of course, can have major effects on blacks' credit usage, as suggested in the previous chapter.

Third, discrimination has restricted blacks to living in ghetto areas. This has made it difficult for middle-class blacks to escape the penalties and inconveniences of having to shop in low-income markets. As will be indicated in later chapters, these markets suffer a particular paucity of low-cost and/or well-managed businesses because they are located in areas that are predominantly poor *and* black.

Finally, discrimination has led to feelings of alienation, frustration, and powerlessness that undoubtedly extend throughout the black income spectrum. These feelings can have marked effects on blacks' mobility and on their effectiveness in combating fraud and deception.

Then there are what might be called cultural differences, which may or may not be the result of all these factors but which tend to set blacks apart, independent of income. Chief among these differences for present purposes are blacks' recent migratory status, different marital structures (i.e., more frequent female-headed households), relative youth and greater fertility, and larger family sizes. These traits can all have significant impact on consumption patterns and consumer problems, as will be seen in the following chapter.

Notes

1. For an excellent history of the black experience, see John Hope Franklin, *From Slavery to Freedom* (New York: Alfred A. Knopf, Inc., 1956).
2. ". . . 'race' as it is known today is a relatively new idea. Only in the last two hundred years or so has an ideology of race claiming scientific validity been added to the rhetoric of national, economic, and social conflict." Michael Banton, *Race Relations* (New York: Basic Books, Inc., Publishers, 1967), p. 12. Banton provides an excellent introduction to the concept of race in several countries.
3. Nathan Glazer and Daniel P. Moynihan, *Beyond the Melting Pot* (Cambridge, Mass.: The M.I.T. Press, 1963), p. 53.
4. U.S. Bureau of the Census, *Current Population Reports,* series P-23, no. 38, "The Social and Economic Status of Negroes in the United States, 1970" (Washington: Government Printing Office, 1971).
5. U.S. Bureau of the Census, *Current Population Reports,* series P-60, no. 81, "Characteristics of the Low Income Population, 1970" (Washington: Government Printing Office, 1971).
6. *Ibid.*
7. U.S. Bureau of the Census, *Current Population Reports,* series P-23, no. 38.
8. Sar A. Levitan, Garth L. Mangum, and Ray Marshall, *Human Resources and Labor Markets* (New York: Harper & Row, Publishers, 1972).
9. U.S. Bureau of the Census, *Current Population Reports,* series P-23, no. 38.

10. Finis Welch, "Black–White Differences in Returns to Schooling," *American Economic Review*, vol. 63, no. 5, December 1973, pp. 893–907.
11. U.S. Bureau of the Census, *Current Population Reports*, series P-23, no. 38.
12. *Ibid.*
13. *Ibid.*
14. *Ibid.*
15. See, for example, E. Earl Baughman, *Black Americans* (New York: Academic Press, Inc., 1971), chap. 3.
16. James S. Coleman, et al., *Equality of Educational Opportunities* (Washington: Government Printing Office, 1966).
17. Shirley H. Rhine, "The Economic Status of Black Americans," *The Conference Board Record*, August 1972, p. 35.
18. U.S. Bureau of the Census, *Current Population Reports*, series P-23, no. 38.
19. *Ibid.*
20. U.S. Bureau of the Census, *Current Population Reports*, series P-23, no. 42, "The Social and Economic Status of the Black Population in the United States, 1971" (Washington: Government Printing Office, 1972), p. 44.
21. U.S. Bureau of the Census, *Current Population Reports*, series P-23, no. 38.
22. *Ibid.* The remaining cases were "other male head."
23. This problem is explicitly discussed in Marcus Alexis, George Haines, Jr., and Leonard S. Simon, "Consumption Behavior of Prisoners: The Case of the Inner City Shopper," in Alan R. Andreasen (ed.), *Improving Inner City Marketing* (Chicago: American Marketing Association, 1972), pp. 25–60.
24. Henry Allen Bullock, "Consumer Motivations in Black and White: Part I," *Harvard Business Review*, vol. 39, no. 3, May–June 1961, p. 96.
25. Herbert McClosky and John H. Schaar, "Psychological Dimensions of Anomy," *American Sociological Review*, vol. 30, October 1965, pp. 14–40.
26. Lewis M. Killian and Charles M. Grigg, "Urbanism, Race, and Anomie," *American Journal of Sociology*, vol. 67, May 1964, pp. 661–65.
27. Raymond A. Bauer and Scott M. Cunningham, *Studies in the Negro Market* (Cambridge, Mass.: Marketing Science Institute, 1970), p. 9.
28. William H. Grier and Price M. Cobbs, *Black Rage* (New York: Basic Books, Inc., Publishers, 1968), p. 31.
29. Kenneth B. Clark and M. P. Clark, "Racial Identification and Preference in Negro Children," in T. M. Newcomb and E. T. Hartley (eds.), *Readings in Social Pyschology* (New York: Holt, Rinehart & Winston, Inc., 1947).
30. Baughman, *op. cit.*

31. Angus Campbell and Howard Schuman, *Racial Attitudes in Fifteen American Cities* (Ann Arbor: Institute for Social Research, University of Michigan, 1968).
32. *Ibid*, p. 62.
33. *Report of the National Advisory Commission on Civil Disorders* (New-York: Bantam Books, Inc., 1968), p. 1.
34. Mildred A. Schwartz, *Trends in White Attitudes toward Negroes* (Chicago: National Opinion Research Center, University of Chicago, 1967).
35. *Ibid.*

5. Consumption Problems of Blacks

A RECURRING ISSUE, in discussions of the nature of black consumption behavior is whether there is something that can be described as uniquely black. The controversy, of course, reflects the major problem noted in the preceding chapter, namely that blackness is highly associated with a number of other characteristics, especially low income. Although research to date has often been anything but effective in separating out effects of these associated variables, a number of patterns are beginning to emerge which tend to suggest that blacks do indeed have different consumption patterns and that the ways in which they are disadvantaged in the marketplace are both similar to and distinct from the ways in which the poor in general are disadvantaged.

In the discussions to follow it should be remembered that in the aggregate a major characteristic of black households is that they are much poorer than white households; one in three blacks is poor compared to only one in ten whites. Thus, again in the aggregate, the problems of black consumers are very much the problems of poor consumers. Partly for this reason, my approach in this chapter will be the same as that in Chapter 3; I shall trace first the budgeting problems of blacks and then their problems in choosing among products, brands, and outlets. This analysis will indicate that being black *and* poor is both different from and worse than just being poor. Further, it will suggest that being black is worse than being white from the standpoint of consumption problems even if one is *not* poor. In sum, it is suggested here that blackness creates its own problems which are both interactive with and additive to the problems of being poor. At least from the standpoint of consumption problems, the concept of a separate black subculture is a useful distinction to make at the present time. Whether it will remain useful when black incomes are raised across the board is not at all clear.

Budgeting Problems

SAVINGS

An integral part of the popular stereotype of blacks in America is that they are "as a race" happy-go-lucky spendthrifts, living for the pleasures of the moment, paying little heed to future needs. If such stereotypes are valid, we might expect to find significantly lower levels of savings behavior by blacks than whites.

Curiously, there has been a marked shift in the prevailing scholarly opinion on this topic over the past 40 years. The conclusion up until 1972 was in opposition to the popular stereotype—that, with income controlled, blacks saved *more* (or dissaved less) on a year-to-year basis than did whites. However, a recent study by Marjorie Galenson, published in 1972, "disposes fairly conclusively of the widely held view that blacks save more." [1]

The early findings are typified by the work of Richard Sterner, who in 1943 found that when changes in assets and liabilities by blacks and whites were compared by income groupings, blacks dissaved less at low income levels and saved more at high income levels than did whites.

Three theories were offered most frequently to explain this finding:

1. THE LACK-OF-ASSETS HYPOTHESIS. This notes that blacks have a lower level of asset holdings (e.g., housing) at each income level and concludes that whites can spend more than blacks because they have more accumulated *past* saving (i.e., assets) to draw upon.

2. THE LACK-OF-CREDIT HYPOTHESIS. This theory, advanced by James Tobin, argued that since blacks have fewer assets, they have weaker bases against which to borrow (and they more often face outright discrimination by lenders).[2] Thus, so the argument goes, whites can go into debt more easily than blacks when their wants exceed their incomes.

3. THE PERMANENT INCOME (OR INCOME MOBILITY) HYPOTHESIS. This hypothesis suggests that whites more frequently have positive expectations of future income growth than blacks do. Whites thus can spend more at given income levels now because they expect to be able to recover these deficits in the future. Blacks are more cautious now because years of past job discrimination tell them they cannot make the same presumption.

A fourth hypothesis was subsequently developed in the work of Brady and Friedman[3] and Duesenberry,[4] who found that black–white differentials disappeared when similar *percentiles* were compared:

4. THE RELATIVE INCOME HYPOTHESIS. One's level of savings is determined, not by absolute income, but by one's income position *relative to*

others with whose income one compares oneself. Thus a black in the fifth decile in the black distribution will save as much as a white in the fifth decile of the white distribution. This hypothesis did appear to fit the data rather well.

In her recent paper, Galenson built upon earlier insights of Tobin[5] and Friend and Schor,[6] suggesting that rather than compare *net* savings behavior of blacks and whites in a given income group, one should investigate separately the behavior of savers and the behavior of dissavers. Galenson, in her study of households of two persons or more under 65 years of age with medium to low incomes ($1,000 to $10,000), found that at all income levels white *savers* save as much as or more than black savers (savings being defined as net changes in assets and liabilities including personal insurance). At the same time, white *dissavers* dissave more than blacks in all but the very highest income groups in her study.

These findings, which were found to hold under alternate definitions of savings and income,[7] pointed out that past reports of higher savings by blacks were, more accurately, reports of higher dissavings by whites. By demonstrating the much greater abilities of whites to dissave, Galenson's analysis supports the lack-of-assets and lack-of-credit hypotheses, as well as the permanent income hypothesis. It points to the fact that blacks are not only handicapped by their lower levels of incomes but *further* handicapped by their lack of assets and their lack of access to credit markets, which could permit them to augment their incomes to meet near-term needs. The results also suggest that they are handicapped in their near-term spending by their discrimination-based belief that things are not going to get very much better for them economically in the near- or even long-term future.

USE OF CREDIT

Do blacks indeed use less credit than whites? Here the direct evidence provides a more complex portrait. For example, the University of Michigan's *Survey of Consumer Finances* showed that in 1969 mean installment debt for blacks was only two-thirds of that for whites, probably because of blacks' lower rate of automobile purchasing.[8] On the other hand, figures from the same study indicate that the proportion of all blacks with *some* installment debt is higher than that for whites and the mean debt is a much higher proportion of black median income.

Race	Percent with Debt	Mean Debt	Mean Debt/ Median Income
White	50	$1,610	19.3%
Black	62	$1,180	30 %

Detailed analyses of the 1968 Michigan survey by Roxanne Hiltz revealed several important findings.[9] First, she found that with income controlled, blacks at all income levels were likely to be using relatively more of eight different kinds of credit than whites, possibly reflecting their inability to get as much credit at *each* source. On the other hand, she found that whites had more different kinds of assets to cover their debts than blacks. As suggested by Tobin and Galenson, total asset position was also found to be much worse for blacks than whites (Table 5-1). Indeed, Professor Hiltz notes, "Whites with incomes under $5,000 have accumulated more financial assets, on the average, than blacks with two or three times as much income." [10] These differences, which appear *not* to have decreased between 1962 and 1968, have major negative effectives on blacks' credit ratings. Finally, with respect to Table 5-1, it should be noted that although black debt is lower than white in amount overall, this relationship is inversely related to income, and indeed at $10,000 income average black debt exceeds that of whites.

Professor Hiltz also evaluated consumers' financial sophistication and found that although *most* respondents knew little about the financial system, blacks were much less knowledgeable than whites. She also notes that as the debt-to-asset ratios would predict, blacks reported paying higher interest on loans than whites, a point discussed at length in a later chapter.

A recent study by Gary Chandler for the National Commission on Consumer Finance[11] found that blacks' use of all types of debt in 1967 was strongly affected by whether they lived in poverty areas or not, other things being equal. He found no differences in debt levels attributable to race within poverty areas but, as Hiltz suggests, much higher levels of debt for blacks than for whites *outside* poverty areas. In fact Chandler found higher levels of debt for both blacks *and* whites in nonpoverty areas, suggesting that *residence* rather than race may be the major source of discrimination in credit availability, a phenomenon that also applies to business insurance in disadvantaged areas.[12]

CONSEQUENCES OF BLACK CREDIT USE

Blacks more often have debts than whites, and as income rises the amount of this debt changes from being less than whites' to being more than whites'. It will also be recalled from Table 3-3 that blacks have been found *much* more likely to default on their debts than whites. This combination of findings on its face would seem to lend credence to the popular stereotype of blacks as present-oriented spendthrifts, inattentive to the future consequences of present debt acquisitions. It will be recalled, however, that an alternative to the careless planner stereotype offered to explain the credit behavior of the poor was the job instability hypothesis that the

TABLE 5-1. Mean Amounts of Assets, Debts, and Total Financial Resources, by Race and Family Income, 1967

Income, $	Assets, $		Debts, $		Total Financial Resources, $[a]	
	Black	*White*	*Black*	*White*	*Black*	*White*
Under 5,000	178	3,055	509	908	697	3,961
5,000–7,499	569	6,393	2,643	2,928	3,321	9,415
7,500–9,999	1,168	3,472	3,804	4,613	5,221	8,156
10,000–14,999	1,066	6,975	6,404	6,389	6,005	13,582
15,000 and over	3,925	34,084	9,633	9,357	13,700	43,501
All incomes	518	8,280	2,021	4,181	2,362	12,538

[a]Includes nine types of assets (amounts in checking accounts, bank savings accounts, savings and loan accounts, credit union accounts, certificates of deposit, stocks, bonds, mutual funds, and yearly premium payments on personal life insurance, since cash value of policies was not available) and six debts (outstanding amounts of first and second mortgages on homes; remaining installment debts on additions and repairs; loans on cars and durables and all other installment loans; and amount borrowed on life insurance). Total assets plus debts do not add up exactly to total resources because the calculations are based on slightly different *N*s due to exclusion of "no answer" codes.

Source: S. Roxanne Hiltz, "Black and White in the Consumer Financial System," *American Journal of Sociology*, vol. 76, no. 6, May, 1971, pp. 987–998. Copyright 1971 by the University of Chicago. Reprinted by permission.

poor got into debt, not because they were reckless, but because they believed at the time it was a wise decision, although later economic setbacks would make it appear to the outside observer to be less than wise. Since Chapter 4 indicated that job instability was much greater for blacks than for whites, it may be hypothesized that greater income instability might explain much of their more frequent use of credit. If this is true, then, as the argument went in Chapter 3, black defaulting debtors ought to report unexpected losses of income as a more frequent cause of their default than overextensions than is the case for whites. Data in Table 5-2 suggest that the hypothesis is well supported, but that the effects of race and income are *not* independent, a point supported by Table 5-1. As predicted, poor blacks do appear to be more often the victims of job instability than whites. They are much less likely than poor whites to see themselves as in over their heads financially and slightly more likely to see themselves as the victims of sudden losses of income. In this sense, one may speculate that they in fact see themselves as reacting very prudently in the face of the greater instability of their lives.

TABLE 5-2. Reasons for Default, by Income and Race

Reasons[a]	Under $4,000, %	$4,000 to $7,999, %	$8,000 and Over, %
Loss of income			
White	54[b]	48	39
Black	57	49	37
Voluntary overextension			
White	27	32	26
Black	13	31	32

[a]Multiple answers permitted.
[b]Percent of individuals.
Source: David Caplovitz, *Debtors in Default*, vol. 1 (New York: Bureau of Applied Social Research, Columbia University, 1971), pp. 9-5 and 9-14.

Data on the middle-income group, however, reveal no such differences in reasons for default between the two races, while for the high-income group, the relationship reverses: blacks are much more likely to see themselves as financially in over their heads and somewhat less likely to feel they are the victims of sudden income losses. This, of course, is in accord with the earlier finding that as incomes rise, blacks become more heavily in debt than whites.

UPPER-INCOME BLACKS AND CREDIT

What then accounts for the fact that blacks, once they achieve a moderately large amount of income, give up their previous prudent behavior and incur more debt than whites of similar incomes, debt that many apparently feel makes them overextended? The most obvious hypothesis one might advance to explain this anomaly draws upon Alexis, Haines, and Simon's conception of inner city residents as *prisoners*. In a recent paper[13] these authors suggest that discrimination and ghettoization hold poor blacks in physical and psychological check, keeping them from achieving full value in the marketplace. If their analogy fits (and they have mixed conclusions), then it might also be useful to think of those blacks who do manage to rise to higher income levels as at least partial *escapees* from the prison economy. Thus their debt accumulation behavior may be seen as an exuberant outward manifestation of a strong pent-up demand. Further, the National Commission on Consumer Finance suggests that one of the reasons blacks in nonpoverty areas have higher debt is "that non-whites go into debt to *move* from poverty areas, or at least to finance the costs of transition" (emphasis added).[14]

The prisoner hypothesis is also supported by various suggestions that blacks are more status conscious than whites in their consideration of product purchases. For example, Feldman and Star find that as income increases, black interest in "living better" as a shopping goal very rapidly increases and for the group over $7,000 actually exceeds that of whites.[15] Leonard Evans has suggested that blacks want the "same brands, same labels as they imagine the *best* white Americans have." [16] If, then, blacks frequently buy "the best" once "the prison shackles" are removed, then it is not surprising that they are in greater debt than whites.

Such behavior, of course, would also be in conformance with the relative income hypothesis advanced earlier. If better-off blacks see themselves as in, say, the top 10% of the black income distribution and see themselves as having to emulate those in the top 10% of the white income distribution (or perhaps even the top 20%), then overspending would be expected.

If the prisoners hypothesis is the more valid, this would suggest a further pernicious consequence of racial discrimination, i.e., that black overindebtedness is a reaction to being pent up in the racial ghetto for so long. On the other hand, if the relative income hypothesis is the more valid, this too could be seen as a negative consequence of racial discrimination. That is, if blacks look to whites for their cues as to the appropriate spending behavior for economic leaders in any community instead of looking to others within their own black community for such cues, this can be seen as a further imposition of a concept of white superiority. Bauer and Cunningham do indeed seem to support this position, concluding that "when asked their social status [middle- and upper-class] Negroes use whites as a reference group, and conclude that even at the same income level they themselves have a lower status." [17] Both hypotheses, then, suggest that even well-off blacks are not immune from the undesirable effects on consumption of racial discrimination.

A hypothesis that avoids this connotation is one that simply suggests that blacks (or perhaps only well-off blacks) are in some cultural sense more willing to use credit than whites. Some support for this hypothesis is found in intentions data reported by Bauer and Cunningham.[18] In response to the question "If you needed a new set of living room furniture but didn't have the ready cash to pay for it, would you prefer to buy it on credit, or would you rather wait until you had saved up the money?" Bauer and Cunningham found that blacks were more likely to give the response favoring credit usage.

	NEGRO	WHITE
Would buy on credit	57%	39%
Would wait until money is saved	43%	61%
N	242	1,877

This finding is also reported by Dalrymple, Robertson and Yoshino[19] and by Bullock.[20] Such willingness to use credit if they can get it may reflect Bauer and Cunningham's finding that upper- and middle-income Negroes "... whatever their disatisfactions might be, ... reflected a sense of relative improvement in their position and in greater future opportunities."[21]

Clearly, because of its substantial public policy import, this question of the effects of discrimination upon upper-income blacks is an area in which considerably more research should be carried out.

Allocation to Product Categories

Given that blacks allocate their incomes between spending and saving differently than whites, do they also allocate the money they do spend differently?

In his excellent review of existing studies Alexis found the answer was yes, that with income controlled:

1. Blacks spend less than whites for food consumed at home, housing, medical care, and automobile transportation (the first three are somewhat surprising in light of the larger sizes of black households).
2. Blacks spend more than whites for clothing and nonautomobile transportation.
3. "There is no consistent racial difference in expenditures for either recreation and leisure or home furnishing and equipment at comparable income levels."[22]

These findings are generally supported by Bauer and Cunningham in their analysis of 1960–61 Bureau of Labor Statistics (BLS) expenditure data for black and white households in 28 cities with over 200,000 population in

1960 (Table 5-3), again with income controlled. They disagree with Alexis on expenditures for house furnishings and equipment, which they find higher for blacks (a point we shall return to below), and on housing, where they find no differences between whites and blacks. They extend Alexis' analysis to point out that blacks also spend *less* for food eaten away from home and spend *more* for personal care, alcoholic beverages and household operations.

TABLE 5-3. Distribution of Urban Family Expenditures for Current Consumption with Income Controlled, by Race, 1960-61[a]

Expenditure Category	Average Percent of Current Consumption	
	White	Negro
Total food expenditures	25.7[b]	24.4
Food prepared at home	20.7	20.0
Food away from home	5.1	4.4
Tobacco	1.8	2.0
Alcoholic beverages	1.7	2.3
Shelter	16.1	16.1
Rented dwelling	8.5	11.3
Owned dwelling	7.1	4.7
Other shelter	0.5	0.1
Fuel, light, refrigeration, and water	4.8	4.6
Household operations	5.8	6.3
House furnishings and equipment	4.6	5.3
Clothing, material, and services	8.9	12.5
Personal care	2.8	3.8
Medical care	7.1	4.5
Recreation	3.5	3.7
Reading	1.0	0.9
Education	0.9	0.5
Transportation	13.1	11.9
Automobiles	11.4	9.5
Other travel and transportation	1.8	2.4
Other expenditures	2.2	1.4
Expenditure for current consumption	100.1	100.3
Value of items received without expenditure	5.1	4.2
Food	0.5	0.4
Shelter	0.5	2.2
Other	4.1	3.6

[a]Income control was obtained by "averaging averages"—that is, the percent for each income group was weighted by 1, summed, and divided by 8, the number of income categories. Income categories under $1,000 and over $15,000 were excluded from the analysis. Total sample size was *8,000* families.

[b]For whites (controlled for income), 25.7% of the total expenditure for current consumption was spent on food.

Source: Raymond A. Bauer and Scott M. Cunningham, *Studies in the Negro Market* (Cambridge, Mass.: Marketing Science Institute, 1970), p. 20.

Clearly, many of these differences can be attributed at least in part to differences in taste and culture. For example, Humes points out that there are greater preferences for lower-cost foods among blacks,[23] and Sterner points out that there is a lower preference for protein among blacks at the lower end of the income scale.[24] These differences in tastes could well account for the lower expenditures for food consumed at home by blacks. On the other hand, larger family sizes and differences in life-style and motivations may well explain much of the higher level of expenditure for clothing among blacks. Differences in life-style could also explain the larger expenditures on personal care. Finally, the unique character of their geographic location in the inner cities of urban centers near to downtown shopping areas and employment opportunities may well account for black's lower automobile and higher nonautomobile transportation expenditures.[25]

Beyond these taste and cultural effects it is difficult to evaluate differences (or lack of differences) between black and white expenditures in certain product categories as evidence of some kind of disadvantage, because of the absence of a common measuring stick. Such is the problem, for example, in comparing housing expenditures. Kain and Quigley in their recent study were required to make a number of assumptions about quantity and quality of housing before concluding that "blacks may pay from five to ten percent more than whites in most urban areas for comparable housing."[26]

A good example of this problem is also found in the data on expenditures for home furnishings and equipment, a category that contains many of the products (e.g., furniture and appliances) in which blacks and the poor are said to find the most exploitation. Bauer and Cunningham find that urban blacks make 5.3% of current consumption expenditures on home furnishings and equipment compared to 4.6% for whites, with income controlled.[27] While this does not agree with Alexis' conclusions, Alexis notes that the more recent studies he reviewed did show this difference.[28] If such a difference does exist, there are three possible explanations:

1. Blacks purchase a greater quantity of goods and services in this category than whites.
2. Blacks purchase the same quantity as whites but purchase better quality.
3. Blacks purchase the same quantity *and* quality as whites but pay higher prices (including credit costs).

First of all, with respect to quantity, there *are* differences between the two groups. Oladipupo, for example, finds much lower levels of appliance ownership by blacks at all levels of income.[29] However, when Bauer and Cunningham divided appliances into necessities, discretionary items, and luxury items, they found that relatively little difference in ownership between blacks and whites existed for *necessities* (refrigerator, range, TV, etc.), although lower-income blacks were somewhat less likely than whites to own *many* such items. With respect to *discretionary items*, blacks were less likely to own such laborsaving appliances as washing machines, vacuum cleaners, mixers, toasters, and coffee makers but more likely to buy furniture, painting or decorating, and record players. They were also less likely to buy innovations in such product categories. With respect to *luxury goods*, Bauer and Cunningham found that "in every income group, and for every product, whites were *more than twice* as likely to own them as were Negroes."[30]

Some of these differences in ownership of discretionary and luxury goods are a function of blacks' lack of credit accessibility, overcrowding in homes, and less frequent home ownership. For example, purchase of a home does tend to increase black consumption of products like washing machines. Whatever the explanation, however, it is clear that blacks' *lower* quantity of appliance and furniture ownership does not explain why they spend *more* dollars for household furnishings and operations than whites.

The second possibility is that blacks buy better-quality appliances than whites. As suggested earlier, the literature does suggest that blacks, particularly those at upper income levels, are likely to be more brand conscious than whites and possibly more concerned with purchasing prestige products than whites. Thus it seems reasonable to conclude that differences in quality levels for given product purchases in the aggregate will to some extent offset lower (or equal) quantities of purchases. However, one must question whether the more frequent purchase of name brands can account for a spending level almost 25% higher. The most likely explanation for this difference is that suggested by the third formulation, namely that blacks pay more for given items. Indeed, Chapter 8 provides ample evidence to support this conclusion. It is partially a problem of blacks having to buy on credit and/or having to shop in higher-priced neighborhood stores and partially a problem of blacks more often being tricked into paying higher charges for given goods. It is, in sum, a pernicious problem that further seriously deflates the actual buying power of meager black incomes.

OTHER COMMENTS

There are two expenditure categories involving purchases of services rather than goods where blacks spend less than whites, food consumed away from home and medical care, where one is tempted also to ascribe the differences to discrimination. Bauer and Cunningham suggest this may be the case in both instances—that past or present discrimination has discouraged blacks from eating out and from seeking medical care from the white medical establishment.[31] It is, however, just as plausible to ascribe these differences to differences in culture and taste. Blacks are more house and family centered than whites, and this rather than discrimination may well account for lower expenditures for food away from home. (It may also account for what seems to the casual observer to be the relatively greater frequency of takeout restaurants in black communities.) Further, with respect to medical care, blacks more often come from Southern and rural backgrounds and as Alexis suggests, ". . . They make greater use of home remedies and patent medicines." [32]

WHITE STANDARDS AND BLACK BEHAVIOR

This last set of speculations confronts us with an issue reminiscent of one raised in Chapter 3. It was suggested there that much of the analysis of the consumption behavior of the poor was misdirected by the application of a middle-class standard of rationality. Against such a standard, the behavior of poor consumers seemed to be in some sense inappropriate and wrong, although it could be shown that such behavior could just as easily be seen as rational *in their circumstances.*

A similar problem crops up in the present context when "white" is suggested as the standard against which black consumption behavior is compared. It is undoubtedly true that many blacks envy whites and try hard to be like them, as implied in Evans's suggestion that blacks want the "same brands . . . as they imagine the *best* white Americans have." [33] And it is undoubtedly also true, as Brimmer's comparison of black expenditures in 1950–51 with those in 1960–61 suggests, that "[the] shifting pattern of outlays by Negro families [as their incomes grow] represents a gradual conversion toward the consuming behavior of white families." [34] The danger for writers and researchers is that they sometimes leap from the use of white attitudes and behavior as points of comparison to the use of them as *standards* or ideals. The latter perspective inevitably then leads to the consideration of deviations from the white norm as indeed deviant in the pejorative sense rather than as evidence of a phenomenon suggested earlier, namely that *black culture is different in some ways from white culture* and that "overspending" in some categories may simply represent basic differences in life-style, tastes, and intragroup norms that basically have little relationship to what whites like and value. As Bullock suggests, ". . . the buying patterns of both Negroes and whites reflect each race's cultural system, and . . . advertisers have so far [1961] taken a distorted approach to the Negro as a consumer." [35] White authors and researchers must constantly be on guard lest they (we) impose their ethnocentrism on a culture that in these days of black nationalism may not want to, and indeed perhaps ought not to, strive to become more and more white.

Choices of Products, Brands, and Outlets

Chapter 3 evaluated the specific consumption problems of the poor in terms of their abilities to achieve their major marketplace goal, the minimization of prices paid. It was found that, contrary to expectations, the poor less often (1) read newspaper ads, (2) did comparison shopping, (3) patronized supermarkets, and (4) purchased private brands, all of which could be considered strategies to reduce market basket costs. It was pointed out, however, that these behaviors were not the result of ignorance or a lack of sophistication—although they undoubtedly were to some extent—as much as they were the product of psychological and physical constraints and perhaps even preferences for local shopping in what turned out to be an atomistic, inefficient local marketing system.

This section traces much of the same ground, asking whether and to what extent these problems also apply to blacks.

PRICE MOTIVATION

Research by Bauer and Cunningham[36] and by Feldman and Star[37] has shown that even with income controlled, blacks more often mention the minimization of price as their major objective when choosing among products than do whites. This finding is also noted by King and DeManche,[38] although these authors found that blacks mention price less often than convenience of location, friendly atmosphere, and the like in the choice of a store for food, a finding also reported in a *Progressive Grocer* study.[39] and by Gensch and Staelin.[40] Bauer and Cunningham further note that blacks are much more likely to be concerned with central rather than peripheral aspects of their shopping experiences and to report somewhat more difficulty making shopping decisions, especially when they are very interested in the products in question.[41] On balance, then, it would seem reasonable to conclude that while blacks may be less concerned about getting the most for their dollars than is the case for whites when choosing stores, once in the store price is much more important to them.

Bauer and Cunningham, however, argue further that this goal, as with other shopping goals and preferences among blacks, is largely a function of whether the consumer is basically a *striver* or a *nonstriver*.[42] A striver is one who sees himself as someone who:

1. Tries to overcome all obstacles.
2. Saves for the future instead of spending for today.

3. Plans ahead all the time.
4. Helps himself instead of relying on government.

Strivers in the Bauer and Cunningham study apparently are striving to be like the white middle class. Their motivations, attitudes, and behaviors are much like whites', and on most questions they respond in much the same way as Bauer's white respondents. They are just the opposite of the poor consumers described in Chapter 2. They are optimistic; they believe that things are changing for the better, that they are having an influence on the change, and that effort will pay off.

Bauer and Cunningham's data suggest that differences in the proportion of blacks who are strivers and non-strivers in their study account for much of the difference in price motivation between the races. Blacks who are nonstrivers are much more likely than strivers to report they check prices and "talk a lot about bargains." However, among whites non-strivers are just as likely to check prices and talk about bargains as strivers.

However, it should be noted that only two in five black Baltimore housewives in Bauer and Cunningham's study were classified as strivers compared to three out of four whites. This is despite the fact that the two samples were drawn from lower-middle- and upper-middle-income census tracts and that the median income for the black households in 1967 was over $7,000. The low level of striving among these middle-class blacks, plus what we may presume to be an even lower level of striving among the dominant black lower class,[43] suggests strongly that the predominant feature of the *entire* black population is *nonstriving.* And since nonstrivers are more price conscious, this again would reinforce the conclusion that blacks in general are more concerned with price than whites.

PROBLEMS IN MINIMIZING PRICE

If it is true that blacks are much more likely than whites to be motivated to seek out low prices for the products they buy, it might also be expected that they would engage in much more cost-minimizing behavior: reading newspaper ads, undertaking comparison shopping, patronizing supermarkets and discount houses, buying private brands, etc. As will be seen, as in the case of the poor the reverse is generally true, although scarcity of income-controlled data makes analysis of these questions difficult in some categories.

INFORMATION-SEEKING BEHAVIOR

Price minimizers ought to read more newspaper ads and/or to undertake more comparison shopping than those who seek other goals in their shopping experiences. A recent study by Portis provides a general overview of the information-seeking behavior of black and white women with respect to clothing choices. Portis found that:

1. Black women reported that they were much less likely than white women to use impersonal advocate sources like newspaper ads.
2. They were much less likely to use personal shopping experiences for information about clothing.
3. They were about equally likely to use personal nonadvocate sources such as friends, relatives, and the like; impersonal advocate sources like magazine articles; and other sources.[44]

These findings hold even when interest in clothing fashions is held constant, although the interaction with income and education is unknown.

Newspaper readership. The fact that blacks use newspaper ads less frequently than whites is supported by the findings of Bauer and Cunningham,[45] Oladipupo,[46] and Bogart[47] that blacks are less often readers of newspapers, preferring to get their news and entertainment more often from television and black-oriented radio. Bogart found this holds true even when several socioeconomic differences between whites and blacks, including income, are held constant. The problem for blacks is that newspapers are of limited interest to them as sources of news because of the papers' sparse coverage of black community events. Thus Greenberg and Dervin found that only 10% of low-income blacks regularly read all of the newspaper compared to 23% of similar-income whites.[48] According to Gibson, it is a matter of approach: "White-oriented media continue to ignore vital dimensions in the lives of nonwhite Americans, and almost without exception these media talk *about* Negroes and not *to* them." [49]

While it is possible that the use of newspapers may be destined to increase with the substantial growth in the number of black-owned and/or black-oriented newspapers, the circulation of such papers is still reasonably small. It remains generally true that the best way to get an action-oriented message to the black community is through black radio, a medium of limited value in giving specific price information.[50]

With respect to ads, it also is true that for poor blacks and for many who are not so poor price-oriented newspaper ads are probably of less value since:

1. For convenience goods and some goods for which people will shop around, blacks are more likely than whites to carry out much of their shopping in small neighborhood outlets rather than in the supermarkets and discount houses which advertise in newspapers.
2. For many durable goods purchases, a critical piece of information (i.e., the cost and availability of credit) is usually not available.

With respect to the latter point, Day and Brandt have found that in making credit purchases blacks are much more interested than whites in securing low weekly or monthly payments, low down payments, and long payment periods. This was true when income was controlled, although blacks with incomes under $7,500 were much more interested in data on these credit possibilities than those with incomes over $7,500.[51] Such data, of course, are rarely provided in newspaper ads.

This is not to say that ads are not of *interest* (rather than use) to blacks. Bogart, for example, points out that blacks have a much more favorable attitude toward advertising than whites, and specifically that 72% of them "look forward" to reading newspaper ads compared to only 66% of whites.[52] Since, as Bogart notes, these differences are attributable largely to educational differences between races, they may reflect advertising's entertainment rather than information value for blacks.

PERSONAL COMPARISON SHOPPING. If blacks use newspapers less than whites and are about as likely to get information from friends, neighbors, and magazines, surely they ought to do more comparison shopping given their greater interest in prices and bargains. But Gensch and Staelin suggest that this is not the case, that blacks have less shopping scope than whites: ". . . concern for quality and prices did not seem to reduce significantly use of the local area, even though it was generally believed to carry merchandise of low quality and high prices." [53] This narrow scope is also the finding in Portis's study,[54] and is further supported by the research of Caplovitz[55] and Feldman and Star.[56]

It will be recalled that in both of the latter studies it was found that the poor generally had narrower shopping scopes than the nonpoor. They more often shopped in local stores and less often went downtown or to the outlying shopping centers. It was found in both studies that blacks did less extensive shopping than whites, and in Feldman and Star this result held true even when income was broadly controlled.

It would seem that this finding is explainable by the constraints hypothesis. Blacks are of course affected by the same time and transportation constraints as poor whites are. But for them the constraints are even tighter since:

1. Blacks are less likely to own automobiles. We have already seen that with income controlled, they spend more of their transportation dollar—and therefore must rely more—on public transportation.
2. Again with income controlled, blacks tend to have larger families than whites.
3. Blacks are more likely to have broken homes and/or to have the adult female in the house working, both of which place extra time constraints on black shoppers.

The effects of racial discrimination. Of course, a fourth major deterrent for extensive comparison shopping outside their own area for blacks both rich and poor is the fear (and/or the experience) of racial discrimination. This inhibition was first highlighted by Martineau in the late 1950s.[57] Martineau noticed in field responses in his studies that there was a considerable sensitivity on the part of blacks to their treatment in stores. Later, in 1961, Henry Bullock wrote a perceptive pair of articles in the *Harvard Business Review* in one of which he noted:

> Apparently, the human relations atmosphere of the large department store elicits some feeling of insecurity from consumers of both races. It places Negroes on the defensive and makes whites more aggressive.
>
> Negroes carry their feeling of rejection into the trading relationships which they experience across racial–cultural lines. . . . [T]hey experienced a compulsion to be on their "best behavior". . . .[58]

Sometimes the fear is greater than the reality. As one shopper is quoted in Bullock's article: "When I would go there, I would get mad. I knew, with all the people they had to wait on, they would make the colored folks wait until last. But they didn't do that. Nowadays, they seem to take you as you come." [59]

That a substantial minority of blacks *still* feel that they will be discriminated against in white stores is attested to in a more recent study by Campbell and Schuman.[60] This study of racial attitudes in 15 Northern cities showed that about one in three blacks, particularly young blacks, felt that black customers were being treated less politely than white customers in downtown stores. And, of course, the racial riots of the mid-1960s gave ample testimony to the fact that blacks had strong feelings of being discriminated against by many of the merchants doing business in black neighborhoods.

That such feelings may be founded in reality is indicated by data from a study of attitudes of a sample of Rochester consumers and a sample of Buffalo inner city merchants.[61] The latter, both black *and* white, clearly had a much less favorable attitude toward black consumers than did the black consumers themselves on such questions as:

- Whether blacks have more appreciation of quality goods.
- Whether blacks are charged higher interest rates.
- Whether store owners are likely to worry about overcharging blacks or selling them used merchandise.
- Whether black customers need to be treated as politely as white customers.

Retailers, however, were no more likely than black consumers to see the latter as more often involved in shoplifting and vandalism than white consumers.

Motivation for extensive personal shopping. In addition to the physical and psychological constraints that inhibit extensive personal shopping, one may hypothesize that greater local shopping by blacks as it was with the poor is the result of stronger motivations to do so. These motivations include some shared with the white poor and some that appear to be uniquely black.

Like the poor, blacks prefer to shop locally because of the need for credit both for durables and (sometimes) for food and clothing. Gensch and Staelin found that need for credit was positively associated with blacks' use of the local shopping area.[62] Day and Brandt also found that minority buyers (primarily blacks and Mexican–Americans) felt that they had significantly poorer chances than whites (with income controlled) of borrowing money from a bank, finance company, or credit union for a consumer purchase and so had to rely on retail outlets where they were as confident as whites of getting credit. Minority credit buyers were also much more likely to go back to dealers where they had previously obtained credit and to rely on the dealer for bank and finance company financing when he would not provide credit directly. Such reliance on dealer credit apparently was particularly constraining for poor minority consumers, 27% of whom said they would have bought elsewhere if they did not have to rely on credit. It will be recalled, however, that Day and Brandt did not find that their automobile-conscious California respondents were particularly constrained to shop for credit near where they lived.[63]

There is also some evidence in the literature that blacks are more interested in personalizing their shopping experiences than even poor whites. Bauer and Cunningham found blacks more likely than whites to indicate that it was "important to be familiar with store clerks," a response that was inversely related to striving and to income for blacks but not related to either for whites.[64] Day and Brandt found that minority buyers were more likely to consider "friendliness of people in the credit department" as an important criterion for choosing a credit source but, in contrast to Bauer and Cunningham, found this criterion positively related to income.[65]

Caplovitz found greater use of peddlers among blacks,[66] a phenomenon which is often a personalizing experience. Interestingly, Caplovitz found that patronage of peddlers was not related to shopping scope for whites but was strongly related to narrowness of shopping scope for blacks and Puerto Ricans. In part, Caplovitz argues that this preference for peddlers (and perhaps for a personalized shopping experience) may stem from black and Puerto Rican households' recent migration from environments like the rural South or the island of Puerto Rico where tradition dictated a much closer, friendlier relationship with the local shopkeepers and the traveling peddlers.

> A background of traditionalized culture also seems to be important. Puerto Ricans and Negroes trade with peddlers far more often than do whites, but this decreases as their educational levels get progressively higher and as they develop broader scope for shopping.[67]

In addition to these motivations for local shopping that are in the main shared by the poor, there are two additional factors inhibiting extensive shopping out of the neighborhood which would seem to be directly a function of blackness. The first of these is the apparently different tastes blacks have in some product categories such as food and clothing and in some service categories (e.g., beauty and barber shops). Such differences in tastes have been well established by Gibson,[68] Bullock,[69] Stafford, Cox, and Higginbotham[70] and others. These differences may well discourage blacks from shopping outside their local area in the belief that assortments and/or service skills may not be appropriate to their tastes.

A second factor that apparently influences some blacks to shop in their own area is the desire to patronize black-owned businesses. In their study of black shoppers in Pittsburgh, Gensch and Staelin found that a substantial minority of blacks, particularly in the younger age groups, felt that black ownership of a business was an important secondary consideration in choosing where to shop.[71]

In general, the effects of physical and psychological constraints and of shopping preferences on black consumer mobility explain the conclusion reported earlier that blacks are more likely to report convenience and friendly service over price as criteria for store choice but *once in the store* seek to minimize price while choosing among products.

Use of supermarkets. As will be seen in subsequent chapters, research has pretty well established that there are perhaps half as many supermarkets per capita in black ghetto areas as there are in the remainder of urban areas and in suburban communities.[72] Those supermarkets are smaller and in many cases older, and they do less business in total and per customer transaction than do stores in non-inner city areas.[73] Certainly if black consumers rely on food outlets in their local community as indicated in the previous section, they will have less access to low-cost supermarkets. Certainly the evidence that in choosing food outlets blacks use a criterion of convenience of location more often than whites would indicate that this is the case. Still, as Alexis, Haines, and Simon have pointed out in a recent paper,[74] there is as yet no definitive research on where, in fact, inner city black consumers do shop. Goodman found that poor black consumers will leave their communities to shop outside the area when there are no supermarkets available inside the area.[75] Goodman's results, however, should be treated with some caution because of the relative affluence of his sample population and his restricted definition of his market area.

A study by Mason and Madden of a less affluent area in a smaller Deep South city [76] (median income $2,765) also found that blacks were more likely to shop in supermarkets than in "mom-and-pops." [77] However, in keeping with the findings in Chapter 3, they found that the median incomes of customers grew as one progressed from mom-and-pops to independent supermarkets to chain supermarkets and then to chain supermarkets outside the area. A problem with this study and Goodman's study is that they were carried out in virtually all-black areas, and so no comparisons between white and black behaviors or preferences can be made where the store structure is controlled. Thus, for example, in Mason and Madden's city area there were five independent supermarkets and two chain supermarkets serving a population of about 7,300 and thus it is not surprising that most blacks used such outlets. The question is whether whites under the same circumstances would patronize them *more*.

Larson did compare a sample of blacks and a sample of whites from one metropolitan area, Chicago.[78] Larson again found that blacks were as likely to prefer chains as whites, although the specific store preferences differed. (Whether "preferences" were equivalent to "use" was not indicated in the study.) Again the results cannot be considered definitive, since the black sample was reasonably affluent (with a median family income in 1966 of $5,750) and no income controls were used in the analysis and since the two samples were drawn from different areas which may or may not have had different market structures.

DISCOUNT HOUSE PATRONAGE. The results of studies of black patronage of discount houses independent of income factors are not at all clear. Feldman and Star found that at lower income levels Chicago blacks in 1962 were less likely in general to patronize discount houses than were whites.[79] However, in his study of shopping patterns for fashionable, household and children's dress goods, Portis found that blacks in New York and Cleveland in 1962 used discount houses more than did whites, although these results were not controlled for income effects.[80] It is possible that these studies can be reconciled by introducing as an intervening variable the need for credit. It may be that for infrequently purchased goods of low to medium price for which people will shop around such as dress goods, blacks who do not need credit will act on their greater price motivation and shop at discount houses. However, for higher-priced items like durables where credit is critical, blacks' fears (or experience) of being unable to get credit may keep them from patronizing the discount houses in white areas. (In the early 1960s when the Feldman and Star and Portis studies were conducted, relatively few discount houses offered credit.) If the theory is correct, one might expect to find relatively few differences between low and high income and between blacks and whites in surveys of discount house use conducted more recently. Undoubtedly, there would still exist differences attributable to the fact that very few discount outlets with wide assortments are located in black communities.

PRIVATE VERSUS NATIONAL BRANDS. A generally consistent assertion about blacks in a wide range of studies in the past has been that they would rather purchase higher quality national brands than private brands. Although Bullock in 1961 concluded that "So far as the brand concept is concerned, black and white consumers are not far apart" [81] (a finding supported in recent research by Dalrymple, Robertson and Yoshino)[82] and although King and DeManche found that *poor* blacks knew more about private brands and purchased more of them than poor whites,[83] Bauer and Cunningham state the more generally accepted case: "The modal pattern of brand preference among Negro users of any [packaged goods] product category is to concentrate on the well known, widely advertised, and generally long-established brands in the particular category." [84] Again, Larson reports that "Negroes do display more loyalty to national products than private labels." [85]

The most common explanation advanced for this phenomenon is that blacks are more status conscious than whites.[86]

> The once prevalent stereotype that Negroes were uninterested in, or incompetent to judge, the quality of goods has long been displaced—with the contrary image now of Negroes being extremely interested in quality, and being even more concerned with the symbolic value of goods than are whites. Although this idea may sometimes be overdrawn, it seems close to the truth.[87]

The most frequently cited basis for this contention is the just-quoted study by Bauer, Cunningham, and Wortzel which reported a finding first attributed to Frank Davis of *Ebony* and subsequently confirmed by Stafford, Cox, and Higginbotham[88] that black per capita consumption of scotch is three times that of whites and that blacks "indicate that drinking of Scotch is associated with high status." [89] Also cited is Akers's findings that a reasonably affluent (median income $6,519) sample of black car owners in Chicago in 1965 "tended to own higher price class automobiles, higher priced models regardless of make, and automobiles, with more cylinders than comparable income white families." [90] This finding contradicted results of earlier studies by Alexis[91] and Mock.[92]

Bauer and Cunningham in a later paper suggest that the main point is that blacks do not buy name brands in *all* categories but only where it is important to them:

> Clearly, these data [on when middle-class blacks consider national brands important] do not support a simple statement that Negroes are "more brand conscious." Rather, they support the statement that Negroes are more brand conscious for products which have more importance to them, and less brand conscious for products which have less importance to them, as shown in prior studies.[93]

Specifically, as reported in Table 5-4, they find that their sample of black women were more national brand conscious than white women of comparable income with respect to clothing and personal care products but less so with respect to durable goods such as TV sets or washing machines, as well as scotch whiskey (which as noted earlier was not the case for black *men.*)[94]

A problem with the Akers and Bauer and Cunningham studies is that they do not find that national brand consciousness is associated with striving for higher status. Akers did *not* find that the fancier cars were more likely to

TABLE 5-4. Importance of National Brands, by Race, Income, and Striver Index

A. By Income
(Percent Who Answered Yes)

	Negro		*White*	
Product	*High*	*Low*	*High*	*Low*
Man's suit	61[a]	48	31	37
Woman's dress	65	67	28	38
Toilet soap	81	80	48	59
Hair preparation	77	73	56	56
Toothpaste	85	76	64	70
Facial tissues	28	39	22	31
TV set	54	55	85	89
Washing machine	77	74	86	91
Scotch whiskey[b]	12	9	32	21
N	104	96	124	71

B. By Striver Index
(Percent Who Answered Yes)

	Negro		*White*	
Product	*Strivers*	*Nonstrivers*	*Strivers*	*Nonstrivers*
Man's suit	53	56	34	31
Woman's dress	50	76	33	29
Toilet soap	73	85	55	52
Hair preparation	69	79	55	55
Toothpaste	81	80	65	71
Facial tissues	34	33	24	33
TV set	78	39	85	90
Washing machine	83	70	88	88
Scotch whiskey[b]	19	5	30	22
N	78	122	149	49

[a]Read as follows: 61% of high-income Negroes say that a national brand is very important when buying a man's suit.
[b]These are Negro women, for whom scotch whiskey presumably does not have the same symbolic significance it does for Negro males.
Source: Raymond A Bauer and Scott M. Cunningham, *Studies in the Negro Market* (Cambridge, Mass.: Marketing Science Institute, 1970), p. 48.

be purchased by those who saw their social status as higher than their fathers' or who expected their future incomes to rise faster.[95] Further, Bauer and Cunningham found that *nonstrivers* were more likely to be national brand conscious for clothing and personal care items than strivers (although the latter were still more brand conscious in these categories than whites). Strivers, however, were more brand conscious than nonstrivers in those categories where whites were more brand conscious, suggesting that the former group may be well acculturated to white middle-class norms. On the other hand, the majority of blacks who are the non-strivers apparently have very different norms of behavior. Thus alternative explanations of black national brand preferences seem to be needed. Six alternative hypotheses suggest themselves.

1. *The relative income hypothesis.* The relative income hypothesis was offered earlier to explain higher expenditure levels and thus greater credit use by upper-income blacks. In the present context, the relative income hypothesis apparently is not helpful. Certainly it is not supported by the earlier argument that a majority of blacks do not necessarily use white standards for their brand name purchases. More specifically, Akers did test the relative income hypothesis against his automobile data and found that blacks and whites in the same position relative to their own income distributions still had differences in the prices of their automobile purchases.[96]

2. *The security hypothesis.* A second alternative explanation for blacks' presumed greater interest in national brand products is that they buy them out of a fear of being "taken" by shopkeepers (especiallly white shopkeepers) should they buy a lower-priced private brand they don't know. Supporters of this position point to blacks' greater anxiety in making marketing decisions and to Bullock's emphasis on blacks' needs for security as a major determinant of their buying behavior.[97] As support for this position, Settle, Faricy, and Mizerski find that black consumers "may perceive themselves as having even less control over effects or outcomes in the marketplace than they do for other areas of activity and other spheres of life." [98] They suggest that blacks may purchase name brands as "a type of risk avoidance. Relying on brand name products may insure some measure of safe decision-making in the market if some blacks perceive that they have little control of outcomes." [99] The explanation would seem to fit the Bauer and Cunningham results reasonably well in that there is probably a lot more risk in getting vastly inferior quality in an off-brand of clothing or personal care products than in washing machines and TV. This explanation would also seem to fit the data that show that in many product categories blacks are less likely to adopt new, untried products than whites.[100]

3. *The compensatory display hypothesis.* The third major hypothesis is that blacks buy national brands because it gives them the prestige and self-esteem denied elsewhere in their lives. Caplovitz has coined the term "compensatory consumption" to suggest the need the disadvantaged have to purchase their way out of their otherwise abject status.[101] As Caplovitz puts it with respect to product categories, "Appliances, automobiles, and the dream of a home of their own can become compensations for blocked social mobility." [102] This notion would also appear useful in explaining the Bauer and Cunningham data, since these data show that it is the *non*strivers who are the more national brand conscious. However, this would only follow if an attitude of nonstriving were associated with feelings of being blocked.

A close reading of the survey questions from which the striver index was constructed does not make such an association obvious.[103]

4. *The expenditure adjustment hypothesis.* A fourth alternative related to the compensatory consumption concept is the suggestion that blacks overspend on some product categories because they are constrained from spending as much as whites in other categories (e.g., housing and eating out). As *Marketing Insights* has put it:

> The Negro has less selectivity in the purchase of a home, of a vacation, of travel, dining, entertainment, etc. This results in a greater expenditure per unit in the things that are available to him. Whites have more places to put their discretionary income while Negroes, even in the same income level as whites, use their dollars differently because of their narrower selectivity.[104]

While this hypothesis might explain greater expenditures by blacks than whites, like the preceding hypothesis it does not explain the difference between strivers and nonstrivers.

5. *The limited shopping scope hypothesis.* This hypothesis suggests that blacks' preference for national brands is related to their shopping scope and to the market structure where they shop. Bauer and Cunningham characterize the shopping values of nonstrivers as "buying inexpensively and enjoying the pleasure of shopping itself, rather than as acquiring *quality at a reasonable price*" and note that nonstriving blacks more often felt it was important to be familiar with store clerks where they shopped.[105] While there is no direct evidence on this subject, it has been suggested elsewhere in this volume that such attitudes are likely to be associated with narrower shopping scope, with dealing heavily with neighborhood outlets. If it is true that nonstriving blacks more often shop in the ghetto and strivers more likely shop outside it, this could well account for nonstrivers' heavier purchases of name brand packaged goods like hair preparations and toilet soaps, since small stores dominate ghetto areas and such stores have very small assortments, stocking only the most popular national brands. And since black strivers presumably also use the atomistic ghetto market more than whites, this could account for the fact that blacks *in general* purchase more packaged national brands than whites.

With respect to durables, Bauer and Cunningham also found that nonstrivers were more willing to use credit.[106] Since blacks have had difficulty getting credit, nonstrivers may pay much more attention to where they can get it than to what model or brand they should buy. Presumably they can get credit more often in ghetto areas and Sturdivant and Wilhelm have shown that ghetto appliance outlets are much more likely to have off-brands than nonghetto outlets.[107] This could explain the nonstrivers' apparent lack of brand consciousness in this category. Strivers, on the other hand, who are less restricted in their credit use, can and presumably do more often venture out into the general market and focus on name brands to the same extent as whites.

6. *The cultural hypothesis.* Bauer and Cunningham continually emphasize that strivers seem to think and behave like whites (although "being white" is not necessarily their goal). Again, what must be considered is that nonstrivers, and by extension the majority of the black population, simply have *different* values, preferences, and behaviors than strivers or whites. The absence of striving attitudes is not necessarily a deviant characteristic, some character flaw. Perhaps nonstrivers simply *choose* to pay more attention to such things as clothing and personal care and less to appliances because different things are important to them. Whether this stems from African roots, from rural Southern backgrounds, or from some influences of urban ghetto life, it may just be, as Fitzhugh suggests, that there is something basically different about being black in America.[108] Our difficulty in satisfactorily reconciling the Bauer and Cunningham data with other hypotheses should at least encourage us to give some serious thought to this final residual hypothesis that there may be important differences between black and white consumption patterns that are purely attributable to race.

Summary and Conclusions

This chapter is filled with complexities and contradictions that overall yield a picture of black consumer problems that are in some ways different and in many respects more serious than those of poor whites. The chapter has shown that despite the fact that they save more on average, blacks are more likely to have some kind of debt. Despite the fact that at the lower end of the income spectrum they have lower average amounts of debt, their net asset position (assets minus debts) is much worse than that of comparable income whites. On the other hand, at the upper end of the income spectrum blacks have not only more different kinds of debt but more debt in absolute amount.

An explanation for these contradictions seems to lie in blacks' generally greater willingness to use credit, which in turn may be the result of the greater employment instability in their lives and their different consumption goals at low and high income levels. At low income levels, where most of the black population presumably are nonstrivers, greater emphasis is given to spending on clothes and personal care products. Few automobiles are purchased because low-income black families live near downtown areas and work opportunities and because family members are more neighborhood centered in their shopping and social orientations. Such purchase preferences mean that merchandise bought on credit is less frequently "big ticket" items which drive up the average credit balance. At the same time such preferences also mean that few assets are accumulated on which future borrowing may be based.

The consequences of their weaker debt-to-asset position are that low-income black consumers will have poorer credit ratings, restricted shopping mobility, and a greater chance of defaulting on their obligations. This, in turn, means that they are more often likely to pay high prices and high interest rates, to have limited product assortments available to them, and to be subjected more frequently to merchant exploitation than comparable-income whites.

The pattern at the upper end of the black income spectrum is less clear. It has been suggested here that greater amounts of debt for blacks than whites may simply be a reaction to a sense of escape from the "ghetto prison." On the other hand, it was also suggested that this could be the result of attempts by strivers to spend on appliances, automobiles, and the like to achieve what they see as a standard equal to the *best* that whites to whom they turn for purchase cues have accumulated. Whatever its causes, greater debt clearly will have the effect of also restricting upper-income blacks' access to credit, and presumably increasing their chances of default and bankruptcy. It also presumably will restrict them more to ghetto markets where they must suffer the disadvantages of having to shop where the poor also shop.

Given these difficulties for both low- and high- income blacks, it is not surprising that despite their apparent greater interest in minimizing price, blacks are less likely to read newspapers or to venture far outside their community to do comparison shopping. In these two respects, they can also be seen as the direct and indirect victims of racial discrimination: one of the reasons they are less likely to read newspapers regularly is that newspapers do an inadequate job of covering news of the black community, and one of the reasons they don't venture farther out of their area is the fear of racial slights. And of course one of the most serious restrictions on black shopping scope is that prejudice keeps most blacks, especially the more affluent blacks, from simply *moving* to where the better shopping alternatives are.

The question of whether blacks use supermarkets and discount houses to minimize prices is not at all clear, although to the extent they are restricted in shopping scope to their own neighborhoods, they will have access to fewer such outlets.

Then there is the evidence that blacks are more likely to buy national brands. It has been suggested that this behavior may also be the indirect result of racial discrimination, as when blacks buy national brands (and fancier cars and other prestige products) to compensate for losses in self-esteem or for blockages to expenditures in other areas (e.g., housing or leisure) that stem from white prejudice. And it has been suggested that such national brand behavior may also be tied in with blacks' restricted shopping scope and credit problems.

In sum, then, the chapter has demonstrated that blacks are in many ways the direct and indirect victims of their race, victims even when they are not poor. They are victims because their race leads to lower incomes and educational levels, which are direct major handicaps in the urban marketplace. But they also suffer from more unstable job patterns, feelings of lost self-esteem, direct blockages of expenditures in certain categories, and residential discrimination. Being black is different and in many respects worse than being poor. Blacks have problems that increased income will not solve by itself, a point that will prove a major theme in considerations of appropriate remedies for the disadvantaged consumer in concluding chapters.

Notes

1. Marjorie Galenson, "Do Blacks Save More?" *American Economic Review*, vol. 62, no. 1, March 1972, p. 211.
2. James Tobin, "Relative Income, Absolute Income and Saving," *Money, Trade and Economic Growth* (New York: Macmillan Publishing Co., Inc., 1951), pp. 135–56.
3. Dorothy S. Brady and Rose D. Friedman, "Savings and Income Distribution," in *Studies in Income and Wealth* (New York: National Bureau of Economic Research, 1947), pp. 247–65.
4. James S. Duesenberry, *Income, Saving and the Theory of Consumer Behavior* (Cambridge, Mass.: Harvard University Press, 1949).
5. James Tobin, *op. cit.*
6. I. Friend and S. Schor, "Who Saves?" *Review of Economic Statistics*, vol. 41, May 1969, pp. 213–45.
7. An alternative formulation added (1) durable goods as savings and (2) income in kind as income.
8. George Katona, William Dunkelberg, Gary Hendricks, and Jay Schmeideskamp, *1969 Survey of Consumer Finances* (Ann Arbor: Survey Research Center, Institute for Social Research, University of Michigan, 1970), p. 31.
9. S. Roxanne Hiltz, "Black and White in the Consumer Financial System," *American Journal of Sociology*, vol. 76, no. 6, May 1971, pp. 987–98.
10. *Ibid.*, p. 991.
11. Gary G. Chandler, "An Analysis of the Debt Level of Central City Families," in National Commission on Consumer Finance, *Consumer Credit in the United States* (Washington: Government Printing Office, 1972), p. 155.
12. See Chapter 7.
13. Marcus Alexis, George Haines, Jr., and Leonard S. Simon, "Consumption Behavior of Prisoners: The Case of the Inner City Shopper," in Alan R. Andreasen (ed.), *Improving Inner City Marketing* (Chicago: American Marketing Association, 1972), pp. 25–60.
14. National Commission on Consumer Finance, *op. cit.*

15. Lawrence P. Feldman and Alvin D. Star, "Racial Factors in Shopping Behavior," in Keith Cox and Ben N. Enis (eds.), *A New Measure of Responsibility for Marketing* (Chicago: American Marketing Association, 1968), pp. 216–26.
16. W. Leonard Evans, Jr., "Ghetto Marketing: What Now?" in Robert L. King (ed.), *Marketing and the New Science of Planning* (Chicago: American Marketing Association, 1968), p. 530. Evans is quoting a study of Social Research, Inc. It is not clear whether Evans himself would accept this finding.
17. Raymond A. Bauer and Scott M. Cunningham, *Studies in the Negro Market* (Cambridge, Mass.: Marketing Science Institute, 1970), p. 8.
18. *Ibid.*, p. 139.
19. Douglas Dalrymple, Thomas Robertson, and Michael Y. Yoshino, "Consumption Behavior across Ethnic Categories," *California Management Review*, vol. 14, Fall 1971, pp. 65–70.
20. Henry A. Bullock, "Consumer Motivation in Black and White: Part 1," *Harvard Business Review*, vol. 39, no. 3, May–June 1961, pp. 89–104.
21. Bauer and Cunningham, *op. cit.*, p. 40.
22. Marcus Alexis, "Some Negro-White Differences in Consumption," *American Journal of Economics and Sociology*, vol. 21, no. 1, January 1962, p. 28.
23. Helen H. Humes, "Family Income and Expenditure in 1947," *Monthly Labor Review*, vol. 68, April 1949, pp. 389–97.
24. Richard Sterner and Edward Mauritz (in collaboration with Lenore Epstein, Ellen Winston, et al.), *The Negro's Share* (New York: Harper & Brothers, 1943).
25. Geographic location also may explain brand choices, as we shall note below.
26. John F. Kain and John M. Quigley, "Housing Market Discrimination, Home Ownership and Savings Behavior," discussion paper no. 148, Institute of Economic Research, Harvard University, Cambridge, Mass., November 1970.
27. Bauer and Cunningham, *op. cit.*, p. 20.
28. Alexis, *op. cit.*
29. Raymond O. Oladipupo, *How Distinct Is the Negro Market?* (New York: Ogilvy and Mather, Inc., 1970).
30. Bauer and Cunningham, *op. cit.*, p. 76.
31. *Ibid.*
32. Alexis, *op. cit.*, p. 26.
33. Evans, *op. cit.*
34. Andrew F. Brimmer, "Economic Trends in the Negro Market," *Marketing Information Guide*, May 1964, p. 4.
35. Henry A. Bullock, "Consumer Motivations in Black and White: Part 2," *Harvard Business Review*, vol. 39, no. 4, July–August 1961, p. 110.

36. Bauer and Cunningham, *op. cit.*
37. Feldman and Star, *op. cit.*
38. Robert L. King and Earl Robert DeManche, "Comparative Acceptance of Selected Private-branded Food Products by Low-Income Negro and White Families," in Philip R. McDonald (ed.), *Marketing Involvement in Society and the Economy* (Chicago: American Marketing Association, 1969), pp. 63–9.
39. *Progressive Grocer*, April 1969.
40. Dennis Gensch and Richard Staelin, "White Attitudes toward Shopping in a Black Neighborhood," working paper no. 16-70-1, Carnegie–Mellon University, Pittsburgh, 1970.
41. Bauer and Cunningham, *op. cit.*, p. 31.
42. *Ibid.*, pp. 33 ff.
43. It should however be noted that Bauer and Cunningham (*ibid.*) in fact did *not* find striving and income to be related for blacks in their relatively affluent sample.
44. Bernard Portis, "Negroes and Fashion Interest," *Journal of Business*, vol. 39, April 1966, pp. 314–23.
45. Bauer and Cunningham, *op. cit.*
46. Oladipupo, *op. cit.*
47. Leo Bogart, "Black Is Often White," *Media/Scope*, vol. 12, no. 11, November 1968, pp. 53 ff.
48. Bradley Greenberg and Brenda Dervin, "Mass Communication among the Urban Poor," *Public Opinion Quarterly*, vol. 34, no. 2, Summer 1970, p. 231.
49. D. Parke Gibson, *The $30 Billion Negro* (New York: Macmillan Publishing Co., Inc., 1969), p. 149.
50. "Black Radio Tells It like It is," *Business Week*, Sept. 7, 1968, pp. 75–6.
51. George S. Day and William K. Brandt, "A Study of Consumer Credit Decisions: Implications for Present and Prospective Legislation," in National Commission on Consumer Finance, *Technical Studies*, vol. 1 (Washington: Government Printing Office, 1973).
52. Bogart, *op. cit.*
53. Dennis H. Gensch and Richard Staelin, "The Appeal of Buying Black," *Journal of Marketing Research*, vol. 9, May 1972, p. 144.
54. Portis, *op. cit.*
55. David Caplovitz, *The Poor Pay More* (New York: The Free Press, 1967), p. 13.
56. Feldman and Star, *op. cit.*
57. Pierre Martineau, "The Personality of the Retail Store," *Harvard Business Review*, vol. 36, no. 1, January–February 1958, p. 55.
58. Bullock, "Consumer Motivations in Black and White: Part 1," *op. cit.*, p. 99.
59. *Ibid.*

60. Angus Campbell and Howard Schuman, *Racial Attitudes in Fifteen American Cities* (Ann Arbor: Institute for Social Research, University of Michigan, June 1968).
61. Alan R. Andreasen, Marcus Alexis, Leonard Simon, and George Haines, Jr., "Comparison of Consumer and Store Manager Attitudes: The Case of Racial Effects in Inner City Retailing," *Proceedings*, Second Annual Conference of the Association for Consumer Research, August 1971.
62. Dennis H. Gensch and Richard Staelin, "The Appeal of Buying Black."
63. Day and Brandt, *op. cit.*
64. Bauer and Cunningham, *op. cit.*, p. 53.
65. Day and Brandt, *op. cit.*
66. Caplovitz, *op. cit.*, pp. 73–7.
67. *Ibid.*, p. 77.
68. Gibson, *op. cit.*
69. Bullock, "Consumer Motivations in Black and White: Part 1."
70. James E. Stafford, Keith K. Cox, and James B. Higginbotham, "Some Consumption Pattern Differences between Urban Whites and Negroes," *Social Science Quarterly*, vol. 49, no. 3, December 1968, pp. 619–30.
71. Gensch and Staelin, "White Attitudes toward Shopping in a Black Neighborhood."
72. See Chapter 6.
73. National Commission on Food Marketing, *Organization and Competition in Food Retailing*, Technical Study no. 7 (Washington: Government Printing Office, 1966).
74. Alexis, Haines, and Simon, *op. cit.*
75. Charles S. Goodman, "Do the Poor Pay More?" *Journal of Marketing*, vol. 32, January 1968, p. 18–24.
76. Joseph Mason and Charles S. Madden, "Food Purchases in a Low Income Negro Neighborhood: The Development of a Socio-economic Behavioral Profile as Related to Movement and Patronage Patterns," *Proceedings*, American Marketing Association Fall Conference 1972, pp. 634–9.
77. *Ibid.*
78. Carl M. Larson, "Racial Brand Usage and Media Exposure Differentials," in Cox and Enis, *op. cit.*, pp. 208–15.
79. Feldman and Star, *op. cit.*
80. Portis, *op. cit.*
81. Bullock, "Consumer Motivations in Black and White: Part 1," *op. cit.*, p. 102.
82. Dalrymple, Robertson, and Yoshino, *op. cit.*
83. King and DeManche, *op. cit.*
84. Bauer and Cunningham, *op. cit.*, p. 91.
85. Larson, *op. cit.*, p. 213.

86. Status conscious is in relation to product quality.
87. Raymond A. Bauer, Scott M. Cunningham, and Lawrence H. Wortzel, "The Marketing Dilemma of Negroes," *Journal of Marketing,* vol. 29, July 1965, p. 2.
88. Stafford, Cox, and Higginbotham, *op. cit.*
89. Bauer, Cunningham, and Wortzel, *op. cit.*, p. 3.
90. Fred C. Akers, "Negro and White Automobile Buying Behavior: New Evidence," *Journal of Marketing Research,* vol. 5, no. 3, August 1968.
91. Alexis, *op. cit.*
92. W. L. Mock, "Negro–White Differences in the Purchase of Automobiles and Household Durable Goods," unpublished doctoral dissertation, University of Michigan, Ann Arbor, 1964.
93. Bauer and Cunningham, *op. cit.*, p. 47.
94. Bauer and Cunningham (*ibid.*) note that this anomaly only "reinforces our general point that the Negro market is not a unitary phenomenon."
95. Akers, *op. cit.*
96. *Ibid.*
97. Bullock, *op. cit.*
98. Robert B. Settle, John H. Faricy, and Richard W. Mizerski, "Racial Differences in Consumer Locus of Control," *Proceedings,* American Marketing Association Fall Conference, 1971, pp. 631–32.
99. *Ibid.*, p. 632.
100. Bauer and Cunningham, *op. cit.*, pp. 85–7.
101. Caplovitz, *op. cit.*, p. 13.
102. *Ibid.*
103. Bauer and Cunningham, *op. cit.*, p. 36.
104. "Is There Really a Negro Market?" *Marketing Insights,* Jan. 29, 1968, p. 14.
105. Bauer and Cunningham, *op. cit.*, pp. 51–3.
106. *Ibid.*, p. 50.
107. Frederick D. Sturdivant and Walter T. Wilhelm, "Poverty, Minorities and Consumer Exploitation," *Social Science Quarterly,* December 1968, pp. 643–50.
108. "The Negro Market: Two Viewpoints," *Media/Scope,* vol. 11, no. 11, November 1967, pp. 70–2 ff.

PART 2

THE DISADVANTAGED MARKETPLACE

6. Market Structure in Disadvantaged Areas[1]

THE PRECEDING CHAPTERS have described in general terms the characteristics and broad consumption problems of the two major disadvantaged groups in this country, the poor and the blacks. The chapters have shown why their defining and associated characteristics—for example, their lack of income and education—tend to lead to the consumption problems found. A major conclusion was that problems of physical and psychological mobility were not causes of disadvantage per se, but only because they put the disadvantaged consumer more frequently in contact with a market structure that was itself the source of poorer selections, higher prices, and exploitative merchant practices.

This and the following three chapters will explicitly consider the nature and operations of markets serving disadvantaged areas. This chapter focuses on the structure of such markets, with particular attention to the ways in which such markets are changing over time. Chapter 7 will concern itself with the problems of merchants operating in such markets. Chapter 8 will discuss the critical problem of price discrimination, and Chapter 9 will consider other major forms of merchant exploitation.

In these considerations, our prototype will be the marketplace faced by black consumers, what has been called by Sturdivant the *ghetto marketplace*,[2] the marketplace in America's urban black central city communities. This focus is adopted for three reasons:

1. Ghetto markets are relatively easy to define geographically. This is not the case for markets serving the poor, some of whom reside in the urban ghettos while others are scattered throughout central city areas.
2. As the analysis to this point has suggested, the market problems of urban blacks represent the extreme case of market-induced disadvantage and so present a more dramatic picture than would be the case for the nonblack poor.

3. Partly as a result of the definable character of ghetto markets and partly as a result of recent interest in black economic development, better data are available for such an analysis.

Inner City Markets

Market structure, the number and size distribution of various types of retail and service outlets, is not a static phenomenon. The structure in an area at any one point in time is only a momentary "photograph" of a process of change over time. This is particularly true of market structures in black ghettos, where rapid changes in aggregate spending power and in racial composition have major effects on the types of businesses existing to serve ghetto consumers. Since in any short-run period different ghetto markets may be at different stages of an underlying change process, a useful approach to understanding ghetto market structure is to try to understand the nature and consequences of this basic process.

Our concern, then, in this chapter will be to establish the major evolutionary processes in typical ghetto markets and to assess their consequences for disadvantaged consumers. The last chapter demonstrated that black consumers seek low prices, as well as wide assortments of quality merchandise, convenience, credit availability, safety, cleanliness, and sometimes, black ownership; this chapter attempts to ascertain the consequences of change for the achievement of these goals.

A BRIEF HISTORY OF RESEARCH

There have appeared in recent years a moderately large number of descriptive studies of market structure in ghetto areas. Such studies have been for the most part one-time undertakings concerned primarily with assessing the nature of black business ownership. To date, there have been six major analytic studies from which an understanding of urban ghetto market dynamics may be built. These studies are by Berry et al., Cox, myself, Haines et al., Sexton, and Aldrich and Reiss. A brief summary of the scope of each study will serve as background for the dynamics model to be presented in the remainder of the chapter.

1. Brian J. L. Berry's pioneering study of commercial structural change from 1948 to 1958 in Chicago[3] provides the only estimate of rates of change in business establishments in urban areas as a function of variables such as income, population, and retail technology. Berry focuses on the consequences of these changes for what he calls commercial blight. A major deficiency in Berry's work, however, is that he did not explicitly consider the nature and effects of changes in population racial composition on market structure

and in particular on black business ownership—a factor critical to an understanding of ghetto market dynamics.

2. William Cox, in his 1969 study of commercial structure in Cleveland,[4] was concerned with developing a model to estimate "ideal" market structure at any point in time. Cox specified that the ideal number of outlets in each store category was basically a function of (*a*) total consumer expenditures in the geographic area and business category under investigation, and (*b*) average selling capacity per outlet in the category (outlet size times average sales per square foot in the business category). Total expenditures in turn were primarily a function of the number of individuals in the area, their after-tax incomes, and their spending habits, with adjustments made for the fact that some of these expenditures will be made outside the area (and at the same time some expenditures of those living outside the area will be made in it). Using this model, Cox recommended a certain number of outlets in a typical ghetto area, Hough area 13. As noted in Table 6-1, these recommendations were well off the mark in many cases, a point returned to below.

Cox, however, was only seeking to estimate an "ideal" number of outlets toward which he felt the market ought to move and was not attempting to explain how the market structure got to be what it was, the concern here. Further, except for some very crude adjustments of spending patterns, he considered the consequences neither of changes in population from white to black nor of substantial increases or decreases in income. As noted in Table 6-2 (p. 111), such changes were particularly marked in his area 13.

3. My 1968–69 study of Buffalo[5] investigated both structural characteristics and race of owner. It was the first such study to suggest racial effects on structure. However, the forcefulness of the study's conclusions was severely restricted by the very small sample of areas observed and by the fact that the data were cross-sectional rather than longitudinal in character. In the latter case for example, the study was unable to tell whether differences in areas' market structure and black ownership were due to their being more or less advanced along some variable continuum—e.g., changes in racial composition—or whether there were important generational differences; blacks who move into white areas now may be in some ways fundamentally different from those who moved in 10 years ago, a contention recently advanced by the Taeubers.[6] The study was, however, suggestive of several of the process components considered below.

4. Haines, Alexis, and Simon have produced a series of papers comparing market structures and outlet characteristics across four market areas of Rochester, New York, that vary in income and racial composition.[7] Tests for similarity of numbers of stores among the areas concluded that there were no differences, which would seem contrary to our earlier assertions. Still, the study did not take account of differences in size distribution of outlets (e.g., for food stores) or in marketing policies, which, as Haines and his colleagues admit, are substantial. They also found that changes in outlet

TABLE 6-1. Recommended and Actual Commercial Structure for Cleveland Market Area 13, 1968

Store Type	Recommended Number of Stores	Actual Number of Stores
TOTAL RETAIL STORES	55	68
Total food group stores	24	25
Grocery & delicatessen stores	15	19
Meat & fish stores	2	2
Fruit & vegetable stores	0	0
Candy, nut, confectionery stores	1	0
Dairy product stores	4	0
Eggs & poultry stores	0	1
Bakery stores	2	2
All other food stores	0	0
Eating & drinking establishments	6	22
General merchandise stores	2	1
Department stores	1	0
Dry goods, general stores	1	1
Variety stores	0	0
Apparel group stores	3	2
Men's & boys' clothing stores	1	0
Women's & girls' clothing stores	1	0
Family clothing stores	0	1
Shoe stores	1	0
Child & infant clothing stores	0	0
Misc. apparel stores	0	1
Furniture & appliance stores	3	3
Furniture stores	1	0
Floor-covering stores	0	0
Draperies, curtains, upholstery stores	0	0
China, glass, metalware stores	0	0
Music stores	1	2
Other home-furnishing stores	0	0
Household appliance stores	1	1
Radio & TV stores	0	0
Automotive group stores	1	1
New & used car dealers	1	0
Used car dealers	0	0
Tires, batteries, accessory stores	0	1
All other automotive stores	0	0
Gasoline stations	6	5
Lumber, building materials, hardware stores	1	4
Lumberyards	0	0
Building materials stores	0	0
Paint, glass, wallpaper stores	0	0
Heating & plumbing stores	0	0
Electrical supply stores	0	0
Hardware stores	1	4

TABLE 6-1. Continued

Store Type	Recommended Number of Stores	Actual Number of Stores
Drug & proprietary stores	5	3
Beverage stores	1	0
Secondhand stores	0	2
Other retail stores	3	0
Fuel, ice dealers	0	0
Feed, farm, garden stores	0	0
Jewelry stores	0	0
Book, stationery stores	0	0
Sporting goods stores	0	0
Florist shops	0	0
Cigar stores	0	0
Cameras, photo supply stores	0	0
All other stores	3	0
TOTAL SERVICE STORES	23	39
Barber & beauty shops	11	15
Cleaning & pressing stores	5	8
Shoe repair, hat-cleaning stores	1	4
Laundry stores	2	3
Funeral service	0	1
Misc. personal service stores	2	1
Auto repair, parking, washing	1	6
Electrical repair stores	0	1
Furniture & upholstery repair stores	0	0
Other repair stores	1	0
TOTAL RETAIL AND SERVICE STORES	78	107

Source: William E. Cox, Jr., "A Commercial Structure Model for a Depressed Neighborhood," *Journal of Marketing,* vol. 33, no. 3, July 1969, p. 8. Published by the American Marketing Association. Reprinted with permission.

TABLE 6-2. Population and Income for Cleveland Market Area 13, 1950, 1960, and 1965

	1950	1960	1965
Total population	17,049	19,334	16,402
Negro population	1,086	15,892	14,984
Percent Negro	6.4%	82.2%	91.4%
Median family income before taxes			
Current dollars	$2,833	$4,598	$4,050
1958 dollars	$3,419	$4,470	$3,719

Source: William E. Cox, Jr., "A Commercial Structure Model for a Depressed Neighborhood," *Journal of Marketing,* vol. 33, no. 3, July 1969, p. 2. Published by the American Marketing Association. Reprinted with permission.

structure over two years were minimal, mainly taking place in the form of differences in entry rates of new outlets across areas. Finally, the team found no differences in market structure between their two black areas and those studied in the aforementioned Cox and Andreasen studies. While this would seem to suggest substantial similarity among ghetto areas of different cities, significantly different procedures in enumerating businesses among the three studies make the results questionable, as do my findings of substantial variation among the eight subareas of Buffalo's ghetto.

5. Sexton analyzed the changes in numbers of supermarkets, superettes, and small food stores in 74 Chicago area communities between 1959 and 1971.[8] Sexton's analysis, like those of Haines et al., are most useful in providing estimates of changes and their causes in both black and nonblack areas. For example, Sexton found the following patterns:

a. From 1959 to 1964, the number of small food stores per family in Chicago was decreasing. They were being replaced by superettes in both black and nonblack areas.

b. From 1964 to 1967, small stores and superettes per family were increasing in black areas relative to white areas (which Sexton interprets as supporting the hypothesis that excessive profits existed in inner city small stores during the period).

c. From 1967 to 1969, small stores per family were decreasing in black areas, probably as a result of urban tensions and riots.

d. From 1969 to 1971, however, the decline in small stores in black areas continued probably indicating lowered profits in such areas. This explanation is given additional credence by Sexton's finding that the number of supermarkets in black areas per family was also decreasing, which also suggests that the disadvantage of immobile ghetto consumers is presently on the increase.

6. Aldrich and Reiss conducted the first longitudinal study of business sites in radically changing neighborhoods. Their data on 431 sites in Boston, Chicago and Washington observed every two years from 1968 to 1972 provide direct evidence of the effects of changes in population racial composition on business survival, vacancy rates, racial ownership of business, and the distribution of business types. The authors' principal conclusion that the business population changes in the same way as the residential population reflects their use of sociology's succession model. This model is also the basis of the analysis reported in this chapter.[9]

The Proposed Model

Urban sociologists have studied processes of black immigration to cities and have proposed as typical of this process what has been called the *suc-*

cession model of residential dynamics.[10] This model assumes that the basic process whereby blacks desegregate an area involves the gradual replacement of existing whites in existing housing by an influx of blacks (as opposed to, say, emigrant blacks moving into new housing in the same area). The process begins with *penetration*, the first "block busting" by a few black families into an area previously all white; then there is *invasion* of a substantial number of black residents into the area, presumably after some "tipping point" representing the upper limit of white tolerance for interracial living is reached; and finally there is *consolidation*, when most whites have left and the area becomes ostensibly black.

Comparisons among regions have shown that the succession model is probably most appropriate for the older Northern industrial centers, more than for Southern or newer urban centers. Finally, urban sociologists have found that in recent years replacement of whites by blacks in expanding black areas often does not change the basic socioeconomic status in the area as measured by occupation, education, and housing status and in some cases serves to upgrade it.[11]

While concerned with relative changes in black and white populations, this research tradition lacks major variables of prime interest to students of market structure, namely changes in aggregate population and aggregate income. Some inferences may be drawn from their work, however. For example, if socioeconomic status as sociologists have defined it does not change as blacks invade an area, it may be expected that even if total population does not change, there will be a decline in aggregate spending power, since a substantial body of research has shown that in the same region blacks earn less than whites of equal education and equal occupational status. Further, if racial change is accompanied by population decline, then aggregate demand should decline significantly, with major impacts on business.

These considerations have led me to propose an alternative three-stage developmental model for understanding change in ghetto business structures. The three stages which seem to adequately fit the Buffalo experience are the following:

I. White equilibrium
II. White-to-black transition (equivalent in time to the sociologists' penetration and invasion stages)
III. Major economic decline (equivalent in time to the consolidation stage)

While this progression is supported in general by the available literature,[12] it is recognized that in some cases in some areas stages II and III will be coterminous or perhaps even reversed. Still, it seems useful to try to separate the effects of the two causes—change in total income and racial change—so as to disaggregate the processes at work, leaving to later research the task of establishing time paths, cutoff points, and magnitudes of effects.

Those uncomfortable with this assumption may wish to consider the stages merely as types. Later sections will discuss several possible answers to the question "What comes after stage III?"

Stage 1. White Equilibrium

Most Northern urban ghetto areas were at one time largely white, although many neighborhoods—often those nearest the central business district—have been established black areas for a long time. When they were white, these areas were often of below-average income, containing large concentrations of whites just emerging from poverty. The market structure during this stage presumably fairly well met the needs of the white residents. Since the areas were often near downtown and passage into and out of the area was not inhibited by racial animosities, a number of large mass merchandise outlets, department stores, five-and-tens, and small supermarkets often dotted the area. Such outlets could depend not only on local patronage but also on transient patronage from neighboring or even distant communities.

Since there was usually a sprinkling of better-off families in the area, it could also usually support a number of specialty stores, some of which catered to special ethnic needs.

Except for random fluctuations in commercial structure, the major change during stage I presumably is a long-term decline in the number of outlets as the result of technological trends in the retail sector and the increased use of automobiles. Berry has estimated that in Chicago between 1948 and 1958, in the absence of other factors, the number of retail establishments declined 5.87% per year due to technological change.[13] This figure, however, is probably high for poorer white areas, where retail structures are antiquated, parking space is limited, and car ownership is low.

Stage II. White-to-Black Transition

As blacks penetrate and begin to invade previously all-white areas, two major factors affecting retail structure are introduced in addition to presumably continuing technological change. First, there is a change in tastes as a greater share of the local market becomes black. This presumably affects the demand for different types of outlets and different product assortments within each outlet. Second, there is presumably a change of business motivation; many white entrepreneurs decide they want to fold up or move out and a rising number of potential black entrepreneurs become anxious to get a piece of the action.

The following sections speculate briefly on how each of these factors might work themselves out. It is assumed that there is little or no decline in aggregate income at this stage, in part because those blacks who move into an area during penetration and invasion stages are generally of higher status than those who follow them later.

CHANGING TASTES

As has already been documented, there are considerable differences in spending/saving behavior and product preferences between blacks and whites. While there is some disagreement about specifics, the following would seem to be reasonable speculations about effects on outlet demand during stage II:

Since at given incomes blacks spend much more for apparel and for personal care, one might expect increased demand for outlets in the following categories:[14]

1. Apparel
2. Dry cleaners
3. Beauty and barber shops
4. Health and beauty aid stores
5. Shoeshine and shoe repair shops
6. Men's tailor-made clothing shops

Since blacks have a narrower shopping scope than whites, less frequently going far for durables they investigate or purchase, in part because of difficulties in getting credit, the demand for shopping and specialty goods in the local community may increase.

Finally, there may be a significant increase in the incidence of nonstore selling, i.e, the use of peddlers and door-to-door salesmen. The consequences of the increased use of peddlers for the marketing system are twofold. First, as shown below, door-to-door salesmen are major sources of exploitation in the marketplace. Second, they take sales away from, and thus limit the demand for, traditional retail and service outlets (although some peddlers, especially in the appliance area, often work for such outlets). No estimate of the extent of the impact of the rise of door-to-door selling on traditional stores exists, however.

CHANGING MOTIVATIONS OF WHITE BUSINESSSMEN

It might reasonably be asked whether, just as white residents seek to flee from the influx of blacks in stage II, white businessmen who in stage I dominated the business structure feel internal (e.g., family) or external pressure to leave also. It is generally assumed that businessmen are more rational in their business decisions, and this may argue that there will not be much of an exodus except as economic considerations dictate—for example, the lowering of profits from selling lower-margin convenience items or the drying up of a market for automobiles or more expensive furniture.

While this may be granted, it is also true that small businessmen and, in particular, small retail and service operators are much less sophisticated than the businessmen of most textbooks. Their motivations for entering business often center on personal and family rather than purely economic considerations such as the need to be independent or to be near family. Those in small retailing and service businesses often live in the community and are on a first-name basis with their customers. For them as well as for many of the customers they serve, their stores are often social as much as business centers. For many of these businessmen, the influx of blacks may portend an estrangement (real or perceived) from their clientele, a reduction in personal contact. Prejudice, to which businessmen are at least as susceptible as nonbusinessmen, may also cause many to move their residences and then their businesses away from "them."

Given the desire to leave, which businesses are most likely to leave? It seems reasonable to speculate that they are the following:

1. Businesses with low reliance on location for sales
2. Businesses with few assets to be liquidated or sold
3. Businesses with salable assets
4. Businesses whose operation involves relatively much physical or otherwise intimate involvement with clients (as in hairdressing shops or funeral parlors)

Whether he *does* leave, however, also depends on whether he can find a buyer—and in a racially changing area, this usually means a black buyer. Thus sales of existing businesses may in the short run be handicapped by the absence of many incoming blacks with substantial resources or borrowing power, although the first wave of black immigrants tends to be of higher status than those who follow.

This absence of a ready supply of black entrepreneurs may also mean that there will be a temporary gap in retail and service outlets in transitional areas during stage II as whites in the first two groups—those with businesses easily transferred or easily liquidated—move out. Black businessmen may not appear quickly enough as replacements and, when they do establish themselves, may well have weaker operations and be more prone to early failure. Data from the Buffalo study found this possibility in areas where transition from black to white was most recent.[15]

Who then *stays* among the white businessmen? Here three groups of businesses are likely to be found:

1. Businesses with large, profitable operations which really couldn't do as well most anywhere else.
2. Businesses which are *unable* to leave. These are presumably the less

successful businesses, those with considerable immovable fixed assets and/or those run by businessmen who have less experience and/or who lack the confidence to move elsewhere.

3. Businesses not necessarily making large profits but whose owners are comfortable or perhaps enthusiastic about serving black customers.

In sum, the net effect of the broad influences in stage II—technological change, change in tastes, and changes in white businessmen's motivations—are far from clear. Yet in the last case at least the implications for market structure are obvious, since business motivations will be a determinant of the supply of outlets as well as of the quality of service available in each outlet.

Stage III. Economic Decline

In stage II aggregate spending power was presumed to be relatively unchanged. In stage III a major decline in aggregate spending power becomes a major determinant of market structure change along with the continuing effects of the population shift from white to black and of technological trends in the retailing sector.

The decline in spending power is made up of one or both of two factors:

1. A decline in population as the accelerating exodus of whites exceeds the immigration of blacks (or, in some cases, where there is a net loss of both groups)[16] or as urban renewal or the expressway bulldozer reduces the housing supply, as in some cities.
2. A decline in average real income as lower-income blacks replace higher-income—but not necessarily higher-education or -occupation —whites and replace higher-income blacks who dominated stage II but who are now moving on to other, better areas into which blacks are now penetrating

Cox's area 13 (Table 6-2) coincidentally provides a good picture of this process. From 1950 to 1960 (roughly stage II) the area grew in income and population. About 12,500 whites left the area to be replaced by 15,000 blacks, while median income in real dollars rose from $3,419 to $4,470. Aggregate, real spending power rose 38%. Then in the 1960–65 period (roughly stage III) both whites *and* blacks left the area and median family income declined 17%, for a net loss in real spending power of perhaps 30%!

Berry in his Chicago study provides separate estimates of the effects of income and population change on the number of establishments. He concludes[17] that:

1. A 1% change in population produces a 1% change in retail establishments.

2. A 1% change in real income produces a 0.86% change in retail establishments.

Applying these rates to Cox's area 13 and ignoring technological change, the effect of which in inner cities is unclear, Berry would predict a decline in retail establishments in only five years, 1960 to 1965, of 30%. It will be recalled from Table 6-1 that Cox estimated an ideal number of outlets for area 13 in 1968 of 78, whereas the actual figure was 107. Three explanations for this discrepancy seem possible. First, the decline in aggregate spending power—population and income—from 1960 to 1968 was simply too rapid for the market to adjust to. While the number of stores may be tending toward the new equilibrium levels, in the short run there may exist in stage III an "overstored" condition. This condition could also be aggravated by the change in racial composition and decline in average income of the area, which make it even harder than in stage II for white businessmen to find buyers for their businesses or their assets. Many of the movable, better-managed businesses will have left in stage II, and those remaining will have more difficulty getting out, a problem that will be increasingly hard to solve the longer they stay in the declining market. The existence of this lag in adjustment of the number of outlets during an economic decline is supported by the Buffalo study, where the number of outlets was more closely correlated with 1960 than 1966 population during a period of decline.[18]

An alternative explanation for Cox's discrepancies is that his estimated average store sizes and sales are not appropriate for inner city markets. One of the changes in stages II and III is a movement away from specialty and shopping goods stores and mass merchandisers toward convenience goods outlets, reducing the size of the "ideal" outlet.

Further, one may ask whether Cox's equations do not underestimate the decline of demand, particularly involving sales to transients, for specialty and shopping goods outlets. In stage III, as blight grows and as the population becomes blacker, transient white customers who earlier shopped in the area on their way to or from the central business district may well stop doing so, cutting down markedly on the flow of outside purchasing power. Such behavior would in part stem from race prejudice, in part from the expectation that assortments in the area are no longer appropriate for whites, and possibly in part from a fear of physical or psychological harm, a problem that also affects many blacks.

Finally, in a more recent paper Cox and Dickinson[19] have suggested that the differences may simply be attributable to random variation. Citing the fact that although Berry found that current population and income accounted for 84% of the variance in retail establishments in Chicago, Cox and Dickinson point out that the bases for the analysis were very large areas averaging over 300,000 population. In their own study of 52 census tracts with average populations of 5,224, they found "a very weak relationship between retail structure and purchasing power ($R^2 = .22$)." They conclude that a population of 10,000 is required for an R^2 of at least .70, implying, as noted, that in smaller areas these variables have little predictive power, requiring the further explanation this chapter seeks to offer.

WHITE BUSINESS MOTIVATIONS

The impact of racial change on white businessmen will continue and indeed be much more intense in stage III. Economically of course, the decline increases white monetary incentives to go elsewhere. Then there are the emotional incentives to leave. In stage II white storekeepers typically served racially mixed clientele; in stage III this will rarely be the case, especially in convenience goods outlets. Further, in stage II, white storekeepers were in a sense indistinguishable to blacks from other whites in the neighborhood who controlled the churches, the welfare agencies, the political parties, and the like. In stage III white merchants will constitute one of the few white power groups still highly visible in the area—another being the police! There is, thus, likely to be in stage III a considerable rise in black concern about "white economic colonialism," by which blacks mean that white businessmen residing outside the area (although they may once have lived in it) come in, take black consumer cash, often hire only other whites to help, and then take their profits back out of the area, which is left without a major source of development capital.

Despite these greatly increasing pressures to leave, the white businessman is in an awkward position. Because of the decline in the area and the absence of experienced blacks with capital, he will find it very difficult to sell out, contributing further to the area's overstored condition. This inability to leave an emotionally and economically depressing setting in many cases will lead to considerable bitterness and frustration on his part, which, given some lingering prejudices or some unfortunate contacts, may be projected onto blacks. The situation will be aggravated if, as is likely to be the case:

1. There are militant black groups in the area actively seeking to push him out.
2. He or his fellow white businessmen are increasingly subject to robberies, arson, and the like.
3. Costs of doing business increase (as Sexton suggests).
4. No efforts are made by city, state, or federal government to improve the inner city business climate.

The consequences of these by-products of structural dynamics for race relations are important and obvious.

ABSENTEE OWNERSHIP

That absentee ownership is a major ghetto problem is attested to by the data in Table 6-3.

Table 6-3 shows that only 2% of white businessmen in Harlem and 30% of white businessmen in Buffalo lived in the ghetto they served. The fact that proportionally more whites live in Buffalo's ghetto is attributable to the fact that Harlem is an older black community whereas many areas in the Buffalo study have only become largely black in the last 10 to 15 years. The lower proportion of black businessmen living in Harlem than in Buffalo's ghetto is further attributable to the fact that other black communities exist in the New York area.

TABLE 6-3. Residence of Ghetto Businessmen in Harlem and Buffalo

Place of Residence	Harlem[a] Whites	Harlem[a] Blacks	Buffalo[b] Whites	Buffalo[b] Blacks
Ghetto	2%	59%	30%	84%
Rest of city	60%	28%	29%	13%
Suburbs	37%	12%	41%	3%

[a]Source: This table is reprinted from *The Merchants of Harlem: A Study of Small Business in a Black Community*, by David Caplovitz (vol. I, Sage Library of Research, 1973), by permission of the Publisher, Sage Publications, Inc.
[b]Source: Alan R. Andreasen, *Inner City Business: A Case Study of Buffalo, N.Y.* (New York: Praeger Publishers, Inc., 1971), p. 108. Copyright Praeger Publishers, Inc., 1971. Reprinted with permission.

Thus the data indicate that a good bulk of management decisions are made by individuals who by evidence of their residence are neither close to nor have a stake in the ghetto community. To the extent, then, that living in a community increases one's ability to meet consumer needs—on the one hand to better know what products and services to offer and on the other to better provide the friendly social atmosphere that many low-income consumers look for along with their goods and services—ghetto residents are more poorly served than residents living elsewhere.

The situation is, at least in one sense, worse than the data above suggest. It was found in the Buffalo study that the larger the business, the more likely it was that the white owner resided outside the inner city area.[20] Since, as shown below, it is further the case that white businesses *on the average* are larger than black businesses, then it is entirely possible that in inner city markets in stage III, as much of Buffalo's ghetto is, as many as 60% of all retail and service sales are made by owners living outside the area.

BLIGHT

In addition to a decline in absolute demand for establishments and increased pressures on white businessmen to leave, stage III is characterized by what Berry calls *blight*.[21] While blight in inner city areas has been occurring for some time, it is greatly accelerated as the population and aggregate income decline. Berry distinguishes four kinds of blight; economic, physical, functional, and frictional.

1. Economic blight. This is simply the underutilization of the set of business premises in a market area. Most of the business premises in the inner city were built during the early part of the century and were designed to serve a much larger market than exists in stage III. The result is economic blight, most evident in the form of vacancies but also found in the use of business premises for residential or other purposes to which they are not well suited. In the Buffalo study, overall vacancy rates of business premises in 1968–69 were 14.5%, ranging from a low of 5% in the relatively wealthy and newer sections of the ghetto (i.e., those still in stage II) to 30% in the older more rapidly declining stage III areas.

Berry's study does not provide an estimate of overall vacancies for Chicago, but it does give some insight into the process of economic blight. In each community there are market centers, ribbons, and scattered sites. In periods of economic decline in ghetto areas in stage III, the principal losses of businesses are usually in the centers, concentrated shopping areas around major intersections. Here are located the specialty and high-price shops that the increasingly poor no longer patronize. Here also are likely to be the more experienced successful businessmen, who can more easily transfer or sell out their businesses. Although these outlets begin emigrating in stage II, in the absence of economic decline the resulting vacancies are quickly refilled, usually with specialty stores and better convenience goods outlets from nearby ribbons (single streets with stores on either or both sides, usually leading away from shopping centers). These in their turn are filled by new convenience and service outlets, so that only limited vacancies appear.

In stage III, however, the movement of specialty stores and mass merchandisers out of centers accelerates. Because of this and because most of the larger and better stores from the ribbons have already moved in, the rents and real estate values in the centers begin to decline. This allows the smaller, less well-capitalized specialty and convenience outlets from ribbons and scattered sites to move into the centers. Because of the economic decline, their places are not refilled and substantial and permanent vacancies come into being. It should be noted, however, that the depressed status of area populations in stage III has a paradoxical dampening effect on the increase in vacancy rates, since poverty leads people to use any available low-cost space, appropriate to commercial needs or not, as living quarters.

In the Buffalo study a comparison of vacancy rates was made between major streets and what were called "off-street" locations, controlling for type of business. Major street locations were those on the seven major traffic arteries in the study area, and off-street locations were all others. Smaller businesses and those catering to local convenience needs were more often found in the off-street locations. In this study, higher vacancies were found in the major street locations. Two explanations for this phenomenon were offered:

First, the fixed costs of operating major street stores (rent, utilities, insurance) are higher than for off-street businesses. In the face of economic decline, these higher break-even volumes threaten profitability more quickly than is the case in off-street stores.

Second, the objectives of major street businessmen may be more economically oriented. The off-street businessmen may more often live above their stores and have extensive personal contacts in their community. "For them, business prospects may sink to a reasonably low level before they will consider giving up their businesses and their role in the neighborhood social life." [22] This interpretation would appear to be supported by data elsewhere in the study that show that major street businesses are newer than off-street businesses. The interpretation would modify Berry's formulation to the extent that it suggests that personal goals of business owners may provide considerable friction in the evolution of business structure use when areas change economically. This friction provides further explanation of the overstored condition noted earlier.

Physical blight. Growing vacancy rates inevitably lead to growing physical deterioration, since outlets no longer in use inevitably decay faster than those in use. But the processes in stages II and III also accelerate physical decay in other ways. First, the geographic shifting of stores toward centers as rental values drop and demand changes means that more outlets are used for purposes for which they weren't originally designed. This means that renovations are needed or, in many cases, premises are underutilized.[23] At the same time the weaker condition of businesses and the smaller capitalization of new black businessmen mean that businesses will less often have the means—and given the declining market, the incentive—to make the necessary improvements in premises.

The Buffalo study offers some information on the extent of physical blight in one inner city community. In this study the interior and exterior of each retail and service business were rated as follows:

> GOOD: General appearance of needing few or no repairs. Premises neat and well cared for. Paint in good condition throughout. Premises may not be new. If occupied, signs and displays of current nature well organized.

FAIR: General appearance of needing some repairs. Minor repairs needed throughout or major repairs in one or two places. Paint peeling in some places. If occupied, premises needing major cleaning. Displays not current and in need of organization.

POOR. General appearance of needing major repairs. Major repairs and/or painting needed throughout. If occupied, premises needing major cleaning. Displays absent or badly in need of organization.[24]

Overall, it was discovered that only about half of all interiors and one-third of all exteriors could be rated "good," and that as expected, conditions were better in stage II than in stage III areas.[25] The data, however, pointed out important relationships between the quality of premises and the ownership of the premises, and between quality and the race of the owner. With one exception (interior condition of white retail businesses), quality was significantly higher when a business owned its own premises. In all cases, with ownership of premises controlled—since blacks much less often own their own buildings—the condition of black-owned businesses was poorer than that of white-owned businesses. The latter probably reflected the more marginal character of black businesses and their lack of capital to acquire the better locations and to modernize.

Since in stage III blacks were more likely to own businesses, premises were less likely to be owned by business owners. The Buffalo data suggest that this may accelerate the extent of physical blight.

FUNCTIONAL BLIGHT. In a sense, functional blight—obsolescence of business structures built many years ago for other purposes and no longer satisfactory for present sales and services—has already been discussed. As Berry points out, over time there has been an increase in specificity in the retail sector's needs for space within given categories.[26] Most inner city properties require extensive modification to meet such needs. Paradoxically, though, this problem is relieved to some extent in stage III as declining incomes reduce the number of cars and thus the need for parking space. Further, declining incomes accelerate the shift toward types of businesses, such as small convenience goods outlets, which have less specific space needs and can more easily use available space.

FRICTIONAL BLIGHT. Frictional blight as defined by Berry "exists when a business has a deleterious effect upon surrounding areas or uses, including transportation arteries, or conversely when these surrounding things have an adverse effect upon the operations of the business." [27]

Berry notes two major kinds of frictional blight in inner cities. First is the effect on traffic congestion of inadequate delivery and loading facilities and the increased pedestrian traffic in business centers. As noted earlier, lower automobile ownership and increased vacancy rates will to some extent mitigate the traffic problem, but higher vacancies may increase fire hazards and police problems. Second is the tendency of physical blight in the business community to increase physical blight in surrounding residential areas. This effect, Berry notes, is not "well documented."

However, since Berry did not consider changes in racial composition of ownership in the process of economic decline, some important sources of frictional blight already noted are omitted. First, in stages II and III white owners of inner city businesses—more often the larger businesses—tend to retain ownership but move their residences outside the area. The effect is to increase the outflow of capital that might otherwise be used for area development. Second, the increased racial discrepancy between business owners and residents increases the antagonism of blacks toward whites, while the inability of whites to extricate themselves from the racially changing area increases their own frustration. These factors may well seriously exacerbate otherwise tense racial relations, an example of frictional blight by Berry's definition.

DECLINE IN MANAGEMENT QUALITY

Another major characteristic of stage III is that businesses on the average become more poorly managed. It is an axiom of business analysis that small businesses in general are badly managed. In many cases this is tautological: small businesses are often small because they are badly managed. But they are also sometimes small because they are new and new managers are usually not yet very good managers. Small businesses are seldom owned by others (e.g., stockholders) who demand good performance. They are often the haven of misfits from other professions who feel that if they could only be their own boss, they could do well. Yet often the reason they couldn't work for others was that they were not very competent.[28] While this is granted, it is argued here that ghetto businesses in stage III are particularly badly managed. There are four basic reasons for this:

First, as noted by Sexton, many large-scale mass merchandisers leave the inner city in stages II and III. Such businesses tend to have more sophisticated systems and procedures as well as better management personnel than the smaller businesses they leave behind.

Second, it will be recalled that in stage III pressures on white businessmen to leave are particularly great and that those businesses that can leave are likely to be those that are better managed (although some extremely profitable businesses will stay behind). Thus one may expect that those whites who do stay behind are likely to be on the average poorer businessmen than those who leave.[29]

Third, in this stage there is a considerable increase in absentee ownership, where the owner no longer lives in the area. A corollary occurrence is that many managership positions in white businesses are turned over to blacks who "front" for the true white owner. To the extent, then, that the owner, however experienced and sophisticated he may be, is physically distant from his market, he is less likely to make sound business decisions, particularly with respect to his marketing programs. This problem will be greatly aggravated in stage III, where the market is changing very rapidly economically and racially. In a related sense, black militants would argue that whites, by definition, cannot make sound decisions about matters relating to blacks. Thus, by this argument, the blacker the market, the poorer must be the management decisions independent of whether the white owner resides or works in the area or not.

Finally, a number of studies have shown that the blacks taking over more and more of the businesses in inner city areas have poorer business backgrounds than the whites with whom they compete. Evidence of this as well as of the poorer quality of white management in the inner city is provided in David Caplovitz's study of Harlem and other New York merchants. His basic results are reported in Table 6-4. These results indicate clearly the weaker background of Harlem merchants, white or black as compared with a contrasting sample of white merchants in a white middle-class area and the weaker experience of blacks than whites in Harlem.[30] These basic findings are supported by the Buffalo study.[31]

TABLE 6–4. Distribution of Harlem and Bay Ridge Merchants According to Index of Business Background

	Harlem Merchants		Bay Ridge
Business Background Index	Blacks	Whites	Merchants
Low	48%	25%	11%
Medium	17%	22%	23%
High	34%	54%	66%
	99%	101%	100%
Number of cases	122	106	53

Source: This table is reprinted from *The Merchants of Harlem: A Study of Small Business in a Black Community*, by David Caplovitz (vol. I, Sage Library of Social Research, 1973), by permission of the Publisher, Sage Publications, Inc.

AND AFTER STAGE III?

At some point, the exodus of white residents will virtually stop, leaving behind a scattering of whites who either are comfortable living in a black community or are without the resources or energy to move elsewhere. A substantial proportion of the remaining whites will presumably be elderly. What happens to the area economically depends on whether there is net black out-migration or in-migration and/or whether average incomes in the area increase or continue to decline. In some areas, the answer is a function of whether public and private policies can be developed to arrest and reverse the decay processes of stage III. In Buffalo, the prognosis is unclear.

To the extent there is increased stability of racial and economic change, several factors should establish a more hospitable business climate:

1. With the pulling out of many specialty goods shops in stage III, competition in many lines of trade will have decreased.
2. Lower rents in center locations will reduce the costs of operation and, along with increased vacancies in the ribbons, will ease the problem for businessmen of obtaining good sites and developing adequate parking facilities.
3. The increasing black population will provide a greater pool from which to draw entrepreneurial, managerial, and employee talent.
4. The continued reduction in the share of white business ownership may reduce the frustration of blacks with absentee investment and their reluctance to let white capital in.
5. If there is a reduction in black frustration, especially if accompanied by a turnaround in median incomes, there may well be reduced losses due to robbery and vandalism.
6. Stability in the area may make insurance more available and possibly of lower cost.

At the present time the prevailing mood in most black areas, as well as the feelings of most white merchants, dictates that the problem of rebuilding ghetto business structures must be largely, if not exclusively, in the hands of black entrepreneurs, a point taken up in a later chapter.

Summary

The discussion of the dynamics of urban commercial structure in the previous sections has made several points:

In Northern industrial centers, changes in the number, types, and quality of retail and service business in ghettos can be better understood as part of a pattern of change over time.

The principal determinants of such change are changes in racial characteristics of the population, changes in aggregate spending power, and technological trends in the retailing sector.

The effects of these determinants are often mediated by other variables such as the motivations of white businessmen; in other cases their effects apparently are lagged over time.

The exodus of white businessmen and their mass merchandise outlets and the relatively slow rate of entry of black businessmen results in considerable hardship for residents in transitional communities in terms of the quality and quantity of outlets available to them and the number of jobs they offer. Specifically, the consequences for inner city consumers in stages II and III (which presumably describe the status of the substantial majority of ghetto communities) are the following:

1. A decline in the number of low-cost mass merchandise outlets in inner city areas. In Buffalo, as the following approximations indicate, the number of supermarkets available to ghetto residents is much less than elsewhere in the city or suburbs:

Inner city	One chain supermarket per 11,000 population
Remainder of city	One chain supermarket per 6,000 population
Suburbs	One chain supermarket per 5,500 population

   There are no broad-line discount houses in Buffalo's ghetto, although a number of small discount outlets specializing in health and beauty aids have appeared in recent years.
2. A disappearance of many specialty outlets, particularly those with higher-priced merchandise.
3. When populations are declining, an overstored condition in many retail outlet categories where the density of outlets is more appropriately designed for earlier times, larger populations and spending power, and a greater amount of transient trade.
4. Poorer management than elsewhere in the metropolitan area.
5. Increased absentee ownership.
6. Physical, economic, functional, and frictional blight.

As the next chapter shows, the weakening competitive structure and other problems in inner city areas also have serious deleterious consequences for the sales, profits, and capital accumulation potential of businesses in disadvantaged areas. These declines in profitability in turn not only accelerate the exodus of sophisticated businesses like the low-cost mass merchandisers but also negatively affect the product and service offerings of the remaining businesses. These deficiencies inevitably further the disadvantage of consumers who patronize local outlets whether through choice or force of circumstances.

Notes

1. Much of the material in this chapter first appeared in Alan R. Andreasen, "Towards a Theory of Inner City Business Dynamics," working paper, School of Management, State University of New York at Buffalo, 1972.
2. Frederick D. Sturdivant, *The Ghetto Marketplace* (New York: The Free Press, 1969).

3. Brian J. L. Berry *et al.*, *Commercial Structure and Commercial Blight*, Department of Geography Research Paper no. 85 (Chicago: University of Chicago, 1963).
4. William E. Cox, Jr., "A Commercial Structure Model for Depressed Neighborhoods," *Journal of Marketing*, vol. 33, no. 3, July 1969, pp. 1–9.
5. Alan R. Andreasen, *Inner City Business: A Case Study of Buffalo, New York* (New York: Praeger Publishers, Inc., 1971).
6. Karl E. Taeuber, and Alma F. Taeuber, *Negroes in Cities* (Chicago: Aldine Publishing Company, 1965).
7. See, for example, George Haines, Jr., Leonard S. Simon, and Marcus Alexis, "Maximum Likelihood Estimation of Central-City Food Trading Areas," *Journal of Marketing Research*, vol. 9, May 1972, pp. 154–9.
8. Donald E. Sexton, Jr. *Groceries in the Ghetto* (Lexington, Mass.: Lexington Books, 1973).
9. Howard Aldrich and Albert J. Reiss, "Continuities in the Study of Ecological Succession: Change in the Race Composition of Neighborhoods and their Businesses," paper presented to the annual meeting of the American Sociological Association, August 1974.
10. Otis Duncan and Beverly Duncan, *The Negro Population of Chicago: A Study of Residential Succession* (Chicago: The University of Chicago Press, 1957).
11. Taeuber and Taeuber, *op. cit.*, p. 5.
12. For example, Berry et al., *op cit.*, p. 175.
13. *Ibid.*, p. 173.
14. See, for example, Allen Pred, "Business Thoroughfares as Expressions of Urban Negro Culture," *Economic Geography*, vol. 39, July 1963, pp. 217–33.
15. Andreasen, *Inner City Business*, p. 38.
16. It should be pointed out that there is no *necessary* reason why there should be a population decline as blacks move in, but in the late 1960s in Buffalo this is what was taking place.
17. Berry et al., *op. cit.*, p. 173.
18. Andreasen, *Inner City Business, op. cit.*, p. 40.
19. William E. Cox, Jr., and Roger Dickinson, "Business Opportunities in the Inner City," in Alan R. Andreasen (ed.), *Improving Inner-City Marketing* (Chicago: American Marketing Association, 1972).
20. Andreasen, *Inner City Business*, p. 111.
21. Berry et al., *op. cit.*, pp. 179–203. The discussion in this section draws heavily on Berry's work.
22. Andreasen, *Inner City Business*, p. 43.
23. Berry found that vacancies in all areas were more likely to occur in businesses of lower-than-average front footage.
24. Andreasen, *Inner City Business*, p. 50.
25. *Ibid.*, p. 85.

26. Berry et al., *op. cit.*, p. 179.
27. Ibid., pp. 180–1.
28. Eli Chinoy, "The Tradition of Opportunity and the Aspirations of Automobile Workers," *American Journal of Sociology*, vol. 57, March 1952, pp. 453–9.
29. The reasons for this are not unlike the reasons why blacks who left the South in the great migration were better educated than those who stayed behind.
30. David Caplovitz, *The Merchants of Harlem: A Study of Small Business in a Black Community* (vol. I, Sage Library of Social Research) (Beverley Hills, Calif.: Sage Publications, Inc., 1973), p. 73.
31. Andreasen, *Inner City Business*.

7. Operating Problems in the Inner City

As Bain,[1] Caves,[2] and others have emphasized in another context, structural defects only create the *chance* of disadvantage. What is perhaps more critical is how in fact the structure performs. In one sense, the structural analysis has already pointed up one performance defect for inner city consumers, namely that mass merchandise outlets are less convenient to consumers who fervently wish to reduce the cost of their purchases. Despite in some cases a moral conviction that pulling out of deprived areas ought to be avoided if at all possible, the principle factor that has driven out such mass merchandisers (or, alternatively, has failed to attract them back) has been the unprofitability of maintaining outlets in poor and black areas. But this unprofitability is not, as it might seem, the simple result of increasing consumer poverty in ghetto areas. Sophisticated merchandisers find that consumers not only have less money to spend but often buy items less profitable to the outlet and, most importantly, that it costs more to serve each customer. A detailed discussion of these problems will offer substantial insight into the problems of most businessmen, sophisticated or not, in serving inner city areas as the consumers there would like to be served.

Profitability in Inner Cities

As recently as 1963 supermarkets in inner city areas were operating at a profit—albeit a much lower profit than in nonpoor areas. Data from a 1963 study conducted for the National Commission on Food Marketing in six major U.S. Cities[3] showed net profit margins of 2.73 cents on the dollar in low-income areas, a figure about 30% lower than that for other, higher-income areas.

The situation, however, has apparently deteriorated considerably. While supermarket profits nationally are down considerably, according to a recent analysis of New England supermarkets reported by Donald Marion and

Charles Goodman it was already unprofitable—not just *less* profitable—to operate supermarkets in low-income areas in 1968, particularly in areas that were both low income *and* black.[4] Marion and Goodman report that supermarkets in low-income areas lost an average of 1.74 cents on every dollar of sales. This situation was relatively better in low-income *white* areas, where losses were 0.94 cents on the dollar, but much worse in poor black areas, where losses were 2.22 cents on every dollar. And while the results of this study may vary from the earlier Food Commission study because of regional differences, conversations with food-retailing executives suggest that the Marion study does indeed reflect a worsening profit picture in low-income areas.

NONFOOD RETAILING

A report by the Federal Trade Commission indicates that the profit picture has been far from bleak for furniture and appliance dealers, at least in the District of Columbia in 1966. This study reported that after-tax profits for low-income area outlets not only were positive but were higher as a percent of sales than for non-low-income area outlets, although their return on equity was lower.[5] It is impossible to tell whether these lower rates of return in inner city areas are due to too low sales volume for a given investment or to too great an investment for given sales. Average volume for the low-income retailers in the study was much less than general market retailers, as noted below:[6]

	AVERAGE ANNUAL SALES
Low-income market retailers	$437,000
General market retailers—Overall	$3,045,000
Appliance, radio, and television	$1,141,000
Furniture and home furnishings	$1,211,000
Department stores	$30,455,000

However, as noted in the discussion of retail structure in low-income areas, durable goods outlets are more often run by white businessmen who have been in the area some time. Thus many stores in these categories may be of a size (and cost) designed for an earlier, higher-volume period. Also, the likelihood is great that such facilities have been subject to considerable physical and functional blight over time, which may make them not only too large but less efficient to operate. Thus the assets may be considerably overvalued, leading to the *reported* lower-than-average rate of return.

A final possible explanation—not unthinkable, given the frequent exploitative practices of ghetto furniture and appliance merchants—is that the profit and equity (and cost) figures reported to the FTC simply should not be believed.

In contrast to these mixed data on inner city business profitability is Caplovitz's study of the perceptions of profitability of businessmen in Harlem in 1967.[7] In this study, subjective data on perceived success, i.e., how respondents felt they were doing currently and how present success compared with the past, were collected on three samples—black businessmen in Harlem, white businessmen in Harlem, and white businessmen in a middle-class neighborhood called Bay Ridge. Scores on a "relative success" index indicate considerable optimism uniformly across the three samples. The index was based upon questions on whether the businessman thought he (1) had made money in 1967, (2) did better or worse in 1967 than in 1966, and (3) thought things would be better in 1968. While equal optimism was found, it may have been for different reasons. The whites in Harlem may feel quite successful because they are relatively so. The previous chapter noted that whites who stay behind often do so because they are quite successful or because moving seems to them a much more awkward and risky alternative. Such a group may well feel they are doing better than they could do in any other circumstances.

Blacks, on the other hand, may well appear optimistic in Caplovitz's data as a reflection of their euphoria at being given a chance at a piece of the action as well as their lack of awareness, given their weak business backgrounds and poorer record-keeping systems, of the true state of things. Some support for this hypothesis is found in the fact that while the feeling of relative success is directly related to gross sales for Harlem and Bay Ridge whites, this is not the case for Harlem blacks.

Unit Sales

Dollar volume is, of course, a major determinant of a firm's profitability. High dollar sales levels in inner city stores are attained by getting many consumers to patronize the store many times and to buy many items each time. In Chapters 3 and 5 we saw that fewer poor than nonpoor consumers patronize supermarkets, although those who did might yield enough customers for the reduced number of outlets available. The data on average sales per store in the National Commission on Food Marketing and Marion studies indicate that this is not so; stores in inner city areas have lower sales than those in non-inner city areas. This difference is to some extent attributable to differences in size among the outlets, but as Marion and Goodman report, outlets in non-inner city areas have more sales per square foot than outlets in the inner city. Their figures are as follows:[8]

	SQUARE FEET OF SELLING AREA	SALES PER SQUARE FOOT PER WEEK
Non-low-income area	13,200	$4.79
White lon-income area	10,505	$4.16
Black low-income area	12,215	$3.18

The next question then is whether the problem of lower sales volume is one of too few customers or one of too small purchases on each customer visit. As the figures below indicate, the answer for predominantly black poor areas is different from that for predominantly white poor areas:[9]

	AVERAGE ANNUAL CUSTOMER VISITS	AVERAGE PURCHASE PER VISIT
Non-low-income area	442,180	$7.43
White low-income area	305,560	$7.43
Black low-income area	375,350	$5.38

The problem for supermarkets in poor white areas seems to be exclusively one of getting more customers more often into their store. Once there, poor white customers apparently spend about as much on groceries as do shoppers in nonpoor areas. As we have seen, the inability to attract more customers is undoubtedly related to poor people's needs for credit and delivery service, as well as to the more frequent lack of automobile transportation. The problem in black areas, however, is both one of increasing customer patronage and one of increasing sales per customer.[10] The problem of attracting more poor black customers may be partially solved by building bigger stores, since the ratio of customer visits in poor black areas to customer visits in nonpoor black areas is not very different from the ratio of their store sizes.

The lower level of sales per customer in poor black areas would seem to be attributable to a combination of factors cited in Chapter 5:

1. Lower rates of automobile ownership preclude relatively more blacks from carrying larger amounts of goods home each store visit.
2. Less certain future income streams may inhibit blacks from doling out many of their available dollars at any one time for food.
3. Larger families and poorer housing conditions may mean there is less storage space for large purchases of groceries.
4. Since female heads of black households work full time, they may have less time for a single major shopping trip and thus may spread their supermarket purchases over more visits (e.g., after work).
5. And as Chapter 6 suggested, the difference may be due to severely diminished transient sales to more affluent (white) customers who no

longer stop in black areas for grocery supplies but may still do so in poor white areas.

(It should be noted that to the extent each of the above explanations implies that given customers spread their purchases over more visits, then the problem is, as in poor white areas, really one of getting more black customers to shop in supermarkets.)

Gross Margin

As noted below, it is more costly to operate in inner city areas. Thus one may ask whether stores in inner city areas require higher gross margin to cover such higher costs. The answer for supermarkets is "possibly," for furniture and appliance outlets "definitely."

Supermarket data from the Marion and Goodman and Food Commission reports would suggest at first glance that food merchandisers in inner city areas secure equal or lower gross margins as compared with non-inner city outlets. However, as Marion and Goodman point out, gross margin in food retailing is a product of both retail prices and wholesale costs, the item mix (i.e., the proportion of relatively high- to relatively low-margin items), and the extent of inventory shrinkage. As Table 7-1 indicates, the latter is a major problem in low-income areas.

Shrinkage is defined to include pilferage by customers, employees, and suppliers as well as pricing and check-out errors, losses on damaged goods, etc. In computations of gross margin, shrinkage is subtracted from initial gross margin to yield the net gross margin. If shrinkage for each area as calculated on grocery items only (meat and produce shrinkage is seldom estimated) is added back to reported gross margins as follows, important differences in *initial* average markup are observed:

	Non-Low-Income Area Stores	Low-Income Area Stores		
		Mainly White	*Mainly Black*	*Overall*
Shrinkage	0.43%	0.56%	2.34%	1.67%
Grocery gross margin	15.07%	14.48%	14.34%	14.59%
Total	15.50%	15.04%	16.68%	16.26%

When shrinkage is added back to grocery gross margins, the gross margins for groceries are about 8% *higher* for stores in predominantly black areas than for the non-low-income area stores. As Table 7-1 shows, gross margins are also higher there in produce and meats. Stores in predominantly

TABLE 7-1. Operating Results for 36 Chain Store Supermarkets in Low-Income and Non-Low-Income Areas, 1968

	Non-Low-Income Area Stores (16)	Low-Income Area Stores: Predominantly White Areas (7)	Low-Income Area Stores: Predominantly Black Areas (13)	Low-Income Area Stores: All Low-Income Area Stores (20)
Total annual sales	$3,285,450	$2,270,300	$2,019,400	$2,107,265
Groc. dept. (% of total)	65.07	65.58	61.61	63.11
Meat dept. (% of total)	26.50	26.08	29.30	28.09
Prod. dept. (% of total)	8.36	8.31	9.03	8.76
Inventory shrinkage (% of groc. dept. sales)	0.43	0.56	2.34	1.67
Gross margin (% of sales)				
Groc. dept.	15.07	14.48	14.34	14.59
Meat dept.	20.57	20.25	21.56	21.07
Prod. dept.	27.94	26.35	30.60	29.00
Total	17.57	16.97	17.60	17.36
Expenses (% of sales)				
Labor	8.54	9.14	9.50	9.36
Rent	1.50	1.66	2.01	1.87
Advertising	0.87	1.00	0.88	0.93
Depreciation and amortization	0.66	0.73	0.98	0.86
Supplies and laundry	0.65	0.57	0.75	0.68
Telephone, heat, light, and power	0.58	0.68	0.98	0.87
Insurance	0.28	0.30	0.29	0.29
Security	0.19	0.39	0.62	0.53
Bad checks	0.05	0.13	0.26	0.21
Other expenses	2.93	3.31	3.55	3.50
Total	16.25	17.91	19.82	19.10

TABLE 7-1. Continued

	Non-Low-Income Area Stores (16)	Low-Income Area Stores: Predominantly White Areas (7)	Low-Income Area Stores: Predominantly Black Areas (13)	Low-Income Area Stores: All Low-Income Area Stores (20)
Pretax net operating profit (% of sales)	1.32	−.94	−2.22	−1.74
Other income	0.66	0.81	0.58	0.67
Net profit (before taxes)	1.98	−0.13	−1.64	−1.07
Avg. cust. purch.	$7.43	$7.43	$5.38	$6.15
Sales/man-hour	$37.28	$36.42	$29.76	$32.27
Sq. ft. selling area	13,200	10,505	12,215	11,617
Age of store (years)	12.4	9.4	11.5	10.8
Rent/sq. ft. selling area	$3.89	$3.91	$3.47	$3.63

Source: Donald Marion and Charles Goodman, "Operating Problems in the Inner City," in Alan R. Andreasen (ed.), *Improving Inner City Marketing* (Chicago: American Marketing Association, 1972), p. 123. Reprinted with permission.

white low-income areas, on the other hand, have lower gross margins than non-low-income areas in all three categories.

There are several explanations for these higher gross margins. First, one is tempted to speculate that since costs of operation are higher in black areas, supermarket managers, contrary to their public statements, do try to get higher prices in their inner city operations. However, one ought not to draw such a conclusion, since differences in *product mix* brought about by differences in taste and/or merchandising strategy may well account for this difference. A third possible explanation for higher initial markups in poor black areas is that lower-quality, lower-cost meat and produce are being sold to blacks at the same prices as better-quality goods are sold to whites. There are some data indicating that inferior-quality meats and produce are sold in inner city areas. These data will be reported in a later chapter. A final, equally plausible explanation is that higher margins may result from blacks buying better cuts of meat and better-quality produce than poor whites in their need for compensatory prestige consumption.[11]

FURNITURE AND APPLIANCE STORES

Furniture and appliance stores serving ghetto areas usually are not low-priced mass merchandisers, and thus it is not surprising that they have higher gross margins than is the case in higher-income areas where discount competition is more often found. What *is* surprising is how really high these margins are. The FTC study referred to earlier, for example, supplies the following data on relative margins in the District of Columbia.[12]

	GROSS MARGIN
Low-income market retailers	60.8%
General market retailers	37.0%
Appliance, radio, and television	30.2%
Furniture and home furnishings	41.2%
Department stores	37.7%

There seem to be three major explanations for this wide discrepancy. First, much of the difference is due to the fact that most inner city furniture and appliance sales are made on credit (92.7% in the District of Columbia case), which typically means very high gross income per item sold. A second cause in many cases is the willingness of some inner city merchants deceptively to charge high prices sometimes for used or otherwise inferior goods. A final, possible explanation is that higher margins in low-income areas are necessary to cover significantly higher costs, a serious and complex problem, as noted below.

Operating Costs

Ranking ahead of demand considerations in the minds of many businessmen as a deterent to operating in the inner city are the day-to-day operating problems and greater costs of operation in inner city areas. It is generally felt that returns on investment in inner city areas are, and will continue to be, much lower than can be obtained in alternative markets because of low volume, pressures to hold down prices, and continually rising costs. That costs of operation are much higher in disadvantaged areas is attested by the National Commission on Food Marketing, Marion and Goodman, and FTC reports. Cost figures for the three studies uniformly indicate higher costs as a percent of sales in the inner city. To understand this, analysis of several cost categories using the Marion and Goodman study as a model (Table 7-1) is necessary.

LABOR

In Marion and Goodman's detailed study, labor costs as a percentage of sales are much higher for both white and black low-income areas. And although labor in many industries is highly fixed over broad levels of output, in food retailing it is highly variable. Stock boys, clerks, and check-out personnel can be added or subtracted relatively easily as volume changes. People like supervisors, managers, meat cutters, and the like cannot, however, and so it is possible that some of the higher percentages for labor costs may be a function of lower volume in inner city stores and thus less efficient use of labor.

Three other explanations are suggested by Marion and Goodman.[13] First, meat sales were substantially higher in black areas, and because of the need for cutting and prepackaging, meat sales have a higher labor component. Second, smaller average transaction sizes noted in black inner city areas probably increase labor costs, since the cost of checking out and bagging orders is relatively fixed over large differences in transaction size.

The final, and in a sense residual, explanation is that the laborers themselves are less efficient. One of the principal findings of the Buffalo study was that white workers in poor black areas were those who were willing for one reason or another to stay behind when the area changed color. One reason white employees leave is that "Many of the better employees refuse to work in stores where they feel their personal well-being is threatened." [14] Indeed in the Buffalo study it was found that those retail categories with lower-than-average white employment were those such as supermarketing which have been subject to higher-than-average neighborhood crime. Since departing white workers have typically had more retail experience, this may explain the lower efficiency of the outlets they leave behind.

In support of the "lower efficiency" hypothesis, Marion and Goodman point to real differences across areas in sales per man-hour. As the figures below indicate, productivity seems to be much lower in black areas but not in poor white areas.[15] This difference adds further credence to the suggestion that white workers leaving black areas is the major source of lowered efficiency.

	SALES PER MAN-HOUR
Non-low-income area	$37.28
White low-income area	$36.42
Black low-income area	$29.76

Lower skills in low-income areas was also found in a U.S. Department of Agriculture study in which 25% more checkout pricing errors were found in low-income areas than high-income areas.[16]

It should be noted here that general incompetence of employees is a universal complaint of food-retailing executives. As two executives testified at a food-pricing hearing:

> *Safeway store manager:* I know it's carelessness because with the standard of employees at the present time, as everybody knows . . . everybody has lowered the standards, for instance, of hiring employees. You don't get, for instance, as ambitious employees as we used to get before, and those employees do make quite a few mistakes sometimes.
>
> *Kroger division manager:* . . . Much, if not most, of our pricing is carried out by part-time personnel, many of whom are high school students and other young people. . . . Frequently, just when they have reached an acceptable level [of pricing performance], they leave us for college, the military service or another job. It becomes quite clear, then, that the speed and frequency in volume of price changes creates human working conditions under which inadvertent errors can occur. . . . [W]hile these errors may occur, they are not by design.[17]

On the other hand, although Caplovitz also found relatively little difference between Bay Ridge and Harlem merchants in the number reporting "having a problem finding competent help",[18] the reasons for not getting good help differ very much between the areas. The basic difference between the two samples reflects pronounced differences in their labor pool. Inner-city merchants find relatively more people interested in working for them but find that even the better applicants lack adequate training and experience and/or are unreliable. Retailers in white middle-class areas, on the other hand, find that their major problem is that the better candidates simply do not want to work in retailing, presumably because of the lower wages there.

Furniture and appliance outlets. There are no directly comparable data on labor costs in the durable goods area. The FTC study (Table 7-2) reports that salary and commissions including officers' salary was 28.2% of sales for 10 low-income market retailers and only 17.8% of sales for 10 comparable general market retailers. This difference reflects three major factors. First, low-income area durable goods retailers place much more emphasis on their sales force for selling—as the discussion of inner city exploitation below will suggest—than, say, on advertising. There are undoubtedly more salesmen for the number of units sold in inner city areas, and each salesman may well get higher salaries and commissions. Further, some of these salesmen especially in black areas, are not necessarily on the selling floor, but go from door to door as peddlers soliciting sales, thus incurring higher labor costs. Second, salesmen do much of the collection work on installment contracts that are such a major component of inner city sales, and in some cases they receive commissions on collections. Third, the higher level of credit sales requires much more clerical help for a given level of sales in inner city furniture and appliance outlets.

ADVERTISING

Food chain advertising expenditures are fixed centrally by region, and the costs are prorated to stores in direct proportion to sales. Thus Marion and Goodman report little difference in advertising-to-sales ratios across outlets, except in poor white areas where special additional campaigns may have been carried out.[19] However, in some areas of the country pressures for chains to advertise in black media are now increasing the outlays specifically attributable to outlets in predominantly black areas.

In furniture and appliance outlets, advertising is a lower percent of sales for low-income than for non-low-income area stores. In the District of Columbia, advertising is 2.1% of sales for the former and 3.9% for the latter.[20] However, since markups are much higher in inner city areas, the dollar outlay per unit sold is much higher, indicating the relative heavy reliance on media to generate sales prospects in poor areas.

INSURANCE

Marion and Goodman's data on insurance expenses do not reveal several of the major problems inner city businesses face with respect to insurance. Again, since insurance is a central office expense, insurance rates were approximately the same for all stores (about 0.29% of sales). However, Marion and Goodman note: "To the extent that a higher incidence of claims from inner city stores forced the insurance rate upward for the entire

TABLE 7–2. Operating Results of 10 Low-Income Market Retailers and 10 General Market Retailers of Furniture and Appliances in the District of Columbia, 1966

Revenue Component	Low-Income Market Retailers	General Market Retailers	Difference in Margins and Ratios: Percentage Points	Difference in Margins and Ratios: Percent of Total
1966 net sales	$5,146,395	$5,405,221		
Sales	100.0%	100.0%		
Cost of goods sold	37.8%	64.5%		
Gross profit margin	62.2%	35.5%	+26.7	100.0
Salary and commission expense[a]	28.2%	17.8%	+10.4	38.9
Advertising expense	2.1%	3.9%	−1.8	−6.7
Bad debt losses[b]	6.7%	0.3%	+6.4	24.0
Other expenses[c]	21.3%	11.2%	+10.1	37.8
Total Expenses	58.3%	33.2%	+25.1	94.0
Net profit return on sales	3.9%	2.3%	+1.6	6.0

[a] Includes officer's salaries.
[b] Includes amounts held back by finance companies to cover bad debt losses.
[c] Other expenses, including taxes, after deduction of other income.
Source: Federal Trade Commission, *Economic Report on Installment Credit and Retail Sales Practices of District of Columbia Retailers* (Washington: Government Printing Office, 1968).

firm, then non-low-income area stores were actually absorbing some of the additional insurance expense which might properly be attributed to stores in low-income areas." [21]

The major problems with respect to insurance in inner cities for all kinds of retail outlets are the inability to secure adequate coverage and higher-than-average costs for whatever coverage can be obtained. Again, Caplovitz's study provides useful data. He found that the extent of coverage varies by size of outlet.[22] Small outlets, which are more often black, have less coverage because they need the money for other purposes or in some cases because they have been refused coverage. Thus when size is controlled, Bay Ridge merchants are less likely to have no insurance and more likely to have multiple policies than Harlem businessmen, and in both respects Harlem blacks are worse off than Harlem whites, a finding confirmed in the Buffalo study.

The Buffalo study further asked those respondents with insurance whether they were satisfied with the amount they had or whether they wanted more.[23] Inner city blacks in both service and retail businesses more often felt that they had too little insurance than did white businessmen. This difference was most pronounced among newer businesses, suggesting that gaps in coverage to some extent may be a function of scarcity of working capital during start-up periods.

The lower levels of insurance coverage in the inner city can be seen as a function of three factors: inability to get new insurance, cancellation of existing insurance, and a greater unwillingness to try to get any insurance on the part of some businessmen. With respect to inability to get desired insurance, Caplovitz reports more difficulty in Harlem than in Bay Ridge, and slightly more difficulty for whites than blacks.[24] The latter finding is contradicted by the Buffalo study.[25] While 60% of Caplovitz's whites were "having trouble" getting insurance, only 53% of his blacks were. This question applied to all those with or without insurance. The Buffalo study asked only those without insurance why this was so. Of blacks without insurance, 48% said they simply "couldn't get coverage" (a smaller percentage because of the slightly stronger wording than Caplovitz used), compared with 40% of whites. Within insurance categories, Caplovitz reports his respondents as saying that fire insurance was hardest to get, followed by theft and riot insurance. In the Buffalo study whites were more than twice as likely to have had their insurance cancelled than were blacks. This finding is supported by Caplovitz, who also found both cancellations and difficulty getting insurance positively related to business size.

As to insurance cost, Caplovitz asked his respondents whether their insurance rates had gone up in the past few years and found that his Bay Ridge respondents were as unlikely as his Harlem respondents to say yes. Interestingly, 51% of Harlem whites paid at least $1,000 for their insurance compared with only 39% of Bay Ridge whites and 19% of Harlem blacks, suggesting that although rates may be going up all over, the base rate may be higher for large white inner city businesses, which are the most obvious targets for riots and burglary in the ghetto.[26]

SECURITY AND RELATED PROBLEMS

As implied throughout this section, many white businessmen—and their employees—fear to locate in the inner city because of rising crime rates there, both street crimes and crimes against businesses, as well as a growing antibusiness hostility that makes it difficult for businessmen to prosecute petty offenders. It has already been reported that low-income stores, especially those in black areas, incur much higher rates of inventory shrinkage. The principle source of the shrinkage is higher pilferage. Marion and Goodman report inner city respondents as laying the blame for most of the losses on children and young people who would "come into the store, scoop up some merchandise or cash from the cash register, and run from the store." [27] Marion and Goodman further note that "white merchants, in particular, felt intimidated by the threat of serious consequences if they were to take positive action against offenders." [28]

Security is only one cost of higher crime rates. The combined costs of shrinkage, security, and bad checks amount to 0.68% of supermarket sales in non-low-income areas, 1.08% in predominantly white low-income areas, and a very substantial 3.22% of sales in black areas. The excess in black areas over non-low-income areas amounts to 2.54% of sales, or, given black stores' average volume, about $50,000 per year per supermarket. Elimination of such unusual losses would turn the pretax profit of stores in black areas from red to black (although the same would not be true for stores in predominantly white areas).

BAD DEBTS

A related item of expense, which, however, typically does not affect chain stores, is bad debts. If the scarce data and individual comments by inner city businessmen are any indication, the problem of bad debts is a major concern of small retailers, especially those in the furniture and appliance business. In the FTC study, bad debt losses were 6.7% of sales for the ten low-income retailers but only 0.3% for the ten matched general retailers.[29] Part of this difference stems, of course, from the fact that almost four times as great a proportion of low-income sales are on installment contracts. Even when this difference is controlled, inner city bad debt losses are clearly five to six times as great as elsewhere.

This difference is one of the prime explanations offered by low-income area retailers to justify their higher prices. As the FTC study put it. "It was evident from analysis of financial statements, finance charges, and retail prices of low-income market retailers that they often charge higher prices anticipating that part of the increased revenue will cover higher collection expenses of their method of doing business".[30] This attitude is also reflected in Caplovitz's interview with merchants in the early sixties, where he concluded, "The high markup in low-quality goods is thus a major device used by the merchants to protect themselves against the risks of their credit business." [31]

It should be noted, of course, that not all the expenses in the FTC study relating to the costs of handling high-risk credit were reflected directly in bad debt costs. Costs of billing machines, interest on borrowed funds, and legal expenses to process the many court actions brought by inner city merchants appear as "other expense," which at 21.3% of sales in the FTC study is almost double that for general market appliance and furniture stores (11.2%).

BUSINESS CREDIT

A final operating problem for inner city merchants that does not show up on balance sheets is the difficulty of securing lines of credit or capital loans in the inner city. Businesses seeking to invest in the area typically need two kinds of financing, bank loans (or their equivalent) for basic investment capital and supplier financing for working capital. The problems in the two categories are somewhat different.

With respect to bank loans, it is not surprising that low-income area businessmen report more difficulty raising capital. Such businesses are often low-volume, high-cost, and poorly managed operations. The areas many of them serve are either in stage II (becoming black) or stage III becoming poor) of inner city economic development, and both stages are likely to be seen as poor economic climates for investment by bankers. Thus loans to inner city businesses are usually seen as very high risk.

In his study of New York merchants Caplovitz found that only 12% of Bay Ridge whites expressed difficulty getting loans, whereas this was the case for 21% of Harlem whites and 39% of Harlem blacks.[32] The relative disadvantage of black merchants relative to white merchants is further elaborated in the Buffalo study.[33] Black businessmen less often get loans than whites due to their smaller size and more recent entry into business, but even when size and length of time in business are controlled, they are less successful in getting such financing. Possibly as a consequence of these problems, Caplovitz found that Harlem whites and especially Harlem blacks were less likely to go to banks for funds (almost all loan rejections were from banks) than to go to other sources like the Small Business

Administration, higher-cost small loan companies, and friends and relatives. Of blacks who did get loans in that study, 30% used the latter sources, compared with 10% of Harlem whites and 14% of Bay Ridge Whites. That blacks are quite discouraged about their ability to get financing was shown in the Buffalo study. Here owners were asked what they thought their chances were of getting a $5,000 loan. Only 30% of black male business owners and 21% of black female owners thought their chances of getting such a loan were excellent, compared with 56% of white males and 30% of white females.[34]

Blacks are also relatively worse off when one looks at data on ability to secure supplier credit. Although Caplovitz found that Harlem whites had no more difficulty than Bay Ridge whites in this regard, even when size of business was controlled, blacks were at least three times as likely as inner city whites to have to pay cash for all their merchandise purchases. This difference applies across all four major business categories in Caplovitz's study.[35] Finally, it should be noted that black businesses not only had to pay cash more often for their supplies but more often bought their supplies at higher prices. Caplovitz found that even when size of business was controlled, blacks were much less likely to buy directly from manufacturers and/or wholesalers and more likely to use higher-priced jobbers.[36]

Summary

This chapter has extended our discussion of the consequences for the disadvantaged consumer of having to shop in inner city areas. Economic decline in poor areas has major effects on the operating problem of inner city businesses. As a direct result of these declining circumstances, volume of sales both in numbers of customers and sales per customer tapers off, labor costs rise, insurance costs rise or insurance becomes unavailable, and security and bad debt costs rise severely. This combination of factors results in operating *losses* for many kinds of business (although not all) and difficulty in securing capital and lines of credit. These problems are particularly severe in black areas, especially for the black businessmen in those areas.

The response of many legitimate businessmen, particularly the more sophisticated, more mobile businessmen, to this profit and capital squeeze has understandably been, as noted in Chapter 6, simply to take their businesses elsewhere. This, of course, has deprived disadvantaged consumers of the close proximity of well-run, usually competitively priced retail and service outlets, particularly the so-called mass merchandisers.

A second response, equally handicapping for disadvantaged consumers, has been for those businessmen who stayed behind to counteract higher costs and lower unit volume by *raising prices*. A third response has been to reduce investment in inventory, store remodeling, expansion, and the like, thus contributing further to the area's economic decay.

The result, in sum, has been that disadvantaged consumers not only have less money to spend but are forced to shop where they have fewer well-run stores to spend it in, narrower assortments within these stores to select from, and higher prices to pay for the items that are available. They must also shop in an economic environment that they see is rapidly decaying around them. This means that being poor and black constitutes a *double penalty* for the disadvantaged as consumers. They have less to spend, and because they *collectively* provide poor markets for business, they receive much less for each dollar they do spend.

Of those businessmen who do not flee the declining markets, not all see disadvantaged consumers as an undesirable market target. Many see their lack of mobility and their presumed lack of market sophistication as a major inducement for the use of unethical merchandising practices, practices that again compound the difficulties of the disadvantaged. It is to these unethical practices that our attention now turns.

Notes

1. Joe S. Bain, *Industrial Organization* (New York: John Wiley & Sons, Inc., 1959).
2. R. Caves, *American Industry: Structure, Conduct, Performance*, 2d ed. (Englewood Cliffs, N.J.: Prentice–Hall, Inc., 1967).
3. National Commission on Food Marketing, *Organization and Competition in Food Retailing*, Technical Study no. 7 (Washington: Government Printing Office, 1966).
4. Donald Marion and Charles Goodman, "Operating Problems of Marketing Firms in Low-Income Areas," in Alan R. Andreasen (ed.), *Improving Inner-City Marketing* (Chicago: American Marketing Association, 1972), pp. 115–48.
5. Federal Trade Commission, *Economic Report on Installment Credit and Retail Sales Practices of District of Columbia Retailers* (Washington: Government Printing Office, 1968).
6. These figures are rounded, and since not all respondents gave profit data in the FTC study, the figures do not necessarily apply to all firms yielding such data.
7. David Caplovitz, *The Merchants of Harlem: A Study of Small Business in a Black Community* (vol. I, Sage Library of Social Research) (Beverly Hills, Calif.: Sage Publications, Inc., 1973), chap. 6.
8. Marion and Goodman, *op. cit.*, p. 123, figures are rounded.
9. *Ibid.*, figures are rounded.

10. Lower levels of sales in all Harlem stores as compared with a middle-income white area are reported by Caplovitz except for outlets selling "high cost items" (Caplovitz, *op. cit.*, p. 12). The exception may be attributable to the fact that such stores in the middle-income area are more often branches or order offices than is the case in Harlem.
11. Yet another explanation, of course, is that these differences are not statistically significant at all.
12. Federal Trade Commission, *op. cit.*
13. Marion and Goodman, *op. cit.*, p. 126.
14. *Ibid.*
15. *Ibid.*, p. 123.
16. United States Department of Agriculture, *Comparison of Prices Paid for Selected Foods in Chain Stores in High and Low Income Areas of Six Cities* (Washington: Government Printing Office, June 1968).
17. *Consumer Problems of the Poor: Supermarket Operations in Low Income Areas and the Federal Response*, Hearings before the Committee on Government Operations, House of Representatives, 90th Congress, 2d Session (Washington: Government Printing Office, 1968), pp. 35–6.
18. Caplovitz, *op. cit.*, p. 81.
19. Marion and Goodman, *op. cit.*, p. 123.
20. Federal Trade Commission, *op. cit.*
21. Marion and Goodman, *op. cit.*, p. 127.
22. Caplovitz, *op. cit.*, p. 96.
23. Alan R. Andreasen, *Inner City Business: A Case Study of Buffalo, New York* (New York: Praeger Publishers, Inc., 1971), pp. 160–9.
24. Caplovitz, *op. cit.*, pp. 96–7.
25. Andreasen, *op. cit.*, p. 163.
26. For a further discussion of insurance problems in disadvantaged areas, see National Advisory Committee on Civil Disorders, *Meeting the Insurance Crisis of Our Cities: A Report by the President's National Advisory Panel on Insurance in Riot-affected Areas* (Washington: Government Printing Office, 1968).
27. Marion and Goodman, *op. cit.*, p. 125.
28. *Ibid.*
29. Federal Trade Commission, *op. cit.*
30. *Ibid.*, p. 19.
31. David Caplovitz, *The Poor Pay More* (New York: The Free Press, 1967), p. 18.
32. Caplovitz, *The Merchants of Harlem*, p. 90.
33. Andreasen, *op. cit.*, pp. 190–1.
34. *Ibid.*, p. 192.
35. Caplovitz, *The Merchants of Harlem*, p. 88.
36. *Ibid.*, p. 84.

PART 3

EXPLOITATION OF THE DISADVANTAGED

8. Price Discrimination in the Inner City

PERHAPS THE MOST DEEPLY FELT FRUSTRATION of most disadvantaged consumers is the sense that they are the victims of price discrimination; that if they weren't poor or black or didn't live where they did, they could buy their food, their clothing, their appliances, even their housing for much less. In the main they believe that this is because they are being cheated, that merchants who usually live outside the area take advantage of their immobility, their lack of education, and their credit problems to gouge them unmercifully at the cash register.

Yet previous chapters have shown that disadvantaged areas are difficult places for merchants to make a profit in at "normal" prices. Higher costs, greater risks, and declining sales all are operating characteristics that exert upward pressure on prices. This suggests that while the allegations made by disadvantaged groups and their spokesmen about price discrimination may be true, their attribution of invidious motivation may be wrong.

This chapter explores the charges and denials in this critical area. First the question of whether price differences do in fact exist is taken up. Then the chapter turns to several important methodological issues that raise basic questions about whether much at all about this critical issue has really been resolved to date.

The Issue

A review of the surprisingly scant research literature on prices paid by disadvantaged consumers suggests that investigators have looked at the problem from one of five alternative perspectives. Stated as research hypotheses, these perspectives are as follows:

I. Prices in stores near disadvantaged consumers on the average are higher than prices in stores near the nondisadvantaged.

II. When the size (as well as efficiency) of outlets is controlled, prices in stores near disadvantaged consumers are higher than prices in stores near the nondisadvantaged.

III. Stores in disadvantaged areas owned by a firm charge higher prices than stores owned by the *same* firm in nondisadvantaged areas.

IV. *Within a given store,* the disadvantaged are charged higher prices than nondisadvantaged consumers.

V. Finally, *wherever they shop,* disadvantaged consumers pay higher prices than nondisadvantaged consumers.

The first three of these formulations are in effect comparisons between areas and do not directly consider prices paid by disadvantaged consumers, only assuming that, for example, stores in disadvantaged areas are primarily patronized by the disadvantaged and stores in nondisadvantaged areas are not. The last two hypotheses confront this price issue directly.

As will be seen in the discussions below, only formulations IV and V could constitute a legal definition of price discrimination and would not do so if haggling were a typical price-setting phenomenon in the line of trade. Thus the term "price discrimination" in the sections to follow is used in what might be called a moral sense where prices presumed to be paid by the disadvantaged are higher than those paid by the nondisadvantaged focusing on the extent to which the disadvantaged come out on the high end of such differences.

A METHODOLOGICAL NOTE. Several of the findings reported below contradict what may be the popular wisdom about price discrimination, namely that the disadvantaged are worse off no matter how the problem is defined. As already suggested, this is partly the result of the fact that the casual reader does not pay close attention to critical definitional differences. Thus if, as is the case, it is found that the average store in poor areas charges more (hypothesis I), this does not mean that given chains charge more in inner city stores (hypothesis III).

Perhaps in greater part the findings contradict popular wisdom because it was founded on a number of methodologically weak early studies which, because they were all that was available at the time, received broad publicity in early congressional hearings on food pricing. As Sexton has recently pointed out: "The conclusions of such studies . . . must be viewed with extreme caution due to methodological difficulties such as inadequate sample sizes, casual sample design, and selective and inaccurate reporting."[1] The studies were carried out by newspapers, consumer action groups, and independent housewives and were often undertaken "to prove a point," as with the New York group that threw out data from chains where *lower* prices in disadvantaged areas were found.

The studies reported below are those that meet reasonably strong tests of methodological rigor. Other issues of methodology will be discussed in the concluding sections of this chapter.

I. THE STRUCTURAL HYPOTHESIS

The first hypothesis says in effect that the average store in disadvantaged areas charges more than the average store in nondisadvantaged areas. Or, put another way, if both disadvantaged and nondisadvantaged consumers shopped in the stores nearest in travel time to them whatever size or type these stores might be, the disadvantaged consumers would pay more. As earlier analyses have suggested, this is a hypothesis that is generally true. It is primarily true because there are fewer supermarkets, discount houses, and department stores and more small, undercapitalized neighborhood outlets in disadvantaged areas. It is a consistent finding in the literature that large mass merchandise outlets have lower prices than small, personal service local businesses. For example, a Bureau of Labor Statistics study in 1966[2] found that prices of large independent food stores were 1% above those of chain stores and small independents 3% higher. Dixon and McLaughlin found the following market basket differences for small stores and supermarkets in Philadelphia:[3]

Area	Supermarket	Small Store	Difference
Higher-income	$8.63	$9.38	8.7%
Inner city	$8.54	$9.01	5.5%

Interestingly, the Dixon and McLaughlin data show that the spread of prices between small and large stores in the higher-income areas is greater than in the inner city, suggesting that small stores in each area may serve very different functions. That is, small stores in low-income areas very often are major sources of everyday food needs for neighborhood residents, whereas in higher-income areas these stores are used more as sources of speciality items and after-hours convenience items for which premium prices can be obtained. These findings however, have not yet been confirmed. For example, Marcus in a study in the Los Angeles area found *both* chains and small "mom-and-pops" more expensive in Watts than in the more affluent Culver City area.[4]

Somewhat higher prices in inner city food stores in Chicago was found in March 1969 by the Task Force on Public Aid of the Church Federation of Greater Chicago.[5] In its study it found higher prices in poor black areas than in poor white areas and found that these sets of prices were both higher than for the rest of the city and the suburbs. As explanation, it pointed out that its inner city sample included more small independent stores because they were where "large numbers of public aid recipients could reasonably be expected to shop." A similar approach and conclusion were reported by Bliss et al. in Cleveland.[6] Studies by Sexton[7] and Focus:

Hope[8] also found higher prices for inner city independents, which are typically smaller outlets, than for chains.

Outside the food category, studies of drug prices have produced mixed results. Wertheimer found higher prices in Buffalo's poor communities,[9] but Hastings and Kunnes,[10] Kotzan and Braucher,[11] and Cady and myself[12] did not find such relationships in Kansas City, Atlanta, and Buffalo.

With respect to durable goods, Caplovitz in *The Poor Pay More* showed that high prices for television sets, phonographs, and washing machines were most likely to be paid to peddlers—a retail phenomenon much more prevalent in poor areas—and to neighborhood stores, although chain stores (large appliance chains specializing in credit and "easy payment" plans) are an important source of higher prices for phonographs.[13] A number of other studies such as the FTC District of Columbia study cited in the previous chapter[14] and studies by Sturdivant and Wilhelm[15] and Hanselman[16] also indicate higher average prices for durables in the inner city. Differences in prices from the FTC study are reported in Table 8-1. Analysis in the previous chapter suggested that these price differences were largely attributable to different methods of sales and heavy reliance on credit merchandising. The FTC study found that "finance charges of low-income retailers are generally somewhat higher than those of general market retailers." [17] This finding is also confirmed by the other two studies. Significantly, in its introduction to its report the FTC said that "there is ample reason, based on information received from consumers by the Federal Trade Commission, to believe that many of the practices found in this survey are also prevalent in the sale of clothing, variety goods, jewelry, and services such as reupholstering and auto repairs." [18]

II. THE STORE SIZE HYPOTHESIS

Implied in the previous discussion is the hypothesis that differences in prices between disadvantaged and nondisadvantaged areas may be largely attributable to differences in the distribution of outlet sizes between the areas. Thus, the question becomes one of whether if the disadvantaged were less immobile and could in fact get to the mass merchandise outlets in their own area, they would pay about as much as they would if they drove all the way out to the more affluent areas.

FOOD PRICES. Perhaps the most thorough study testing this hypothesis was that carried out on February 8 and 9, 1968, by the Department of Agriculture.[19] This study investigated prices in 134 stores of two chains in each of six cities for products in 17 categories, with two brands designated for each packaged and canned product. Because of difficulties in controlling for quality, no produce was included in the study's market basket for pricing.[20] The dates chosen for the study "represent a time period when

TABLE 8-1. Average "Retail Prices" of District of Columbia Retailers on Best-Selling Items of Appliances and Furniture in 1966, Assuming Wholesale Cost of $100 for Each Item

	Average "Retail Price" in Dollars[a] Assuming $100 Wholesale Cost of –			
		General Market Retailers		
Merchandise Item	Low-Income Market Retailers	Appliance Stores[b]	Furniture Stores[b]	Department Stores
Television set	187	131	140	134
Carpet	200		160	150
Refrigerator	202	132	133	153
Washing machine	204	133	148	155
Stereo–phonograph	211	149	157	153
Freezer	216	133		151
Dryer	217	135	138	160
Furniture	228		190	202
Vacuum cleaner	237	136	143	157
Radio	250	130	161	139
Sewing machine	297	196		174

[a]These are cash prices and do not reflect separately imposed finance charges.
[b]Appliance and furniture stores have been classified on the basis of their principal merchandise lines. Furniture stores carry appliances as a substantial secondary merchandise line, and for this reason average "retail prices" of appliances sold by furniture stores are included in this table.
Source: Federal Trade Commission, *Economic Report on Installment Credit and Retail Sales Practices of District of Columbia Retailers* (Washington: Government Printing Office, 1968).

the patronage of retail food stores by Food Stamp participants and welfare recipients was likely to be relatively high".[21] Stores in each chain were divided into low and high income area stores based on area income and the extent of Food Stamp redemption in stores themselves.[22] The basic finding of the study was that when store size was controlled, "the differences in average prices paid in high and low income area stores were no greater than would be expected on the basis of the variation among stores within an income area." [23] This finding for supermarkets was replicated in the Dixon and McLaughlin study previously cited,[24] although these researchers found lower prices for smaller independents in low-income areas.

A study of a wider selection of 66 stores in low-, middle-, and high-income areas of Phoenix was carried out in July 1968 by Louis H. Grossman, using the Dixon–McLaughlin market basket.[25] While, as in other studies, Grossman found considerable range in total costs across his study districts (a low of $7.77 and a high of $8.36) he again concludes that "a negative correlation between income and food prices does not exist".[26] In fact, in three of the four low-income areas consumers could buy Grossman's market basket at their average supermarket at *less* than the Phoenix average. Grossman also controlled for ownership type (e.g., national chain, local chain, independent) and again found great variation even within chains on a single day but no apparent relationship with income.

An extensive study of 117 of a "wide spectrum" of name brand food and nonfood items was carried out by Richard Teach in Buffalo, New York, in 1969.[27] The study was carried out in 18 supermarkets in low-income ($3,000 to $5,000 1960 median income) and high-income ($7,500 to $10,000 income) areas. Instead of using raw prices in computing his indexes, Teach used actual consumer purchase data for three families with similar socioeconomic characteristics (including low income) to weight his market basket. Teach also found no significant differences between areas for the supermarket market basket, although some results were mixed. In support of the hypothesis, however, Teach did find that the lowest six stores in price were in the suburbs and the highest five were in the core area.

Two studies disagree with these general findings. Donaldson and Strangeways found slightly higher prices for an 111-item market basket for chain and large independents in poor and near-poor areas of Atlanta, Georgia, in July, 1969.[28] The range of difference was 1 to 2 percentage points, although no statistical test was applied to determine whether these differences were in fact significant. Marcus (as noted above) also found higher supermarket prices in Watts than in Culver City, although his approach to the problem of substituting for missing brands leaves the results somewhat unclear.[29]

Drug prices. Hastings and Kunnes[30] found significant differences in prices among types of pharmacies selling in low- and high-income areas.

Medical students priced digoxin (Lanoxin) in all pharmacies in census tracts with incomes under $3,000 and over $8,000 in Kansas City. The results, reported in Table 8-2, show that while there were few overall differences between areas in prices of the drug, there were significant differences among types of outlets. Consumers residing in low-income areas obtained significantly *better* prices in professional (i.e., selling drugs only) or chain pharmacies than in the slightly more prevalent independent variety pharmacies.

TABLE 8-2. Mean Prices for Digoxin, by Store Type and Area Income

	Low-Income Area[a]	High-Income Area[b]
Independent, drugs only	$2.71 (3)[c]	$3.19 (10)
Independent, variety	3.26 (8)	2.59 (7)
Chain,[d] variety	1.90 (7)	2.29 (5)
Overall Average	$2.64 (18)	$2.79 (22)

[a]Median family income under $3,000.
[b]Median family income over $8,000.
[c]Number of outlets.
[d]Four or more outlets under single ownership.
Source: Adapted from Glenn E. Hastings and Richard Kunnes, "Predicting Prescription Prices," *New England Journal of Medicine,* vol. 277, no. 12, Sept. 21, 1967, p. 626. Reprinted by permission.

The problem, as noted in the next section, is that this study, like others, doesn't indicate who shopped in the outlets in question. Chapter 6 showed that poor areas often border on central city shopping areas, and it is thus possible that some or all of the chain variety drug outlets in poor areas do not really serve those areas. Indeed, Hastings and Kunnes refer to such outlets as "central city chain drugstores" and note that they have heavy competition from each other and from independents. (No chain variety outlet had *few* competitors.) Still, to the extent the poor can and do shop in such outlets, they get lower prices. These findings are confirmed in a second study by Kotzan and Braucher,[31] who found lowest prices for Darvon in Atlanta in what they called "promotional discount drug outlets," three of which were located in "the most economically depressed areas."

III. BETWEEN-STORE DISCRIMINATION

Do given retailers charge one set of prices in one area and another set in another area in order to maximize profits? For example, does A&P charge more in low-income areas of Cleveland than in high-income areas? This question is one that most frequently arouses the ire of inner city consumer groups at government hearings. For example, at hearings before the House

Government Operations Committee in 1968, a Bedford-Stuyvesant area group reported the following price discrepancies for a market basket of goods for five supermarket chains on November 14, 1967:[32]

	AREA		
	FLATBUSH	BED.–STUY.	DIFFERENCE
A&P	$10.08	$10.29	2.1%
Waldbaum's	$8.33	$8.41	1.0%
Key Food	$11.82	$12.60	6.5%
Royal Farms	$10.31	$10.31	
Associated Foods	$10.25	$10.32	0.68%

On the other hand, an earlier 1966 study by Massive Economic Neighborhood Development Inc. in New York found no evidence that A&P charged higher prices in East Harlem than in upper-income areas, but evidence that another chain, Sloan Food, charged as much as 15% more in Harlem.[33] In St. Louis the Human Development Corporation found prices in one poverty area store of one chain 15% higher than in one of its affluent area stores.[34] It found poverty area stores for Kroger 2½% higher than non-poverty area stores and 7½% higher for Associated Food Stores, a cooperative of individually owned and wholesaler-affiliated stores.

Despite their methodological weaknesses, such "studies" considerably inflamed the rhetoric in the early years of the debate on inner city price discrimination. As already noted, the methodology of such studies is uniformly suspect (although each for different reasons). There have been relatively few methodologically sound investigations of the between-store hypothesis.

Perhaps the most thorough such study was again that conducted by the Department of Agriculture, pricing 17 items in food chains in six cities.[35] In only one instance did it find a chain charging significantly higher prices in low-income areas, and the study noted: "Even for this chain, differences were small for most of the 19 items where deviations were found".[36] Grossman in his study of Phoenix chains and independents found stores in a given chain both higher and lower in inner city areas.[37] Echoing the conflicting results, Brinzo et al. in Cleveland found one chain with a store higher priced in the inner city, one with a store lower priced, and two chains with no difference.[38]

Other results were as follows: Conway compared pairs of outlets in four chains in St. Louis and concluded, "No unequivocal statement can be made that national food chains charge different prices in poverty area stores. . . ." [39] A Better Business Bureau study in the same city a year later, however, did find one chain charging higher prices (based on a smaller market basket of goods) in poor areas.[40] In New York, Wright reported no discrimination within chains.[41] Finally, in its studies in the District of Columbia and San Francisco in 1969 the Federal Trade Commission found some incidences of higher food pricing in low-income areas but claimed there was no "intentional discrimination" against low-income areas.[42]

To the writer's knowledge, similar studies within ownership groups have not been made in the drug and durables category.

Finally, Sexton has pointed out that to the extent no significant differences in prices between outlets exist within chains while higher costs do exist in outlets in disadvantaged areas, chains that do not discriminate are in fact subsidizing low prices in disadvantaged areas from profits made in nondisadvantaged area stores.[43]

IV. WITHIN-STORE PRICE DISCRIMINATION

Within-store price discrimination is an accepted operating practice in many lines of business. Used and new car salesmen set initial bargaining positions (usually by manipulating the trade-in value) depending on the customer's likely sophistication, the time of the model year, the general state of the economy, and so on. And, indeed, a certain amount of haggling is expected in these and several other product categories (e.g., antiques, houses). In such instances, the unsophisticated shopper is not likely to get as low prices as would a sophisticated shopper. To the extent that the disadvantaged are less sophisticated in such product categories, they are worse off.

In many product categories (e.g., appliances, drugs) it has been historically assumed that within a given store all customers are charged about the same cash price, or if they buy on credit, the same credit price. There is now considerable evidence that this is not true and that being black in particular is a major (and time-honored) source of disadvantage. As usual, however, the findings are not uniform.

With respect to drugs, Hastings and Kunnes found that poorly dressed black student–consumers more often paid high prices for digoxin than well-dressed white student-consumers.[44] They found:

> In the thirty-nine pharmacies where both Negro and white students completed purchases, the former paid more than the latter seventeen times. The white students paid more on six occasions. On nine occasions (23 percent of the purchases) the Negro purchaser paid at least fifteen percent more than his white counterpart. Only once did a white student pay fifteen percent more than a Negro student.[45]

The reader should be aware that most drug studies have found a surprisingly high variation of prices for a given drug *within stores*. In 59% of the cases in the Hastings and Kunnes study, different prices were charged the two customers. Such apparent flexibility in pricing leaves great *opportunity* for discrimination.[46] It should also be noted that the Hastings-Kunnes study did not make clear whether the source of discrimination was the Negro's race or the fact that he was poorly dressed. In their later Atlanta study of Darvon purchases, Kotzan and Braucher did control for these factors and found no discrimination due to *either* race or dress.[47]

In the durable goods area the pattern is somewhat clearer. In disadvantaged areas variable pricing is a way of life. As noted by Caplovitz in his early interview of Harlem businessmen for *The Poor Pay More*.

> . . . in East Harlem, there are hardly any "one price" stores. In keeping with a multi-price policy, price tags are conspicuously absent from the merchandise. The customer has to ask, "how much?," and the answer he gets will depend on several things. If the merchant considers him a poor risk, if he thinks the customer is naive, or if the customer was referred to him by another merchant or a peddler to whom he must pay a commission, the price will be higher.[48]

Most often these factors are apparently closely associated, at least in the merchant's view, with income and race.

In a 1967 study Sturdivant and Wilhelm observed prices quoted to three couples shopping in the Los Angeles area for portable TV sets.[49] The three couples—Negro, Mexican–American, and "Anglo"—were given identical credit profiles and similar briefings and sent out to price models of 19-inch portable black and white TVs in stores of comparable size in three areas—the Watts area, the largely Mexican-American East Los Angeles area, and suburban, white Culver City. As the investigators note, the shoppers, to make the results as realistic as possible, "did everything necessary to obtain price data, except sign the contract." Sturdivant and Wilhelm found only infrequent cases of discrimination in the *cash* prices quoted the couples. No differences were found in Watts; all couples were quoted the same (high) price. In Culver City two stores quoted the same prices to all, and one quoted a $10 higher price to the two minority couples. Finally, in East L. A. one store quoted $6 higher prices to the minority couples. The remaining East L. A. store quoted the lowest price to the Negro couple, the next lowest to the Anglo couple, and the highest to the Mexican–Americans!

Cash prices, however, are not a particularly useful basis for comparison, since most poor families pay on time. The crucial question, then, is whether there was any discrimination in what they would have to pay *including finance charges*. Here the findings are mixed. In East L. A., despite the fact that the Anglos were quoted the lowest cash prices, they were charged the *highest* prices when finance charges were included. On the other hand, in two of three cases in Culver City the Anglos were quoted the lowest rates including finance charges. In the Watts area highest rates were charged the blacks in one store and the Mexican–Americans in another.

What can one conclude from these data?

1. The principal means of discrimination in prices was credit charges, which varied from as little as 7% of the quoted price to as high as 82%!
2. There was discrimination among customers, but it didn't always correspond to racial or ethnic status. In three of the eight analyses, Anglos were charged the highest prices after finance charges. It must be remembered, however, that their credit profile gave them a disadvantaged—i.e., poor—status.
3. Many of the stores were charging illegal and highly exploitative rates of interest. In one Culver City store the Mexican and black couples were charged rates of 42% and 44% respectively. In one Watts store the Anglo and black couples were asked 50% rates and the Mexican–Americans 82%.
4. Although the blacks and Mexican-American couples were discriminated against in two Culver City stores, "in no case did they have to pay more than in ghetto stores" and in some cases much less.

An interesting replication and extension of the Sturdivant–Wilhelm study was carried out in the summer of 1970 by William Hanselman in Portland.[50] Noting possible confounding effects in the earlier study, Hanselman sought to control for both race *and* income status in seeking out possible cases of price discrimination. Using differences in clothing, appearance, and behavior[51] to indicate income status, two black and two white couples visited four stores each in low-income black and middle-income white areas, pricing 18-inch portable black-and-white TVs.

Hanselman's results agree with the earlier study in several ways. Credit charges were the principal means of discrimination among customers. A comparison of credit costs across couples and areas in Table 8-3 shows the expected patterns across race and income. That is, more favorable terms were received by whites than blacks, and by middle-income, more sophisticated shoppers than low-income, inexperienced shoppers. Credit costs, however, were lower for the disadvantaged in the low-income area than in the middle-income area, although cash prices were usually higher. The major surprise in the data was the fact that the highest credit charge was quoted to the low-income white couple in the middle-income area. The credit charge for this couple was more than double that for the middle-income white couple in the same area. However, one should note that the credit charge for the three disadvantaged couples (low- and middle-income black and low-income white) was at least 20% greater than that for the middle-income white couple in the low-income area and 60% greater in the middle-income area.

TABLE 8–3. Average Carrying Charges, by Area, Race, and Income Level, Portland, Oregon, 1970

Area	Low-Inc. Blacks	Low-Inc. Whites	Combined Low-Inc.	Mid-Inc. Blacks	Mid-Inc. Whites	Combined Mid-Inc.	Combined Black Avg.	Combined White Avg.
Middle-Income area	$20.25	$28.25	$24.25	$21.00	$13.25	$17.12	$20.62	$20.75
Low-income area	$17.75	$17.50	$17.62	$20.25	$14.25	$17.25	$19.00	$15.87
Average both areas	$19.00	$22.88	$20.94	$20.62	$13.75	$17.19	$19.81	$18.31

Note: Carrying charges are total credit price minus retail price.
Source: William Hanselman, "The Basis for Market Discrimination: Race or Poverty," unpublished paper, Portland State University, 1970, p. 25.

Finally, Hanselman noted that, in addition to regular interest charges, "Disadvantaged shoppers would have been charged up to 13% of cash payment price for credit 'application' or 'registration' fees in a number of stores in both areas" [52] as well as more often asked to pay for nonrefusable television stands. Such items were never charged to middle-income white shoppers.

Several patterns begin to emerge from the Hanselman data:

1. As found in the FTC study (Table 8-1), cash prices in disadvantaged areas are higher than in nondisadvantaged areas. This higher-pricing technique is presumably used by most inner city merchants in part to cover their higher credit costs, as well as to exploit the disadvantaged consumer's credit problems.
2. Confirmation of the preceding point is indicated by the fact that middle-income area retailers charge higher carrying charges to disadvantaged consumers than do low-income area retailers. They must do so because they haven't "protected themselves" through higher cash prices. (Higher interest rates in the middle-income Culver City area than in the disadvantaged Watts and Mexican–American East L. A. areas were also found in the Sturdivant–Wilhelm study *if* one eliminates Watts store 3, which asked exorbitant and illegal carrying charges averaging 65% of cash prices from the three couples).
3. While higher cash prices and/or higher carrying charges for the poor may be justified by the higher risks and higher costs involved in offering them credit, one wonders whether costs that are *double* (i.e., low-income carrying charges were about twice those of middle-income whites in Hanselman's middle-income area) are really justified.[53]
4. Whatever the justification for overcharging the poor, there is apparently *no* justification for higher interest rates charged middle-income blacks[54] or for the practice of loading the disadvantaged with numerous credit "extras" that merely reflect their lack of credit mobility and perhaps their lack of sophistication.

Pricing on welfare check days. A special case of price discrimination within outlets is the oft-repeated charge that food outlets selectively raise prices just before welfare checks are issued and then lower them to "normal" several days later. As noted in earlier chapters, a problem for the poor is that their low incomes do not stretch far. This is a particular problem for those on welfare, who theoretically have few funds coming in between welfare checks and so presumably buy moderately large quantities whenever the checks are issued and then try to "scrape by" until the next check comes. Prices raised just before these welfare "paydays" thus would particularly discriminate against the welfare poor.

Typical of early evidence on this subject were reports to a special consumer inquiry of the House Government Operations Committee in 1968.[55]

For example, the Consumer Action Program of Bedford–Stuyvesant, Inc., found that prices for a market basket of 20 items developed from resident shopping lists were increased between 1.2% and 3.4% in five chain stores in Bedford–Stuyvesant between November 14 and November 16, 1967 (welfare check day), and remained unchanged or declined in outlets of the same chains in middle-income Flatbush.[56] These findings were supported by testimony of Arthur Ross, Commissioner of Labor Statistics, U.S. Department of Labor, on the basis of data on Watts; testimony of Deputy Mayor Timothy Costello of New York City, who found a 15% increase in ghetto food costs after welfare check day (no comparison with nonghetto stores was reported); and comments of the Director and Deputy Director of the U.S. Office of Economic Opportunity's (OEO) Community Action Program based on data in California and (again) Bedford–Stuyvesant.[57]

The Government Operations Committee report itself states that despite chain store criticism of methodology, "There is considerable evidence to support the case of those who charged such price hiking".[58] On the other side of the question, Dixon and McLaughlin's study quoted earlier did not find that prices in Philadelphia in November, 1967, rose after welfare checks were distributed although prices were only studied over one week's time.[59]

In response to much of this clamor, a more extensive study on this issue was carried out by the U.S. Department of Agriculture in the spring and summer of 1969.[60] The Department purchased 16 food products "frequently purchased by low income families" in 26 supermarkets and neighborhood stores in seven cities[61] on the same day one week before and shortly after welfare checks were issued. Results showed essentially no differences between the two purchase dates. About 8% of the items increased in price, and 6.3% decreased. In only 2 of 261 outlets studied did the surveyors find significantly more increases than decreases in prices—one store in Cleveland and one in Newark. The study attributed price changes mainly to:

1. Lack of price marking, which presumably led to check-out errors (8.7% of *marked* items were over- or undercharged). This was particularly a problem in neighborhood stores, where three-quarters of all price changes were attributable to unmarked items.
2. Advertised specials which were added or deleted between periods.
3. A general rise in prices, which may account for the fact that slightly more items increased than decreased between the two periods.

V. PRICES AND ACTUAL SHOPPING BEHAVIOR

Each of the four preceding hypotheses and the data that support them make assumptions about where the disadvantaged shop. Where discrimination was found in disadvantaged areas, this was assumed to be evidence that the poor were discriminated against. Alexis, Haines, and Simon point out that their review of black–white consumption expenditures has brought out that studies on this subject have almost all assumed a normally operating market. Studies of prices paid, on the other hand, have almost always assumed a prison market.[62] Again, as Sexton puts it, "If the stores sampled are not patronized by blacks and the brands sampled not purchased by blacks, these data cannot show whether or not blacks pay more." [63] Since research by Charles Goodman has suggested that perhaps blacks are not as immobile as many thought,[64] we must reasonably ask the question of whether the disadvantaged pay more wherever they shop.

Only two studies have sought to look at prices actually paid for food by consumers. Both studies used panel data for Chicago. The first study, by Frank, Green, and Sieber, did not have the present subject as its principal interest and concluded only that whites tended to pay higher prices per unit than nonwhites without further explanation.[65]

The more extensive study is Sexton's investigation of prices actually paid for three products over 1 to 2½ years by black and white members of a *Chicago Tribune* consumer panel.[66] Although Sexton reported only purchases of blacks in their own community and although the black sample was relatively affluent (median income over $6,000) and the sample of products small, his findings do parallel those reported earlier:

1. Blacks in black city areas pay more than whites in white city areas, who in turn pay more than whites in suburban areas.
2. These differences are largely attributable to price differences among affiliated and nonaffiliated independents. No significant differences within chains were found.
3. "Although there was a slight tendency for low-income families to pay more than medium-income families, no systematic pattern appeared between prices paid by medium-income and high-income families." [67]

The only study in the durable goods area that has investigated prices actually paid by consumers is Caplovitz's early study. Caplovitz found that low-income consumers were more likely to pay a "high" price and that race and ethnic background were related to price paid.[68] Caplovitz's basic findings are shown in the following table (figures in parentheses are number of cases):

	Percent Paying "High" Price		
Appliance	*White*	*Negro*	*Puerto Rican*
Television	26 (61)	43 (83)	47 (142)
Phonograph	17 (18)	48 (52)	56 (70)
Washing Machine	18 (27)	33 (27)	53 (64)

This relationship held when purchases of TVs were separated into cash and credit. However, again as already noted, credit payment much more often resulted in high prices. Caplovitz suggests the important point that the propensity to charge high credit prices is strongly related to store type. While noting that the patterns are only "suggestive," Caplovitz states:

> In the large, bureaucratic stores where prices are standardized, the race of the customer does not affect the price. The neighborhood merchants and peddlers, on the other hand, are specialists in a more personal system of credit and apparently do take the race of the customer into account.[69]

This point will be taken up in the next chapter.

Conclusions

The analysis of research results above points to the following tentative conclusions with respect to the five formulations of the price discrimination problem:

1. Prices in disadvantaged areas for both durables and nondurables are higher on average than in nondisadvantaged areas.
2. With respect to food purchases at least, a substantial portion of this difference is attributable to differences in market structure. Disadvantaged areas have more small, higher-cost independent supermarkets and mom-and-pops than nondisadvantaged areas, which more often have low-cost supermarkets. Whether the structure hypothesis applies to other categories of expenditure is not now known.
3. Prices among outlets owned by the same organization appear not to discriminate against the poor, at least with respect to food. It is possible that this may be a recent phenomenon reflecting a change in chain store practice, as Honig suggests.[70]
4. Durable goods outlets do discriminate markedly among customers on the basis of race and income. This discrimination appears most often in charges for credit purchases rather than in cash prices. Drug outlets also discriminate among customers on prescription drug prices, but there the pattern is not yet clear.
5. There appears to be little support, at least after 1969, for the charge that food stores charge more on welfare check days. This, too, may reflect a recent change in supermarket chain policy.
6. There is relatively little evidence on what the disadvantaged do in fact pay for their durables and nondurables. The studies that do exist tend to confirm the general findings that disadvantaged status is strongly related to paying high cash and higher credit prices.

Some Unresolved Questions

The price discrimination question is, in fact, linked to earlier consideration of the consumption patterns of disadvantaged consumers in Chapters 3 and 5. There it was learned that the disadvantaged allocated their available expenditures differently than the nondisadvantaged, but left unresolved was the question of whether, for example, poor families were able to get as much value as the nonpoor for the money spent annually on food, house furnishings and equipment, etc. It has since been demonstrated that to the extent the poor must buy food in their own communities or appliances on credit and interest costs are included in the expenditure figures, they do indeed receive less value. And it has been further shown that disadvantaged consumers buying furniture and appliances on credit pay a double penalty, since it is in credit sales that sellers most often charge discriminatory higher prices. It has also been shown that to the extent the disadvantaged more often shop smaller neighborhood stores for food, drugs, and appliances, they will pay, on average, higher prices and presumably receive less value.

But what of those who can and do pay cash or who can and do shop at the neighborhood supermarket? Do they get as much value as those outside disadvantaged areas? The studies reported in the earlier sections of this chapter suggest that at least as far as these studies go, they probably are charged the same prices. However, to assume that equal prices mean that the disadvantaged who pay cash do in fact get as much value for their annual expenditures, one must be assured that (1) the items that have been studied are a representative sample of all items purchased in each category (e.g., food, drugs, house furnishings and equipment) and (2) the satisfactions from purchases received by the disadvantaged and nondisadvantaged are equivalent (i.e., one is not comparing apples and oranges). We shall now turn to these unresolved questions.

REPRESENTATIVENESS

In no sense have any of the studies reported above purported to study prices of a truly representative sample of expenditure within a category. The drug and appliance studies were the most deficient in this regard, in that at most each included only five or six product items, usually chosen for their high volume of sales and/or for their availability in both low- and high-income areas. On the other hand, the food studies did investigate samples of up to 120 items. Since the realities of field research costs made it impossible to study all prices of all possible food items, investigators sampled products that bulked large in the low-income food budget. Thus:

> Products purchased were carefully selected to represent kinds commonly used by families.[71]
>
> The commodities to be priced were selected to represent a large proportion of the household food budget of low income families.[72]

Undoubtedly such market baskets were chosen to discover whether the disadvantaged face discrimination in their *major* food expenditures. There is a question, however, as to whether or not it is with these products that one is *likely* to find discrimination if it exists. A well-developed marketing theory suggests that if a food retailer seriously wishes to increase his markups in inner city outlets through selective price increases, his strategy is to keep his prices essentially competitive on those items on which consumers decide whether or not to transfer their patronage to other outlets.[73] These items are essentially those 200 or so products which are heavily advertised by most chain outlets and about which most consumers have a reasonably good sense of "normal prices" so that they would be quickly aware if a store got "out of line." These, then, are the products where a smart retailer would specifically *not* discriminate among outlets in rich and poor areas. Since they are also the products studied in virtually all food price studies to date, it is not surprising that most such studies have detected few differences. It is entirely possible that if price studies sampled *all* offered products (or perhaps items in the second volume tier), the differences many poor people *feel* exist might well appear.

VALUE

A more thorny question is whether, even in the absence of cash price differences, there are marked differences in the value received by disadvantaged as against nondisadvantaged consumers. Are the goods equal in quality? Are the secondary satisfactions offered by outlets—broad assortments, attractive layouts, or extended hours of operation—equivalent? If in either or both of these cases disadvantaged consumers receive less value, then they are in fact being discriminated against.

MERCHANDISE QUALITY

A major complaint of disadvantaged consumer groups at hearings on supermarket operations has been that meat and produce in low-income areas are inferior in quality to meat and produce in other areas, that a head of lettuce in Harlem is something less than an equally large head of lettuce in Westchester. A problem of course in this regard—one that caused a number of researchers whose work was discussed above to eliminate meat and produce from their market baskets—is the difficulty of judging quality. However, some reasonably good data do exist.

Testimony at a hearing before the Government Operations Committee in 1967 tended to bear out the claim that food is inferior in low-income stores.[74] Also, despite prior warnings to supermarket managers, Bureau of Labor Statistics investigators still found in a 1966 study that food was generally inferior in low-income area stores.[75] Testimony by the Commissioner of Labor Statistics was that this was particularly apparent for lettuce and fruits. In general, he reported that "those items where there would be variations in the quality were of lower quality in the low-income neighborhood".[76]

Testimony in 1966 by the deputy mayor of New York was in the same vein:

> . . . I'm afraid that you will not find either the environment there [in New York's ghetto supermarkets] or the quality of merchandise provided there to be equal to that which you [committee members] might find in your own residential neighborhoods. It is in quality particularly that the supermarkets don't come up—supermarkets in the ghetto areas don't come up to the supermarkets in other areas in the city.[77]

Two informal studies by the *St. Louis Post-Dispatch* also found inferior produce in low-income stores of the National and Kroger chains.[78] It was found that in low-income area Kroger stores there was much more fat and bone in pork chops and more fat in hamburger.[79]

Perhaps the most thorough study was a study of meat quality by the U.S. Department of Agriculture in connection with its 1968 food-pricing study.[80] For three of the meat items purchased in that study, the following laboratory tests were made:

Frankfurters—percentage of total protein, total water, and water added
Ground beef (store ground and in casings)—percentage of total protein, total water, water added, and fat
Pork chops—percentage of total fat and total bone

With respect to store-ground beef the study found that 7% of the samples from low-income stores were above the USDA standard of 30% fat set for beef centrally ground and packed in casings,[81] compared with only 2% of the high-income store samples. In contrast, 22% of the latter samples were lean (less than 20% fat), compared with 7% of the low-income samples.

Only 13 of 244 frankfurters tested had water content that was above federal standards. These were equally likely to be from low- and high-income area stores. Fat in pork chops was slightly higher in low-income stores but, according to the study, "not enough so to be considered statistically significant".[82]

Obtaining inferior merchandise is also a considerable problem in durable goods purchases. Caplovitz's recent study of defaulting debtors reported that 13% of defaulters listed (1) the delivery of defective merchandise, (2) the delivery of used merchandise instead of new, and (3) the failure to deliver all merchandise ordered as at least partial reasons why they stopped paying on their accounts.[83] A sample complaint was as follows:

> The set was not the same as the one I had ordered from the pictures. It was longer and lower. . . . I told them I wouldn't pay for it and they said they would pick it up but instead they turned it over to a lawyer. . . . *He said it would be a new set, but I'm pretty sure it was a used set. . . . He said it would cost $356, but when I received the book it was $456* . . . . I made a couple of payments, but then I stopped because I didn't want that phonograph and they were supposed to come by and pick it up.[84]

AVAILABLE SERVICES

Chapter 6 showed that outlets in disadvantaged areas are more likely to be small, undercapitalized, and in an advanced state of physical and economic blight. These problems lead to seriously diminished services for the poor. One consequence is a limitation in assortment variety. There are many more small outlets within store categories in poor communities, and most of these are badly understocked because there are so many of them. But limited assortments are also a problem for food chains, as the following data on the variety of goods offered in supermarkets from a USDA study indicate:[85]

	HIGH-INCOME AREA		LOW-INCOME AREA	
VARIETY OFFERED	*Number*	*Percent*	*Number*	*Percent*
Limited	5	7	7	11
Average	32	48	36	55
Extensive	30	45	22	34
Total	67	100	65	100

Related data are provided in Caplovitz's study of Harlem businesses, where interviewers ranked respondents on the amount of stock on hand.[86] In this study 60% of white-owned Harlem stores and 45% of black-owned stores were rated as "well supplied" with stock, whereas the corresponding figure in middle-class Bay Ridge was 75%. The differences for stores selling small- and high-cost items are revealing (figures in parentheses are number of cases):

	PERCENT WELL STOCKED		
	Harlem Blacks	*Harlem Whites*	*Bay Ridge*
Small-cost stores	43 (44)	45 (40)	83 (23)
High-cost stores	48 (21)	74 (38)	77 (13)

In the main, small-cost stores include food stores and miscellaneous and general merchandise stores selling inexpensive items (e.g., five-and-tens). High-cost stores include apparel, jewelry, automotive accessory, and home furnishings stores. In the latter category, Harlem whites offer about as good assortments as Bay Ridge stores, while Harlem whites are more like Harlem blacks in the small-cost category, both about one-half as often rated well stocked as Bay Ridge merchants. This difference probably reflects inner city business dynamics as described in Chapter 5. The whites remaining in black areas are either well-capitalized, successful outlets or small, weak, immovable outlets.

"Well stocked," however, doesn't necessarily mean well stocked with quality items. As Sturdivant and Wilhelm found: "When national brands are carried by a ghetto appliance dealer, he generally stocks only the lower end of the line. . . . Furthermore, off-brand merchandise tends to make up a substantial part of the ghetto dealer's stock."[87]

A second problem for the disadvantaged already noted is that the outlets they patronize are much less attractive places to be in. Almost all studies seem to confirm this. For example, the USDA found the following levels of store quality in low- and high-income areas:[88]

	High-Income Area		Low-Income Area	
	Number	*Percent*	*Number*	*Percent*
Neatness				
Poor	3	4	11	16
Average	25	37	28	42
Well kept	39	58	28	42
Cleanliness				
Fair	7	11	18	27
Average	30	46	34	51
Excellent	28	43	15	22

Of high-income area stores, 43% were rated excellent on cleanliness, compared with only 22% of low-income area stores. This finding would lend support to the complaint of low-income consumers that the meat and produce they buy are inferior in that a less cleanly maintained store is likely to be more frequently selling unsanitary products.

A similar result was found by Bliss et al. for independent food stores in Cleveland. In a ranking of overall "conditions of store," 31% of low-income area stores were rated "poor" or "fair." No store in the high-income area was rated poor, and only 16% were rated fair.[89]

There appears to be one respect, however, in which low-income area stores offer more value than high-income area stores. This is in their extended hours of operation. Data in this regard are offered by Caplovitz's study of Harlem and Bay Ridge merchants.[90] Mean number of hours open in four store categories was greater in all categories in Harlem than in Bay Ridge, with black businesses in Harlem open longer hours than white businesses. Caplovitz's data also show relatively little relationship between business size and hours of operation. If anything, larger businesses are open slightly longer hours (much longer hours for black Harlem businesses) than smaller businesses. In the Bliss study in Cleveland, 30% of low-income area supermarkets were open 13 or more hours a day, compared with only 15% of high-income area supermarkets.[91]

There is a second way in which the disadvantaged may be benefited by the offerings in their area. As noted in Chapters 3 and 5, they are much more likely to look for personal attention in the outlets they patronize. And, indeed, the frequent small stores in the area where they shop, while necessarily charging higher prices, do in fact offer much more personalized sales help and opportunities for social interaction than one could find in the mass merchandise outlets that are more the norm in affluent neighborhoods.

Summary

This chapter has made several central points. First, the evidence suggests that there is now little outright discrimination in prices between disadvantaged and nondisadvantaged areas by food chain outlets on equivalent items and that some chains in fact may be subsidizing their losing inner city stores. This finding is, however, subject to some qualifications. First, it is not clear that the quality of goods offered or the quality of stores themselves are equivalent across areas. Second, it is not clear that prices of the *right* products have been studied and thus not clear that an absence of differences in prices is what one *ought* to expect. And finally, even if these other qualifications were satisfied, it would still be possible that although there is now no discrimination, there may well have been discrimination in the very recent past—as the disadvantaged have asserted—and we have only discovered that chains have recently stopped the politically risky practice.

Even if it is only a possible approximation to the answer to the chain store pricing question, it is true that there is relatively wide agreement that the disadvantaged pay more for food primarily because they shop more often in small, higher-priced neighborhood stores. But even here, it is not completely clear whether they choose this strategy out of necessity or because they prefer to.

Finally, with respect to durable goods the evidence points much more strongly toward chicanery, deceit, and discrimination both in the charging of higher prices, especially where credit is involved, and in the provision of inferior goods. That such chicanery and deceit does not stop with pricing practices is a theme taken up in the next chapter.

Notes

1. Donald E. Sexton, Jr., "Comparing the Costs of Food to Blacks and to Whites: A Survey," *Journal of Marketing*, vol. 35, July 1971, p. 41.
2. U.S. Department of Labor, Bureau of Labor Statistics, "Prices Charged in Stores in Low and High Income Areas of Six Large Cities, February, 1966," in *Special Studies in Food Marketing*, Technical Study no. 10 (Washington: National Commission on Food Marketing, June 1966), pp. 121–44.
3. Donald F. Dixon and Daniel J. McLaughlin, Jr., "Do the Inner City Poor Pay More for Food?" *Economic and Business Bulletin*, vol. 20, Spring 1969, pp. 6–12.
4. Burton H. Marcus, "Similarity of Ghetto and Non-Ghetto Food Costs," *Journal of Marketing Research*, vol. 6, August 1969, pp. 365–8.
5. Task Force on Public Aid of the Church Federation of Greater Chicago, "Summary of Results of Food Pricing Survey," as reported in Sexton, *op. cit.*, p. 42.
6. Philip E. Bliss, Michale D. Durovchik, James W. Feldhouse, Richard L. Janus, and Walter F. Mog, "Do the Poor Pay More for Food in the Independent Stores?" Unpublished paper, Cleveland: Graduate School of Business, Western Reserve University, May 1967.
7. Donald E. Sexton, Jr., "Do Blacks Pay More?" *Journal of Marketing Research*, vol. 8, November 1971, pp. 420–6.
8. Focus: Hope, Inc., *Comparison of Grocery and Drug Prices and Services in the Greater Detroit Area*, in Sexton, "Comparing the Costs of Food to Blacks and to Whites," p. 42.
9. Albert Wertheimer, "Prescription Drug Prices: Art, Science or Whim," paper presented to Section on Economics and Administrative Science, Academy of Pharmaceutical Sciences, American Pharmaceutical Association Annual Meeting, San Francisco, Mar. 31, 1971.
10. Glenn E. Hastings and Richard Kunnes, "Predicting Prescription Prices," *New England Journal of Medicine*, vol. 277, Sept. 21, 1967, pp. 625–8.
11. Jeffrey A. Kotzan and Charles L. Braucher, "A Multivariate Analysis of Retail Prescription Prices," *Journal of Marketing Research*, vol. 7, November 1970, pp. 517–20.
12. John F. Cady and Alan R. Andreasen, "Price Levels, Price Practices and Price Discrimination in the Retail Market for Prescription Drugs," *Journal of Consumer Affairs* (forthcoming).
13. David Caplovitz, *The Poor Pay More* (New York: The Free Press, 1967), p. 85.
14. Federal Trade Commission, *Economic Report on Installment Credit and Retail Sales Practices of District of Columbia Retailers* (Washington: Government Printing Office, 1968).

15. Frederick D. Sturdivant and Walter D. Wilhelm, "Poverty, Minorities and Consumer Exploitation," *Social Science Quarterly*, December 1968, pp. 643–50.
16. William Hanselman, "The Basis for Market Discrimination: Race or Poverty," unpublished paper, Portland State University, Portland, Oregon, 1970.
17. Federal Trade Commission, *op. cit.*, p. 17.
18. *Ibid.*, p. 9.
19. U.S. Department of Agriculture, *Comparison of Prices Paid for Selected Foods in Chainstores in High and Low Income Areas of Six Cities* (Washington: Government Printing Office, 1971).
20. The products purchased were milk, margarine, eggs, baby food, green beans, fruit cocktail, evaporated milk, rice, flour, sugar, bread, regular coffee, frankfurters, ground beef in casings, store-ground beef, pork chops, and whole chickens.
21. U.S. Department of Agriculture, *op. cit.*, p. 4.
22. One city did not participate in the Food Stamp program.
23. U.S. Department of Agriculture, *op. cit.*, pp. 1–2.
24. Dixon and McLaughlin, *op. cit.*
25. Louis H. Grossman, "Comparative Prices of a Market Basket in Phoenix," *Arizona Business Bulletin*, vol. 15, no. 10 (Dec. 1968), pp. 267–77.
26. *Ibid.*
27. Richard Teach, "Supermarket Pricing Practices in Various Areas of a Large City," working paper no. 53, School of Management, State University of New York at Buffalo, undated.
28. Loraine Donaldson and Raymond S. Strangeways, "Food Prices in Low Income Areas: The Case of Beuhler's Supermarkets, Atlanta, Georgia," Urban Life Center, Georgia State University, November 1969.
29. Marcus, *op. cit.*
30. Hastings and Kunnes, *op. cit.*
31. Kotzan and Braucher, *op. cit.*
32. U.S. House of Representatives Government Operations Committee, *Consumer Problems of the Poor: Supermarket Operations in Low-Income Areas and the Federal Response, Hearings* (Washington: Government Printing Office, 1968), p. 30.
33. *Ibid.*
34. *Ibid.*
35. U.S. Department of Agriculture, *op. cit.*
36. *Ibid.*, p. 2.
37. Grossman, *op. cit.*
38. John S. Brinzo, Daniel Craig, Franklin J. Cristiano, James J. Hunt, Calvin C. Meury, and Walter J. Tornstrom, "Do the Poor Pay More for Food," Unpublished paper, Graduate School of Business, Western Reserve University, January 1967.

39. Edward B. Conway, "Comparison of Retail Food Prices in Food Chain Outlets: Poverty Area versus Non-Poverty Area Stores," quoted in Sexton, "Comparing the Costs of Food to Blacks and to Whites," p. 43.
40. Better Business Bureau of Greater St. Louis, Inc., *Comparative Study: Food Prices and Quality Practices of Major Chains in the St. Louis, Missouri Metropolitan Area,* quoted in Sexton, "Comparing the Costs of Food to Blacks and to Whites," p. 43.
41. Carlton E. Wright, "Summer Participation in the Program of the New York City Council on Consumer Affairs," Summer 1967.
42. Federal Trade Commission, *Economic Report on Food Chain Selling Practices in the District of Columbia and San Francisco* (Washington: Government Printing Office, 1969).
43. Sexton, "Do Blacks Pay More?" p. 425.
44. Hastings and Kunnes, *op. cit.*
45. *Ibid.*, p. 627.
46. *Ibid.*
47. Kotzan and Braucher, *op. cit.*
48. Caplovitz, *op. cit.*, p. 17.
49. Sturdivant and Wilhelm, *op. cit.*
50. Hanselman, *op. cit.*
51. "Poverty couples were coached to not act as 'shopping wise' or 'buyer-sophisticated' as the middle-income pairs. The former would allow themselves to be 'led' by the salesman's presentation." *Ibid.*, pp. 18–9.
52. *Ibid.*, p. 31.
53. Additional discussion of the problem of discrimination against the poor is found in National Commission on Consumer Finance, *Consumer Credit in the United States* (Washington: Government Printing Office, 1972), pp. 156–60.
54. It is *possible* that the higher default rates for blacks reported in Table 3-3 apply to middle-class blacks. No data on this point could be discovered.
55. U.S. House of Representatives Government Operations Committee, *op. cit.*
56. *Ibid.*, p. 19.
57. *Ibid.*
58. *Ibid*, p. 24.
59. Dixon and McLaughlin, *op. cit.*
60. U.S. Department of Agriculture, Economic Research Service, *Food Prices before and after Distribution of Welfare Checks . . . Low-Income Areas, Seven Cities, 1969* (Washington: Government Printing Office, September 1970).
61. Washington, Detroit, Boston, Newark, Jackson, Miss., Cleveland, and Oakland.

62. Marcus Alexis, George Haines, Jr., and Leonard Simon, "Consumption Behavior of Prisoners: The Case of the Inner City Shopper," in Alan R. Andreasen (ed.), *Improving Inner-City Marketing* (Chicago: American Marketing Association, 1972), p. 49.
63. Sexton, "Do Blacks Pay More?" p. 420.
64. Charles S. Goodman, "Do the Poor Pay More?" *Journal of Marketing*, vol. 32, January 1968, pp. 18–24.
65. Ronald E. Frank, Paul E. Green, and Harry F. Sieber, Jr., "Household Correlates of Purchase Price for Grocery Products," *Journal of Marketing Research*, vol. 4, February 1967, pp. 54–8.
66. Sexton, "Do Blacks Pay More?"
67. *Ibid.*, p. 426.
68. Caplovitz, *op. cit.*, p. 91.
69. *Ibid.*, p. 92.
70. David Honig, "The Market Research Report," paper presented at the Twelfth Annual Meeting, The Institute of Management Sciences, Detroit, Mich., Oct. 2, 1971.
71. U.S. Department of Agriculture, *Comparison of Prices Paid for Selected Foods in Chainstores in High and Low Income Areas of Six Cities*, p. 4.
72. Dixon and McLaughlin, *op. cit.*, p. 11.
73. Bob R. Holdren, *The Structure of a Retail Market and the Market Behavior of Retail Units* (Englewood Cliffs, N.J.: Prentice–Hall, Inc., 1960).
74. U.S. House of Representatives Government Operations Committee, *op. cit.*
75. U.S. Department of Labor, Bureau of Labor Statistics, *A Study of Prices Charged in Food Stores Located in Low and Higher Income Areas in Six Large Cities* (Washington: Government Printing Office, 1966), pp. 1–28.
76. U.S. House of Representatives Government Operations Committee, *op. cit.*, p. 28.
77. *Ibid.*, p. 29.
78. *Ibid.*
79. It has been alleged that chains "dump" older, inferior produce from suburban stores into poor area stores. Honig, with some imaginative methodology, was unable to detect such behavior in Rochester (Honig, *op. cit.*)
80. U.S. Department of Agriculture, *Comparison of Prices Paid for Selected Foods in Chainstores in High and Low Income Areas of Six Cities.*
81. This standard applies to meat centrally ground and packed in casings and not to meat ground in stores.
82. U.S. Department of Agriculture, *Comparison of Prices Paid for Selected Foods in Chainstores in High and Low Income Areas of Six Cities*, p. 2.
83. David Caplovitz, *Debtors in Default* (New York: Columbia University Bureau of Applied Social Research, 1971), pp. 6–17–8.
84. David Caplovitz, *Consumers in Trouble* (New York: The Free Press, 1974), p. 101.

85. U.S. Department of Agriculture, *Comparison of Prices Paid for Selected Foods in Chainstores in High and Low Income Areas of Six Cities*, p. 18.
86. David Caplovitz, *The Merchants of Harlem* (Beverly Hills, Calif.: Sage Publications, Inc., 1973), p. 61.
87. Sturdivant and Wilhelm, *op. cit.*, p. 645.
88. U.S. Department of Agriculture, *Comparisons of Prices Paid for Selected Foods in Chainstores in High and Low Income Areas of Six Cities.*
89. Bliss et al., *op. cit.*
90. Caplovitz, *The Merchants of Harlem*, p. 50.
91. Bliss et al., *op. cit.*

9. Exploitation: Trapping the Unwary

DISCRIMINATORY PRICING is only one element in the chain of relationships between merchant and customer that can lead disadvantaged consumers to seriously misallocate their disposable incomes. For the exploitative merchant who has few scruples about how he takes advantage of handicapped customers, there exists a wide array of techniques for cadging extra dollars from unwary clients. These techniques are of three broad types with respect to their legal status and their acceptance outside the disadvantaged marketplace:

1. Techniques that are legal and widely practiced in specific states, such as the use of "holder in due course" provisions of many state laws that absolve finance companies and banks from responsibility for deceit involved in contracts they buy and that have especially serious consequences for disadvantaged consumers
2. Techniques that are presently legal in some or all states but are generally regarded as unethical by most honest businessmen, such as the securing of an installment purchase with goods still being paid for under earlier contracts (cross collateral) or charging different prices for the same item in different outlets of the same supermarket chain
3. Techniques that are clearly illegal such as the use of bait advertising or outright misrepresentation.

Since the kinds of remedies one might provide in each of these cases is clearly different these distinctions will be retained throughout the sections to follow.

A second useful distinction is between exploitative practices that pertain solely to credit transactions and those that do not. This distinction is useful for two reasons. First, the law applying to the two sets of practices differs in many states. Second, the distinction helps to emphasize the overwhelmingly important role consumer credit plays in the psychological and economic injury of disadvantaged consumers.

Finally, it is useful to distinguish among the kinds of consequences exploitation has for the disadvantaged consumer. First, there are techniques that divert consumers from purchasing items they would have purchased had they not been subject to the exploitative practice. Second, there are techniques that cause the disadvantaged consumer to pay more for a given item than he would have in the absence of the exploitative practice. Finally, there are practices that seriously increase the total cost to disadvantaged consumers of defaulting on a consumer credit transaction. A summary of these distinctions with examples is presented in Figure 9-1.

This chapter first presents an overview of several of the principal techniques summarized in Figure 9-1 (with the exception of price and interest rate discrimination, which were discussed in the previous chapter). This largely descriptive section will be concluded with a discussion of the specific impact of exploitation on the disadvantaged. Here, our principal thesis will be that many techniques, both legal and illegal, that can exploit all consumers have particularly serious impact on the disadvantaged and thus, where legal, deserve serious reconsideration as to their continued legal support and, where illegal, deserve much more vigorous detection and punishment.

Techniques for Diverting Purchases and Increasing Their Costs

The range of techniques used by exploitative merchants to entice poor, and minority consumers to purchase products that they often cannot afford and to pay more than they need to for those they do buy are seemingly endless. For example, the Better Business Bureau has cataloged (and continues to catalog) over 800 types of sales fraud and deception.[1] Senator Warren Magnuson and Jean Carper have noted, however, that these tactics can be separated into five basic categories: the "special low price," the bait and switch, chain referrals, the "free" gimmick, and the fear-sell.[2]

THE "SPECIAL LOW PRICE"

This tactic seeks to convince the buyer that what is being offered is a bargain unavailable to most (if not all) others. A good example of this approach is that reported by Magnuson and Carper[3] as being used by a Mr. G. in Arkansas. Mr. G. poses as a representative of a major aluminum company and tells his victims that the victim's house has been selected to demonstrate the "before and after" results of new aluminum siding. Because of this special honor, the victim will get his siding at bargain factory rates. These bargain rates, of course, turn out to be higher than those of other siding companies in the area.

FIGURE 9–1. An Overview of Consumer Exploitation

Effect	Transaction	Legal[a] and Accepted	Legal[a] but Unethical	Illegal
Divert purchases	All purchases	Puffery	"Special low prices" "Free" gimmicks Fear-sells	Bait and switch Chain referrals Other deception and fraud
Increase purchase costs	Credit only All purchases	High interest charges Monopoly pricing	Excessive fees Within-chain price discrimination	Illegal interest charges Hidden charges
Increase default	Credit only	Default judgment	Balloon payments	Collusive repossession

[a]Legal in at least some states.

THE BAIT AND SWITCH

The general approach here is to lure customers into a store with an advertisement, e.g., window display, for an exceedingly good bargain (the bait) and then convince the customer he should take another, usually higher-priced item often of an inferior brand (the switch). This is not merely an effort to upgrade a sale, a practice engaged in by most salesmen. The merchant has *no intention* of ever selling the bait item. Many ploys are used to ensure this: the item turns out to be "sold out," the only sample left has a dent or a crack or is dirty, it operates poorly (the downgrading of merchandise is known in the trade as "burning"), or it is, as a salesman might put it, "just not right for someone of your good taste." Magnuson and Carper quote one store manager referring to a bait television set as saying, "Any [salesman] who lets that set go out the door goes with it." [4] A good example of the technique is found in *The Poor Pay More* in the testimony of a 28-year-old black housewife:[5]

> I saw an advertisement in the paper *for a $49 Hi-Fi set*. The ad said: "Phone for free demonstration," so I did. The salesman came a few days later, bringing a set that was different from the one I saw advertised. I told him it wasn't the set I saw in the paper, but he said it was, so we hassled for a while. He kept high-pressuring me, saying he had one in the car he knew I would like. So finally, I told him to bring it up. He did, and played it for me.
>
> *I asked him to leave it so my husband could hear it, but he said "no." Then I asked him to come back later when my husband would be home and he said "no" again. Well, I decided to gamble and signed the papers.* [Later they mailed a coupon book. The set came to $175.]
>
> He asked me for a down-payment, so I gave him my old radio and got $10 off. *And right after that, my husband came in. He didn't want the set, but the salesman told him we couldn't return it.* Later my husband examined the set. The salesman had said it contained four woofers and two tweeters, but my husband found out they didn't exist. We called the store, but they said we couldn't change it, so we had to pay the full amount.
>
> Once the set stopped working. We phoned the store and got free repairs. *But the second time the set broke down, we called the store and were told that the company no longer dealt in Hi-Fi sets, only in sewing machines.*

Advertisements which have been the basis of formal bait-and-switch complaints initiated by the Federal Trade Commission in a pilot poverty area program include the following:[6]

Broadloom Carpet—3 rooms wall to wall—carpet and padding and installation—no extra charges—$109

Sewing machines—recond., guar., $14.95 up

Sewing machine—SINGER slant needle, like new, repossessed, bal. $58, $5 mo.

Frigidaire 1 H.P.
6000 BTU . . . $144

RCA Victor 19 in. Portable TV tuner carrying handle, telescoping antenna built in. . . . $112

Western BEEF Round-up. A carload of top quality beef. Guaranteed tender, delicious beef halves, includes all top cuts of steaks and roasts 29 lb. Example: 300 lbs only $6.69 a week for 13 weeks

VACUUMS—Recond. Electrolux GE Hoovers, $9.95 guar., will del.

The FTC notes that offers of free home demonstrations in many of these cases were simply a way of getting salesmen into the homes. In many cases door-to-door salesmen received no commissions on the advertised bait items sold.

THE CHAIN REFERRAL

This technique, also practiced by Mr. G. in Arkansas, is very simple. Victims are told that if they buy the item and refer friends to the company as prospective customers, they will receive commissions for all sales that result, commissions that (so goes the "pitch") will quickly pay the cost of the merchandise. While salesmen often claim that there will be very high commission earnings, a Post Office study found that in one case only 5% of the customers referred ever bought.[7] A more recent variation on these schemes is the so-called pyramid club, which seems more concerned with enticing people to secure distributorships than in selling final products.[8]

THE "FREE" GIMMICK

This technique also closely resembles a traditional marketing technique. It says that "if you buy our product we will throw in, absolutely free, this. . . ." The most common sources of fraud in this area are the food freezer sales organizations. Under many deceptive food freezer plans consumers are offered a "free" freezer if they agree to buy so much frozen food per month from the vendor. The result often is that they obtain poor food that is sometimes inedible and is always overpriced enough to easily cover the cost of the freezer. The deception is that the "free" gimmick is not free, but has its cost built into the price of the tie-in item.

In another free gimmick approach the advertiser states that he is "going to send you absolutely free this wonderful product"; all you have to pay for is the cabinet, stand, shipping costs, service contract, etc., which, of course, cover the cost of the basic product. Two categories in which this approach is often used are sewing machines and door-to-door magazine subscription sales. In the latter case, the victim–customer is merely asked to pay the postage and handling which, of course, often exceed $100 and equal or exceed the value of the magazines if ordered directly from the publisher. The prospective customer is advised that this "free service" is possible because publishers are seeking to boost their circulation "since they make their real profits from advertising." The free gimmick magazine sale has largely replaced an older approach in this business, where the salesman represented himself as working his way through college.

THE FEAR-SELL

Again, the premise is simple: convince the victim–customer as graphically as possible that unless the product or service is acquired, dire consequences will befall him, his family, and/or his property. Often the danger is nonexistent, as with tree surgeons cutting down slightly rotted but basically stable and healthy trees or chimney repairmen fixing "clogged" chimneys. Often the danger is in fact created by the salesman himself and his cohorts.

Historically, the best known fear-sell was that practiced by the Holland Furnace Co. for over 30 years. Beginning in the 1930s, Holland Furnace would send one of its 5,000 employees in 500 offices to households posing as "safety inspectors," who, in one approach, would tear down furnaces and refuse to rebuild them, claiming they were too dangerous to be allowed to operate again. The "inspector" would then tell the victim–customer about a friend who could correct the problem or provide a new furnace (often bringing in parts from the last house "inspected"). The Holland Furnace Co. used variations of this technique until finally closed down in 1965 by the Federal Trade Commission.[9]

OTHER TECHNIQUES

Among the assorted other approaches noted by Magnuson and Carper are:

1. Collections for phony charities.
2. Earning schemes. "Earn money in your spare time by buying this item [vending machine, etc.]."
3. Delivery of unsolicited merchandise followed by dunning letters.
4. Phony home improvement schemes, e.g., silver-painted rope "lightning rod" cables, motor oil–covered "asphalt" driveways, paint that lasts until the next rainstorm.[10]
5. Nonaccredited correspondence and vocational schools.
6. Land development frauds.

The Better Business Bureau catalogs in its monthly newsletter the seemingly endless variations and combinations of these techniques which are still being perpetrated.

IMPACT ON THE DISADVANTAGED

While a later section will discuss the general susceptibility of the disadvantaged to exploitation, it is important to note that several of the above techniques have special appeal to those who are poor and/or black. For example, it was noted earlier that the disadvantaged are particularly interested in minimizing prices. Thus they are much more likely to be susceptible to techniques such as the "special low price," the "free" gimmick, and the bait and switch, which play upon this strong need. Salesmen in disadvantaged areas are particularly effective in using switching tactics that subtly touch upon the disadvantaged consumers' embarrassment with their poverty. ("You wouldn't want to have *this* inexpensive model in *your* house, would you?")

Also playing upon the disadvantaged consumers' concern with their poverty are deceptions involving products and services that promise to give them or their children some chance of escaping that poverty. These would include schemes involving subscriptions to magazines or encyclopedias as well as schemes that promise disadvantaged people lucrative earnings in their "spare time" or correspondence or vocational courses that "guarantee exciting new and financially rewarding careers." It is a particular irony of this aspect of disadvantaged consumers' problems that just those acquisitions or enrollments that are expected to relieve them of a major part of their disadvantaged status serve only to drive them further "into the hole." They become overburdened financially with payments they cannot meet, and as a consequence can end up in court, without a job, without their acquisitions yet still with a debt, the subjects of harassment, and the holders of bad credit records against future purchases.

This does not always mean that the goods or services themselves were defective (although this is often the case, as will be documented below). For example, encyclopedias are very often excellently written, comprehensive, and accurate and truly can be of great value to children and adults for homework, leisure reading, and the like. But the critical point is that an encyclopedia "can be" of great value. What value is it likely to be to an eighth-grade disadvantaged child reading at the third-grade level, who has no incentive to do homework and no place to do it in because he or she lives in an overcrowded, run-down apartment? Such a child often also has no *time* to do homework because he or she either must work part or full time to supplement the family income or must baby-sit or do household chores so that both parents (or the female head of the household) can work. The parents, when they are around, can provide little incentive or help in using the encyclopedia because they themselves may have only a sixth- or eighth-grade education. And many of them may well have serious difficulties with the English language.

This, of course, raises the question of business morality. Many of the techniques used to sell encyclopedias, including the free gimmick and the special low price, are clearly illegal. But simply selling an encyclopedia enthusiastically to a family that very likely cannot use it and perhaps cannot afford to pay for it but that can be induced to contract for it because of the *hope* it represents is perfectly legal. On the other hand, in the judgment of critics of the business community as well as most reputable businessmen, it is behavior that is highly immoral. And indeed most reputable encyclopedia manufacturers claim that it is their policy not to encourage such sales. Still, the policy seems not well policed. The salesmen who are attracted to this area seem to have few scruples,[11] and the commission payment system in the industry puts the burden on them to get as many sales as they can, no matter to whom the encyclopedias are sold. Their behavior is impossible to legislate against. Thus ways must be found to bring more pressure to bear on unethical businesses from inside the business establishment and to allow consumers more easily to escape contracts entered into under high-pressure circumstances.

Credit, Contracts, and the Disadvantaged Consumer

The need for credit severely constrains the shopping scope and thus the merchandise alternatives of the disadvantaged and in many cases substantially increases the prices they must pay, both through higher-than-average cash prices and through higher interest rates. But the tremendous growth of credit noted in Chapter 3 also affords both the ethical *and* the unscrupulous merchant many more opportunities for increasing profits through exploiting the disadvantaged. As economist Helen Nelson, recent president of the Consumers Federation of America once stated, "More money is being taken from Americans at penpoint than by gunpoint, and the pen often makes it legal." [12] The principal reason for this is that credit sales involve *consumer contracts* and contractual obligations are protected even in many iniquitous situations by courts of law. Thus, to understand this aspect of consumer credit a brief digression into the nature of consumer contract law is necessary.

CONSUMER CONTRACT LAW

Much of consumer contract law has its roots in the law of commercial contracts. Many of the assumptions of commercial law, such as a person's freedom to make a contract and (barring unconscionability) the requirement that a person be held to what he or she has signed, apply equally to contracts between businesses and consumers. However, many key assumptions *do not*. Among such assumptions are that:

The parties have relatively equal powers to bargain about the terms of the contract prior to signing.

Both parties have full knowledge of the contents of the document prior to signing.

The contract contains *all* that is material to the agreement between the parties. For example, verbal promises by the seller or his salesman not written into the contract have no standing. (Courts vary in their strictness as to each of the above assumptions.)

A consumer engaged in contract transactions is presumed to have three essential characteristics:[13]

1. He knows that he should, and wants to, shop around for best buys when purchasing goods and services.
2. He is competent to decide which product offers the greatest value for the least money.
3. He knows his legal rights (and liabilities) in the event of a postsale legal conflict with the seller and is prepared to use all available remedies in such a conflict.

Competence to ascertain best values is something that eludes all of us as consumers. But as the material in Part I suggested and as will be documented further below, none of these "essential characteristics" are characteristics of disadvantaged consumers.

As a consequence of these and other difficulties discussed below, the basic assumption of contract law that the two parties are equals in making the contract is far from the truth. This inequality leads to a great many abuses:

1. The disadvantaged consumer is likely to place very heavy reliance on representations made by the salesman. This is likely for several reasons:

The consumer is, of course, less knowledgeable about products, contracts, and his rights, and because of his frequent lack of education he may be reluctant to admit he cannot understand the contract before him.

If he is Spanish–American (or a recently immigrated foreigner), he may have difficulty with the language and so will have to rely on translations by salesmen who speak his language.

If he is old, his eyesight may make it difficult to read the contract, and he will want the salesman's help.

He may want to ingratiate himself with the salesperson because, for many, making such social contacts is a major goal of the shopping experience.

Finally, he may rely on the salesman because he feels such an attitude will help ensure that he gets the credit he so desperately needs to be able to acquire the merchandise.

2. The disadvantaged consumer may place heavy reliance on the fact that he is offered a preprinted *form contract.* Instead of there being a contract fully negotiated and drawn up by equals, the seller creates the contract in his own interest and presents it to the consumer as his only option. Since the contract appears to be in routine usage, the less knowledgeable consumer may feel that it is the form he will encounter anywhere or perhaps that it is "the law." Thus he may feel he can do no better by shopping around. Further, he may be comforted to think that an accepted contract form is not likely to contain many really onerous clauses since such clauses would have been struck down in court over time. Finally, the credit-starved consumer may readily believe the merchant's assertion that he must accept the contract and its terms if he wants any credit at all. The corollary of this belief is, of course, that the more the consumer believes he is beholden to a given "generous" merchant, the more he can be made to accept exploitative provisions.

Among the legal but often onerous terms and clauses that, depending on the state, the merchant may be able to introduce into consumer contracts are the following:

Accelerated payment. In the event of a default (i.e., one or more missed payments) or some other action by the buyer prohibited by the contract, all remaining payments become due immediately. Under this clause, a consumer wishing to reinstate a contract by repaying missed installments (plus a penalty) cannot do so. This permits an unscrupulous merchant, after the consumer has paid most of the contract (and in many cases already produced a substantial profit for the merchant), to force the consumer in the event of some temporary lapse in payments into default and into giving up the product for resale to meet the debt. (The resale procedure itself can be a major source of further profits to the seller, as described below.)

Balloon payments. This technique makes the last payment in the payment stream very large. This approach is desirable for business firms that wish to retain cash until the last possible moment, and possibly it is also desirable for some consumers with seasonal or sporadic jobs. For most, however, it can have the effect in consumer transactions of forcing unwary disadvantaged consumers into defaulting after payment of most of their contracts. It is also a technique that permits sellers to appear to reduce the average size of payment (i.e., all but the balloon payment), and, as discussed earlier, the payment size, not the cash price or interest rate, is often of first importance to the disadvantaged consumer.

A security interest in some item unrelated to the purchase or to the relationship with the seller or in any and all property of the debtor including future property. This, of course, can give the seller claim to major possessions of the unsuspecting buyer in the event of a default on some minor item.

Cross-collateral security (often used in conjunction with "add-on" purchases). This clause is used when the buyer purchases several items either at the same time or on different occasions from the same seller. It requires that payments be credited on a *pro rata* basis to all outstanding debts, having the effect that the buyer does not obtain title to *any* of the goods until they are *all* paid for. As Caplovitz has noted, a consumer practice among ghetto merchants is to watch customer payments until they are about complete and then sell him another item on credit.[14] This practice not only keeps the customer in the merchant's clutches but also permits the use of the cross-collateral security technique, which in the event of default allows the merchant to repossess all the merchandise the customer ever bought from him even if, for example, the customer had paid an amount that would have paid off all the merchandise except some small portion of the last item if separate contracts had been used.

Confession of judgment. This clause, which is now outlawed in most states, in effect waives the buyer's right to trial. The buyer agrees in advance that in the event or anticipation of a default on the debt he authorizes "an attorney of any court of record" to accept the seller's claim that the judgment is valid. This saves the seller much time and court costs. It precludes the buyer from facing the creditor in court or from raising arguments about the seller's alleged unethical behavior. No notice of the impending judgment is sent the buyer, and he only learns about it after, say, his wages are garnisheed or some of his household goods are repossessed. The creditor needn't use a collection agency because the court collects the debt without charge (except for attorney's fees). It was estimated that as much as $22 million was collected from 34,000 people in Cook County in Illinois in 1966 by means of confession of judgment.[15]

Disclaimer of salesmen's oral representations. This clause, of course, discourages customers from claiming in court that they were deceived by salesmen.

There are, of course, a host of other techniques that unscrupulous sellers employ to turn consumer contracts to their advantage, including (1) the use of blank forms disguised as "shipping orders" or "approvals for credit check" that are subsequently filled in to the seller's advantage; (2) the use of legal language and small print to disguise the true nature of the merchandise, interest costs, and extra charges; and (3) the use of the fact of the contract as the basis of extra charges such as "contract preparation." A final major advantage of the contract, for those who avail themselves of it, is that it permits the seller to place a major obstruction in the way of buyers he deceives who wish to get their money back. This obstruction involves the sale of the credit contract to a finance company or bank.

ENTER THE FINANCE COMPANY

A common practice for businesses that are hard pressed for capital or that do not wish to be in the finance or collection business is to sell their credit contracts to a financial institution—typically a bank or finance company—soon after acquiring them. The financial firm buys the contract for an amount usually equal to some portion of the unpaid cash balance of the contract (although as noted below a kickback or "holdback" may also be involved). This practice, known variously as "assigning," "discounting," or "factoring one's paper," is another legally protected device borrowed from industrial credit transactions. In the industrial setting, discounting increases the flow of capital and makes business in general more efficient because, theoretically, it allows debt obligations to be held by those agencies which can do so at the least cost.

There are few drawbacks to this procedure in industrial settings, since both parties to the discounting transaction as well as the original buyer–debtor are quite familiar with the technique including the potential problems involved. These problems typically stem from the so-called holder-in-due-course doctrine, which specifies that if the contract was assigned, in the event of default those who have purchased a credit contract in an "arm's length" transaction (i.e. where the parties are independent) are free from a buyer's claims against the seller. Although acceptable in commercial credit transactions, holder-in-due-course provisions in consumer credit transactions can have pernicious effects, particularly for disadvantaged consumers. To understand why this is so, it will be useful to describe a typical transaction taking undue advantage of the holder protection.

Suppose an unsuspecting disadvantaged buyer buys a refrigerator from Exploitative Enterprises, Inc., and signs a 24-month contract with EEI to pay the inflated cash price, extras, and the highest possible (but legal) interest charges. Since most states now require notification if a contract is to be discounted to a financial institution, EEI is careful to have the buyer sign (among other papers) a slip indicating he was aware that the contract would be sold to the Unscrupulous Finance Co. If the buyer raises any questions, the unethical seller might tell him simply that UFC "handles the paper work."

Once the paper is discounted—assuming it is an arm's length transaction[16]—the buyer will be required to pay the *holder* of his contract who acquired it *in* the *due course* of a regular business transaction his regular monthly or weekly payments no matter what may go wrong with the transaction between the buyer and the original seller. Thus if, for example, the refrigerator was found to be used instead of new or if it broke down and the seller refused to fix it under guarantee, the buyer cannot stop payment to force the seller to make good on the original obligation. He might very well be able to do this if the seller still held the contract, since the seller would be reluctant to go to court on a default and risk having his deception brought to light. However, under holder protection, the finance company can claim that it is not responsible for the seller's transgressions and that its only relationship with the buyer is a financial one. In states where holder is permitted, the law will usually back him absolutely on this issue. The buyer must keep paying. If he does not keep paying—perhaps feeling he has a right to until the matter is straightened out—the finance company will bring default proceedings, which could lead to loss of possession, court action, and attendant difficulties.

The principal legal method of recovery open to the buyer in such a case is to bring a legal action against the seller to make him perform on the contract or to repay losses to the buyer. His discovery of this double bind—i.e., that he must (1) keep paying for a product about which he was deceived and (2) lay out legal costs plus time and inconvenience to recover these losses—comes as a shock to many an unsophisticated buyer (especially those whose notice of the original discounting transaction was somehow "lost in transit"). As Caplovitz has shown, many simply do not understand what is happening to them.[17] In such instances, it is not difficult to understand why a buyer would feel that "the system" is somehow against him when it makes him pay *and* go to court over a product about which he was cheated and which, in some cases, no longer works.

For the more knowledgeable students of this issue it is also difficult to understand how a system could be permitted to continue that absolves the finance company of any responsibility for the honesty of the seller or the original transaction at all (although the finance company may consider these factors to some extent in determining whether to give the retailer a kickback or to require him to put up a "holdback" reserve to cover expected losses). The most reprehensible cases are those financial institutions that buy the contracts of the fly-by-night sellers who have little intention of staying behind in the community to make good on their sales of shoddy aluminum siding, driveway repaving, swimming pool installations, and the like. Discovery of such intentions would not be difficult for most established financial institutions.

It should be noted that not all retailers discount their credit obligations and many of those who retain their contracts seldom sue customers. Many retain these obligations because they feel that doing so will increase their revenues. This is likely to be the case for two reasons, both premised upon the merchant's keeping close contact with customers by having them come in each month with (or mail) their payments. First, such an approach permits the merchant to adjust the credit terms to meet family circumstances. When illness or unemployment strikes, payments can be reduced or temporarily forgiven. The expectation would be that such flexibility and intimate knowledge of the customer's financial circumstances will ensure that everything will be paid eventually and perhaps something new purchased. Further, the merchant's goodwill should be enhanced, possibly drawing in other customers through favorable word-of-mouth advertising. Second, as noted earlier, this close contact with the buyer will undoubtedly allow the merchant to suggest new credit purchases as the account is about to be closed out, knowledge of which he would not have had if he had discounted the contract.

Not all retailers tie the sale of credit and the sale of merchandise together. Sometimes the retailer, instead of making an installment contract for the purchase, will arrange for the consumer to obtain a personal loan to pay for the purchase (or sometimes just for the down payment, letting the rest of purchase price be financed by regular installment contracts). This procedure, of course, immediately gives the finance company "holder-like" protection, since the two transactions are separate. It also frees the financial transaction from restrictions, such as lower interest rate ceilings in some states, that are more binding for installment sales contracts. Greater use of this approach, as noted below, might well be expected as holder protection is reduced or eliminated.

CONTRACTING PRACTICES OF LOW-INCOME MERCHANTS

To secure a broad picture of the pattern of credit-granting practices of low-income merchants, reference may again be made to the FTC study of Washington, D.C., retailers.[18] In this study data were collected on 18 low-income market retailers—14 furniture dealers, two appliance dealers, and two sellers of miscellaneous items—and compared with general market department stores, furniture dealers, and appliance dealers in the District of Columbia. The 18 low-income dealers were estimated to account for between 35% and 44% of sales of furniture and appliances to low-income customers in the District of Columbia area.

Several important characteristics of low-income merchants' credit practices are immediately obvious from the results reported in Table 9-1. First, almost *all* sales of low-income merchants (92.7%) involved installment contracts, compared with only about one-third of all dollar sales of general market furniture and appliance dealers. (Only one in five department store sales is on an installment contract, which reflects these stores' different product mix and their heavy use of revolving charge accounts.) These figures

TABLE 9-1. Installment Contract Practices of Low-Income and General Market Retailers, Washington, D.C., 1966

	All Contracts		Assigned Contracts			Unassigned Contracts		
	Sales, %	Avg. Value, $	Contracts, %	Avg. Value, $	Interest Rate, %[a]	Contracts, %	Avg. Value, $	Interest Rate, %[a]
Low-income market retailers	92.7	140	19.8	298	25	80.2	124	23[b]
General market retailers	26.5	147	37.9	261	21[c]	62.1	116	19[c]
Appliance, radio, and television	33.7	210	98.3	212	24	1.7	141	18
Furniture and home furnishings	39.8	359	57.1	383	18	42.9	332	16
Department stores	20.6	100	None			100.0	100	20

[a]Effective annual rate.
[b]One low-income market retailer has been omitted, because it made no separate charges for installment financing.
[c]Weighted average.
Source: Federal Trade Commission, *Economic Report on Installment Credit and Retail Sales Practices of District of Columbia Retailers* (Washington: Government Printing Office, 1968).

again stress (1) the critical role of installment credit in allowing the disadvantaged to acquire the discretionary items they need and want and (2) the critical role of installment credit in the profitability of low-income marketers.

The second feature one notes in the data is that the average value of installment contracts of low-income area retailers is much less than that of general market appliance and furniture stores. (It will be remembered that all but two low-income retailers were appliance or furniture stores.) This finding agrees with earlier data reporting the lower dollar value of indebtedness of poor and black consumers, compared with white middle-class customers.

A third finding in Table 9-1 is perhaps more surprising: low-income marketers are *less* likely to assign their contracts to finance companies or banks than are general market retailers. Only one in five such contracts is assigned, compared with almost all (98.3%) of general market appliance contracts and three in five (57.1%) of furniture contracts. No department store contracts were assigned in 1966. Finance companies were assigned almost all the appliance store contracts in the District of Columbia area but only one-third of the contracts from furniture dealers, the remainder going to banks. Low-income market retailers were slightly less likely to concentrate their assignments on a few finance companies than were general market retailers.

In both the low-income and general markets, it is the larger contracts that are assigned. This undoubtedly is due to the fact that larger contracts (1) tie up more of the firm's capital and (2) represent a greater risk. The risk element is undoubtedly much more of a factor for low-income market retailers, since the value of their assigned contracts is 2.4 times as great as that of their unassigned contracts, compared with only 1.25 times as great for general market furniture and appliance dealers.

As earlier analyses have led us to expect, low-income merchants tend to charge higher rates of interest as reported in Table 9-1. As other FTC data indicate, almost one-half (47.9%) of all low-income contracts carried effective annual interest rates of 26% or more. Less than ½% of general market retailers' contracts carried interest rates this high. Only 4% of low-income contracts were under 18%, compared with 28.5% of general market contracts.[19]

The interest rate data offer a second set of reasons why low-income market retailers assign only one in five of their installment contracts to financial agencies. First, there is the fact that much more risk is involved in such contracts and low-income marketers may have difficulty in assigning them unless the financial institution feels the interest rates are high enough to cover the risk. If the interest rates are not high enough, substantial holdback funds may be required. As the FTC study found, "Low-income market retailers were unable to assign a significant volume of installment contracts at less than 26 percent (effective annual rate) without some form of holdback arrangement."[20] As noted earlier, the holdback arrangement requires the retailer to set up a reserve which the finance company holds against possible losses. This extra cost, of course, would significantly discourage low-income retailers from assigning as many *lower*-interest contracts as would a general market retailer. At the other end of the interest rate scale, they may also not wish to give up the contracts from the nearly 50% of their customers from whom they can get a substantial 26% rate of interest or higher. Thus, for example, the FTC study showed that the 18 low-income retailers did not assign *any* of the $360,000 worth of contracts (7.1% of their total) from which they were able to get the highest rates of interest (33%). They also retained virtually all (98.4%) of their contracts earning 18% or less interest (35% of all contracts).

In addition to these economic reasons it is also possible that low-income marketers keep more of their "paper" because their customers need flexible credit and because they want to know when their customers are about to pay off their contracts so that they, the merchants, can keep the customers continually in their debt.

Finally, it is essential to point out the important role finance charges play in generating revenues for low-income marketers. They sell almost all their merchandise (92.7%) on installments, keep 80% of these contracts themselves, and obtain an average 23% interest per annum on the unpaid balance. Although the FTC study provides no direct data, if we assume that for both low-income and general market retailers most installment contracts were in equal payments for a 24-month period and net sales were not greatly different in 1965 than they were in 1966, then revenues from finance charges would have constituted somewhere in the order of 15% of total revenues for low-income marketers, compared with less than 1% for general market furniture and appliance outlets.

It is likely that the costs of generating these revenues, including the very high bad debt losses noted in Table 7-2, are less than the revenues themselves. This may well explain why low-income merchants are not overly reluctant to promote credit sales in poor areas or to keep their installment paper themselves.

JUDGMENTS, GARNISHMENTS, AND REPOSSESSIONS

Perhaps the most striking finding of the FTC study was the excessively frequent rate at which low-income retailers go to court in their own name to collect on their unassigned installment contracts and 30-day and revolving credit accounts. In 1966, the 18 low-income retailers in the study *filed 3,030 suits in their own names, or one suit for every $2,599 in net sales.*[21] This compared to only 260 suits for the 44 general market furniture and appliance dealers in the study, the equivalent of one suit for every $199,000 in net sales. Such figures, of course, do not include additional suits brought by finance companies or collection agencies on contracts *originating* from low-income or general market retailers which were not included in the FTC study. Needless to say, the FTC report had little difficulty concluding: "Clearly, a number of low-income market retailers have come to view the courts as an integral part of their credit-collection system and in so doing have put a heavy burden on our legal system." [22]

What involvement in this legal system and the processes that accompany it means for disadvantaged consumers is a topic to which we shall now turn our attention.

Consequences of Missed Payments

Table 3-3 demonstrated that disadvantaged consumers (particularly blacks) are more likely than those who are not disadvantaged to default on consumer contracts. When this happens but before court action is taken on the default, the disadvantaged consumer usually will be subject to pressure to pay his obligation. This pressure may range from simple computerized reminders of the overdue amount to vicious harassment, by mail, by phone, or in person. An example of such harassment is a collection letter allegedly emanating from a large Philadelphia bank described by Magnuson and Carper. The couple who received this letter owed $40 on a $225 debt. The note was crudely written on the back of a bank envelope and said:

> WE GUESS YOU WANT THE PIG TREATMENT
> AND WE KNOW HOW TO TREAT PIGS!
> WE WILL TELL EVERYBODY THAT YOU
> ARE NOT WORTHY OF TRUST!! [23]

Heavy harassment such as this, Caplovitz has found, is most likely to come from collection agencies and small loan companies, followed by door-to-door sellers and finance companies.[24] Least likely to harass defaulting debtors are general market retailers and credit unions. Harassment is most likely to be directed at the disadvantaged. As noted in Table 9-2, Caplovitz found that the poor were more likely to be harassed than the nonpoor and blacks more than whites, with income controlled. Interestingly, while there is a strong income effect for whites, there is little such effect for blacks. This suggests that while creditors make distinctions among whites according to income, they tend to treat all blacks alike. Such treatment again points to the overwhelming burden of racial discrimination that most blacks in America must bear not only in schooling, housing, and employment but also in the marketplace.

What, then, becomes of the consumers who do default on consumer contracts and end up in court? Is this an opportunity for further exploitation? The answer, not surprisingly, is yes. Exploitation in this regard is

TABLE 9-2. Percent of Defaulting Debtors Harassed, by Income and Race

Income	Whites, %	Blacks, %
Under $4000	65	62
$4000 to $7,999	53	62
$8000 and over	47	57

Source: David Caplovitz, *Debtors in Default* (New York: Columbia University Bureau of Applied Social Research, 1971), p. 10–20.

manifested in three aspects of the default process: (1) service of process, (2) repossession and sale of merchandise, and (3) deficiency judgments. The principal source of difficulty with respect to service of process is the time-honored practice known popularly as "sewer service."

"SEWER SERVICE" [25]

A problem faced by many low-income consumers in default is that they are not notified that a court action is imminent. This, of course, would always be the case where confession of judgment was possible. However, in cases where confession is not possible, then the lawyer for the creditor must arrange for service of a summons personally on the accused debtor before the case may proceed. Since collection lawyers typically handle a great many such cases, service of summons is usually subcontracted to a process-serving agency or to sheriffs, who typically receive a flat fee for each subpoena served and *nothing* for those not served. Poorly paid, frequently harassed process servers must then serve the summons on the debtor and return a sworn affidavit stating that the process was personally served and where and when. When no attempt to serve is ever made, this is known as "sewer service." This tactic, according to the assistant attorney general of New York, is:

> . . . the fraudulent service of a summons or summons and complaint usually either by destroying it [throwing it down a sewer], by leaving it under a door or mailbox, or by leaving it with a person known not to be the defendant; and then executing an affidavit stating that summons was personally delivered to and left with the defendant.[26]

If the defendant does not appear in court for whatever reason, it is difficult to prove that he was *not* served a summons.

Notices of intended garnishments in most states must also be served on the now-guilty borrower a specified number of days before notifying employers. In New York State this service is carried out by a city marshal acting as an agent of the court. There is here also the potential for sewer service. Again, if no process is served, the debtor is severely deprived of due process—of his day in court to confront an exploitative retailer, if that be the case. Needless to say, sewer service is very much in the short-run interest of the exploiting low-income merchants.

Evidence of the relatively widespread use of sewer service is methodologically weak—as often is the case in this entire subject area—but *cumulatively* quite impressive. Of 18 sworn services in New York City, an investigator from the New York State attorney general's office found nonexistent addresses in some cases, that one house had been closed for eight years, seven cases where the defendant had moved several months earlier from the address where the service was allegedly made, that one defendant had died the day before "service," and, that one address was a school where the defendant had never worked![27]

Of 612 default judgments studied in a second study by the New York attorney general's office, 201 defendants could not be located by the Post Office Department at the address where service was said to have been made, although some of these could have moved since the service date six weeks earlier. (Many may have "skipped." As noted earlier, many of those who are involved in credit defaults are often unstable in employment and/or residence.) Of 411 who presumably received the mail questionnaire, 140 responded. Of these, 128 said they had not been served. Even assuming *all* the nonrespondents had been served properly and, say, *half* of the nonlocatable addresses had moved "naturally," the resulting sewer service rate is better than *one in three*.[28] A further study of 96 default judgments by the same office about two weeks after service found 31 not at the address where service was said to have been made and 20 respondents denying service, a "sewer rate" of at least 50%.[29] Evidence collected by the Congress of Racial Equality (CORE) on times and places of service found "numerous examples of service sworn to have been effected [by the same server] at different places at the same time."[30] Other cases were found of service of summons indicated before the time a court clerk stamped it as valid for service.

Similar complaints are made of sewer service by city marshals.[31] In a small study on housing cases, Mobilization for Youth found that "only 5 of the 22 persons who had experienced income executions [garnishments] said that they had been given advance notice."[32] Such findings for both marshals and process servers are backed up by public statements by lawyers, workers with youth, and the state attorney general.

Are the disadvantaged more subject to sewer service? The consensus seems to be "yes." This point was made impressively in a study by CORE of all cases brought in New York County Civil Court by 12 corporations. CORE found that default judgments (judgments where the debtor does not appear in court), although not all due to sewer service, occurred in only 73.5% of cases involving R. H. Macy & Co. but 97% of those cases involving Harlem merchants. One merchant had *all* default judgments.[33] To some extent, this difference is explainable by the fact that service among the poor and minorities is a difficult job. The disadvantaged are harder to find and when found are more willing to use threats against servers. Most process servers are highly reluctant to go into ghetto areas, fearing for their personal safety. Some lawyers argue that service to the poor is not really necessary, since they seldom have defenses. On the other hand, it is known that because of fraudulent elements in contracts involving the poor, there is much more incentive for collection lawyers to *encourage* sewer service.

Yet it is also known that the consequences of sewer service for the disadvantaged are much greater. First, they are much more likely to lose all their possessions in default suits. Second, because they typically have less job seniority, they are more likely to lose their jobs should employers learn of garnishment proceedings (although this is illegal for first garnishments). Third, even where they have no defenses, many disadvantaged defendants are anxious to have "a day in court," and even when they do not want such an opportunity, the surprise (to them) of learning of a default judgment when they never knew a court case was pending gives the disadvantaged one more reason to believe the entire legal system is designed to block and suppress them.

Fourth, notice of impending trial gives the defendant time to secure a lawyer. Securing a lawyer with or without a defense often secures an out-of-court settlement in and of itself. As a lawyer for the poor has said: "The other side folds when a lawyer enters the picture for the defendant. We are constantly being bought out. It is merely a matter of equalization of power." [34] Even when this does not happen, the defendants often have a number of defenses inherent in the making of the contract itself. Finally, even where defenses are absent, the defendant has a chance to try to settle the matter before judgment is entered.

GARNISHMENT AND REPOSSESSION

Once a judgment has been entered by a court, the next step in the process is for the holder of the contract to attach some assets of the buyer for payment of the debt. This usually means either attachment of the buyer's wages (garnishment) or repossession of the item involved in the defaulted contract, items included as cross collateral in the contract, or other possessions of the buyer. (Such actions may also be possible *before* a court action.)

Garnishment of wages often compounds the consequences of default for the disadvantaged consumer, since garnishment often has led to dismissal by employers who either did not want the trouble of deducting wages from the defaulter's salary or felt that garnishment was evidence of faulty character in the worker. Although federal and state laws now make it very difficult to discharge employees except in cases of multiple garnishments,[35] other grounds for dismissal can often be found. The pity in cases where loss of job results is that as suggested above, the use of credit, which may have been undertaken as a mark of hope or in the expectation that a new job will mean that the family has finally broken the cycle of poverty, can itself serve as the instrument to drive the family back from hope into another, perhaps deeper, round of poverty and despair.

While dismissal because of garnishment is not itself, strictly speaking, a practice of exploitative merchants, the potential for garnishment and job loss *is* often used by merchants as a basis for harassment of recalcitrant debtors. A debtor, particularly a disadvantaged debtor, may well find himself the recipient of a letter like that cited by Kenneth Block in the *Brooklyn Law Review:* "We are holding you responsible for this debt and unless arrangements are made to pay it, we will notify [name of debtor's employer] concerning this matter. They frown upon employees owing these kinds of debts." [36] One in three respondents in Caplovitz's study of defaulting debtors reported that calls to employers were used as a technique to secure payment of their debts.[37]

Repossession has its seamy side too, whether the repossession involves the courts or not. The problems here are in the *manner* of repossession and in the manner of disposal of the goods. In the first instance, marshals can be very disruptive in the process of repossession, not only acquiring the levied goods but also indirectly notifying neighbors of the consumer's predicament. This again can be a focus for harassment by creditors, who can threaten the defaulter with considerable embarrassment should he refuse to pay or should he choose to contest a default action.

In the disposal of goods, the danger is that the sale will not be conducted as a normal business transaction in which a repossessed item is sold for a fair price. Most states require that such sales involve reasonable publicity, notice to the defaulter (who could conceivably have a friend buy back his merchandise), and a reasonable attempt to secure a fair price. Often this procedure involves a public auction. The auction, however, has been the focus of many allegations of collusion between auctioneers and creditors. They collude frequently to keep the prices low and in some instances to sell the item back to the original merchant so that he can make a second profit on it, while at the same time assuring the auctioneer of healthy fees, storages charges, and the like. Repossessions and sales involve procedures typically understood and monitored by a relatively few specialists. Since they also usually are kept relatively quiet, they represent exploitative practices to which the disadvantaged, with their lack of education and market sophistication, may be especially susceptible.

Caplovitz has reported a number of instances in which the value obtained at auction is less than a fair market price. For example, he quotes the February–March 1969 issue of OEO's *Clearinghouse Bulletin* as follows:

> Plaintiff, General Motors Acceptance Corporation, sold the defendant a 1962 Oldsmobile sedan for $2,315.72 (total time sales price). Upon alleged

> default, plaintiff repossessed the automobile and resold it for $75.00. At the time of resale the automobile had an alleged resale value of $840.[38]

As a second example, he reports the case of one of his respondents whose car was purchased for $2,200 and sold at auction three months later for $200. Caplovitz remarks with some irony, "The planned obsolescence of our economy notwithstanding, it seems quite remarkable that an automobile priced at $2,200 could lose 90 per cent of its value in three month's time." [39]

It is important to note, however, that retailers in general are reluctant to repossess merchandise from their customers. The two main reasons for this are that (1) the goods often have limited value because of extensive use and, in the case of inner city retailers, because they were shoddy to begin with, and (2) the seller does not want to lose goodwill in the community. Repossession is mainly a threat to be used against reluctant payers. Sometimes the merchant does repossess "not to regain his equity, but to punish a customer he feels is trying to cheat him." [40] Given the strong social network and facile interpersonal communication in disadvantaged areas, the lesson is not lost on the merchant's other customers, both his customers and those of his fellow low-income market merchants.

DEFICIENCY JUDGMENTS

Once the merchandise has been repossessed and sold, the proceeds are to be used to pay off the outstanding debt plus whatever other costs have been incurred. If any money is left over, it goes to the defaulter. If the receipts are *not* sufficient to meet the outstanding obligations, the buyer *still owes* what remains. This *deficiency* on the debt may or may not be the subject of further court action. Thus in extreme circumstances the buyer may end up as did Mr. Aiken in a well-known New York City Case:

> Mr. Aiken purchased a Delco battery for his 1955 Oldsmobile from a retail auto store for $29.30 plus a "credit service charge" of $5.70 pledging his car as collateral. The contract was sold to Imperial Discount Corporation and after paying $23.25 on his contract, Aiken defaulted. His car was repossessed and sold at auction after which Imperial took him to court for the deficiency of $128.80 computed in the following manner:

Balance due	$ 11.75
Late charge	.25
Attorney fees	16.80
Repossessing charge	45.00
Auctioneer's fees	35.00
Storage for 28 days	70.00
	$178.80
Sale of auto	50.00
Deficiency	$128.80[41]

Several points about the Aiken case should be noted. First, apropos an earlier discussion, note how little was obtained at auction for the car. Imperial realized only $50 for what was presumably a five- or six-year-old Oldsmobile. Second, a judge was reviewing this case only because *Imperial* had brought it to court, not Aiken. If it had not come to court, if Aiken had paid what was still due, no one would have known of Imperial's unconscionable practices. Third, as often happens with the disadvantaged, Aiken never appeared in court. As the judge noted:

> When the defendant's journey [into indebtedness] . . . reached its unsought destination in this court, the defendant was *sans* his battery, *sans* his automobile, and confronted with a demand for "judgment for $128.80, together with interest, costs, and disbursements of this action." The futility of trying to free himself of the engulfing accumulation of charges must have so overwhelmed the defendant, that he failed to answer the summons and complaint, and thus this inquest.[42]

Fourth, the judge noted that all the actions taken by Imperial were "seemingly sanctioned by the Retail Installment Sales Act" of New York and thus, taken one by one, were perfectly legal. Finally, it may be sadly noted that despite the fact the judge was "shocked by the mountainous pyramiding of charges" [43] all he was able to do was to dismiss Imperial's request for a second judgment. Aiken was still left without his battery, without his car, and without his $23.25. The machinations of the law, although helpful in some respects, could not remove the tragedy that had befallen Aiken, who at the end of the inquest presumably could no longer drive to work, and presumably now had a bad credit record because of his original default. Cases like Aiken's only serve as reminders of how resolute the laws can often be in unwittingly carrying out low-income marketers' programs for systematically exploiting the disadvantaged.

CONSEQUENCES

The consequences of this deceit, of the harassment, and, for many, of the experience of going through default and court proceedings can be substantial, extending not only to the consumer's economic circumstances but often to his health, marital status, and the like. Caplovitz summarizes his analysis of the effects of default on defaulting consumers as follows:

> In sum, debt problems can be extremely costly and debilitating. Law suits against default-debtors can result in job loss, undoubtedly in magnitudes greater than our data, collected so soon after the debt problem, indicate. They can undermine health in at least two ways: by producing the psychosomatic symptoms often associated with anxiety and worry, and by forcing the debtor

to so skimp on his budget that he neglects health needs. They can interfere with the debtor's marriage as debt problems become a source of contention between spouses; and finally they force the debtor to lower his standard of living, a process that might well further undermine his health and marriage. These findings would suggest that the current system of resolving disputes between creditors and debtors is far too costly both to the debtors and to society at large.[44]

Who Is Exploited?

The preceding sections have outlined some of the principal techniques employed by unscrupulous merchants and their sometimes unwitting allies to exploit consumers. In the course of this exposition bits and pieces of evidence and many speculations have been reported as to who are likely to be the victims of such practices. The present section examines this issue directly.

An unfortunate problem encountered at the outset is that there are no reliable statistics available to estimate the true incidence of exploitation in America. There are two basic reasons for this. First, most incidents of exploitation go undetected by their victims. This is a function of the skill of merchants, the growing complexity of products, and the extensive use of complex credit contracts. Second, perhaps nine out of ten detected incidents are not reported,[45] for several reasons:

The victim may feel the dollar amount involved isn't worth the effort of "making a fuss."

He may feel that in the game of *caveat emptor* he was beaten by a "better" opponent and "ought to take my medicine gracefully."

He may not know where to go to report his experience.

Even if he knows where to report, he may feel that it will be fruitless because of the weakness or disinterest of prosecuting agencies.

Finally, if he is disadvantaged, he may fear to "blow the whistle" on what he feels is his only credit source.

Be this as it may, it may still be asked whether the disadvantaged are likely to be more vulnerable to consumer exploitation. As we have suggested earlier, the answer again seems to be yes:[46]

1. Their ability to consume is hindered by restricted incomes. The disadvantaged are almost as frequently subjected to the blandishments of advertisers proclaiming the virtues of the materially secure life as are the middle classes, and, it may be argued that the disadvantaged, because of their *lack* of material possessions, are more sensitive to such messages. Two-

thirds to three-quarters of their incomes must go for the most basic necessities of life. The promise of easy payments, free gifts, and the materially good life may well blur the vision of such individuals.

2. They have a greater need for credit. Many disadvantaged families because of their characteristics—unsteady job history, minority racial status, old age, and broken family structure—will be classified as poor credit risks by most lenders despite the fact that they often can pay off modest debts. Others, of course, may already be well burdened with debts and other obligations and find it hard to get further credit. For such families, the exorbitant price of merchandise and its accompanying high credit cost may be seen simply as what one has to pay to get the needed credit.

3. They have a stronger present orientation. The orientation of the disadvantaged toward the present very much lends itself to impulsive buying. An impulsive buyer is the ideal prospect for many swindlers. Indeed, many door-to-door salesmen try to see the husband and wife together so that the "I must ask my husband" dodge cannot be invoked.

On the other hand, one may argue that a present-oriented consumer may care less than others if he is defrauded, being unconcerned about whether he pays or not. Indeed, with his frequently gloomy perspective, he may well expect things to be worse, not requiring that he pay. "Why not get the TV now? So what if they repossess it in a few months, at least we can watch television in the meantime!"

4. The disadvantaged lack education and shopping sophistication. The swindler finds particularly good customers among the disadvantaged, since he expects the consumer not to understand much about contracts and "formalities," such as confessions of judgment, and to be unlikely to read legal language carefully or to peruse contracts disguised as receipts. An elderly Washington, D.C., woman is the "ideal": "I only meant to have signed on the slipboard of the delivery man that I received the set. . . . I am not so good in reading and writing and I do not understand words and meanings which are in a sales contract."[47] This lack of education and sophistication is also likely to mean that the victim, if and when he discovers he has been swindled, will not know where to go for legal assistance. Middle-class customers more often call in lawyers. In cases involving the poor, lawyers by their mere presence can often get the seller or finance company to remedy a fraudulent situation or at least to discontinue pursuit of the victim.

5. The disadvantaged have greater needs for attention and respect. A problem for the elderly and minorities is that their contacts with the outside world are often fraught with rebuffs, insults, and discourtesies. Racial minorities are quite familiar with the subtleties with which prejudice can manifest itself. Thus to be confronted by a salesman who acts deferential and seems to take a genuine interest in his customer is often a very flattering experience. Such flattery often causes the victim to ignore fraud or deception

or perhaps to forgive it when it appears. Magnuson and Carper cite a good example of a company playing on this need:

> One home-improvement company working the Negro ghettos in Washington, D.C., pointedly used all-white work crews, whom the company representative in the presence of the Negro homeowner always referred to as "boys." [48]

TYPES OF DECEPTION

About the only extensive statistical data available on the incidence of exploitation is found in David Caplovitz's recent study of consumers who were brought to court in one or another of four major cities because they had defaulted on their debts.[49] While it is entirely possible that defaulting debtors may not be representative of all debtors, these data do give us a beginning insight into who is deceived, how they are deceived, and by whom.

Caplovitz asked his respondents several questions about deception. He asked:

1. Whether they had been misinformed or were not told something critical about their purchase or were not given promised merchandise.
2. Whether the true cost was higher than that quoted at the time of sale.
3. Whether the respondent received a copy of the contract at the time of sale.

The latter two requirements are part of the state law in the four states Caplovitz studied.

Caplovitz found that 36% of his respondents believed they were misinformed about their purchases, 46% found the actual price higher than the quoted price (24% found it at least 25% greater), and 54% did not receive a contract at the time of sale. When these findings were combined, Caplovitz found that only 29% of all defaulting debtors said they were *not* involved in transactions involving some form of deception.

WHO IS DECEIVED?

In general, Caplovitz found relatively little difference across income classes in perceived exposure to the three kinds of deception, although the differences are in the expected direction. However, with income controlled, blacks were more likely to feel they were deceived than were whites, again supporting the conclusion that race is a burden for blacks in the marketplace whether they are poor or not. Caplovitz also found that lack of education is a serious burden in exposing debtors to deception. Even though this is the case, however, he still found that 64% of those defaulting debtors with at least some college education perceived some deception.

WHO DOES THE DECEIVING?

A major thesis of this book has been that the problems of disadvantaged consumers stem from three sources—consumer characteristics, marketplace characteristics, and exploitation, which are inextricably interrelated. Caplovitz offers strong confirmation for this thesis. First of all, as indicated in Table 9-3, he points out that the amount of deception is strongly related to the type of outlet. Direct sellers (door-to-door salesmen) are the worst offenders, followed closely by automobile dealers (principally used car dealers), low-income retailers, and then general retailers. We have already seen in other chapters that the likelihood of patronizing any one of these sellers is directly related to one's consumer characteristics. These seller preferences are likely to explain many of Caplovitz's data on who is deceived. This is well illustrated in Caplovitz's data on black defaulters in Table 9-3. This table shows that blacks are much more frequently deceived than whites, almost entirely because they are much more active patrons of direct sellers (a fact noted in Chapter 5) *and*, crucially, because direct sellers more frequently deceive blacks.

TABLE 9-3. Extent of Deception, by Race and Type of Seller

	Whites		Blacks	
Type of Seller	*% of Sellers*	*% High Deception*[a]	*% of Sellers*	*% High Deception*[a]
Direct seller	17	50	34	64
Automobile dealer	39	58	25	56
Low-income retailer	13	45	26	41
General retailer	31	23	15	27
	100		100	

[a]High deception includes respondents reporting two or more instances of deception.
Source: David Caplovitz, *Consumers in Trouble* (New York: The Free Press, 1974), p. 43.

A somewhat different kind of pattern appears with respect to education. The benefits of education seem to accrue only to those who dealt with automobile dealers—perhaps, Caplovitz speculates, because they more often dealt with new rather than used car dealers. Education appears not to have any effect on direct sellers or low-income retailers. Caplovitz concludes:

> Type of seller is the critical determinant of the amount of deception that takes place in the transaction. Whether the debtor is rich or poor, black or

white, of high or low education is important primarily because such characteristics channel debtors to particular types of sellers. But when the financially better off debtor, or the well-educated one, makes a purchase from a direct seller or a low-income retailer, he is just as vulnerable to deception as the poor and uneducated debtor.[50]

Thus who one is affects one's susceptibility to exploitation, but it does so by trapping consumers in disadvantaged markets into dealing with sellers who are often not adverse to misrepresenting merchandise and prices, failing to provide copies of contracts, and presumably using the legal system to further their private economic and, in the case of racial discrimination, personal ends. That efforts to improve the lot of the disadvantaged consumer must proceed along three fronts is obvious. It is to an analysis of such efforts our attention now turns.

Notes

1. Warren G. Magnuson and Jean Carper, *The Dark Side of the Marketplace* (Englewood Cliffs, N.J.: Prentice–Hall, Inc., 1968), p. 8.
2. *Ibid.*, p. 9.
3. *Ibid.*, pp. 3–6.
4. *Ibid.*, p. 11.
5. David Caplovitz, *The Poor Pay More* (New York: The Free Press, 1967), pp. 142–3.
6. Federal Trade Commission, *Report On District of Columbia Consumer Protection Program* (Washington: Government Printing Office, June 1968), pp. 7–8.
7. Magnuson and Carper, *op. cit.*, p. 14.
8. The pyramid club operates by splitting territories for the sale of some product (e.g., cosmetics). To secure a franchise, a distributor pays a fee. He can then split *his* territory and collect his own fees. His customers can then resell their territories, and so on.
9. See "Translating Sympathy for Deceived Consumers into Effective Programs for Protection," *University of Pennsylvania Law Review*, vol. 114, no. 3, January 1966, pp. 444–5.
10. Magnuson and Carper, *op. cit.*, pp. 24–5.
11. *Ibid.*, pp. 18–21.
12. *Ibid.*, p. 8.
13. Eric Schnapper, "Consumer Legislation and the Poor," *Yale Law Journal*, vol. 76 (1967), p. 748.
14. Caplovitz, *op. cit.*, p. 25.
15. Magnuson and Carper, *op. cit.*, p. 109.

16. We shall consider in Chapter 12 arguments that may be used to prove the transaction was not "arm's length."
17. Caplovitz, *op. cit.*, p. 152.
18. Federal Trade Commission, *Economic Report on Installment Credit and Retail Sales Practices of District of Columbia Retailers* (Washington: Government Printing Office, 1968).
19. *Ibid.*
20. *Ibid.*, p. 31.
21. *Ibid.*, p. 34.
22. *Ibid.*
23. Magnuson and Carper, *op. cit.*, p. 52.
24. David Caplovitz, *Consumers in Trouble* (New York: The Free Press, 1974), p. 183.
25. See, for example, "Abuse of Process: Sewer Service," *Columbia Journal of Law and Social Problems*, vol. 3, June 1967, pp. 17–39.
26. *Public Hearing, Abuses in the Service of Process, Before Louis J. Lefkowitz, Attorney General of the State of New York* (1966).
27. "Abuse of Process: Sewer Service," p. 17.
28. *Ibid.*, p. 18.
29. *Ibid.*
30. *Ibid.*, p. 19.
31. In New York City, city marshals are responsible for, among other things, income executions and are required to notify the debtor 20 days before contacting the debtor's employer.
32. "Abuse of Process: Sewer Service," p. 20.
33. *Ibid.*, pp. 18–9.
34. *Ibid.*, p. 21.
35. The Federal Consumer Protection Act of 1968 makes it illegal to fire an employee for a single garnishment.
36. Kenneth M. Block, "Creditor's Pre-Judgment Communication to Debtor's Employer: An Evaluation," *Brooklyn Law Review*, no. 1, Fall 1969, p. 98.
37. Caplovitz, *Consumers in Trouble*, p. 181.
38. David Caplovitz, *Debtors in Default* (New York: Columbia University Bureau of Applied Social Research, 1970), p. 6–16.
39. *Ibid.*, pp. 6–7.
40. Caplovitz, *The Poor Pay More*, p. 21.
41. *Imperial Discount Corp. v. Aiken*, 38 Misc. 2d 187, 238 N.Y.S. 2d 269.
42. *Ibid.*
43. *Ibid.*
44. Caplovitz, *Consumers in Trouble*, p. 289.
45. Magnuson and Carper, *op. cit.*, p. 8.

46. The following numbered paragraphs are closely based upon George Fisk and Alan R. Andreasen, "Exploitative Retailing: Prologue for a Race Riot," in Alan R. Andreasen (ed), *Improving Inner-City Marketing* (Chicago: American Marketing Association, 1972), pp. 70–72.
47. Magnuson and Carper, *op. cit.*, p. 35.
48. *Ibid.*, p. 40.
49. Caplovitz, *Consumers in Trouble*, chapter 3. The material in this and the following sections is drawn primarily from this source.
50. *Ibid.*, p. 45.

PART 4

SOLUTIONS

10. Building Consumer Self-Reliance

The early sections of this volume have shown that the problems of disadvantaged consumers stem from three complex, interrelated sources—their own personal characteristics, the marketplace they typically patronize, and the exploitative practices of many of the merchants with whom they come in contact. It therefore will come as no surprise to the reader that the discussion of proposed solutions falls into three parts corresponding to the three basic sources of difficulty. Thus the next chapter, Chapter 11, considers strategies to improve low-income marketplaces, focusing specifically on the special problems of improving market structures in black ghettos. Chapter 12 will consider approaches to the regulation of merchant exploitation primarily through the passage and enforcement of federal, state, and local legislation.

The present chapter is concerned with strategies to correct problems stemming primarily from the disadvantaged consumer's own characteristics. Here the discussion, in the main, is of programs that will eliminate differences that set the disadvantaged apart from those who are not so disadvantaged. This will be a concern of Chapter 12 too, but Chapter 12, as well as Chapter 13, will be more frequently concerned with programs that can benefit *both* disadvantaged *and* nondisadvantaged consumers.

In this chapter a principal theme will be the development of programs that will permit disadvantaged consumers to better look out for their own interests. This emphasis on self-reliance lies at the heart of conservative economic philosophy, which abhors tinkering with the marketplace directly and relies instead on the force of individual choice and resultant competitive pressures to correct any temporary inequities.[1] Certainly it has been demonstrated earlier that the level of competition is quite weak in most low-income market areas and obviously in need of reinvigorating. However, there is a serious question as to whether, in the short run, programs designed to make disadvantaged consumers more self-reliant are very likely to be implemented or, if implemented, will prove to be *enough* to restore effective competition in disadvantaged areas. What is rather more likely is, for example, that programs will be developed that will make *some* disadvantaged consumers mobile enough to *escape* the disadvantaged marketplace, leaving those remaining behind *worse off* than before implementation of the programs.

In the main, the chapter proceeds by considering first the two major personal handicaps of disadvantaged consumers discussed in Chapters 2 through 5, poverty and race, and then discusses problems related to characteristics associated with poverty and race, such as limited education. In passing there will be consideration of several informational programs, including unit pricing, open dating, and nutritional labeling, which, although intended to help all consumers, have been touted as having especially important benefits for the disadvantaged in helping them to make better market choices, thus better facilitating the working of the market mechanism.

Eliminating Poverty

Perhaps the single most pervasive and punishing characteristic of disadvantaged consumers is their poverty. Because their incomes are low and unstable, the poor must:

Spend more than they take in.
Restrict their shopping scope.
Forgo stocking up on bargains.
Make substantial use of credit.
More often default on their debts.
More often live in neighborhoods with impoverished marketplaces.
More often patronize sellers who will exploit them.

Many of their encounters with the marketplace lead inexorably to worsening rather than bettering of their poverty status. It would seem obvious, therefore, that major improvements in the size and stability of the poor's incomes should have important beneficial effects on their status as consumers. Indeed, some would argue that this is the *only* way one *should* seek such effects, that allocating equivalent funds to direct meddling in the marketplace will only lead to a serious misdirection of resources and lower levels of aggregate consumer satisfaction.

THREE APPROACHES

Robert Lampman, director of the Institute for Research on Poverty, has suggested that proposals to eliminate poverty fall into three general categories depending on the basic causes one assumes underlie existing low incomes.[2] In brief, Lampman suggests that the solutions appropriate to the three causes could be described as (1) making the system work better, (2) adapting the system to the poor, and (3) adapting the poor to the system.

MAKING THE SYSTEM WORK BETTER. Since the extent of poverty is closely related to the ability of individuals to secure and hold well-paying jobs and since the availability of such jobs depends on the current strength of the economy, many economists argue that a major improvement in the rate of decline of poverty will come about from policies to increase economic growth and reduce unemployment. Such policies include both monetary and fiscal measures, incentives to industrial investment, deficit financing, and general tax cuts.

There is considerable merit in this argument in that the postulated inverse relationship between poverty and growth does exist, as noted earlier. However, while economic growth may be promoted on other grounds, its *efficiency* for reducing poverty is quite poor. That is to say, relatively few cents of a given dollar in expenditures to promote economic growth actually benefit the poor. The primary benefactors of such policies are likely to be the rest of the population, those who get higher profits or growth in stock value or who can demand higher wages or who have their taxes cut. Moreover, many poor don't benefit *at all* from some of these policies. For example, most economists regard a 3% to 5% unemployment rate in the U.S. as a minimum feasible level under very rapid growth; they think a lower level risks runaway inflation. And, of course, those who comprise the residual 3% to 5% are the hard core poor.

There are other issues that might arise in connection with programs to stimulate economic growth. These issues have to do with *how* the programs work and whether their secondary effects may not be detrimental to the poor. That is:

1. If an economic growth policy involves *inflation,* one must ask whether the poor will suffer more than the rest of the population. The answer here is likely to be yes if inflation hits nondiscretionary expenditure items harder than other items, as appears to be the case in the inflation of the mid-1970s. It will also be true if the fixed transfer payments, which as noted earlier make up 45% of the poor's present incomes, are not adjusted upward to keep up with the rate of inflation.[3]
2. If an economic growth policy involves across-the-board *tax cuts,* the poor *who do not pay taxes* will receive no direct benefits from the program and may well be left relatively worse off than before. This will be particularly true if increased demand from the nonpoor sector raises the prices the poor must pay.

CHANGING THE SYSTEM. Those who believe that growth policies are inadequate point to the fact that many people are in poverty because of (1) events that happen to them—being born into a poor family, losing a wage earner through death or disability, etc., (2) barriers that prevent them from moving out of poverty—being nonwhite, living in segregated areas with poor schools, etc., and (3) an absence of ability or motivation that would encourage them to *try* to escape poverty. All three areas, so this argument runs, require direct action.

In essence, most of the approaches designed to alter the socioeconomic system to more directly attack these problems involve some kind of transfer of money from the more affluent to the less affluent sectors of society. Such transfers could be direct, such as the graduated income tax, unemployment compensation, old age, survivors, disability, and health insurance, public welfare, veterans' benefits, and medicare, or indirect, such as assistance for day care centers in low-income areas that would allow female heads of poor households to work full time.

The arguments against programs that seek to change the system, however, are that they tinker with the system in arbitrary ways, they eat up a lot of costs administratively, and they often benefit the middle class (e.g., administrators of programs, private entrepreneurs) more than the poor. Green estimates that only one-half of such transfer payments go to those defined as poor before the payments.[4]

With public welfare programs, the one set of programs specifically aimed at the poor, the major problem is that they only cover a subset of the poor, those with specific reasons for being in poverty, i.e., the blind, children in families without a "breadwinner," the totally disabled, and the aged. However, as noted in Chapter 2, a very substantial proportion of the poor are quite able bodied and in "normal" households but simply do not earn enough money each year. Such households are effectively barred from welfare assistance. Welfare is also criticized because payments are uneven across states, causing some dislocation of indigent populations and increased welfare burdens on Northern urban centers. It has also tended to submit the poor to many indignities and has encouraged them to lie and cheat in order to prove eligibility and in order to maximize their receipts under the program. Most seriously, welfare tends not to reward behavior that would get recipients off the welfare roles. This last criticism leads us to consider the final major set of programs to reduce poverty, those concerned with motivation.

CHANGING THE POOR. The major problem with poverty according to poverty cycle theorists is that it tends to *breed more poverty*. Programs that are supposed to provide temporary support prove self-sustaining because once on, people are very slow to get off a given program, thus prolonging the drain on public coffers. What is needed is some program or set of programs that will break the cycle of poverty by affecting the motivations of the poor. With the major exception of McClelland and Winter's program to directly affect achievement motivation,[5] most programs in this area have involved some form of job training, under the theory that if the poor got used to working, learned a skill, and began to believe in themselves as productive people, they could eventually be launched into the major labor stream and off the public dole. The major criticism of such programs in the past is that they have typically had fixed time horizons; participants entered a program for a fixed period of time, were subjected to special attention and treatment, and as a result often thrived. However, when program participation ended, participants often fell back into their old patterns. What was lacking, many believe, was some continuing incentive built into the entire payment scheme independent of specific programs. Such an incentive is a central feature of the negative income tax approach to income enhancement. Since such an approach represents the near-term solution to the poverty problem most likely to be enacted within the next decade, further attention will be given to it here.

INCOME MAINTENANCE AND NEGATIVE TAXES

Negative tax schemes were first proposed by Friedman,[6] Tobin,[7] and others over a decade ago. As currently under consideration, such programs have two basic features; an *income floor* and a *work incentive*. The income floor is merely a basic level of "income continuity" below which the country feels no household should be forced to live. This floor level of income varies by household size although not by age of family head or by rural versus urban residence (as in the Orshansky model.)[8] In the Nixon administration's version of such a program (the Family Assistance Program), this floor amount was $2,400.

The work incentive is introduced through the use of what has been called an effective tax rate. The rate is the proportion of earnings the household makes itself which it must give up to the government while it is in the program. Several alternative rates have already been subject to formal experimentation.[9] The matter of what rate is most effective is still highly controversial, since it is not clear which rate (and what income floor) will minimize the country's long-term support costs.[10]

At the moment, debate on family assistance programs (FAPs) is relatively dormant pending further experimentation. It seems likely that the subject will remain a prominent domestic issue for several years. To date, however, most of the debate on the issue has focused on the consequences of income supplements for employment rates, work effort, work force characteristics, population migration, other public assistance programs, and state and local financing[11] and has largely ignored the effects on consumption patterns—other than to state the obvious, that giving the poor more money to spend will allow them to buy more and will cause some shifts in the way they allocate their budgets away from necessities toward discretionary expenditures.[12]

The critical question with respect to consumption that has not been discussed to date is whether income supplement programs will significantly *remove barriers* to effective consumption faced by disadvantaged poor consumers. Specifically, there are two sets of basic questions:

1. What will be the extent and nature of improvements in spending power accruing to poor consumers from increased income? Will these improvements be greater than the absolute gains in income?
2. What residual problems will *not* be resolved by an income enhancement program?

It turns out that there are surprisingly few data to answer these questions, and thus estimation of likely consequences is highly speculative. It is clear however, that an income supplement program would have major impact on three critical sources of difficulty for disadvantaged consumers:

1. The program would substantially increase their average level of income.[13] This should permit the disadvantaged to obtain auto transportation, to purchase bargains when they are available, and to move their residences out of disadvantaged neighborhoods.
2. It would make their incomes more *stable* by providing a basic floor of earnings below which the family would never fall. This would give them more planning information that could reduce overextensions of credit. It should mean that they would be less likely to default on loans because of sudden losses of income. And finally, it should make them better credit risks, which could lead to access to more credit at lower cost.
3. Finally, it should get more poor family heads (and other members of the family) working. This would further increase the family's income stability and its credit rating. It might well increase the family's faith in the system and its own self-confidence, which in turn could increase its willingness to shop outside the neighborhood and its willingness to combat deception when it is encountered.

Certainly these are the consequences one would *hope* would follow from the implementation of an income supplement program of some form. And certainly they are the consequences that *would* accrue to *many* of those now disadvantaged. But the question is *how many?* And, further, what would become of those who did not reap these benefits?

Three questions are critical in determining the effects on disadvantaged consumers of the implementation of a major income supplement program:

1. How will poor people's debt accumulation behavior change?
2. Will they become more mobile?
3. What will be the response of businessmen in disadvantaged areas?

1. Use of credit. Research has well demonstrated that sustainable long-term increases in income as envisioned under an income supplement program will lead to increases in short-term debt, to additions to liquid and contractual saving, and to greater discretionary expenditures, primarily on durable goods.[14] In their study of families' responses to income changes in 1964–65, Katona and Mueller were further able to conclude tentatively that income increases lead to fewer increases in debt for those with incomes under $7,500 than for those over $7,500.[15] It is unfortunate in the present context, however, that past studies have not specifically focused on the poor and have not considered permanent increases which amount to 50% or 100% or more of family incomes. Despite such lack of specific research evidence, it does seem reasonable to conclude that the income effect suggested previously will apply. That is, after the implementation of an income supplement program more of the poor will become debtors; and the average size of their debts will increase, partly because many of the poor will acquire auto transportation. What is not known, and what is quite critical, is what will happen to the distribution of debt-to-income ratios for poor families. What proportion of those now overcommitted (i.e., with debt-to-income ratios over 20%) will use their newly found added income to put themselves in more financially respectable circumstances? Further, will any of the less committed debtors and nondebtors now become overcommitted?

The answer to these questions depends in part on whether the poor can effectively budget their substantially greater new incomes and whether there exists any pent-up demand among some segments of the poor that will result in short-term splurges of credit spending? With respect to planning, it is entirely possible, as Richards has suggested,[16] that the poor, particularly those who are not well educated or who have not held white-collar jobs, are much poorer planners than the nonpoor. Even if it really is the case, as suggested in an earlier chapter, that the disadvantaged do carry out some planning but have been frustrated by their lack of a critical piece of planning data, their likely future income, one might ask whether such past planning experience is likely to be very relevant to their new, more affluent, more stable circumstances. Certainly one would expect that the poor would need a period of time to adapt to such new circumstances, a period during which they could accumulate burdensome new debt obligations.

With respect to pent-up demand, we have seen that a substantial proportion of the poor are black and that blacks are more disposed to use credit as their incomes increase than are whites and to more rapidly increase their average indebtedness. Poor black households may well behave as if they had pent-up demand under income supplement programs. Thus, in sum, it seems at least *possible*, although this must be considered rank speculation at this point, that the initiation of a FAP-type program in the short run may well *increase* the debt-to-income ratios of the poor in as many cases as it decreases them. All other things equal, this increased relative indebtedness will leave a significant segment of the poor *more* restricted to trading with local merchants and peddlers (even if they've used their income increases to buy automobiles!) and *more* subject to high prices, exploitation, and possibly default (although their increased income stability ought to reduce the chances of their defaulting due to sudden losses of income).

2. CONSUMER MOBILITY. If some disadvantaged consumers may become less mobile under an income guarantee program because of their credit problems, surely the remainder will use their improved (or at least unchanged) credit status, their newly acquired automobiles, and their greater abilities to withstand financial mistakes in unknown markets to become more mobile, to leave their impoverished and exploitative marketplace (either on a day-to-day basis or permanently through a residential move) in order to obtain the lower prices, wider assortments, and better credit terms of the general market. While this will certainly be true for many—perhaps most—disadvantaged consumers (barring dramatic changes in their local marketplace, a point to be discussed below), there exist several groups for which the *opportunity* for increased mobility may not lead to the *fact* of increased mobility. In addition to those who become overcommitted to debt, this would certainly be the case for the aged and the disabled poor, who will not be physically able to move about more, and the case for those who have difficulty with the English language, who undoubtedly will remain reluctant to deal with sellers not speaking their native tongue. Then there are some members of the black community who will be relatively unwilling to venture far from their own area because of fears of racial slights elsewhere, because of desires to support minority enterprise, or because of preferences for dealing in their own cultural milieu. And certainly, an FAP program will not of itself very greatly speed up the residential migration of blacks to the more affluent markets in all-white neighborhoods.

Finally, there is a group of poor whites and blacks who will not become more mobile because their major goals in shopping involve, not price minimization, but making important social contacts with peddlers, store clerks, neighbors, and friends in their local neighborhoods.

In sum, then, it seems likely that income supplement programs will produce two major classes of potential benefactors, those who become more mobile and those who do not. It may be expected that those who leave their local markets will become significantly less disadvantaged as consumers. They will obtain lower prices, better assortments, better credit terms, and less exploitation. What happens to those who choose *not to leave* or who cannot leave because of physical or language handicaps or because they have overburdened themselves with debt depends on what happens to their local markets.

3. MERCHANT RESPONSE. Economic theory would suggest that a sudden increase in buying power in an area—as would be the case under an income

supplement program—will prove a potent magnet drawing more competitors into the area, including mass merchandisers, who will broaden the available service and merchandise offerings, drive prices and credit costs down, and provide serious, hopefully fatal, competition to those who exploit the disadvantaged. A first difficulty with this theory is that although *available* spending power will increase, increased mobility will draw more customers out of the area, not only for discretionary items but also for basic necessities like food and clothing. It is entirely likely that in the short run the result may be that *actual* spending in disadvantaged areas will decline rather than increase. This discouraging event will be intensified by the growing economic blight in poor areas described in Chapter 6, racial animosities that linger in poor areas that are also black or Spanish–American, and the fact that no appreciable customers patronage comes *into* these areas. These factors, when coupled with the fact that there are growing investment opportunities outside of poor areas, especially in the suburbs, make it exceedingly unlikely that, in the absence of other programs to stimulate business development in disadvantaged areas, the better merchandisers will reenter poor areas or will even slow down their present rate of exodus. If such merchants do not come to populate poor areas in significant numbers, this should further accelerate the exodus of the newly affluent, which, in a further turn of the wheel, should drive out even more good merchants.

The net result then, may be that disadvantaged marketplaces after FAP will contain only the weakest merchants plus the few more experienced merchants who stay behind because of substantial opportunities for exploitation and higher profits. While the latter's markets may shrink in total, so may their competition. Further, those customers left to them will be those who are the least mobile. For these reasons—i.e., less competition and less mobile customers—the remaining merchants may well be emboldened to become even more exploitative than they were previously. At the same time, because of increased overstoring and their overall weaker business backgrounds, the remainder may well become more marginal, thereby reducing assortments, raising prices, and allowing further physical deterioration of the commercial structure in disadvantaged areas.

SUMMARY

The discussion of the likely impact of an income supplement program on disadvantaged consumers has suggested three possible outcomes that are the opposite of those that conventional theory might predict:

1. In the absence of programs to help the poor to budget their newly increased incomes and to secure the best credit terms, some of them may well get into *more* rather than less debt in relation to income

than was the case before the program. This would seem to be a much more likely possibility for blacks than for disadvantaged whites.

2. Since perhaps the majority of disadvantaged consumers will use their increased incomes to take their purchasing power *out* of the area, in the absence of other business development programs those who do *not* become more mobile will find themselves with more restricted assortments, perhaps higher prices, and an even more unattractive commercial environment than they did before the implementation of the income supplement program.
3. Because of the changing character of their clientele and their competition, in the absence of better governmental control the more unconscionable merchants may become more rather than less exploitative under income supplement programs.

A major conclusion to be drawn from the above speculations is one that will be emphasized several times in these concluding chapters, namely that programs to eliminate sources of disadvantage to some consumers may have deleterious effects on others and thus efforts must proceed along several fronts simultaneously. Single programs may work well for some disadvantaged consumers but may have side effects for others that could seriously impair or perhaps defeat the overall objectives of these critical reforms.

Eliminating Racial Discrimination

Chapters 4 and 5 pointed out that the principal sources of market disadvantage for blacks are fourfold:

1. Black incomes are lower and more unstable than white incomes.
2. Blacks are likely to have had less education than whites.
3. Blacks, whether poor or not, are likely to be segregated residentially into areas with inferior market structures.
4. Many blacks lack self-esteem and confidence in their dealings with the marketplace.

The discussion in the earlier chapters, however, also pointed out that we have not been altogether successful in separating out preferences and behaviors that are the product of these disadvantages from preferences and behaviors that are merely the product of cultural differences between blacks and whites. Still it seems reasonable to conclude that black disadvantages are responsible at least in part for the fact that blacks are more likely to get into debt and to default more often on their debts, are more restricted in their shopping scope, are discouraged from expenditures in some categories, and apparently in some cases feel they must rely more on national brands for security, compensatory prestige, and the like.

The obvious major solution to black disadvantage, of course, is the elimination of racial prejudice. This involves the elimination of direct manifestations of prejudice in discrimination in jobs, education, housing, and the like as well as the indirect manifestations of prejudice in interracial personal contacts. Such solutions would primarily involve changes in the attitudes and behavior of whites. At the same time, efforts can be made to build black pride and self-confidence that can minimize the *effects* of white prejudices. It is well beyond the scope of this book to deal with the broad problem of reducing white discrimination in housing or schools or that of building black pride.[17] It is, however, appropriate to discuss ways of eliminating racial prejudice as it appears *within the marketing system*. Such prejudice can appear in three critical areas of the system:

1. Minority employment
2. Personal contacts between white salespeople and black customers
3. Promotional activities directed at black consumers

MINORITY EMPLOYMENT

One would imagine that white retail and service businesses in minority areas would employ substantial numbers of minority personnel. First of all, potential black employees are closer at hand; most white employees have moved away sometime earlier and presumably are reluctant to come back to areas where racial tensions run high. Second, minority employees are likely to be more effective salespeople in dealing with minority customers. They are more likely to know their customers' tastes, to "speak their language," and to provide the social contacts that many poor minority customers apparently seek. Third, the extensive use of minority employees should ease the resentment some black organizations and individuals feel about "parasitic" white businessmen remaining in black areas.

Despite this apparent logic, data on white business employment of minority workers in Buffalo's inner city, where perhaps 85% of the labor force is black, suggest that black employment in retail and service businesses is markedly less than one would expect.[18] These data, reported in Table 10-1, indicate that only about 43% of all full-time jobs in white retail and service businesses in the inner city go to blacks and only about 64% of the part-time jobs. While, in contrast, black businesses fill virtually all their full- and part-time jobs with blacks, such businesses are much smaller than white businesses and have many fewer jobs to offer. As a result, overall, blacks have only about 59% of the full-time marketing jobs and about 79% of the part-time jobs (black businesses more often rely on part-time employees).[19]

TABLE 10-1. Percent of Full- and Part-Time Jobs Held by Blacks in White-Owned Businesses

Type of Business	Percent of Full-Time Employees	Percent of Part-Time Employees
Contracting	10.5	33.3
Manufacturing	15.9	22.5
Transportation	5.9	18.4
Wholesaling	9.6	40.7
Total CMTW	13.7	25.2
Retailing		
Groceries, delicatessens	45.8	63.5
Supermarkets	76.5	91.9
Other food	33.3	85.8
Automotive, service stations	31.0	42.9
Apparel (new)	45.9	58.4
Home furnishings, music	21.7	61.2
Restaurants	51.2	20.0
Bars, taverns	73.6	65.7
Building materials, hardware	4.9	60.0
General merchandise	17.4	66.7
Drugstores	62.8	87.8
Liquor stores	72.8	72.4
Secondhand stores	40.0	40.0
Other retailers	12.5	25.0
Total retailing	42.9	64.7
Services		
Dry cleaners	83.6	92.4
Beauty shops	50.0	0
Barber shops	0	0
Other personal	9.3	29.4
Auto repair	20.6	81.3
Other repair	7.1	33.3
Other services	20.0	33.3
Total services	43.7	61.5
Finance, insurance, real estate	30.8	34.5
Total—all businesses	21.5	48.3

Source: Alan R. Andreasen, *Inner City Business: A Case Study of Buffalo, N.Y.* (New York: Praeger Publishers, Inc., 1971), p. 148. Copyright 1971 by Praeger Publishers, Inc. Reprinted with permission.

It is quite likely that this pattern stems at least in major part from white employers' reluctance to hire black workers. Thus the variation in black employment across the retail and service categories in Table 10-1 depends on white *employees'* willingness to seek or retain work in areas that have become almost black and that are declining economically and physically. Analysis of white employment data suggests that the threat of robbery is a major deterrent to white employment, while the potential for high earnings (often through the exploitation of blacks) seems to keep whites in the area.[20]

It would seem, therefore, that in black areas the marketing system itself has some important responsibilities in upgrading black employment. Putting more blacks into full-time jobs would have several benefits for the black community *and* in return would substantially benefit inner city businesses. Among the benefits to the community, greater black employment would:

1. Provide more jobs, and therefore more income, to black householders, which, as noted, can have many subsequent benefits through increased buying power.
2. Provide more jobs close to home where blacks are not handicapped by their lack of transportation.
3. Keep black expenditures in white stores from leaving the area; recycle money that would otherwise leave as white wages. This is seen as a particular handicap to the development of minority business and to the minority community in general by Davis[21] and others.
4. Provide visible, nearby success symbols for black youth (who may not physically see successful black foremen but can easily be impressed by a capable, prospering clothing, home furnishings, automobile, or general merchandise salesman).
5. Help train blacks for future entrepreneurship positions (see next chapter).
6. Give more black clerk–consumers knowledge about retail transactions.
7. As already noted, give those black consumers who wish it more opportunities for social interaction during the shopping experience.
8. In general, give blacks a more favorable attitude toward whites and the white business establishment; afford them fewer opportunities for feeling they are blocked from their legitimate goals by white prejudice and intransigence. Conceivably this could have positive effects on blacks' willingness to use the courts and the Better Business Bureau in cases of merchant exploitation.

For white-owned businesses, the hiring of more blacks can have the following benefits:

1. It will broaden the pool of talent from which they can select.

2. It may increase their penetration of the black market, which presumably is growing more and more to dominate their market area, since black sales staff members presumably are more knowledgeable about black needs and can talk more easily with black customers.
3. It should relieve some of the pressures from, and feelings of alienation held by, black nationalist groups—particularly if some profit sharing or other involvement in ownership is included with increased employment.[22]
4. It may well contribute to the education of white employees (and owners) about the feelings and aspirations of blacks in America. This could importantly reduce some of the tensions and correct some of the misconceptions and stereotypes that so often lead to prejudicial behavior on the part of whites. (This is a point taken up in the next section.)
5. In the long run it may help strengthen the community economically, reduce the leakage of customers to non-inner city markets and otherwise improve the market environment to which the white businessman is presumably committed.

FINDING MINORITY EMPLOYEES

Given blacks' educational problems and the fact that they have in the past been effectively barred from important retail positions, it is not surprising to hear white retailers complain about the difficulty of getting competent black help. In Buffalo, difficulty in finding competent personnel was the single most frequently mentioned *major* problem for white businessmen (getting training in specific skills, perhaps not surprisingly, was the most frequently mentioned problem for black businessmen).[23]

In my experience in research and consulting in the inner city, there are three possible solutions to these problems frequently overlooked by white businessmen:

1. CAST A WIDER NET. The fundamental failing in minority hiring for many white businessmen is that they tend to go about it using traditional methods. When they have an opening, they place a sign in the window, list themselves with the state employment service, and perhaps place a want ad in the major newspapers. As noted in Chapter 5, white newspapers are not a particularly effective way to reach blacks. The other two approaches are also likely to be ineffective in that they rely on chance or black aggressiveness to find good minority workers. To rely on *chance* in the white community is not a bad strategy, given the reasonably moderate skills needed in retailing and the reasonably high levels of education and business experience of available white workers. But in the black community, relying

on walk-ins means that most applicants by force of their personal history will have little experience and often inadequate education. *Black aggressiveness* also is of limited value, since capable blacks are unlikely to be very interested in retail or service careers or to be willing to trust "whitey" without reason to do so.

What is necessary is that white businessmen seek black employees in nontraditional ways. This means contacting black action groups or the "pulpit network" of black ministers. Both groups often are well aware of which capable blacks are "looking to make a move." Also it means using local, black-oriented media, black newspapers and black radio, to promote job availabilities. These media are much more effectively attended to by the community and have high credibility. They also can carry the message that the advertiser is an employer who cares about the community enough to pay it *special* attention.

2. Develop training programs. There is undeniably a scarcity of capable black retail and service workers. In addition to casting more widely into the existing pool, white employers must work to *expand* the pool. Although white firms have sometimes been involved in training programs to help start minority enterprises which might be future competitors (see Chapter 11), they have done relatively less to provide themselves with good employees to meet their own immediate needs.

Clearly, the initiation of training programs is beyond the scope of small individual businessmen in the inner city. What is needed is a joint effort either through area associations (such as chambers of commerce or neighborhood businessmen's associations) or through associations of businessmen in similar lines of trade (delicatessen owners, hardware dealers, etc.). While discussion of the details of such a program is beyond the scope of this volume, an ideal mix would be between some form of classroom training (including "remedial" English and mathematics) and in-store apprenticeships, possibly carried out through the major retailers in the metropolitan area. Such programs could be funded by inner city businessmen, local and national foundations, and federal job-training grants.

3. Get involved in the community. As dramatically highlighted by the riots of the mid-1960s and innumerable hearings after them, white businesses in the ghetto have a very serious "image" problem. A major difficulty for white firms sincerely interested in contributing to inner city growth is overcoming black feelings of alienation, suspicion, and often hatred of whites and white businesses in general. Looking for more able black workers, therefore, also means convincing the black community the firm cares. There are several general guidelines for achieving such an end. One approach is that suggested by Greater New York Operation Breadbasket as reasonable objectives for white business organizations. These objectives are outlined in Figure 10-1.

FIGURE 10-1. Business Objectives Suggested by the Greater New York Operation Breadbasket

1. *Hiring,* where, to begin making up for years of deliberate injustice, a fair range of blacks must be employed *in all categories* [emphasis added].
2. *Training* of trainable blacks in every technical and professional skill utilized by the company.
3. *Promotion* of blacks on an equitable basis, taking into consideration the culturally induced handicaps imposed upon them.
4. *Buying* products and utilizing services of new and struggling black businesses in order to begin making up for the years in which they were forced out of business. This includes the total range of services from pest control to insurance and major contracting.
5. *Depositing* funds of significant size in black-owned banks in a manner that will guarantee maximum leverage for the black community.
6. *Advertising* in black-owned media at least in proportion to business done in the black community, both directly and indirectly. Also, having advertising and public relations handled by black companies.
7. *Philanthropy* also must be geared to black community needs. Because of past and present handicaps these needs, almost without exception, are far higher than white-related needs. Most corporations are far off base in this area.
8. *Cooperation* with SCLC [Southern Christian Leadership Conference, Operation Breadbasket's "parent" organization] in whatever way they can to ensure that all other corporations do their share in taking the responsibility needed to bring equity and to keep the peaceful climate in which we can advance toward fulfullment.

Source: Greater New York Operation Breadbasket, 1972.

A more simplified program specifically designed for retailers is one proposed by Allvine and Star.[24] These authors contrast the successes of several chains and small businesses in inner city areas with the experience of Red Rooster in Chicago[25] and McDonald's in Cleveland[26] and suggest the key to success can be summarized as a "CRASH program":[27]

Communicate with and become part of the local community.
Run a clean, modern, and well-lighted store.
Add minority group manufactured products to store (and chain) assortments and use minority group services.
Stock a product–service mix desired by local community (for chains, at area-wide uniform prices).
Hire minority group employees, store managers and executives.

While such a program of action is a highly desirable voluntary strategy for those retail and service organizations seeking to increase their effectiveness and seeking to attract more black workers, the growth in strength of Operation Breadbasket and the recent emergence of PUSH[28] suggest that the time may not be far off when white organizations, at least the major ones, will be strongly pressured through economic boycotts to adopt these programs under much less pleasant circumstances. Blacks seem to be more and more willing to accept Rev. Leon Sullivan's recommendation, "don't shop where you can't work." [29]

BATTLING PREJUDICIAL BEHAVIOR

Prejudice is manifested not only in the broad policies and practices of white institutions but also in the day-to-day practices of individual white functionaries who most deal with individual blacks. Racism thus is both institutional *and* individual. Unfortunately, institutionalized racism is somewhat easier to deal with, once identified, than is individual racism.

Thus it may be that the real problem in inner city markets is not that stores sometime systematically charge higher prices or install poorer managers in their inner city outlets, but that *individual* white employees and managers treat *individual* black customers as if they were less intelligent, less discriminating, and more likely to shoplift. It is not hard to see that such treatment if it is pervasive can be much more damaging to blacks as individuals and as a culture than institutionalized behaviors that simply cheat them of their money. As noted in Chapter 5, white retailers (and presumably white employees) do indeed have a highly negative attitude toward blacks, one that presumably manifests itself in prejudicial treatment. (It will be recalled that one in three blacks felt downtown stores treated blacks less well.)[30] Whites, of course, may behave as they do out of fear and suspicion as well as prejudice. Grier and Cobbs suggest the possibilities: "Cultural stereotypes of the savage rapist–Negro express the fear that the black man will turn on his tormentors. . . . White merchants who have contact with black people have uneasy feelings when they see a tight mouth, a hard look, and an angry black face." [31]

It has always struck me that among black contacts with whites, interactions with retail salespeople must be much more frequent than any other kind of contact, particularly for black adults. Thus it would seem desirable to put as much emphasis on ensuring that these contacts are prejudice-free as the society seems to have put on improving contacts between blacks and white policemen, teachers, and social workers in the past.

What is needed is the development of "educational" programs (in the broadest sense) that will acquaint white retail and service personnel working in ghetto areas with the nature and consequences of prejudice as it applies to minority Americans and with what they can and should do about it. The problem is partly white ignorance: "White Americans have developed a high skill in the art of misunderstanding black people." [32] Partly it is a matter of redirecting white energies. As Whitney Young is quoted as saying:

"There are far too many white people telling Negroes what they need . . . and far too few white people telling other white citizens to get off the Negro's back." [33]

One major American marketing firm, the Pepsi-Cola Company, has developed a program in this area, in which I have been involved, that could well serve as a model for distributors, retailers, and others who have or who intend to develop a significant commitment to selling to and hiring from minority communities. Pepsi-Cola for several years has operated its aggressive Management Institute (PCMI). Until 1969 PCMI focused on bread-and-butter management subjects, such as "marketing to chain stores" and "getting the most from your people." In 1970, at the instigation of aggressive young staff members and with the encouragement of the firm's vice-president for special markets, H. Naylor Fitzhugh, PCMI initiated an experimental course entitled "The Black Community: Opportunity and Challenge." First presented to selected top management of Pepsi franchises, the three-day course has now been run many times, including presentations to both top management and lower-level personnel in specific franchises. Such lower-level personnel include route managers who must deal directly in the inner city market and production supervisors who must hire, train, and manage minority workers.

With a biracial faculty including Prof. Marcus Alexis of Northwestern University, Benjamin Wright of Clairol Corporation, Rev. William Jones of Greater New York Operation Breadbasket, and myself, the seminar uses live actors, films, role playing, lectures, and the like to achieve the following goals:

1. To acquaint participants with the nature and historical roots of the black experience in America
2. To permit insight into the nature, causes, and possible solutions of interpersonal prejudice problems
3. To acquaint participants with the dimensions of the minority market and the special problems of dealing with it
4. To acquaint participants with the efforts of other firms to deal with minority hiring and marketing problems
5. To afford participants an opportunity to set goals and develop specific plans for themselves and their firms in response to the opportunity and challenge presented in the program

The program appears to have been quite successful. Discussions have been spirited. Participants genuinely seem to change their perceptions and attitudes. Several changes in franchise and company operating programs have resulted. PCMI is now considering making the program available to some of its customers, including chain stores and service stations, that have precisely the same kind of "opportunities and challenges" in the minority marketplace.

PROMOTION AND BLACKS

While blacks form their images of themselves, their values, and their aspirations in part through direct contacts with others, both whites and blacks, they also form them indirectly through their perception of how "people like them" are portrayed in novels, movies, television, and advertisements. Thus marketers have a second major opportunity to affect black self-esteem in the way that they treat blacks in their television and radio commercials and print advertisements.

Here the problems are twofold, of both *quantity* and *quality—how often* blacks are included in product advertisements and *how well* they are portrayed when they do appear.

1. Quantity of blacks. Part of the problem is quantity. As Kassarjian,[34] Dominick and Greenberg,[35] Cox,[36] and others have demonstrated, at least until fairly recently blacks have been underrepresented in television and magazine advertisements, although the trend is clearly upward. For example, Dominick and Greenberg found the following proportion of product ads with blacks in them from the 1967 TV season through the 1969 season:

	1967	1968	1969
Daytime	4%	7%	10%
Prime time	3%	6%	8%

Blacks appear in two types of commercials, those which are all-black and are designed primarily for the black consumer market and those in which blacks appear along with whites. Dominick and Greenberg found that all-black ads obtain a better representation during the day; of product and non-product ads with blacks, one in three daytime ads and one in five prime-time ads were all-black. They also found that in ads in which blacks appeared there was an average of about *six people* per ad whereas in white-only ads there was an average of *two* people per ad. These data make one suspect that most of the racially mixed ads were those in which blacks were the "eleventh man" included for "representativeness." [37] It would seem, then, that these "integrated ads" may represent little more than tokenism, adding black models primarily because of pressures from the NAACP, CORE, and others to increase the number of black ads and to increase the amount of black employment, but using blacks only where they are reasonably inconspicuous parts of "mob scenes."

If this reasoning is correct, then only about 3% of all daytime product ads and 2% of prime-time TV ads were directed specifically at black consumers. This is despite the fact that blacks comprised about 12% of the population and perhaps 7% of total U.S. consumer buying power in 1969.[38]

This underrepresentation of black ads has two principal causes. First, there is the feeling of many white advertisers that black-only ads or the "excessive" use of blacks in integrated ads will alienate white consumers, especially those in the South and those of lower socioeconomic status, thereby creating a "white advertising backlash." In the last three years, several studies devoted to this specific topic have appeared.[39] Those studies have generally denied the likelihood of a widespread white backlash. The principal findings are as follows:

1. All-black or integrated ads appear to get more attention from whites than all-white ads.[40]
2. As a group, whites apparently do *not* evaluate ads with blacks in them more poorly than all-white ads.[41] Perhaps the strongest evidence in this regard is that reported by Schlinger and Plummer.[42] Based on standard copy tests at the Leo Burnett advertising agency and in-theater tests within a program context, Schlinger and Plummer found that white adults (as opposed to the presumably more liberal college students used in other studies) showed no difference in responses to an all-black and an all-white television commercial, and tentatively concluded that "the mere presence or absence of prominently shown blacks may not make much difference to most whites."
3. No major demographic differences among whites have been discovered in responses to black commercials.[43] However, Cagley and Cardozo[44] found that highly prejudiced respondents, as expected, were much more likely to respond negatively to an all-black commercial.
4. Stafford, Birdwell, and Van Tassel found that a negative response to black ads may depend on the product category, but suggest that; "From a practical standpoint, it might be concluded that whites are generally indifferent to well-conceived integrated advertisements." [45]

A second cause of underrepresentation of blacks in commercials is the argument that it is not really necessary if one wishes to attract the black market. Some, pointing to Bullock's conclusion that "Negroes want to be identified with the general American Society and all its peoples," [46] have said that blacks really have little trouble identifying with white ads and will respond to them as much as to black ads. Others, pointing to Bauer and Cunningham's work suggesting that relatively affluent blacks look to whites for cues to behavior,[47] have suggested that blacks might well respond *more* to white ads than to black ads. However, the analysis in Chapter 5 and in earlier sections of this chapter has suggested that neither of these assumptions is likely to be valid, that rather, as one authority has suggested:

> The first "blunder" of advertising and marketing people in assessing the Negro market ". . . is in assuming that the Negro wants to be white. He doesn't want to be white or act white. If anything he is getting more nationalistic and prouder of his color all the time".[48]

And the research evidence tends to support this contention. Blacks in a study by Barban[49] and in the studies reported by Schlinger and Plummer[50] were more likely, in the latter case *much* more likely, to respond favorably to black ads than they were to all-white ads.

Thus it would seem that there is no good rationale for keeping the quantity of black advertising below the black community's share of the population or its share of sales in particular product markets. Increased all-black advertising would have considerable benefits in advertising effectiveness for those firms with significant black market shares, as indicated in Larson's study of brand preferences of Chicago blacks.[51] The benefits could also accrue to brand manufacturers and retailers seeking a major foothold in the black market. Parke Gibson notes that those firms that get a positive "racial reaction" can make major improvements in their shares of the black market particularly if their competitors fail to respond:

> The previous conditioning of Negroes and their constant social upheaval have conditioned them to *think, consider,* and *respond* as Negroes. . . . It is important for those who want to sell more products and services to Negroes to know that from all indications the Negro's growing awareness of his buying power is making him a more selective customer. In the future, his "racial reaction" to a given company, product, or service will become even more meaningful, and when properly used, a more favorable image can mean increased sales.[52]

Perhaps more importantly, increased use of blacks in advertising can have a major impact on blacks' image of themselves. An absence of blacks on television and magazines gives blacks the sense that they are truly Ralph Ellison's "invisible man," [53] forgotten by the rest of society, led to believe that white behavior and values are the standards he should use. Gibson suggests there can be benefits here for both blacks and whites:

> When a group of people have been conditioned for years to feel inferior by exclusion from the socially acceptable, all-American image portrayed by advertising in America, and thus to be dependent, it cannot turn itself around in a brief period of time.
>
> What integrated advertising can do is to increase the acceptance of the Negro as a purchaser of goods and services; it can lift the self-image or esteem of the Negro; it can give whites new images of the Negro and other minority groups; and it can make advertising more realistic.[54]

2. Quality. Increasing the number of blacks in advertisements and the number of all-black ads is a necessary but not sufficient condition for the improvement of the image of blacks held by both blacks and whites. *How* blacks are portrayed in the ads is critical. Here there are again two problems. First, there is the realism problem. Blacks have been frequently annoyed by the lack of realistic portrayal of blacks in ads. Often this comes about when whites try to depict upper-status blacks either as a well-meaning gesture or because they think it will occasion emulation among other blacks. As one

observer notes: "A Negro on water skis with a sunny Florida background, for instance, isn't realistic. In Negro-directed ad copy, . . . beware of preaching. 'There are many subtleties to observe or to stay away from.' " [55]

The second problem is to insure that the portraits do not stereotype, that they do in fact present a healthy positive image. This has been far from the case in the past. As Shuey, King, and Griffith have shown, in 1949 and 1950 *three-quarters* of the blacks included in advertisements in five mass circulation magazines were portrayed in the traditional stereotyped roles of servants to others (maids, waiters, chauffeurs).[56] The stereotypes, however, have changed since 1959. Both Cox[57] and Kassarjian[58] have shown that by the end of the 1960s the most prominent use of blacks was in their roles as entertainment or sports figure or as figures in some Caribbean or African setting. Cox found that in 1967–68 in the same five mass magazines studied by Shuey et al. these roles were included in 55% of all advertisements with blacks in them.

While one might argue that this stereotype is not as demeaning as that of the 1950s (only 8% of 1967–68 roles were as servants), still it gives millions of American blacks the sense that foreigners or entertainers or athletes are the only blacks that the white marketing establishment is willing to recognize. It also suggests that white marketers are again playing it safe by showing blacks in roles that are nonthreatening to whites (as were blacks as servants). Finally, it tends to suggest that black success comes only with musical, athletic, or comic talent, and since such talent is *largely* something that cannot be developed, this can only contribute to the remaining blacks' feelings of the hopelessness of their aspirations.

What is needed, of course, is the more frequent portrayal of blacks as knowledgeable, sophisticated consumers and as successful employees, businessmen, teachers, doctors, and lawyers—positive images, just as whites are shown of themselves. Research by Guest[59] suggests that such messages should not be threatening to whites. And they could do a great deal to help blacks overcome feelings of invisibility and inferiority that have in the past seriously disadvantaged them as consumers and as human beings.

Lack of Education

Most consumers are restricted in their dealings with *most* sellers in the marketplace in terms of their knowledge about available alternatives, the nature of contracts, and the legal recourses available in the event of difficulty. For sellers, these matters are critical to the success of their principal livelihood; for buyers they are usually subjects of transient interest, things to be learned, if possible, as need arises. "The Chinese say the buyer needs a thousand eyes—the seller but one. Marketing wants to keep it that way." [60] Part of the reason they want to keep it "that way" is that this disparity in knowledge and interest can represent a major source of market power.

There is only limited evidence as to whether the disadvantaged consumers we have been studying here are less knowledgeable in the marketplace than those who are not so disadvantaged. An earlier chapter noted that the poor and the undereducated know less about interest rates, that they know less about where to go for legal assistance, and that they tend to gather less information before making major decisions. There is also circumstantial evidence that they are less knowledgeable. It is known that they have had less formal education and that they less often have white-collar jobs that can teach them how to cope with the paper work found in credit transactions. They more often have come from rural or foreign backgrounds which have limited applicability to urban markets, they read less, and they sometimes have serious language problems.

Their deficiencies in market knowledge are compounded by the fact that, because of who they are and where they shop, in many respects they need to know *more* than the average consumer. They have stronger requirements to stretch a limited budget and have less ability to absorb the costs of a wrong decision.[61] When they buy major durables, they almost always use credit and must face the substantial paper work this involves. At the same time the sellers they face are more willing than other sellers to deceive and exploit them and are much less reluctant to use the complex legal system to enforce their will.

If, then, their characteristics and the markets they face leave the disadvantaged with a greater *knowledge gap* than the nondisadvantaged, programs of action to diminish their disadvantaged status ought to include serious efforts to reduce this gap. Such efforts, if successful, could redress the balance of informational power in disadvantaged markets, thereby working toward the elimination of many of the practices which now succeed primarily due to the ignorance and vulnerability of their disadvantaged victims.

There are two basic approaches to the problem of the consumer knowledge gap; one starts at the consumer side of the transaction, the other at the market side. The first approach is to equip the consumer with more basic skills and knowledge than he presently has so that he can take more effective action or can seek out further information as needs arise. The alternative approach is to force the marketplace to provide more information than it volunteers now. The two approaches, which can be labeled respectively "educating consumers" and "increasing market information," are not, as noted below, substitutes for each other.

CONSUMER EDUCATION

Perhaps the most comprehensive study of consumer education in the U.S. was the Purdue consumer education study conducted for the U.S. Office of Education in 1968–69.[62] In this study, the authors distinguished three basic types of information that can be part of any consumer education program:

Type I: Information to improve the consumer's shopping abilities in the private sector
Type II: Information to improve purchasing skills for coping with the public sector
Type III: Information about legislation and enforcement for the protection of consumers

There are two very broad sources of consumer education, one that emphasizes face-to-face communications with *individuals* and one that seeks education of large numbers of consumers in a more indirect fashion. The former is suggested by Caplovitz and others as the more effective medium for getting specific messages across. As Caplovitz points out, "Direct, personal contact clarifies and reinforces messages and provides social support for the intended change in behavior."[63] While this is, of course, well documented and should motivate agencies in contact with the disadvantaged to incorporate or enlarge consumer-counseling activities, it is unlikely that such efforts will make a very great dent in the consumer knowledge problem, given the cramped financial and staffing conditions of most such agencies and given that the disadvantaged must somehow know about and volunteer to use their services. Thus the principal concern here will be with programs that can reach larger numbers of consumers.

Five major channels are now employed to impart the three types of information to large numbers of consumers. The channels range from being quite distant in space and time from the consumer's actual need to being available virtually at the point of sale:

1. Formal primary or secondary classroom training programs either as separate courses or through presentation of materials integrated into other courses such as English, social studies, and home economics
2. Voluntary adult education programs
3. Distribution of special written consumer education materials in the form of books, magazines, or brochures
4. Presentation of special topics in the mass media, particularly radio, television, and the newspapers
5. Presentation of point-of-sale information such as that printed on contracts, packages, and supermarket shelves

The last-mentioned channel will be discussed later in the chapter.

CLASSROOM TRAINING

Classroom training (channels 1 and 2) has the major advantage that it can give extended treatment to a wide range of subjects, integrating them into a comprehensive philosophy or strategic posture. It is possible that such training, particularly when it is a required part of primary or secondary school curricula, can have a major long-term effect on disadvantaged consumers, especially if it overcomes a major fault noted in the Purdue study, that of concentrating excessively on type I information (shopping skills) and focusing to a lesser degree on type III information (consumer self-protection). Formal classroom approaches, however, have distinct disadvantages, disadvantages which vary somewhat between primary–secondary and adult education programs.

1. PRIMARY–SECONDARY PROGRAMS. While these programs can cover virtually all future disadvantaged consumers, the information is given at a time when the student may see little relevance in the topic for his or her immediate or future needs. Although it is likely that more disadvantaged than nondisadvantaged children are involved in shopping activities at an earlier age, their involvement is more as a messenger than as a decision maker.

Also the children of many disadvantaged families (i.e., those with the highest probability of themselves being disadvantaged in the future) are just those who have the least confidence in the ultimate payoff from education and thus may be even less receptive than most students to material that might seem irrelevant to them.

2. ADULT EDUCATION. Here the motivation of those who attend is likely to be much higher than among primary and secondary school students. The need is presumably seen as more immediate and attendees are presumably more willing to accept "formal schooling." The major problem, however, is whether *many* disadvantaged adults will volunteer to attend such courses at all. Many of their characteristics would seem to mitigate against it. Most disadvantaged adults will not have gone very far in school and so may have a negative or disinterested view of classroom education. Many are heads of large families and many times their spouse is absent. As a consequence they may feel they have little time to fit in a several-nights course on a subject that may not seem of immediate value. This would be a particular problem, as would disadvantaged people's lack of transportation, if they had to travel some distance to a central school, church, or library for the desired classes.

Some success in surmounting the motivation problem has been achieved by programs that tie adult consumer education with the process of credit granting. For example, S. Kann and Sons Company in Washington, D.C., in October 1968 agreed to begin giving $50 of credit in their department stores to low-income individuals referred to them by the United Planning Organization of Washington.[64] These individuals were required to take a consumer education course before being referred. At first, UPO required participants to take only one "credit education" class, but because some of the first 500 participants seemed to need further education, subsequent groups were required to attend *five* two-hour sessions.

A similar program that did not specifically promise credit availability upon "graduation" from a consumer education course was that developed among four major U.S. chains—Sears, Montgomery Ward, Federated Department Stores, and J. C. Penney—and the industry-sponsored National Foundation for Consumer Credit.[65] In this program consumer education was quite intensive, comprising eight weeks of two-hour classes per week. Only about 40 to 45 people completed each of the first two classes, and a number of problems were encountered:

> Among the operating problems encountered in running the two courses were these: selection of a convenient class location; getting people to turn out for class; baby-sitting services, and the communications gap between the low-income person and the visiting lecturer. As one observer of the program put it, ironically the low-income participants knew more about certain topics as they affected the poor than did some of the visiting experts.[66]

These problems again highlighted the possibility that adult education in disadvantaged areas will not make very great contributions to the reduction of the disadvantaged consumer's knowledge gap.

3. WRITTEN MATERIALS. Written materials have the advantage that they can be systematic, comprehensive, and topical. The information is in more or less permanent form, sometimes well indexed, for handy reference when specific problems arise. The information comes to the consumer for him to absorb when he can, rather than requiring, as in the previous examples, that he come to the information to absorb it when *others* are willing to offer it.

The written materials on consumer problems are wide ranging. Books on consumer problems range from Douglas Matthews's book on how to use the small claims courts[67] to a Nader, Dodge, and Hotchkiss manual on what to do when your car turns out to be a lemon,[68] Goody Solomon's *Radical Consumer's Handbook*,[69] and Poriss's and Callenbach's books on living well cheaply.[70] Periodicals devoted to consumer problems include *Changing Times*, *Consumers' Research*, and *Consumer Reports*. Free materials include the bulletins of local Better Business Bureaus and the President's Office of Consumer Affairs.

The problems with these media materials are several. First, many of them are expensive. For example, Poriss's book *How to Live Cheap but Good* as of December 10, 1972 was only available at $6.95. Subscriptions to *Consumer Reports* are $11 a year ($27 for three years). These, then, unless obtained in sometimes inconvenient libraries, require substantial outlays the disadvantaged seldom possess. Second, even the free materials require that needy consumers seek them out, that they visit a bookstore (usually there are few in disadvantaged areas) or, in the case of magazines and bulletins, find the proper forms and mailing addresses to request a subscription. Some of the free materials are particularly difficult to obtain.[71] Congressman

Benjamin Rosenthal of New York notes that although the BBB distributes a lot of material, "it is important to understand that a great deal of the best BBB literature [i.e. that containing names of offending businesses] never reaches the average consumer." [72]

A third and perhaps more fundamental problem is that the use of written materials also poses a motivation problem for the poor. It requires some interest in and affinity for the printed word, especially when the materials are written in reasonably sophisticated or technical language. As discussed earlier, this is a quality relatively infrequently found among the disadvantaged. As a result, materials specifically written to help disadvantaged consumers usually end up in the hands of those who have the least need for them. As Colston Warne of Consumers Union concludes about his own organization's publication, *Consumer Reports*:

> Thus far, it has reached a substantial band of eager and sophisticated consumers who could probably, in their own right, avoid most purchasing pitfalls, with an assist from technically trained neighbors and associates. . . . [T]he consumer testing movement . . . has thus far become a vehicle for product choice of the better educated members of the more affluent societies.[73]

Some recent, informally reported efforts to provide consumer information in the form of comic books or as simple readers in both English and Spanish and in large type for the elderly may prove more fruitful approaches to overcoming the problems to which Colston Warne has alluded.

Media presentations. Newspapers are also not very effective communications channels for educating the disadvantaged. Again, they involve the printed word. Further, although their cost is low, the disadvantaged are less likely to subscribe to them. Those who do subscribe will find that consumer materials, except for the reporting of specific frauds, typically appear on "the women's page." One suspects that such pages are underread by the disadvantaged. Placement near the comics or the sports section or even with the food advertising might make such materials much more accessible to the disadvantaged. Finally, it should be noted that the recent addition by many newspapers of "action columns" that are often devoted to specific consumer complaints of readers may have significantly increased the newspapers' educational role among the disadvantaged, although the magnitude of this increase (if any) has not been researched to date.

SUMMARY

If, then, newspapers are less-than-effective methods for consumer education among the disadvantaged, if books and magazines are expensive and free bulletins as often not very accessible, if adult education can only reach a very few well-motivated disadvantaged consumers, and if primary or high school education is really only a long-run (and possibly ineffective) solution, what really can be done?

In this writer's view, the channels with the greatest opportunity for success in educating the disadvantaged are radio and television, although they have to date been used very rarely for that purpose. These media have a number of important advantages that correct the disadvantages of the various channels previously discussed:

They are free and reach perhaps more than 95% of disadvantaged homes.

They are attended to by the disadvantaged more than any other medium is. As Greenberg and Dervin have shown, the poor are much more likely to put in long hours watching television than the nonpoor, and blacks many more hours listening to radio than whites.[74]

They involve oral rather than written communication. The messages are relatively painless to absorb.

They come *to* the disadvantaged where they are, rather than require the disadvantaged to come to them in some fashion.

The potential for meaningful improvements in disadvantaged consumer knowledge through these channels would appear to be substantial. This does not, however, mean using 15- or 30-minute programs, as is now the case in some areas, since they make too severe demands on the disadvantaged consumer, who must (1) make a conscious effort to tune in and (2) pay attention for an extended period of time. Rather, commercial formats of 30 or 60 seconds duration should be employed and scheduled over an extended time period at intervals during peak *viewing* hours for the poor and peak *listening* hours for blacks. Television scheduling of such "commercials" should minimize the use of UHF stations, since the television sets of the poor are less frequently equipped for UHF reception. Major advertising agencies should be employed to give professional polish to the messages, which presumably would focus on type III information. Efforts should be made not to make the messages overly serious. Entertaining formats, celebrities, music, drama, and lead-ins by figures popular in the local disadvantaged communities should be used extensively. While the "commercials" could in the main be developed nationally, room in local schedules should be made for local messages, since many of the frauds perpetrated on the disadvantaged are essentially local in character.

The potential for improving the disadvantaged consumer's lot inherent in these programs should make them appealing to educational foundations as well as to the public service interests of advertising agencies and their associations, which would have to provide the creative and financial backing needed to make the venture viable. Some initial efforts in this direction are now being made by the Better Business Bureau.

Removing Market Restrictions

A fourth approach to building self-reliance suggested in many quarters is to remove restrictions that now limit the disadvantaged consumer's choices. One such set of restrictions is those keeping banks out of the high-risk consumer loan market. As the 1972 report of the National Commission on Consumer Finance points out,[75] restriction is achieved in most states by direct prohibitions as to the kinds of loans that can be made by banks and/or by setting ceilings on interest rates that banks charge on consumer loans that are substantially lower than those that can be charged by finance companies. The result is that the two institutions end up serving different clienteles:

> When . . . the ceiling applicable to a given type of credit for one class of lenders is substantially below that of another class of lenders, the former class will be forced to serve mainly low risk borrowers the latter, high-ceiling class will tend to serve relatively higher risk borrowers. This artificial segmentation of the market obviously, restricts inter-institutional rivalry.[76]

This "artificial segmentation" also means that the disadvantaged will be *forced* into the hands of just those credit-granting retailers and small loan companies which are the major source of deception, harassment, and excessive use of the courts in disadvantaged areas.

The Commission's recommendations are not only to lift these restrictions on banks but, in general, to substantially increase competition in the consumer loan market by easing barriers to entry and otherwise encouraging interinstitutional competition. Among the Commission's major recommendations are the following:

> a. . . . under prescribed conditions savings and loan associations and mutual savings banks [should] be allowed to make secured and unsecured consumer loans up to amounts not to aggregate in excess of 10 percent of total assets;[77]
>
> b. . . . the only criterion for entry (license) in the finance company segment of the consumer credit market [should] be good character, and . . . the right to market entry [should] not be based on any minimum capital requirements or convenience and advantage regulations.
>
> c. The Commission recommends that direct bank entry in the relatively high risk segment of the personal loan market be made feasible by:
>
> (1) Permitting banks to make small loans under the rate structure permitted for finance companies;
>
> (2) Encouraging banks to establish *de novo* small loan offices as subsidiary or affiliated separate corporate entities. Regardless of corporate

structure, these small loan offices, whether separate or within other bank offices, should be subject to the same examination and supervisory procedures applied to other licensed finance companies;

(3) Exempting consumer loans from the current requirement that bank loan production offices obtain approval for each loan from the bank's main office; and

(4) Prohibiting the acquisition of finance companies by banks when banks are permitted to establish *de novo* small loan offices.[78]

Increasing Market Information

In recent months, following on the growth and successes of the consumerism movement, there has been a very rapid growth of public interest in various programs that would force marketers to make more information available to consumers at the point of sale. The assumption of such programs has been that more information would permit consumers to make better decisions, which could only help them as well as make the market system function more effectively. Several steps in this direction have already been taken. Marketers have been required in recent years to make available to consumers in various parts of the country information such as the following:

1. Annual interest rates on credit purchases and other finance charges (Consumer Credit Protection Act, 1968)
2. Health risks of smoking cigarettes (Cigarette Labeling Act, 1966)
3. Prices per unit of measure for food items in large chains (in the states of Massachusetts, Rhode Island, Connecticut, and Maryland and in New York City)[79]

Among the pieces of information that the many consumer groups feel ought to be made available in the future include:

1. Unit prices for food in *all* states
2. Nutritional contents of all food products[80]
3. Freshness dating of food (stamping a date on a package signifying the date after which the product should not be sold)[81]
4. Posted prices of prescription drugs[82]

Because of its central role in potentially solving some of the problems faced by disadvantaged consumers discussed in this volume, the focus here will be on the benefits and potential failings of programs to provide unit-pricing information to the disadvantaged.

UNIT PRICING

Scholars and consumer advocates have frequently cited Friedman's 1966 finding that even when given adequate time for detailed computational analysis, college-educated shoppers could not consistently pick the lowest-priced item in 20 staple product categories, and in fact on average paid prices about 9% higher than the minimum they could have paid.[83] The major problem, critics note, is that the marketplace is rampant with odd sizes, unusual price combinations, and the like that make comparisons on a price-per-unit basis impossible. For example, the reader might ask himself which of the following hypothetical product sets of, say, tomato juice has the least cost per ounce:

BRAND	SIZE	PRICE
A	32 ounces	45 cents
A	20 ounces	Two for 55 cents
B	48 ounces	69 cents
B	28 ounces	Two for 79 cents

Contrary to what many consumers might assume, the answer is that smallest size is in the least expensive per unit measure and the largest size in the most expensive.[84] Consumers could save the 9% Friedman found they lost plus the value of the time they spent trying to calculate the lowest-cost alternative if only stores provided them with the cost per unit of measure for all items sold, as is already done for meat and produce.[85] And Houston has indeed shown that unit pricing does make it easier for consumers to find lowest-cost alternatives.[86]

It is suggested that unit pricing would be of particular value to the disadvantaged, since it is they who are most interested in saving money. It is also they who might find the problem of calculating unit costs on their own most difficult and burdensome. Thus a particular concern of unit-pricing studies to date has been to see whether the disadvantaged, principally the poor, will benefit from mandatory unit pricing more than the nonpoor.

PAST STUDIES. Perhaps the most thorough test on unit pricing to date was that carried out in six Kroger stores in Toledo, Ohio, in 1970 as reported by McCullough and Padberg.[87] In this test a blue and white label 1 inch by 2½ inches, containing the name of the product and its line number, size, price, and price per unit, was placed on shelves for about 5,000 different items for 16 weeks in the six test stores, three each in high- and low-income areas. Television and newspaper coverage informed potential buyers of the innovation. An informational notice was also placed in grocery bags in test stores.

Two main questions were at issue: what does it cost to operate a unit-pricing system and what are the benefits to consumers?

COSTS. The following costs were reported for the experiment. The authors claim that the costs are relevant for all computerized chains and large voluntary groups, which account for 90% of U.S. grocery store sales:

	DIRECT COSTS	INDIRECT COSTS
Installation		
Division level (total)	$8,885.64	$471.38
Store level (one store)	$449.15	$3.85
Annual maintenance		
Division level (total)	$11,873.26	Not Applicable
Store level (one store)	$2,073.24	$2,098.25

Other stores which have experimented with unit pricing have reported lower costs than Kroger, although their analyses may not have been as comprehensive.[88]

DEMAND. There have been two approaches to measuring the effects of unit pricing on consumers. The first involves measuring case sales within test stores to see if there is a shift toward lower-priced items. The second approach involves survey data asking consumers whether they saw, understood, or used unit-pricing information. The first approach is imperfect in that it doesn't necessarily reflect all the effects of unit pricing on sales, the second because there is a likely tendency for consumers to report more knowledge and use than was actually the case.

Studies of case sales have, in most cases, shown little or no shifting to lower-price products. This was the finding of McCullough and Padberg, Block and his colleagues,[89] and also Jewel Tea.[90] Isakson and Maurizi take issue with these results on statistical grounds and point out that McCullough and Padberg did not control for package size variety or for the possibility of brand preferences.[91] When they make such controls (e.g., for the fact that someone who is loyal to a brand may use unit price data to switch to the lowest-unit-priced package size of *his brand* but not necessarily to other brands), they *do* find significant effects from unit pricing. McCullough and Padberg and Isakson and Maurizi agree, however, that unit pricing does not have much effect on low-income consumers. Isakson and Maurizi do find effects for middle- and high-income consumers, where McCullough and Padberg do not, and such effects may indirectly aid low-income consumers by exerting downward pressure on prices.

The finding of few effects in low-income areas is strongly supported by interview data collected in various studies. These data almost uniformly show that the disadvantaged are less likely to have known about or to claim to have used unit-pricing information, with education and actual experience apparently the most critical determinants here.[92]

The McCullough and Padberg data offer one explanation of this unexpected result. As indicated in Table 10-2, the problem appears to be that the disadvantaged are less likely to *know* about the labels and less likely to have *understood* them than the nondisadvantaged. But once they *do* know about the labels, they are more likely to use them. Thus, for example, only 23.9% of those with grade school education and 28.8% of those with incomes under $4,000 knew about *and* understood unit pricing, compared with 59.6% of those who were college graduates and 58.2% of those who had incomes over $16,000. However, 72.1% of those with low education used this information once they got it, compared with 67.3% of the college graduates. Two in three of those with incomes under $4,000 used the information once obtained, compared with 57.7% of the knowledgeable rich.

Summary. Monroe and LaPlaca point out that there are a number of important methodological and theoretical questions still unresolved by the unit-pricing studies conducted to date. For example, it is not at all clear that the measure of success of unit pricing ought to be only whether consumers gravitated toward lower-priced items. It is possible that many of the 30% of McCullough and Padberg's respondents who used the unit-pricing data did so to *upgrade* their purchase—e.g., by noting that a "better" brand is only fractionally higher priced on a unit basis than a cheaper brand one has been purchasing. Further, it seems likely that past evaluation studies of unit pricing were often undertaken too soon after the systems' installation before the kind of learning that is required for such a "new product" has really been completed.

Despite these unresolved issues, it does seem quite clear that the disadvantaged have benefited much less than the nondisadvantaged from unit-pricing programs. However, it is also clear that the problem here lies in the fact that there have not been special efforts to *teach* the disadvantaged what unit pricing is and how it can contribute to their major goal of minimizing prices. If such efforts can be made and if unit pricing is adopted more widely, the disadvantaged may benefit substantially. That wider adoption is likely is suggested by the comments of chain store people that the costs of the system are worth it, not so much because it affects consumers, but because the system involved helps retailers significantly in controlling their merchandise flows. Chains in some communities have already adopted unit pricing voluntarily, partly because of its potential as a tactic for differentiating firms from their competition.

The implementation of unit pricing on a wide scale, however, is still not likely to benefit the nondisadvantaged more than the disadvantaged for two reasons. First, it is unlikely that unit pricing will be forced on smaller

TABLE 10–2. Reported Response to Unit Pricing in Toledo Kroger Stores, 1970, by Income and Education

	Education					
	Grade School	Some High	High Grad.	Some College	College Grad.	Total
Saw labels	50.0%	60.8%	68.9%	68.2%	72.1%	65.5%
Understood lables[a]	47.7%	71.1%	75.0%	80.9%	82.7%	74.0%
Used labels[b]	72.1%	66.7%	60.4%	65.8%	67.3%	64.2%
Original base	174	309	639	277	182	

	Income				
	Less than $4,000	$4,000 to $7,999	$8,000 to $16,000	Over $16,000	Total
Saw labels	46.0%	61.5%	72.9%	71.8%	65.6%
Understood labels[a]	62.6%	76.4%	76.3%	81.1%	75.5%
Used labels[b]	66.7%	66.9%	65.8%	57.7%	64.9%
Original base	213	338	616	177	

[a] As a percentage of those who saw the labels.
[b] As a percentage of those who understood the labels.
Source: T. David McCullough and Daniel I. Padberg, "Unit Pricing in Supermarkets: Alternatives, Costs, and Consumer Reactions," *Search: Agriculture,* vol. 1, No. 6, January 1971, pp. 17–9.

outlets, where, according to McCullough and Padberg, costs of the system could run as high as 8% of sales or more. It is, of course, these smaller outlets that the disadvantaged must—or choose to—patronize most often. And second, the existence of unit-pricing data, even if understood, does not always mean the disadvantaged can buy the item with the lower unit price. Often such items are the large economy size, where the *total* outlay is more than the disadvantaged consumer can usually afford. Unit pricing would, however, still allow him or her to minimize costs within a given dollar constraint.

Other Approaches

There have been several other approaches to the problem of building more self-reliance among disadvantaged consumers. Three of these are the food-buying club, the cooperative and the credit union.

FOOD-BUYING CLUBS

Food-buying clubs are small groups of 20 to 300 families who pool their purchasing power in order to buy selected food items directly from wholesale markets.[93] The clubs collect orders from members once a week, then selected club members visit wholesale markets the next day and buy in case load lots. Overnight the items are rebagged, and orders are made available the next morning at central locations (garage, church basement, neighborhood center, etc.). Sales are almost always for cash, although experienced clubs may allow well-known and trusted members some credit.

The clubs, which may be sponsored or subsidized by one or more poverty agencies or church groups, typically focus either on meat and produce, where they can save members 30% to 35% and significantly improve the quality available, or focus on canned and dry goods, where savings are a more modest 10%.[94] Meat and produce, however, are much more difficult items to deal in: more skilled buyers are needed, storage and other equipment must be acquired (e.g., meat-cutting tools), and perishability can be a major source of losses. Canned goods are much easier to manage.

Besides the direct savings to members, food-buying clubs have additional benefits. First, they help educate members, particularly those who volunteer to do the buying or the preparing of individual orders. Skills in food selection and in simple accounting can be developed, and a more general knowledge of how food systems operate can be engendered. Second, the clubs most importantly can help build self-reliance among the disadvantaged. Although the numbers of people involved in buying clubs are reasonably small, the sense of community control over some aspect of their consumer lives is significantly increased. Because of this sense of control, the club can also be the base for other related consumer activities, such as consumer education programs and cooperatives.

COOPERATIVES

Despite their success in Europe and their success in some U.S. farm communities, cooperatives, where the consumers of a retail outlet own the outlet itself, have rarely been successful in urban areas. As Cox and Seidman have pointed out, there are six characteristics that tend to mark successful U.S. coops:[95]

1. Emphasis on food marketing
2. Relatively little competition from large-scale efficient retailers
3. Highly educated customers
4. Capable leadership dedicated to cooperative principles
5. Experienced, professional management
6. Large, modern, fully competitive stores

Although food cooperatives have been tried in several disadvantaged areas and although several successful food-buying clubs have considered expanding in this direction, there are these basic problems with such operations:

The membership will not be highly educated, which means they will less likely understand the concept of savings in the form of dividends to members at the end of a fiscal period. Members may be difficult to hold if dividends are not produced in the first year or two and, as is likely, if prices are no lower than at other, perhaps more convenient chain outlets.

As noted in the next chapter, leadership and experienced personnel are not likely to be available in disadvantaged areas. The chain food business is a very difficult one to operate in the best of circumstances, with profits often well under 2% of each sales dollar. A cooperative food outlet in a disadvantaged area would have two serious disadvantages:

1. It would be faced with all the operating problems faced by chains in disadvantaged areas outlined in Chapter 7.
2. As a single outlet, it would not have the buying power of multiple-outlet major chains.

Thus it is unlikely that prices could be lower than in competing chains. If they are not *higher*, losses may well ensue. Yet if they *are* higher, it will be much harder to get community members to support the cooperative venture.

This is not to say that the cooperative idea could not be successful in other retail categories. For example, much of the high pricing and fraud in poor areas comes from furniture and appliance outlets. Such retail categories may provide enough profit "cushion" to allow for real consumer savings even while managerial skill is being developed, as well as provide serious relief for disadvantaged consumers from exploitative merchants. Shadden[96] describes just such a furniture co-op in a black area of Chicago in the mid-sixties; by making arrangements with wholesalers and manufacturers to ship directly to consumers, it could save its members 30% to 50% on top-quality furniture. It is claimed that the co-op was able to save its members $119,642.87 over a five-year period.

CREDIT UNIONS

Credit unions are nonprofit organizations again owned by their members, who make deposits either individually or through payroll-savings programs. In return, members can start Christmas clubs, get money orders or traveler's checks, get financial advice, or, most importantly, obtain loans at reasonable rates of interest. The credit union can increase its base by investing its funds in selected safe securities and/or by borrowing from other banks.

In the late 1960s there were about 750 state and federal credit unions in the U.S. catering specifically to low-income households.[97] Such credit unions, which include about ⅓% of all credit unions in the country, are characterized by the following features:

1. Small. Average membership for federally charted low-income credit unions was 279 in 1968 compared with 835 for all federal credit unions. Assets of the former averaged $45,000 and the latter $550,000. Partly as a consequence, average loans for low-income credit unions were $372 and for all others $945.

2. Heavy expenses. Expenses for federally charted low-income credit unions were 53.8% of gross income in 1968 compared with only 38.4% for all credit unions.

3. High delinquency ratios. Low-income members were slower paying on their loans; 8.3% of their loans were delinquent in 1968, compared with 3% of all loans). However, losses were still only ½% for low-income credit unions, compared with ¼% for all credit unions.

4. Weak membership base. Most credit unions are organized around occupational groups, unions, businesses, or types of business (e.g., federal employees). Since 87.5% of all federal credit unions had such a base in 1968, deposits, often as payroll deductions, were fairly steady and communication among members was relatively easy. Given that the disadvantaged

have poor work histories and those who could get work would probably join regular credit unions if they could, it is not surprising that only 16.8% of low-income credit unions were occupationally based, so that most of them lacked steady deposits and the communications advantages of other credit unions. Most low-income credit unions were organized around fraternal, religious, community action, or residential groupings. While the fraternal and religious groups have an independent life that can help sustain the credit union over a considerable period of time, community action bases tend to come and go and residential bases tend to be particularly fluid in low-income areas. In 1968, over 44% of all state and federal low-income credit unions were related in some way to the Office of Economic Opportunity, a relatively weak base given the recent dismantling of many OEO programs.

5. INSUFFICIENT MANPOWER. Finally, as with other cooperative ventures in disadvantaged areas, there has been a serious problem of finding capable indigenous leadership and management to staff the low-income credit unions.

As a result of the above problems, there is in most low-income credit unions a continuing need to bolster operations in terms of both manpower and assets. William G. Kaye and Associates have suggested that some of these problems could be helped by more active involvement of banks in low-income credit unions, a move that would give more stability and expertise to the credit union and would have important payoffs for the banks.[98]

CONCLUSIONS

Barring involvement of major outside support, it seems unlikely that credit unions or other cooperative ventures will very often be successful in disadvantaged communities. In these areas the population is likely to be less understanding of the cooperative concept and more apathetic about and distrustful of self-organizing ventures. The disadvantaged often are heavily weighted down with their own problems and fatalistic about what will happen to them. However, in recent years they have begun to organize more frequently to fight for what they want and against what they don't want. One organization, the Consumers Education and Protective Association in Philadelphia, has been particularly effective in banding black consumers together for self-protection, primarily through picketing campaigns directed against offending merchants, banks, and finance companies.[99] With over 4,000 members and seven branches in 1969, the CEPA has become a powerful consumer-protective force in the Philadelphia area, winning the respect of many businessmen, police, and politicians. As the association's founder put it, "We are simply engaging in a constitutionally protected power and it is a terrific power when exerted." [100]

In the main, however, community cooperation in disadvantaged areas has not been very successful to date. Whether this reflects merely a lack of organizational imagination and leadership or a deeper, more fundamental problem of consumer attitude and motivation is an issue discussed at greater length later.

Summary

It is unarguable that disadvantaged consumers ought to be made more self-reliant through programs of income enhancement and consumer education, through the reduction of racial prejudice and the increase of consumer information in the marketplace, and through efforts to help them band together to help themselves. Such approaches to the disadvantaged consumer problem clearly do least damage to the market system in terms of imposing changes directly on the system itself. They merely make one group of consumers better able to impose its needs and wants on the marketplace itself.

Just as unarguably, the programs recommended in this chapter (1) in many cases are not likely to be actively initiated in the near term, (2) in other cases are likely to have their effects only in the long run, and (3) in still other cases may have short-term side effects that are *not* in the disadvantaged consumer's best interests. For these reasons, efforts must be made along other fronts. Inner city marketplaces must be restructured to benefit those who do *not* become more mobile and more sophisticated. Individual merchants must be restrained from taking advantage of consumers who are yet to be organized and/or are still uneducated as consumers. Finally, some agency must be established to take responsibility for planning, coordinating, and monitoring efforts along these general fronts.

It is to these remaining program elements that attention is turned in the remaining three chapters.

Notes

1. Milton Friedman, *Capitalism and Freedom* (Chicago: The University of Chicago Press, 1962).
2. Robert J. Lampman, "Ends and Means in the War on Poverty" in Leo Fishman (ed.), *Poverty amid Affluence* (New Haven, Conn.: Yale University Press, 1966), pp. 212–29.
3. For an analysis of the relationship between changes in prices and poverty see Charles E. Metcalf, "The Size Distribution of Personal Income during

the Business Cycle," *American Economic Review*, vol. 59, no. 4, part 1, September 1969, pp. 657–69. Metcalf concludes: "Increases in real wages and employment rates tend to improve the relative position of low income families *which are labor-force oriented*, and to lower the relative, but not the absolute, position of high income families. With the exception noted in the text, increases in the price level have a parallel effect" (p. 667; emphasis added).

4. Christopher Green, "Income Guarantee Alternatives," in Robert E. Will and Harold G. Vatter, *Poverty in Affluence*, 2d ed. (New York: Harcourt, Brace & World, Inc., 1970), p. 198.
5. David McClelland and David G. Winter, *Motivating Economic Achievement* (New York: The Free Press, 1969).
6. Friedman, *op. cit.*
7. James Tobin, Joseph Pechman, and Peter Mieszkowski, "Is a Negative Income Tax Practical," *Yale Law Journal*, vol. 77, 1967.
8. Mollie Orshansky, "Counting the Poor: Another Look at the Poverty Profile," *Social Security Bulletin*, January 1965, pp. 3–28, and Mollie Orshansky, "Who's Who among the Poor: A Demographic View of Poverty," *Social Security Bulletin*, July 1965, pp. 3–30.
9. Some preliminary results of the study with respect to consumption patterns are reported in an unpublished paper, Consumption Patterns in the New Jersey Experiment, Princeton, N.J., Mathematica, Feb. 10, 1972.
10. Daniel P. Moynihan, "Annals of Politics: History of the Family Assistance Plan," *New Yorker*, January 13, 1973, pp. 34–42 ff.
11. See, for example, President's Commission on Income Maintenance Programs, *Technical Studies* (Washington: Government Printing Office, 1970).
12. The expected changes are indicated in Tables 3-1 and 3-2.
13. President's Commission on Income Maintenance Programs, *op. cit.*, p. 154.
14. George Katona and Eva Mueller, *Consumer Response to Income Increases* (Washington: The Brookings Institution, 1968).
15. *Ibid.*, p. 126.
16. Louise C. Richards, "Consumer Practices of the Poor," in Lola M. Ireland (ed.), *Low-Income Life Styles* (Washington: U.S. Department of Health, Education, and Welfare, 1966), pp. 24 ff.
17. We shall, however, consider in Chapter 11 the tactic of building minority business and training minority businessmen, which many consider a major requirement for the growth of black pride.
18. Alan R. Andreasen, *Inner City Business: A Case Study of Buffalo, New York* (New York: Praeger Publishers, Inc., 1972), pp. 145–9.
19. *Ibid.*
20. *Ibid.*, pp. 146 and 154.
21. Frank G. Davis, *The Economics of Black Community Development* (Chicago: Markham Publishing Company, 1972).

22. Robert Little and Thaddeus Spratlen, "Alternative Forms of Ownership for Inner City Business," in Alan R. Andreasen (ed.), *Improving Inner-City Marketing* (Chicago: American Marketing Association, 1972), pp. 179–204.
23. Andreasen, *Inner City Business*, p. 159.
24. Fred C. Allvine and Alvin D. Star, "The Role of White-owned Businesses in the Inner City," in Andreasen, *Improving Inner-City Marketing*, pp. 149–76.
25. *Ibid.*, pp. 160–2.
26. *Ibid.*, pp. 167–70.
27. *Ibid.*, p. 158.
28. PUSH, an acronym for People United to Save Humanity, is based in Chicago and is headed by Rev. Jesse Jackson. Its goals are similar to those of Operation Breadbasket.
29. Allvine and Star, *op. cit.*, p. 155.
30. Angus Campbell and Howard Schuman, *Racial Attitudes in Fifteen American Cities* (Ann Arbor: Institute for Social Research, University of Michigan, June 1968).
31. William H. Grier and Price M. Cobbs, *Black Rage* (New York: Basic Books, Inc., Publishers, 1968), p. 66.
32. *Ibid.*, p. 210.
33. Nathan Wright, Jr., *Let's Work Together* (New York: Hawthorn Books, Inc., 1968), p. 25.
34. Harold H. Kassarjian, "The Negro and American Advertising, 1946–65," *Journal of Marketing Research*, vol. 6, no. 1, February 1969, pp. 29–39.
35. Joseph R. Dominick and Bradley S. Greenberg, "Three Seasons of Blacks on Television," *Journal of Advertising Research*, vol. 10, no. 2, April 1970, pp. 21–8.
36. Keith K. Cox, "Social Effects of Integrated Advertising," *Journal of Advertising Research*, vol. 10, no. 2, April 1970, pp. 41–44.
37. Dominick and Greenberg, *op. cit.*, p. 24.
38. It is possible that blacks represent a higher proportion of sales of those products advertised on television, as opposed to all products.
39. Mary Jane Schlinger and Joseph T. Plummer, "Advertising in Black and White," *Journal of Marketing Research*, vol. 9, May 1972, pp. 149–53; Arnold M. Barban, "The Dilemma of 'Integrated' Advertising," *Journal of Business*, University of Chicago, Chicago, vol. 42, no. 4, October 1969, pp. 477–96; Arnold M. Barban and Edward W. Cundiff, "Negro and White Response to Advertising Stimuli," *Journal of Marketing Research*, vol. 1, no. 4, November 1964, pp. 53–56; James Stafford, Al Birdwell, and Charles Van Tassel, "Integrated Advertising: White Backlash?" *Journal of Advertising Research*, vol. 10. no. 2, April 1970, pp. 15–20; Lester Guest, "How Negro Models Affect Company Image," *Journal of Advertising Research*, vol. 10, no. 2, April 1970, pp. 29–34; and William V.

Muse, "Product Related Response to Use of Black Models in Advertising," *Journal of Marketing Research*, vol. 8, February 1971, pp. 107–9.

40. Schlinger and Plummer, *op. cit.*, and Guest, *op. cit.*
41. Guest, *op. cit.*; Muse, *op. cit.*; Barban, *op. cit.*; and Stafford, Birdwell, and Van Tassel, *op. cit.*
42. Schlinger and Plummer, *op. cit.*
43. See, for example, *ibid.*
44. James W. Cagley and Richard N. Cardozo, "White Response to Integrated Advertising," *Journal of Advertising Research*, vol. 10, no. 2, April 1970, pp. 35–40.
45. Stafford, Birdwell, and Van Tassel, *op. cit.*, p. 20.
46. Henry A. Bullock, "Consumer Motivation in Black and White: Part 1," *Harvard Business Review*, vol. 39, no. 3, May–June 1961, pp. 89–104.
47. Raymond A. Bauer and Scott M. Cunningham, *Studies in the Negro Market* (Cambridge: Marketing Science Institute, 1970), p. 8.
48. "The Negro Market: Two Viewpoints," *Media/Scope*, vol. 11, no. 11, November 1967, pp. 70–2 ff.
49. Barban, *op. cit.*, p. 495. However, Barban concludes that "special construction of advertisements with only Negro models does not seem to strengthen the advertiser's position greatly among Negroes."
50. Schlinger and Plummer, *op. cit.*
51. Carl M. Larson, "Racial Brand Usage and Media Exposure Differentials," in Keith Cox and Ben M. Enis (eds.), *A New Measure of Responsibility for Marketing*, Proceedings of the American Marketing Association National Conference, June 1966, pp. 208–15.
52. D. Parke Gibson, *The $30 Billion Negro* (New York: Macmillian Publishing Co., Inc., 1969), p. 58.
53. Ralph Ellison, *The Invisible Man* (New York: Random House, Inc., 1947).
54. Gibson, *op. cit.*, p. 168.
55. "The Negro Market: Two Viewpoints."
56. Audrey M. Shuey, Nancy King, and Barbara Griffith, "Stereotyping of Negroes and Whites: An Analysis of Magazine Pictures," *Public Opinion Quarterly*, vol. 17, no. 2, Summer 1953, pp. 281–7.
57. Cox, *op. cit.*
58. Kassarjian, *op. cit.*
59. Guest, *op. cit.*
60. Quotation reported in E. B. Weiss, "Marketers Fiddle while Consumers Burn," *Harvard Business Review*, July–August 1968, p. 47.
61. On the other hand, it is possible that the disadvantaged make what are in some sense simpler decisions.
62. J. N. Uhl, "The Purdue Consumer Education Study: Some Findings and Implications,'" *Journal of Consumer Affairs*, vol. 4, no. 2, Winter 1970, pp. 124–34.

63. David Caplovitz, *The Poor Pay More* (New York: The Free Press, 1967), p. 185.
64. William Kaye and Associates, *Consumer Credit and the Low Income Consumer* (Rockville, Md.: Urban Coalition, 1969), pp. 39–40.
65. *Ibid.*, pp. 42–3.
66. *Ibid.*, p. 43.
67. Douglas Matthews, *Sue the B*st*rds: The Victim's Handbook* (New York: Arbor House Publishing Co., Inc., 1973).
68. Ralph Nader, Lowell Dodge, and Ralph Hotchkiss, *What to Do with Your Bad Car* (New York: Bantam Books, Inc., 1972).
69. Goody L. Solomon, *The Radical Consumer's Handbook* (New York: Ballantine Books, Inc., 1972).
70. Martin Poriss, *How to Live Cheap but Good* (New York: American Heritage Publishing Co., Inc., 1972); Ernest Callenbach, *Living Poor with Style* (New York: Bantam Books, 1972).
71. See, for example, letter from New Orleans Regional Office of the Federal Trade Commission to Congressman Benjamin Rosenthal, June 16, 1971, quoted in Hon. Benjamin S. Rosenthal, "Report on the Better Business Bureaus," *Congressional Record*, Dec. 17, 1971, p. E13774.
72. Rosenthal, *op. cit.*
73. Colston E. Warne, "Consumer Action Programs of the Consumers Union of United States," in Ralph M. Gaedeke and Warren W. Etcheson (eds.), *Consumerism: Viewpoints from Business, Government and the Public Interest* (San Francisco: Canfield Press, 1972), p. 109.
74. Bradley Greenberg and Brenda Dervin, "Mass Communication among the Urban Poor," *Public Opinion Quarterly*, vol. 34, no. 2, Summer 1970, p. 231.
75. National Commission on Consumer Finance, *Consumer Credit in the United States* (Washington: Government Printing Office, December 1972), pp. 91–149.
76. *Ibid.*, p. 137.
77. This is also a recommendation found in *The Report of the President's Commission on Financial Structure and Regulation* (Washington: Government Printing Office, 1972).
78. National Commission on Consumer, Finance, *op. cit.*, p. 138.
79. Kent B. Monroe and Peter J. LaPlaca, "What Are the Benefits of Unit Pricing?" *Journal of Marketing*, vol. 36, July 1972, pp. 16–22.
80. Edward H. Asam and Louis P. Bucklin, "Nutrition Labelling for Canned Goods: A Study of Consumer Response," *Journal of Marketing*, vol. 37, no. 2, April 1973, pp. 32–7.
81. Monroe P. Friedman, "Consumer Responses to Unit Pricing, Open Dating, and Nutrient Labeling," in M. Venkatesen (ed.), *Proceedings*, Third Annual Conference 1972 of the Association for Consumer Research (Iowa City: Association for Consumer Research, 1973), pp. 361–69.

82. Nathaniel Sheppard, Jr., "Few Prescription Drug Prices Posted Here despite New Law," *New York Times*, Sept. 23, 1972, p. 53.
83. Monroe P. Friedman, "Consumer Confusion in the Selection of Supermarket Products," *Journal of Applied Psychology*, vol. 50, December 1966, pp. 529–34.
84. The prices per ounce for the four alternatives are 1.406, 1.375, 1.438, and 1.41 cents.
85. Hans R. Isakson and Alex Maurizi, "The Consumer Economics of Unit Pricing," *Journal of Marketing Research*, vol. 10, August 1973, pp. 277–85.
86. Michael J. Houston, "The Effect of Unit Pricing on Choices of Brand and Size in Economic Shopping," *Journal of Marketing*, vol. 36, no. 3, July 1972, pp. 51–4.
87. T. David McCullough and Daniel Padberg, "Unit Pricing in Supermarkets: Alternatives, Costs, and Consumer Reaction," *Search: Agriculture*, vol. 1, no. 6, January 1971.
88. Monroe and LaPlaca, *op. cit.*
89. Carl Block, Robert Schooler, and David Erickson, "Consumer Reaction to Unit Pricing: An Empircal Study," *Mississippi Valley Journal of Business and Economics*, vol. 7, Winter 1971–2, pp. 36–46.
90. Monroe and LaPlaca, *op. cit.*
91. Isakson and Maurizi, *op. cit.*
92. Monroe and LaPlaca, *op. cit.*, p. 19.
93. Michael Avery, *Food Buying Clubs*, a report prepared for the Human Resources Administration, City of New York, September 1967.
94. Of course, the risks in dealing in canned goods are extremely low.
95. William E. Cox, Jr., and Sue R. Seidman, "Cooperatives in the Ghetto: A Brief History of the Cooperative Movement," *Proceedings*, American Marketing Association Fall Conference, August 1969.
96. Harry S. Shadden, Jr., *A Model Consumer Action Program for Low Income Neighborhoods* (Chicago: Department of Church Planning, Church Federation of Greater Chicago, May 1966).
97. Kaye and Associates, *op. cit.*, pp. 28–9.
98. *Ibid.*, pp. 32–3.
99. Jean Carper, "Defense against Gouging," *The Nation*, Nov. 3, 1969.
100. *Ibid.*

11. Inner City Business Development

THE SECOND MAJOR SET of causal factors creating market difficulties for disadvantaged consumers arise from the fragmented, deteriorated, overpriced, and understocked market structure they patronize either by choice or by force of psychological or physical barriers to mobility. Earlier analysis suggested that these market conditions are in part the result of four factors:

1. Low and often declining total spending power available to many inner city areas
2. High operating costs
3. Low average quality of management
4. An absence of low-cost mass merchandisers

Strategies for the elimination of the first factor were discussed in the preceding chapter. This chapter will consider what might be done about the other three problems in the absence of any great upsurge of spending power in poor areas.

Responsibility for Inner City Business Development

THE ROLE OF WHITE MASS MERCHANDISERS

Given highly profitable alternative uses of their capital, it seems highly unlikely that major white mass merchandisers will reenter disadvantaged markets in the near future without significant financial and manpower assistance from federal, state or local agencies. A number of proposals to achieve this end, including direct subsidies for losses incurred, accelerated tax write-offs, joint ownership forms, special leaseback arrangements for land and buildings, and special insurance pools, have been offered by Cross and others.[1] To date there has been little enthusiasm on the part of governments to adopt such proposals despite their obvious benefits to the disadvantaged. The reasons for such lack of enthusiasm undoubtedly include the following:

1. In the absence of a major reversal of the flow of buying power from poor areas, it is entirely possible that the provision of outside financial support for major mass merchandisers in disadvantaged areas could continue indefinitely. If, also, such support were tied to loss levels, it is further possible that the amounts of subsidies could increase substantially over time. Such a perpetual drain of public resources would be very difficult to justify politically.
2. Special treatment of selected, powerful mass merchants would undoubtedly raise vociferous objections from local retailers in disadvantaged areas, who would suffer severely from new vigorous, yet subsidized competition in areas where the "pickings" are already very slim. The local merchants' objections would likely be taken up by the small business community generally, which has most powerful lobbies at the federal and state levels.
3. Support for some businessmen over others at the retail level, would likely prove an interference with the marketplace that would also be generally unpalatable to those of a conservative political persuasion. They and the small merchants could carry a strong media counteroffensive to the general public on this issue.
4. Finally, subsidies for white-owned businesses of any kind to enter minority disadvantaged communities would also be challenged vigorously by minority Americans who feel that white businesses are already too much of a drain on the community's depleted stock of wealth and too much competition for fledgling minority businesses.

If, then, political exigencies make it unlikely that in the near term there will be a new infusion of outside white retail capital into disadvantaged areas, responsibility for improvements in these markets must fall to the merchants already there and to future entrepreneurs drawn from the local population. This challenge presents itself most dramatically in black communities, where needs of improving the retail structure often coincide with needs to develop a strong minority business sector. Because of this strong coincidence of interests and, further, because minority markets were the primary basis of analysis in earlier discussions, these markets will again serve as our principal focus of interest in this chapter.

It should be noted at the outset, however, that whether minority individuals wish to accept the challenge of developing their own markets or whether they must do so by default because no one else is really very much concerned with inner city market development is moot. The principal burden *will* rest with them, and the challenge then is to establish and evaluate alternative proposals for helping them meet that burden. Principally, the proposals revolve around four elements necessary for successful minority business development: people, organization, training, and financing. In order to discuss alternative proposals in each of these areas, it is first necessary to assess the current state of minority business enterprise and to try to unravel the several causes of its presently weak condition.

PRESENT STATUS OF BLACK ENTERPRISE

According to a government survey, there were approximately 322,000 minority-owned business enterprises in the United States in 1969.[2] Of these, about one-half, 163,000, were black owned.[3] These black businesses represented 2.2% of all U.S. firms and were responsible for only ⅓% of all receipts. For retail and service businesses only, blacks did slightly better, owning 2.6% all firms but still getting only ⅔% of all receipts. These figures, of course, compare most unfavorably with earlier indications that blacks comprise about 12% of the total U.S. population and about 7% of total consumer buying power.

Part of the reason that black businesses are so few and so small is that virtually all of them are concentrated in ghettos where economic conditions are very depressed. Still one might expect that within these markets, blacks ought to have a very substantial share of outlets and sales. The answer, as indicated in Table 11-1, is that, at least if the inner city of Buffalo, New York, is representative, this is not the case. Blacks still own only 57% of the retail and service establishments in their own community, representing only 38.3% of sales and 36% of total employees. This, of course, means that black businesses are smaller on average than white businesses. This is partly because blacks choose (or are forced) to concentrate in business categories where the average business, white *or* black, is small. For example, 33.4% of all black businesses in Buffalo's inner city were in the grocery, delicatessen, or beauty and barber shop category—all notoriously small operations. But blacks' businesses are also small because *within* most categories their businesses tend to be smaller. Thus, as can be seen by comparing percent of establishments and percent of sales in Table 11-1, only in the restaurant, bar, and liquor store categories are black businesses bigger in sales than white businesses in the ghetto and in the first two cases only slightly bigger. On the other hand, white businesses are *much* bigger than black businesses in major categories such as groceries and delicatessens, other food, service stations, home furnishings, dry cleaners, and auto repair.

The Buffalo study also found that, black businesses have other characteristics which compare unfavorably with their inner city white counterparts:

1. They are much newer in terms of years in business and thus have less market experience. Median age of black retail and service businesses was 5 years, as against about 15 years for white businesses.

TABLE 11-1. Black Shares of Establishments, Sales, and Full-Time Employee Equivalents, by Business Type

Type of Business	Establishments[a]	Sales[b]	Employees
Retailing			
Groceries, delicatessens	64.7	42.0	33.7
Supermarkets	14.3	c	c
Other food	43.5	20.0	50.9
Automotive, service stations	43.9	30.4	32.2
Apparel (new)	50.0	41.1	23.4
Home furnishings, music	26.7	7.7	21.9
Restaurants	61.7	68.7	64.8
Bars, taverns	41.8	46.2	45.1
Building materials, hardware	4.8	c	39.6
General merchandise	16.7	c	5.0
Drugstores	16.7	c	10.6
Liquor stores	36.4	49.1	39.0
Secondhand stores	47.1	26.2	0
Other retailers	50.0	51.0	15.4
Total retailing	47.2	31.7	30.5
Services			
Dry cleaners	60.9	31.4	30.8
Beauty shops	94.8	c	91.6
Barber shops	91.7	c	100.0
Other personal	54.5	25.7	29.5
Auto repair	44.3	16.0	27.9
Other repair	65.0	65.4	31.1
Other services	85.8	83.8	83.3
Total Services	73.1	45.1	41.7
Total	57.0	38.3	36.0

[a]Calculations exclude businesses where ownership not ascertained.
[b]Responses were obtained from 61% of respondents.
[c]Fewer than five cases for one race.
Source: Alan R Andreasen, *Inner City Business: A Case Study of Buffalo, N.Y.* (New York: Praeger Publishers, Inc., 1971), p. 62. Copyright 1971 by Praeger Publishers, Inc. Reprinted with permission.

2. They are less often on major streets. Of white retail and service businesses, 74% have such choice locations compared with 56% of black businesses.
3. They more often have premises rated in fair or poor physical condition both inside and outside.
4. They less often offer services such as credit, off-street parking, and delivery to their customers.
5. They more often report operating problems, especially with respect to bookkeeping, financial management, and obtaining insurance.

Clearly, then, blacks are in a very weak position in terms of business ownership even within their own community. Blacks are also not very often managers of the businesses of others. In 1970, "Negroes and others" comprised only 4% of those classified as salaried managers, administrators, etc., many of whom were undoubtedly in low-level managerial positions and not in the private business sector.[4] In the Buffalo study, less than 8% of all managerial positions in white inner city businesses were held by blacks.[5] The longer-term trend in black employment in these categories is significantly upward, as it is in the more broadly defined category of white-collar workers.[6] It is clear, however, that despite this considerable progress there are still very few blacks with major managerial positions in white-owned business enterprises, just as there are very few blacks who are managers of major retail and service ventures of their own.

Missing Blacks in Management: An Overview

Three different hypotheses—although not really called that—have been advanced over the years to explain the very obvious fact that there are very few blacks in business either as entrepreneurs or as managers working for others. The three hypotheses might be called the *black inferiority hypothesis*, the *direct white discrimination hypothesis*, and the *legacy-of-discrimination hypothesis*. Each obviously has its champions, and each has its echoes in other areas where blacks do less well than whites—in employment, in education, and in housing. Each hypothesis, if true, has particular implications for policy on how one might correct the circumstances.

THE BLACK INFERIORITY HYPOTHESIS

This hypothesis argues quite simply that blacks do not have, nor are they likely to acquire, the basic skills needed to succeed in business. Comments from white merchants in Drake and Cayton's classic study of Chicago business in the thirties state the argument:

> Most of the colored people you find in business are failures. I don't know what causes this, whether they don't grasp the principles of business or whether they want to start right out on the top as big shots. . . . I really think they've got too much ego. . . .
>
> They don't have the dough to invest in business. . . . [T]hey don't have the brains either . . . [I]t takes brains to make a good businessman.
>
> The happy, carefree nature of the Negroes in seeking lines of least resistance in the conduct of their business is largely responsible for the high credit risk tabulated against them.[7]

Despite many examples to the contrary, many whites feel blacks don't have the motivation or the skills needed for business—attention to detail, willingness to work long, hard hours, awareness of basic concepts of pricing, inventory control, bookkeeping, financing, and the like. This presumed lack of skills, coupled with their lack of capital and credit, would make it almost certain they would fail. Their frequent actual failure is then taken as a sign by whites that blacks are indeed inferior.

But this argument sounds not unlike the controversy about black–white differences in IQ scores and in scholastic achievement. Is poor performance on some examination evidence of basic inferiority or is it strongly, even totally, conditioned by other circumstances: low personal motivation to perform, little family support for performance in the area, poor physical and intellectual settings for learning for those who have overcome the first two hurdles, and, finally, low expectations of those in control of the means to and rewards of success? The sections to follow will suggest that these factors have their analogy in the case of black business development, so that it is virtually impossible to establish or reject the validity of the black inferiority hypothesis in business.

THE DIRECT WHITE DISCRIMINATION HYPOTHESIS

This hypothesis suggests that the problem of black business ownership is not inherent in blacks, but in the direct discriminatory practices of whites in positions to control black access to training, financing, and business opportunities necessary to mount a viable set of business enterprises. Advocates of this hypothesis point out that in the latter half of the nineteenth century and the early twentieth century there was a large and active Negro business community. Several major black insurance companies, banks, catering firms, and undertakers sprang up during this period, in many cases thriving on the "colored" business white firms refused to take. While not all these firms were successful—most were not long lived—they did reflect business vigor that somehow died in the twentieth century.[8]

Several writers have suggested that early black businesses didn't die, but were killed by conspiring white bankers who refused them the finances to develop, by white insurance companies that wouldn't insure them, by white wholesalers who wouldn't give them credit to help them build inventories, by white politicians who wouldn't build them parking spaces or provide adequate police, garbage, or street-cleaning services, and by white realtors and businessmen who conspired to keep blacks from the best business locations.[9] As Drake and Cayton found in the 1930s:

> All of Bronzeville [Chicago's major black ghetto] believes what a grocer states: "If we could get better locations our businesses would be better. The location I have is only fair—it is too far from the corner; but two white

merchants keep the best places leased in order to prevent any Negro business from getting them. . . ." [10]

Those who favor the direct discrimination hypothesis also believe that it is largely the result of economic rivalry. As Hodge and Hodge have put it, ". . . discriminatory policies may be induced by the economic interest of certain groups in protecting themselves from competition with workers willing to accept or unable to demand conditions of employment fully commensurate with those enjoyed by the discriminating body." [11] As Glenn earlier put it more succinctly, ". . . discrimination and its supporting prejudice persist mainly because majority people gain from them." [12]

The Hodges' basic argument in this context is that whites stand to gain greater monetary rewards if blacks are excluded from the business community. Obviously the principal beneficiaries are presumed to be the white entrepreneurs and white employees in the ghetto, and it is presumed that other businesses, banks, suppliers, insurance companies, and real estate agents conspire with them consciously or unconsciously to gain this end. The benefits the whites presumably get are more jobs for "our own people," higher profits, and perhaps the psychological pleasure of being economically "in" while others are "out."

It is, however, difficult to prove a case of conscious discrimination setting up barriers to black entry. Certainly other conditions could motivate such behavior. As noted earlier:

1. Many black consumers are psychological or physical captives of the merchants in inner city markets and thus, in theory, can be charged higher prices, enticed into unconscionable sales contracts, and otherwise exploited. The market is reasonably distinct, with a different demand schedule for many products, particularly those in the high-cost durables category. As a low-income area merchant put it: "People do not shop in this area. Each person who comes into the store wants to buy something and is a potential customer. It is just up to who catches him." [13] Another notes that "the amount of goods sold a customer depends not on the customer but on the merchant's willingness to extend him credit." [14] Still another says, "They advertise three rooms of furniture for $149 and the customers swarm in. *They end up buying a $400 bedroom set for $600 and none of us can believe how easy it is to make these sales.*" [15]
2. Little or no white business competition has been entering the market for some years now, thus minimizing the risk of potentially strong competition from this source.
3. Whites might expect that strong black business competitors would be less willing to exploit black customers and/or would be less willing to collude with existing whites to bring this about.
4. A final motivation to keep black businessmen out stems again from

the inferiority hypothesis. If whites feel, as the Chicago merchant quoted earlier,[16] that blacks don't have "the brains" for business, they may believe that, to the extent blacks know little about sound operating practices, (*a*) more will enter business than the market can support, and/or (*b*) more will engage in pricing or credit practices that, if matched by others, would reduce profits intolerably.

On the other hand, circumstantial evidence does indicate that white businessmen have been successful in keeping black business in check. First, the aforementioned numerous cases of exploitation and higher prices reported in inner city areas can be construed as evidence of weak competition. Second, there is ample direct evidence that these blacks who have come in as businessmen have very weak business backgrounds. Finally, Caplovitz has reported examples of specific collusive behavior:

> In East Harlem, as the interviewers learned, T.O.'s [customer turnovers] extend beyond the store. When a merchant finds himself with a customer who seems to be a greater risk than he is prepared to accept, he does not send the customer away. Instead, he will tell the customer that he happens to be out of the item he wants, but that it can be obtained at the store of his "friend" or "cousin," just a few blocks away. The merchant will then take the customer to a storekeeper with a less conservative credit policy.[17]

On the other side of the argument is the evidence from the Marion and Goodman and FTC studies[18] that ghetto profits for white businesses are lower than elsewhere, and in the food area nonexistent. This, however, is not proof of an absence of discrimination, since discrimination can have other objectives. For example, it can promote stability or it can be necessary to maintain present, albeit low, profit levels. Since many ghetto areas are in stage III (economic decline), limited entry of new businesses, even given the exodus of many white businesses, may be necessary to maintain the profit status quo for those remaining.

A second argument against the white discrimination hypothesis is that whites need not discriminate because they really have little to fear. They have the best locations, the biggest businesses, and the "best business brains." They presumably can take comfort from the fact that a very high percentage of black businessmen will fail and fail quickly. Again, the arguments here do not remove the worry that "excessive" numbers of businessmen, no matter how weak or how transient, will drive prices and profits down further.

Third, one may argue that pressure on white businessmen within minority communities is now so great that (1) they do not dare try to encourage discrimination, and (2) they are more likely to be spending their time looking for ways to sell out profitably to prospective black businessmen. The first point is weak, however, because discriminatory practices "behind the scenes" or in the form of "hard-nosed business tactics" may not be readily apparent to the bulk of the minority community. The second point carries somewhat more weight, since the Buffalo study showed that 35.8% of white ghetto retail and service business owners in 1969 "probably" or "definitely" planned to discontinue their businesses within "the next couple of years." [19] This is not to say, however, that even these businessmen would not have an interest in maintaining some barriers to black entry if it helped to keep the selling price of their business up. And, this still leaves the 51% who "probably" or "definitely" wouldn't leave the area, who may well have had a strong interest in promoting antiblack discrimination. Many such businessmen are currently seeking to minimize black community pressures by "going underground" and putting a black co-owner or manager "out front."

A final argument is that the *appearance* of discrimination is only the result of sound business practice: suppliers give less credit and bankers fewer loans to black businessmen simply because they *are* poorer businessmen, poorer risks. This may well be the case, but it is clear that many such decisions are not based on hard data, but require judgments about character, ability, and the like. The hypothesis here does not argue that the process of discrimination involves misleading or outright suppression of data about black businessmen. It simply says that key white businessmen, in judging "the intangibles," may be unduly influenced in a negative way by the color of the applicant's skin. In some cases this is a communication problem for both parties. In most cases, however, the problem may be that the key businessman knows nothing about blacks and bases his judgments on what he hears. And what he hears may well be what inner city white merchants—to whom he may well pay the most attention in these cases—want him to hear.

THE LEGACY-OF-DISCRIMINATION HYPOTHESIS

This third hypothesis probably best fits the current scene. It suggests that the weakness in black business today is no longer primarily the direct result of day-to-day discrimination in employment, education, financing, and the like, but is for the most part a consequence of years of *past* discrimination. In effect, it links together the two preceding hypotheses, stating that:

1. Blacks are not inferior, but they often behave *as if* they were because years of discrimination and disparagement have kept them from building the necessary skills and have made them often *feel* that they are less adequate.
2. Whites do not consciously discriminate, but by taking what they believe to be "sound business decisions," they act in ways that result in continued barriers to black development.

The problems of black feelings of inferiority are well exemplified by the problems of black males. From the days of slavery, whites have made it extremely difficult for black males to become strong and dominant individuals in their families and in their communities. Under slavery, the black man was often wrenched from his family in Africa and from his cultural roots. In America on the plantation, he was often forced to breed with whomever the master chose. He was not allowed to maintain a legal marriage, to have any rights to his offspring, or to be able to protect them from adversity or the whims of the master himself. Today, institutions such as welfare continue to put similar pressures on the black man as head of his household. Job discrimination has meant that he is often out of work, and when he does work, he often can bring in little money. As a consequence he often leaves home, "moves around," and accumulates a job history that worsens his employment problems.

This problem is often exaggerated by the fact that the women around him are in some important ways stronger than he is. They more often have good jobs at better pay relative to white women and work more steadily. Black women often hold families together and are principal sources of motivation and education for the children. They often have had more education, since it usually was more profitable for a black man to get out to work earlier.

The result of this legacy of discrimination has been what many describe as a loss of self-esteem and ambition for black males, who often feel that the deck is stacked against them and there is little point in trying to succeed in white society. This, of course, is a major problem in an area that is so heavily dominated by whites as the business sector. Also, a number of other contributing forces that discourage blacks from business careers could be considered part of the legacy of discrimination:

1. Very few role models exist for the potential businessman to emulate. Very few black businessmen succeed, and fewer to a degree that could greatly influence impressionable youth. At the national level, for success models they have any number of alternatives to choose from the worlds of entertainment, athletics, and politics. For other ethnic groups such important role figures very often were businessmen. But one is hard put to think of more than a handful of black businessmen of national prominence. Curiously, the black probably most closely identified with black business development is a minister, Leon Sullivan, recently elected to the General Motors Board of Directors.

   At the local level, it has been said that the "businessmen" who have the most visible signs of success—the cars, the diamond rings, the girls—and who will most impress young black kids are often the neighborhood's numbers men, pimps, and pushers. It is not an idle question to ask how many potentially good entrepreneurs are drawn into such careers for lack of legitimate outlets for their skills.

2. Most black youths have very few friends, immediate family, or more distant relatives who are in business or have been in business in the past, and again, the likelihood that they are or were successful in business is poor. Further, school segregation keeps blacks from seeing many whites in favorable business roles or from absorbing white students' probusiness motivations.
3. Compounding the fact that there are few success models to emulate, the potential black businessman finds peers, family and responsible adults actively discouraging him from entering a business career. Youths with ability and ambition are encouraged to become doctors, lawyers, teachers, ministers, and social workers, and more recently to become active in poverty and related work. Davis and White report what is probably not an atypical comment of a high school counselor, who said that "business was for the drop-outs." [20]
4. Finally, in the black community consumer demands put no particular pressure on blacks to get into business. There is no real black monopoly. As Glazer and Moynihan point out:

> There was no local demand for a Buitoni or a La Rosa to make pasta, for a Goodman and a Manischevitz and a Shapiro to supply matzos and kosher wine. The only demand was for undertakers, hairdressers, and cosmetics. As we know, in time these small beginnings in supplying members of one's own ethnic community might grow into sizable enterprises which laid fee on a world of customers that extended beyond the initial ethnic base.[21]

The problem in part is the result of the fact that there has been in the past little racial solidarity among black people to buy from "our own kind." While this has been a major support to other ethnic businessmen, recent efforts by black activist groups to stimulate "buy black" programs have often met with the same passive results that irritated black businessmen in Chicago in the late 1930s. There, Drake and Cayton found that "businessmen are convinced that one of the main problems facing them is the power of 'the white man's psychology.' 'Negroes,' they feel, 'have never learned to patronize their own.' " [22]

Needs

While it is not yet clear what the principal explanation for the lack of significant numbers of black enterprises in the past has been, it is evident that the time has now come for major improvements in the situation. It is also evident that if the condition of black enterprise is to be improved significantly, four separate goals have to be achieved:

1. There must be a significant increase in the number and quality of minority individuals, both men and women, who choose careers in

business management, both as self-employed entrepreneurs and as managers for non-minority-owned businesses.
2. There must be a significant improvement in the methods of detecting and developing market opportunities for prospective managers and entrepreneurs.
3. There must be a significant increase in the quantity and type of financial assistance available to minority entrepreneurs.
4. There must be some increase in the quantity and quality of managerial assistance available to fledgling minority entrepreneurs.

In this writer's judgment, the third and fourth requirements are somewhat less critical than the first two, since increases in the pool of minority management talent and in the number of soundly conceived business opportunities will go a long way toward solving financial problems and will significantly reduce the need for managerial advice and assistance. While this is not to deny that more lenient financial policies and more managerial advice are quite necessary during the present interim period, in the sections to follow attention will be focused on the more fundamental problems of generating *talent* and *opportunities*.

INCREASING THE POOL OF MINORITY MANAGEMENT TALENT

In one sense, the problem of securing more minority entrepreneurs appears circular. More entrepreneurs will appear only after we have more entrepreneurs—i.e., more models of successful minority individuals, men and women, who are "getting their piece of the economic action." These models presumably will spur others to accumulate the necessary experience and basic education to "take the plunge." This circularity, on the other hand, would seem encouraging since it implies that if we can begin to accelerate the growth in the number of talented blacks who choose business management careers, the process may well continue of its own momentum. But how to begin?

It would seem that there are three basic problems in increasing the pool of minority managerial talent. These three areas concern motivation, advanced education, and managerial training.

1. MOTIVATION. A critical problem to be overcome is the fact many talented blacks, particularly young blacks, believe that business management is a career for "dropouts," for those who can't make it as doctors, lawyers, social workers, and the like. They believe that there is little chance for advancement for them in white organizations except in "black jobs" (e.g., vice-president for urban affairs or minority hiring or special markets). Nor do they believe that banks or white businesses will let them become serious entrepreneurs. As a consequence they seldom seek out the necessary

training, either academically or on the job, that would prepare them to be successful managers. As the Buffalo study showed, it is only after several years of experience working for others that black males typically turn to working for themselves, often choosing such careers for the wrong reasons (i.e., as escape from something else), being very poorly prepared for such a change, and not very willing or able to be retrained.[23]

This is the "circularity problem" again. How do we get blacks to believe there is a chance for them to move easily into management careers when they see few blacks already there? Clearly, there has been an increase in black involvement in management positions in white businesses in the very recent past, and one would hope this increase would accelerate in the near future. The problem thus would seem to be one of mounting an effective propaganda campaign in local minority areas with a particular focus on minority youth, to apprise them of this fact. Such a campaign, also touching on related matters, would include:

Publicizing more widely the success of blacks in the community who have already made it in white businesses as well as in their own businesses. These potential role models could be written up in the local black and white press, visit black high schools, make presentations to career seminars, etc.

Providing more contact for black youth with business through meaningful summer job programs where business management can be seen firsthand. Class visits to carefully selected businesses could be scheduled and followed by realistic talks with senior executives about careers in the business world.

Promoting school desegregation as a means to increase minority students' opportunities for learning business vocabulary and some business management techniques informally from white students with relatives in business.

Providing more courses in business management at the high school level and introducing more business materials into high school social studies and history courses to give students a sense of the subject area and possibly a taste of what it would be like to be a responsible operating manager.

Convening conferences of guidance counselors and teachers from predominantly black high schools along with local businessmen and deans of area business schools to inform the counselors of increased opportunities for blacks in businesses and business schools.

It presumably need not be said that the *promise* of important future careers for blacks in business must be borne out in reality over the next 10 years. The danger, of course, is in overselling black opportunities, establishing expectations that are not fulfilled. This can only lead to further distrust of the white business establishment and possibly to a reversal of the process presently started.

2. ADVANCED EDUCATION. Assuming black motivations can be enhanced, the next step is to get more motivated blacks funneled into management training programs and business colleges. In both cases there will be a short-run problem of entrance qualifications; blacks, even the talented ones, will less often meet the qualifications usually set by white institutions, primarily grade point averages and aptitude test scores. This is a problem, however, that many institutions seem to be overcoming, recognizing that to apply normal standards will continue to penalize blacks for the results of past discrimination and that the critical issue of standards is not so much one of entrance requirements as one of *exit* requirements; upon leaving training programs or four years of college, blacks should meet the same standards as whites even if it means giving them extra training and/or extra time to meet the given exit requirements.

With respect to college training in business, it should be pointed out that although such training may be very useful for careers in managing for others, as Davis and White suggest it is not always true that advanced study is necessarily helpful in building entrepreneurial skills.[24] At least at the present time, those better business schools that are making major efforts to increase their minority student enrollments are generally geared toward training top management and thus are largely irrelevant to the needs of minority entrepreneurs. And those second- and third-quality schools that could provide more immediately relevant training either are not enrolling many minority students or, as in the case of many predominantly black Southern colleges, have a business faculty that is often undertrained and seriously overworked. But academic training, wherever it is obtained, *is* essential to entry into most management training in white businesses, and given the value of *this* training, an academic degree in the long run is potentially very valuable in improving inner city business management.

3. MANAGEMENT TRAINING. The problems of bringing minority members into management training programs, entrance standards problem aside, are substantial. There are potential conflicts with threatened coworkers, the trainee's own fears of inadequacy, and, perhaps most importantly, white management's insecurities about upgrading minority workers to supervise whites or bringing them into contact with white customers. These management insecurities can prove particularly frustrating to talented blacks. In this regard the experience of George Fraser, a 29-year-old black with a master's degree in business from Columbia University, is probably not untypical. After graduating from school, he went to work for a "Midwest steel company," eventually obtaining an in-house sales position where he followed up on orders from the field. Despite supervisors' favorable reports on his work, Fraser found that "I wanted to move to outside sales, where the real opportunities lie, but they kept putting me off. . . . I guess they felt I wouldn't be able to move in the same country club circles as the other

salesmen. On the outside, after all, you don't really sell steel—you sell yourself and the company." [25] George Fraser soon left the company.

There is therefore a serious problem in educating *white* management if more blacks are to be given important managerial responsibility and experience. Again, the Pepsi-Cola Management Institute "Black Community" program discussed in the preceding chapter provides a good model for such education.

Finally, it should be emphasized that more efforts can be made by white businesses to give older potential black entrepreneurs meaningful, relevant training in retail management. A sound prototype in this area is the program of the Men's Wear Retailers Association, whose members agree to train blacks who wish to go into the men's wear business in the members' own businesses for a specified period of time before the black entrepreneurs buy into these businesses or strike out on their own, sometimes as competitors.[26] Such valuable retail management experience is otherwise very difficult for blacks to obtain.

Finding Business Opportunities

It has been noted on several occasions earlier in this volume that a major problem for disadvantaged consumers is that their marketplace lacks many large-scale, well-run retail and service enterprises and has an excess of small, undercapitalized, overpriced, poorly managed mom-and-pop outlets. Similarly, the problem for black businessmen is that they are usually the ones who *run* the small marginal outlets. Indeed, the Buffalo study showed that one-half of all black retail and service enterprises had *sales* under $8,400! [27] Thus, given that white large-scale businesses are unlikely to return to the area and many that are already there will attempt to leave in the near future, the solution for both black consumers and black businessmen is to find ways of putting the latter into larger operations.

One of the broad set of techniques for achieving this end proposed by Cross,[28] Little and Spratlen,[29] and others is to match black interests with white expertise and capital through some form of joint venture. A number of different formats exist or have been proposed to achieve black–white cooperation. The formats vary primarily in the extent to which whites retain ownership and/or control.[30]

RELATIONSHIPS INVOLVING OUTSIDE WHITE CONTROL

At one extreme, there is the *wholly owned subsidiary.* This may be simply a branch of a parent company, a neighborhood A&P or a Walgreen's drugstore fully identified with the parent and benefiting from centralized promotion, pricing, supervision, and auditing. A variation is where the subsidiary is under a different name and perhaps is in a different business altogether. Here the control of the parent company is less, involving such things as financing, providing some personnel, giving general advice, and assisting in accounting and auditing. In both cases, the store in the black community would be managed and staffed by blacks. The black manager would be given an amount of autonomy depending on the type of business, company policy, and his own experience. In many cases, he would share in the store's profits.

The advantages of such an ownership form are several. First, the community may benefit in that this may be the only arrangement under which a low-cost mass merchandizer will come into the area. The community also benefits from the jobs provided. To the extent the manager participates in a profit-sharing plan, the community retains some of the profits that normally would flow back out to the white community. The manager benefits from having broad, detailed assistance from the parent company in most decision areas; he doesn't have to invest any of his own money yet shares in the profits; the parent company takes almost all the risks. The job, needless to say, is a good stepping-stone to a higher position in the parent company or into private enterprise.

The primary disadvantages, of course, are that the white-owned parent company takes most of the profits and that the manager has really little autonomy. Further, except to the extent the parent company becomes actively involved in the community, the community will have little or no control of company decisions about the subsidiary—e.g., whether to close the branch in the expectation of higher profits elsewhere.

A variation on the above type of arrangement is what is called the corporate spin-off, where the black outlet initially operates as a wholly owned subsidiary but eventually is taken over by the manager, the employees, and/or some community group.

The alternative which appears to involve the next greatest degree of outside parent company control is what Little and Spratlen call the *idea franchise*. In this type of franchise, which they distinguish from the distribution franchise (to be discussed below), the franchiser's intention is "to sell and maintain an image and a packaged set of operational procedures which result in a service of uniform quality. Standardized operations, common architectural styles, and proven promotional techniques which provide 'instant recognition' of the service are common characteristics." [31] Such franchises, which include most so-called fast food franchises, often are very tightly controlled from a central location, although they vary in the extent to which the franchise participates in profits.

While franchising offers considerable potential for disadvantaged area businesses, recent investigations by Dickinson point out some of the disadvantages of this approach:[32]

1. Franchise packages have seldom been created or merchandised for the black community, but in the main for the white suburbs.
2. Many franchise packages are seen by blacks as establishment enterprises "with the attendant negative connotations."
3. "The very concept of franchising is a type of colonialism [where] a more powerful entity is dealing with a less powerful entity."
4. Franchise fees costs may be high compared with what one gets.
5. Many franchises require few skills, pay little, and underutilize black skills.
6. Down payments are often required in excess of available black capital.
7. Many franchisers let franchises (often using the name of a national sports or entertainment celebrity) before the franchise idea is well perfected or before the franchise company is well organized or capitalized. Unsophisticated entrepreneurs may believe that since the franchise *idea* seems to work well and to be more or less foolproof, so must all franchise *systems*—which, of course, is not true. For example, the Department of Commerce booklet *Franchise Company Data for Equal Opportunity in Business* lists hundreds of franchises but attests only that each one does not discriminate.[33]
8. Franchise contracts contain many of the traps of consumer credit contracts in that they are usually drafted by corporation lawyers for the benefit of the franchiser. The black entrepreneur is often at a considerable disadvantage in understanding contracts which in the course of events may bind him to a poor franchise or even make it difficult for him to *keep* a good one.
9. Franchise systems designed for white suburbs and white entrepreneurs often have fairly rigid high expectations as to performance in early years, yet start-up time and problems may be much greater than normal for black businesses.

The next degree of control is involved in *voluntary chain organizations.* Such organizations typically are sponsored by wholesalers, e.g., the Rexall Drug and IGA Food chains, but they may also be sponsored by a group of retailers. Typically, sponsoring wholesalers conduct joint advertising and promotions for all outlets, provide management assistance, centralized accounting, and in some cases assistance in securing financing. A major advantage for ghetto outlets of these kinds of arrangements is that they guarantee a supply of low-cost merchandise with available and reasonable credit terms. Ownership of the outlet, however, is totally in the hands of the individual proprietor.

Another approach is what Little and Spratlen call *distributor franchises.*[34] Here the franchiser's objective is not to sell an operating package, but, as in the cases of General Motors, General Electric, and Texaco, to secure outlets for his goods. Again franchises are individually owned, but the franchisers will provide management assistance and will produce and share in the cost of advertising and promotion. And, of course, they provide a stable source of well-priced merchandise, again, with available credit terms. As in all the organizational forms mentioned above, considerable assistance will be given in finding good locations, which is an important advantage for blacks.

RELATIONSHIPS INVOLVING OUTSIDE BLACK CONTROL

All the above alternatives involve outside white organizations participating in some way or another in the management of minority business. A number of other alternatives have been developed or proposed in the minority enterprise area which involve outside *black* organizations in management decisions. Principal among these are the following:

Consumer cooperatives have already been discussed as a viable way for black consumers to cut costs in several areas, although their success to date has been limited. In a sense, the cooperative does not involve outside influence. The involvement of consumers in decision making, however, often results in decision by committee, and often the interests that consumers represent are primarily *community* interests. Thus the decisions taken may not always be sound from the *business's* standpoint.

One alternative approach of obvious merit is the black *holding company,* or *conglomerate.* Here a central parent firm provides financing, managerial guidance, and the like for diversified enterprises. This approach has been used by Action Industries and the Green Power Foundation in Los Angeles, by the National Economic Growth and Reconstruction Organization (NEGRO) and the Harlem Commonwealth Council. Perhaps the most widely known undertaking of this type relevant to marketing and retailing is Rev. Leon Sullivan's Progress Plaza in Philadelphia. Using a combination of funds from his own parishioners, foundation grants, and bank loans, Reverend Sullivan established the shopping plaza in November 1968. It cost $1.7 million and contains 16 outlets. There is a branch of a Philadelphia bank, and several outlets are branches of national retail chains. All are managed by blacks. In addition, 10 shops are wholly owned by blacks. The plaza apparently has been quite successful. The holding company that owns the plaza is also owner of Progress Aerospace Enterprises and Progress Garment Manufacturing Company.[35]

A similar project is El Mercado de Los Angeles, a Mexican–American marketplace with 40 businesses organized as a local development corporation with all stockholders required to be from the local East Los Angeles community.[36]

RELATIONS WITHOUT OUTSIDE CONTROL

The above approaches involve relationships that do or can impinge upon decision-making freedom in black enterprises. There are in addition to these a great number of formal and informal relationships between outside organizations and black business to provide the latter facilitating assistance in specific functional areas of marketing, selling, finance, voluntary management advice, etc. Among the more prominent of these are the following:

Many major white organizations have assisted fledgling black businesses by entering into *purchase contracts* guaranteeing to buy a specific amount of output for a specific period of time during the critical start-up years of a new business. Most examples of such arrangements are in the manufacturing area. For example, Xerox was the first customer for metal stampings and transformers from Fighton, an offshoot of FIGHT, a militant black group founded with help of Saul Alinsky in Rochester. A similar arrangement was General Electric's agreement to buy electronic components from Leon Sullivan's Progress Aerospace Enterprises. A number of such contracts have been let by government agencies including the General Services Administration and the Federal Aviation Agency under the provisions of Section 8 of the Small Business Act.[37]

In the area of retail and service marketing, examples include agreements worked out between Chicago supermarkets and Operation Breadbasket to stock products of black-owned manufacturers—Joe Louis milk, Baldwin ice cream, and Golden Crown lemon juice—and the agreement by Kodak to contract out some of its repair work to Camura, Inc., a black-owned repair shop to which Kodak also made available technical help and training.

Another form of white assistance is through *minority enterprise small business investment corporations* (MESBICs), a new approach recently developed by the Office of Minority Business Enterprise theoretically to channel the interest and capital of major corporations and other investors into black capitalism ventures. The MESBIC is like other small business investment corporations (SBICs), but with a focus on minority ownership. It is created when a business or other body puts up $150,000, which is then matched two for one by the Small Business Administration. The resulting pool can then be used as a basis for direct loans or loan guarantees to minority businesses. The MESBIC provides only capital, with no influence on management. Its major feature is its drawing of government into partnership, thereby pyramiding the value of a corporation's initial contribution.

While the form has the potential to be of help to minority enterprise, its track record has to date not been very good.[38]

THE COMMUNITY DEVELOPMENT CORPORATION

A more fundamental change in the capitalist system has been proposed as a basic part of the Community Self-Determination Act initiated by CORE and its former director, Roy Innis. The act's basic philosophy is that "the control of goods and services flowing through a distinct geographical area inhabited by a distinct population group [should] be in the hands of those indigenous to the area." [39] The essential vehicle for such control would be federally chartered community development corporations (CDCs) which would "acquire, create, and encourage" all business in the geographic area or in some cases permit outside investment with the proviso that newly built facilities be turned over to the CDC once they were stable. Some part of the profits in some CDCs would be turned into community project funds for recreation, health services, or education.

As McClaughery has noted, the bill has been the subject of a great deal of controversy.[40] Perhaps the two major criticisms refer to the basic "separatist economics" philosophy behind the bill and the likely inefficiencies the CDC model might encourage. In the first regard, economist Frank Davis has argued that either an increase in effective demand in ghetto areas must come from social welfare payments from the white community or "the black community must be allowed to own and organize the private capital resources in the black ghettos and make up the deficiency in the aggregate wage bill out of community receipts of profits, rent, interest, and dividends." [41] Others have argued that closing up the black community will keep out many mass merchandisers needed for low-cost goods and for jobs. As Sturdivant has argued, because the CDC is restricted to the ghetto, its economic base is poor and it cannot expand into wealthy areas.[42] Major sources of inefficiencies, critics feel, would be the elimination of incentives for individual businesses and the fact that major business decisions by a community-wide board of managers would be subject to possible political and other nonbusiness influences. On the other hand, one might refer to the analysis of Chapter 6 to suggest that community monopolies would permit the establishment of optimum-sized businesses and the elimination of much of the present overstoring.

Critics like Sturdivant feel that there are viable alternatives to the CDC model, such as El Mercado and Progress Plaza, that do not require a territorial monopoly.[43] Supporters, however, feel that the old economic models based on free enterprise have hurt blacks in the past and will provide slow if any improvement in the future. Quite simply they feel that the new approaches must be tried before black patience is exhausted.[44]

The Community Self-Determination Act has not been passed to date. However, the Office of Economic Opportunity, through its Special Impact Program, has set up community economic development groups called community development corporations. The CDCs are given OEO funds to start up, buy out, make loans to, and otherwise guide minority businesses. Policies for the CDCs are totally set by minority community members. Among the better-known CDCs are the following:

Hough Area Development Corporation, Cleveland
Black Economic Union, Kansas City, Missouri
Bedford–Stuyvesant Restoration and Development Corporation, Brooklyn, New York
Circle, Inc., Roxbury, Massachusetts
United Durham, Inc., Durham, North Carolina
Harlem Commonwealth Council, Inc., New York
New Jersey State Development Corporation, Trenton

A recent evaluation of CDCs in 11 locations including several of the above by Cromwell and Merrill generally gives the CDC concept good marks. They note that 13 of the 47 ventures sponsored in the 11 areas were in the black by June 1971, and say, "This fact . . . lead[s] the authors to see real value in the CDC movement." [45] Stein, writing in the same journal, is more forceful: "*How successful are the CDCs? Damn successful!*" [46] However, Cromwell and Merrill find that ventures wholly owned by the CDCs, although larger and therefore providing more jobs than non-wholly owned ventures, also tend to have lower profits. The authors suggest this may be due to (1) a lack of "drive and commitment of a managing entrepreneur/owner" or (2) a greater emphasis on nonprofit goals in wholly owned CDCs; they conclude that "CDCs should consider more variety in ownership patterns than in the past." [47] Finally, they also conclude that "venture financial performance will suffer significantly if compromises are made on the quality of management," [48] a point made in the previous section, and again point out that CDCs should not allow social goals to become so prominent (e.g., by deciding to "grow your own manager") that the long-term viability of the business venture is threatened.

OTHER NATIONAL ADVISORY, COORDINATING, AND FINANCING GROUPS

In addition to the above, there are a number of national organizations involved in helping minority businesses in various ways, including providing advice and financial assistance. These include the Interracial Council on Business Opportunity, the National Business League, some chapters of the Urban League, the Council for Equal Business Opportunity, and the Urban

Coalition. The advantages such organizations have rest on their national status, which allows them to:

1. Draw on wider sources of capital, advice, and staff.
2. Compare experiences in diverse settings.
3. Spread their risk capital among more widely diversified opportunities.
4. Select among a wider pool of candidate businesses.
5. Provide avenues of advancement for capable personnel.

Predicting Business Needs

While the varied organizational forms discussed in the previous section can serve importantly to minimize the risks in inner city business ventures and thus improve business opportunities, there still remains the critical question of what *kinds* of businesses these ventures ought to be. There is no denying the truism that a knowledgeable entrepreneur with sound financial backing and a flair for merchandising can make a success in almost any business, given reasonable demand and competitive conditions. Still, for most potential minority businessmen, the problem of finding favorable demand and competitive conditions will be most critical to their success. In the short run, the problem is to find a specific type of business and a location within the inner city area that has the highest probability of future success. More critically, since the success of a business venture depends on what will happen over the longer run, the problem is finding types of business where the demand is likely to be growing or where competitive conditions are likely to be easing. The latter information would be especially useful in directing potential businessmen toward particular kinds of apprenticeships and/or formal training experiences.

In effect, what is needed is some model of how inner city markets are changing over time in terms of demand for particular kinds of business and in terms of likely entry and exit of businesses competing for this demand. As noted in Chapter 6, Cox,[49] Berry et al.,[50] Haines et al., [51] and others have made a major beginning toward answering these questions. Cox in particular has developed a computerized analytic procedure using readily accessible federal and local data that estimates at one point in time the *ideal* number of outlets in specific inner city store categories with which the *present* number of such outlets might be compared. While an important beginning, Cox's model has some conceptual difficulties.[52] More importantly, it does not explicitly *predict* ideal or existing outlets over the medium-to-long-run period. Yet it is this forecast of future conditions that truly ought to be the basis of the prospective businessman's decision.

It is clear what such a forecasting model ought to contain. These major parameters are specified in Figure 11-1. Here, as noted, business opportunity

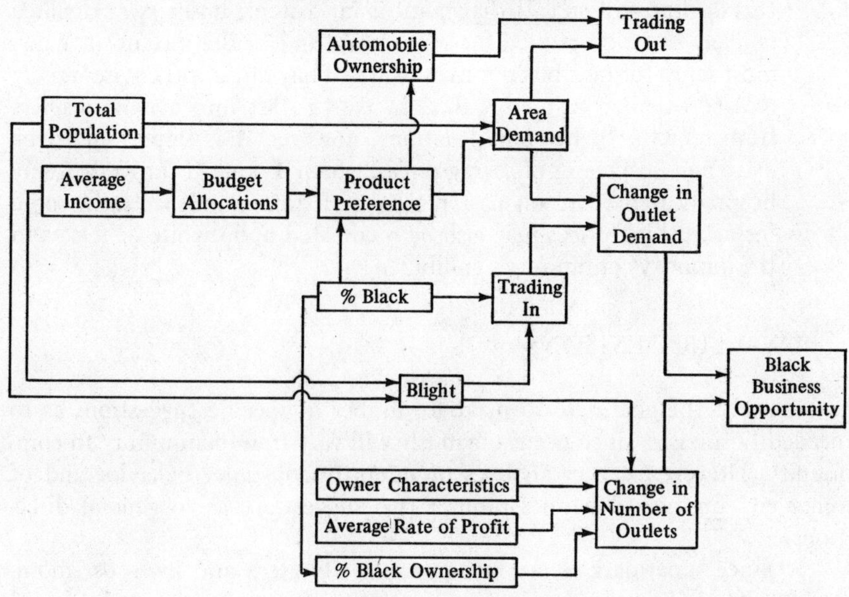

FIGURE 11-1 *A Model of Inner City Business Dynamics*

is seen as a function of demand changes and changes in existing businesses. Each of these in turn is influenced by a series of relatively obvious variables. Some important beginnings in estimating some of the parameters in this model are found in the work of Sexton[53] and Aldrich and Reiss.[54] Clearly, the task of completing the model should be a major near-term research goal for those interested in this critical problem area if we are to provide any sounder planning data for minority businessmen and for the rationalization of inner city market structures.

In the absence of such a comprehensive model, some rules of thumb have been developed from the Buffalo study:

1. It must be ascertained whether the market area under consideration fits the model described in Chapter 6 and, if so, whether it is currently in stage II or stage III.
2. If the area is in stage II, it must be remembered that (*a*) a major change in tastes and preferences is taking place as the area goes from white to black and thus the existing business structure is not necessarily a good predictor of what will be needed in future; (*b*) there is likely at some point to be a rapid exodus of white residents which may cause a serious overstored condition. Some such pressures *will* be exerted in this period as transient business dries up.
3. If the area is in stage III, where there is a decline in population and/or average spending power, it is important to try to estimate when

this decline will end. If that point is far distant, business in the area is likely to be overstored for some time, and in the interim it makes most sense for new businessmen to try to buy out or otherwise merely replace existing businesses than to try to start into a new business from scratch. In buy-out situations, however, it is important to be extremely suspicious of asking prices, which if honestly arrived at may be predicated more on past results than future prospects. In some instances high prices may also be predicated upon white beliefs as to the minority community's gullibility.

TWO SUGGESTIONS

It is not the goal here to make a number of specific suggestions as to needed businesses, since needs obviously will vary from community to community. However, earlier analyses of minority consumer behavior and of inner city business dynamics prompt two suggestions as to general directions:

1. Since supermarkets are rare in inner city areas and high-cost mom-and-pop food stores predominate, some form of operation must be found that:

Will offer low prices.

Can be conveniently located in several parts of the community (since residents less frequently have access to automobile transportation).

Requires limited capital (this is scarce in the community).

Is easy to manage, given the limited managerial skills available.

A form of operation that could meet these criteria is what might be called the *community retail food warehouse outlet* (CRFWO). The CRFWO concept is based on the design of early supermarkets and early discount houses. Retail frills are eliminated, assortment breadth is kept very narrow, and customers do most of the work. Basically, the operation would proceed as follows:

Store locations of modest to large size near heavy population centers would be selected, provided only that the locations permitted easy access for truck delivery. (The high vacancy rate in poor areas should make location not a major problem; the larger the space, given that it is near many customers, the better.)

A range of perhaps 100 of the most popular *dry* grocery items (canned goods, paper products, and the like) would then be selected and the most popular *brand* in the local community in each category determined. These 100 items would constitute the store's *only* inventory.

Inventory would be purchased in caseload lots, trucked to the store by store personnel or the supplier, and *stacked on the floor* with the carton tops cut off. Signs indicating product, size, and price (including price per unit or serving) would be posted above each stack of cartons. This would comprise the *total* floor display.

A table (a door and two sawhorses would be fine) with a cash register would be placed at the exit. Baskets would be carried by shoppers to pick up items (and never taken out of the store). Items would not be price-marked, since the limited assortment would permit the check-out person to memorize all the prices. Customers could be given a small refund if they bagged their own groceries.

Sales would be only for cash. Payments to all suppliers, landlords, etc., would be solely by check.

Because of limited staffing and operating needs, the outlet could stay open very long hours.

Over time, the selection of products and brands could be experimented with to determine the optimum mix. Shoppers will surely make suggestions. Possibly with the accumulation of profits some produce, dairy, and frozen foods equipment *might* be added and the assortments broadened.

The advantages of this type of operation are several. Little capital is needed—just enough for a cash register, baskets, a desk, supplies, and possibly a truck, with a little working capital left over. Little labor is needed, since there is no price marking, shelf stocking, bagging, repairs of equipment, and the like. This fact, together with the ability of the store to buy in case load lots, will keep costs and therefore prices down, especially if locations are well chosen. Management should be relatively easy because all transactions will be recorded and counts of inventory should be very easy to make.

The major risks will still be shoplifting, crime, and consumer disinterest. If, however, the CRFWO can be developed from some community base, a food-buying club or a CDC, and/or is operated under some form of customer ownership, and if the manager of each outlet is given a significant profit (not sales) incentive, these problems ought to be limited. In the eventuality these problems cannot be resolved, the CRFWO has the final advantage that it is very easy to liquidate!

2. A second suggestion is related to the general problem of considerable overstoring in a great many retail and service categories. As noted, this overstoring tends to reduce (or more typically eliminate) the profitability of most outlets in these categories and at the same time tends to limit the assortments, raise the prices, and reduce the services available to minority consumers. The problem here is to find a way to introduce scale economies into these overstored categories without necessarily driving any of the existing minority entrepreneurs out of business. The obvious answer would seem to be some form of *retailer cooperation.* Among the possibilities:

Cooperation in purchasing. This would have two benefits. First, pooling purchases would reduce each outlet's average merchandise cost.

Second, depending on the nature of the cooperative arrangement, it could also afford access to supplier credit heretofore unavailable.

Joint purchase of business services. Most small retailers do not use accountants or bookkeepers or have access to advice on marketing, inventory management, financing, and the like. A group of retailers in similar (even different) categories could pool their limited discretionary expense funds to acquire such services, e.g. the advice of a concerned university professor or business consultant. Even if such consultants are not hired, the businessmen in the course of discussion of such a step may learn the virtue of sharing problems and solutions with each other. It has been my experience that although, across the board, minority small businessmen (like *most* small businessmen) are not very experienced, each has one or two areas in which he is reasonably expert. Thus while business sophistication is lacking on an individual basis, collectively—if they can be brought together and stimulated to interact—the merchants possess a considerable pool of basic skills.

Cooperation in selling. Here the objective would be to combine facilities in some fashion while still maintaining the integrity of each business. The mall concept could prove a useful model here. For example, a large abandoned building such as a vacant factory could be rented by a group of dissimilar merchants who would then divide up the space with or without formal partitions, hire their own security, advertise jointly, and otherwise work collectively to bring customers into the mall, relying then on their individual skills to capture their share of trade once the customers were inside.[55] Such collectivities could also respond to the disadvantaged community's frequent desire to combine socializing with shopping by making the mall a center of community activity—amateur art displays, children's shows, dance workshops, political speeches, perhaps even rummage sales!

Each of these forms of cooperation could also be the basis for soliciting financial assistance from various federal programs, foundations, and local CDCs. The major hurdle to overcome, of course, will be in securing cooperation among the merchants in the first place. Small businessmen in general tend to be quite individualistic, and inner city people in particular seem to be highly suspicious of using any form of organization to achieve their goals, since they feel organizations have so often mistreated them in the past. This form of cooperation thus would seem most feasible if engineered by a successful, trusted indigenous business leader or some other prominent community figure who, like a Leon Sullivan, could serve as its principal salesman, inspiration, and guide until it could stand on its own feet. Alternatively, the organizational stimulus could well come from a local development group such as a Model Cities agency or a CDC. A CDC might be particularly appropriate if it were seeking to achieve some of the rationalizing ends intended in the Community Self-Determination Act without having the proposed monopoly power.

Business versus Market Development: A Paradox

This chapter began by asserting that improvements in minority market structures are inextricably bound up in the improvement of minority businesses and businessmen and then suggested several ways in which the improvement of minority businesses and businessmen could be (and in some cases is being) achieved. As a concluding note, it must be pointed out that there is considerable possibility that strategies to improve minority business prospects may become (or may be) in conflict with the goal of improving market structures for disadvantaged consumers. To assess this possibility, let us consider several goals of the minority economic development movement:

TO INCREASE THE NUMBER OF MINORITY MEMBERS IN BUSINESS. This goal in the short run may well lead to excessive focus on the small mom-and-pop outlets that minority businessmen have traditionally operated because the requirements for the capital and experience that are so scarce in the minority community are small for these businesses. Putting many blacks in such small businesses in order to show a rapid increase in minority businessmen, however, is likely not to be in the interest of inner city consumers, since it will perpetuate the small, high-cost and high-priced, overstored and understocked structural conditions of the present market. It will, of course, also not be in the interest of minority businessmen, as the failure rate in these categories is very high.

TO BUILD SIGNIFICANT ENTERPRISES THAT THE COMMUNITY CAN BE PROUD OF. With this goal the danger for consumers is that the emphasis will not be on building significant retailing and service outlets but on building significant manufacturing outlets, where employment can be high and the risks of failure *reasonably* low. And it has been this writer's experience that when minority economic planners think of building significant enterprises in the *retail* sector, they invariably think of supermarkets (often thinking they can "reduce prices for our people"). Supermarkets, as noted earlier, are in a very competitive business which exists on very small percentage profits (or, as is typical, losses.) The potential for creating another glaring case of failure and frustration for minority businessmen *and* consumers is quite high. Few development organizations seem to think of encouraging the formation of stripped-down, limited-assortment-and-frills superettes catering to low-income families or of furniture and appliance outlets, in both of which the chances for significantly reducing the amount of inner city exploitation are substantial. In both cases the business can be "significant" and the benefits to consumers substantial.

TO REDUCE THE PRESENCE AND POWER OF WHITE COLONIALIST BUSINESSMEN. Of course, the paradox of this goal is that, at least in the short run, protecting minority business will drive out or keep away those mass merchandisers—Sears, Penney, Woolworth's, A&P—which, as Sturdivant has pointed out, can significantly lower prices and give better service to minority consumers.[56]

TO GIVE MINORITY CONSUMERS MORE BUSINESSES RUN BY MEMBERS OF THEIR OWN RACE AND ETHNIC GROUP. Here the presumption is sometimes that this will make most, if not all, minority consumers happier even if it means sacrificing some assortment breadth or quality or price. While there is evidence that buying from minority-owned businesses is a consideration of perhaps one in three minority members, there is no evidence that even these more ethnically or racially conscious consumers would trade off very much quality or service for this satisfaction. Indeed, minority businessmen frequently allege that their people *prefer* to buy from "whitey." [57]

There is frequent neglect in much of the minority development rhetoric of the fact that changing the color of management in a deviant market system will not of itself necessarily do away with many of the problems that now keep prices high and businesses relatively unprofitable:

1. Street crime and violence that keep transient customers away and some minority consumers from shopping at nighttime will not disappear, although minority store owners may be somewhat more willing to take personal action or bring court action against thieves or vandals than would a white store owner, who might fear that such a response could lead to a major "incident."
2. The deteriorated condition of store premises will not improve until the capital and profit positions of most businesses improve *and* spending power in the area increases.
3. The problem of shoplifting and bad checks will probably not improve significantly until the economic condition of the families in the area improves.
4. Problems of securing motivated, hardworking, and responsible help will not abate noticeably in the short run with a change in the race of ownership, although, as noted above, the presence of more successful minority businessmen may inspire more minority youth to consider business careers and to apply themselves more assiduously to summer, part-time, and apprentice jobs in minority-owned businesses.
5. As long as minority businesses remain small, great amounts of capital are not going to "stay in the community," nor is minority political

power likely to grow substantially. One should not expect significant improvements in street repairs, street cleaning, or garbage collection because of an ownership change.

6. Exploitation will also not necessarily disappear with a change in skin color. While greater informal pressure can be brought to bear on "brothers" who exploit, it is not unreasonable to expect that a community which respects "hustling" as much as the black community does is going to produce a lot of businessmen who do just that.

Conclusion

The major hope for rationalizing the market structure in areas most heavily patronized by disadvantaged consumers is in rapid growth in the number and quality of minority enterprises. While several programs are slowly materializing and others are proposed to achieve these ends, the goals of minority business developers are not necessarily the same as those of minority consumers. Further, a change in race does not necessarily mean the elimination of several other key operating problems in inner city areas. It is thus the major recommendation of this chapter that minority business developers, particularly those CDCs given mandates over relatively wide geographic areas, be forced to consider explicitly the impact of their programs and proposals on minority consumers. As Sturdivant has noted with respect to ghetto shoppers, "Real progress will come only if we can find some way to extend into the ghettos the highly advanced, competitive retailing system that has so successfully served other sectors of the economy." [58] Marketing scholars have for a long time been saying that successful marketing enterprises start their planning with consumer needs. As suggested in this chapter, this maxim ought to be equally valid for inner city market developments.

Notes

1. Theodore L. Cross, *Black Capitalism: Strategy for Business in the Ghetto* (New York: Atheneum Publishers, 1969).
2. U.S. Bureau of the Census, *Minority-owned Business: 1969*, series MB-1 (Washington: Government Printing Office, 1971), p. 1.
3. It should be emphasized that although blacks are the dominant minority group, they own only about one-half the minority businesses.
4. U.S. Bureau of the Census, *Current Population Reports*, series P-23, no. 38, "The Social and Economic Status of Negroes in the United States, 1970" (Washington: Government Printing Office, 1971), p. 61.

5. Alan R. Andreasen, *Inner City Business: A Case Study of Buffalo, New York* (New York: Praeger Publishers, Inc., 1972), p. 91.
6. U.S. Bureau of the Census, *Current Population Reports*, p. 59.
7. St. Clair Drake and Horace R. Cayton, *Black Metropolis: A Study of Negro Life in a Northern City*, vol. II (New York: Harper & Row, Publishers, 1945), p. 453.
8. Edward H. Jones, *Blacks in Business* (New York: Grossett & Dunlap, Inc., 1971).
9. *Ibid.*
10. Drake and Cayton, *op. cit.*, p. 448.
11. Robert W. Hodge and Patricia Hodge, "Occupational Assimilation as a Competitive Process," *American Journal of Sociology*, vol. 71, no. 3, November 1965, p. 251.
12. Norval D. Glenn, "Occupational Benefits to Whites from the Subordination of Negroes," *American Sociological Review*, vol. 28, June 1963, pp. 447–8.
13. David Caplovitz, *The Poor Pay More* (New York: The Free Press, 1967), p. 19.
14. *Ibid.*
15. *Ibid.*, p. 29.
16. Drake and Cayton, *op. cit.*, p. 453.
17. Caplovitz, *op. cit.*, p. 17.
18. Donald Marion and Charles Goodman, "Operating Problems of Marketing Firms in Low-Income Areas," in Alan R. Andreasen (ed.), *Improving Inner-City Marketing* (Chicago: American Marketing Association, 1972); and Federal Trade Commission, *Economic Report on Installment Credit and Retail Sales Practices of District of Columbia Retailers* (Washington: Superintendent of Documents, March 1968).
19. Andreasen, *Inner City Business*, p. 173.
20. Harry L. Davis and Wilford L. White, "Finding, Motivating, and Training Entrepreneurs and Managers for Inner City Businesses," in Andreasen, *Improving Inner-City Marketing*, p. 212.
21. Nathan Glazer and Daniel P. Moynihan, *Beyond the Melting Pot* (Cambridge, Mass. M.I.T. Press and Harvard University Press, 1963), p. 33.
22. Drake and Cayton, *op. cit.*, p. 439.
23. Andreasen, *Inner City Business*, pp. 99–101.
24. Davis and White, *op. cit.*, pp. 220–2.
25. Thomas J. Bray, "Black Executives Face Many Special Problems," in Editors of the Wall Street Journal, *Business and Blacks* (Princeton, N.J.: Dow Jones Books, 1970), p. 122.
26. Jones, *op. cit.*, pp. 106–7.
27. Andreasen, *Inner City Business*, p. 65.
28. Cross, *op. cit.*

29. Robert Little and Thaddeus Spratlen, "Alternative Forms of Ownership for Inner City Business," in Andreasen, *Improving Inner-City Marketing,* pp. 179–204.
30. For excellent discussions of alternative ownership programs and of community academic development in general, see *Law and Contemporary Problems,* vol. 36, no. 1, Winter 1970–71, and no. 2, Spring 1971.
31. Little and Spratlen, *op. cit.,* p. 187.
32. Roger Dickinson, "Franchising and the Inner City," unpublished paper, Rutgers University, 1970.
33. U.S. Department of Commerce, *Franchise Company Data for Equal Opportunity in Business* (Washington: Business and Defense Services Administration, U.S. Department of Commerce, 1967).
34. Little and Spratlen, *op. cit.,* p. 187.
35. Frederick D. Sturdivant, "The Limits of Black Capitalism," *Harvard Business Review,* January–February 1969, pp. 122–8.
36. *Ibid.*
37. See almost any issue of U.S. Department of Commerce, *OMBE Outlook.*
38. David Madway, "Minority Enterprise Financing: Mired or Moving," *Review of Black Political Economy,* vol. 3, no. 3, Spring 1973, pp. 87–93.
39. Roy Innis, "Separatist Economics: A New Social Contract," in William F. Haddad and G. Douglas Pugh (eds.), *Black Economic Development* (Englewood Cliffs, N.J.: Prentice–Hall, Inc., 1969), p. 52.
40. John McClaughery, "Black Ownership and National Politics," in Haddad and Pugh, *op. cit.,* pp. 38–49.
41. Frank G. Davis, *The Economics of Black Community Development* (New York: Markham Publishing Company, 1972), p. 142.
42. Sturdivant, *op. cit.*
43. *Ibid.*
44. Perhaps the best argument here is made by Davis, *op. cit.*
45. Jerry Cromwell and Peter Merrill, "Minority Business Performance and the Community Development Corporation," *Review of Black Political Economy,* vol. 3, no. 3, Spring 1973, p. 78.
46. Barry A. Stein, "How Successful are CDCs? An Interim Response," *Review of Black Political Economy,* vol. 3, no. 3, Spring 1973, p. 98.
47. Cromwell and Merrill, *op. cit.,* p. 78.
48. *Ibid.,* p. 77.
49. William E. Cox, Jr., "A Commercial Structure Model for Depressed Neighborhoods," *Journal of Marketing,* vol. 33, no. 3, July 1969, pp. 1–9.
50. Brian J. L. Berry, et al., *Commercial Structure and Commercial Blight,* Department of Geography Research Paper no. 85 (Chicago: University of Chicago, 1963).
51. George H. Haines, Leonard S. Simon, and Marcus Alexis, "Maximum Likelihood Estimation of Central-City Food Trading Areas," *Journal of Marketing Research,* vol. 9, May 1972, pp. 154–9.

52. For example, as noted in Chapter 6, the model takes relatively little account of the racial characteristics of his area 13.
53. Donald E. Sexton, Jr., *Groceries in the Ghetto* (Lexington, Mass.: Lexington Books, 1973).
54. Howard Aldrich and Albert J. Reiss, Jr., "Continuities in the Study of Ecological Succession: Changes in the Race Composition of Neighborhoods and Their Businesses," paper presented at the American Sociological Association, August 1974.
55. This, of course, is the approach of early department stores and many present discount houses.
56. Sturdivant, *op. cit.*
57. Drake and Cayton, *op. cit.*, pp. 439–43.
58. Frederick D. Sturdivant, "Better Deal for Ghetto Shoppers," *Harvard Business Review*, March–April 1968, p. 136.

12. Preventing Merchant Exploitation

The solutions proposed in the preceding two chapters, increasing consumer self-reliance and improving market structures in disadvantaged areas, will have important effects in limiting merchant exploitation. Indeed, in the long run, making the market mechanism more competitive will prove a more effective check on the shady marketer than any number of extramarket pressures. Still, as also suggested in these preceding chapters, the necessary improvement in competitive forces is a long way off if it is ever realistically achievable. Thus, at least in the short run, there is a serious need for more effective programs to cut down the exploitative practices facing disadvantaged consumers.

Such programs, which are the principle focus of this chapter, come from two related sources: from the passage of *laws* and *regulations* prohibiting specific practices and from the actions of *agencies*, both governmental and nongovernmental, which try to enforce the given laws and regulations. However, since the general nature of *existing* laws was considered in Chapter 9, the discussion of laws and regulations in this chapter will be focused on proposed *changes* in legislation. And since the results of these proposed changes depend in great measure on the effectiveness of existing regulatory and coordinating agencies, the chapter will begin with an evaluation of these agencies.

Agencies of Consumer Protection

There are four basic types of agencies concerned with the prevention of merchant exploitation. These types are distinguished by their basic functions:

1. *The Self-regulatory agencies.* These are the business associations that seek to police the actions of their own members.

2. *The judicial agencies.* These are the lawyers, judges, and court systems that seek to bring exploitative merchants to justice through private litigation.
3. *The government prosecutorial agencies.* These include the state and federal attorneys general as well as various state and local consumer protection agencies which seek to dispense consumer information, mediate disputes, or bring court action against exploitative merchants on behalf of the general public.
4. *The government regulatory agencies.* These include federal, state, and local agencies given responsibilities for regulating certain practices (e.g., the Federal Trade Commission and local departments of weights and measures) or for regulating certain industries (e.g., the Food and Drug Administration and Consumer Product Safety Commission).

As noted below in the discussion of the FTC, there is often some overlap between groups 3 and 4.

BUSINESS SELF-REGULATION

There are many business agencies and associations that have taken upon themselves a self-regulatory function. Most trade associations have codes of ethics for their members, which they seek to uphold through their powers of withholding membership. Radio and television stations subscribe to the codes of the National Association of Broadcasters. Individual media such as the *New York Times* have detailed guidelines as to acceptable practices to which they hold their advertisers.[1] More significantly, as a result of the growing interest in consumerism, a substantial number of manufacturers have established consumer affairs departments at the executive level and have "cool lines" to service complaints made directly by consumers about their specific products. Several industries have recently established complaint-handling procedures for disputes between industry members and consumers. Among such programs are the Furniture Industry Consumer Action Panel, Major Appliance Consumer Action Panel, Automobile Industry Consumer Action Panel, and Carpet and Rug Institute Consumer Action Panel.

It is unlikely, however, that most disadvantaged consumers will be aware of the possible help they could get from these sources, with the possible exception of the manufacturers' "cool lines," since they are not all that well known and it is not always known how one lodges a complaint through them. The agency most disadvantaged consumers seem to think of first is the local Better Business Bureau.[2]

THE BETTER BUSINESS BUREAU

The Better Business Bureau in local communities is "an independent agency of business, organized as a nonprofit corporation which is financed entirely by membership dues or subscriptions voluntarily paid to it by responsible business and professional firms." [3] The Bureau thus is clearly first and foremost an arm of business, and, until very recently its activities in the consumer protection area, while sometimes effective, tended more to be like those of "a businessman's protective association often syphoning off consumer complaints that would be better directed to other agencies." [4]

The BBB carries out six major activities impinging on consumer interests:

1. Providing information prior to purchase
2. Helping to adjust "misunderstandings" or to pass on to sellers complaints after purchase
3. Promulgating and administering advertising standards
4. Where both advertising and selling abuses are involved and voluntary compliance has not worked, requesting action at state, federal, and local levels where appropriate
5. Lobbying against most consumer protection legislation
6. Carrying out consumer education by distributing booklets and producing radio and television spots describing major frauds and suggesting dos and don'ts for consumers

In cases of suspected exploitation, the Bureau has no power to require resolution of differences. It must rely on suasion, where its two principal tools are the threat of withdrawal of membership (which the exploiting firm may be boasting about in its advertising or on its premises) and the threat of subjecting the firm to "the pitiless glare of publicity" in its monthly consumer brochure or in its releases to the general media. If the case is serious enough to warrant the latter, the BBB may also threaten to send the complaint on to a federal or local agency with more power. The Bureau claims, however, that stronger action is seldom necessary, that from 50% to 90% of consumer complaints are merely "misunderstandings" which are quickly cleared up once the seller is informed of the nature of the complaint—and is aware of the involvement of the Bureau. (This is a claim frequently heard in the consumer protection field—that the involvement of a third party, e.g., state consumer protection agency or a private lawyer, leads to speedy disposition of problems as "misunderstandings.")

Criticism of the bureau. In 1971, the Bureau came under a great deal of criticism in a study commissioned by Congressman Benjamin S. Rosenthal. The study concluded that although the BBB handled as many as 8 million complaints a year in only 139 offices, "BBB services are of little value to the buying public. In some instances, their efforts actually have a counter-productive impact on the consumer." [5] Specifically, Congressman Rosenthal made the following criticisms:

1. "Local Bureaus are trapped in an almost insurmountable conflict-of-interest between service to consumers, on the one hand, and financial dependence on business, on the other. By every objective standard BBBs serve as the agents of the business community and reflect all the biases of that community. . . ."
2. Bureaus do not expel offending or clearly unethical members.
3. Telephone reports prior to purchase are "misleading, inaccurate, incomplete and couched in vague generalities." For example, in a small study Rosenthal's staff telephoned BBBs in four cities for reports on 25 firms against which a federal, state, or local agency had recently taken enforcement action. The study found only *one* instance where any government action was mentioned and only three other instances where the firm was the subject of critical reports.
4. The Bureau's complaint adjustment procedure is successful only when issues are not controversial.
5. The Bureau's frequent claims of high rates of success are due to excessive reliance on the seller's report of successful adjudication of a complaint and the "negative option" consumer reporting plan, which allows the Bureau to believe that a complaint has been settled satisfactorily if the consumer does *not* contact it again or reply to the Bureau's follow-up inquiry.
6. Bureaus "lack aggressiveness and initiative" in sending serious complaints on to federal, state, or local agencies, although *when asked* they do tend to cooperate "fully and freely."
7. Despite their claim to be a consumer protection agency, "BBBs frequently oppose the enactment of new consumer protection laws and . . . often work behind the scenes to defeat such legislation."
8. Despite their claims to be consumer educators, ". . . [most] of the best BBB literature concerning abusive marketplace practices, including the names of offending firms, is circulated only to the BBB membership and not to the public-at-large." [6]

The BBB has responded aggressively in recent months to these criticisms. It has sought to improve its complaint-handling procedures. It has begun establishing a major national data bank on consumer frauds and has begun establishing arbitration panels in several communities. The latter is perhaps the most promising initiative, but it is still based on the BBB's unwillingness to take a strong stand against its members, which it asks only to *volunteer* to be bound by such arbitration. In the New York metropolitan area, 1,361 companies have agreed to settle disputes by BBB arbitration. Disputes arbitrated by the 364 volunteer arbitrators are, under a revision in the New York Commercial Code, enforceable in the State Supreme Court.[7] Despite such advances it is still highly questionable whether an agency sponsored by business and requiring voluntary cooperation from its members can ever be effective in dealing with the worst offenders in disadvantaged areas, many of whom do not belong to BBBs. Indeed, a recent study has indicated that even among traditional members the Bureau has failed to gain widespread support for voluntary arbitration.[8]

Suggestions for improvement in the BBB's effectiveness will be considered later in this chapter.

THE NEXT STEP

If a consumer cannot secure satisfaction through informal intervention by the BBB, his next course of action would be to have a formal complaint brought. Here the alternatives are to bring a private action or to ask an agency at some level of government to take the necessary action. A number of issues of fact and objectives will determine which is the best choice:

1. How much money can be spent? If little or none, private litigation is impossible unless (*a*) the amount at issue is below the *maximum* of local small claims courts or (*b*) a class of consumers with identical complaints can be formed to bring suit.
2. Is the seller in some way involved in interstate commerce? If not, it may be impossible to secure action by a federal agency.
3. What outcome of the litigation process does the consumer desire? Does he wish (*a*) to have the seller punished, (*b*) to have some practice of his stopped, (*c*) to receive some compensation for personal loss, or (*d*) some combination of the above? If damages are sought by the consumer for himself, they can only be secured by private litigation although having a successfully prosecuted government case (e.g., an antitrust conviction) as a precedent will greatly improve chances of success and can reduce some of the costs of a private suit.
4. What kinds of laws seem to have been violated? For instance, can the customer prove *intent* to deceive, in which case a proceeding under criminal fraud statutes can be brought privately or by a city or state district attorney? If not, a state or local consumer protection agency is probably the preferred prosecutor.

THE JUDICIAL AGENCIES: PRIVATE LITIGATION

If the disadvantaged consumer seeks corrective action in his specific case and/or if he wants damages, then he may consider private litigation. Here there are two major alternatives: personal litigation in *small claims court*, usually without the help of a lawyer, or litigation with the help of a lawyer in regular civil or criminal courts. We shall consider each of these approaches in turn.

SMALL CLAIMS COURT. As of October 1971 all but three states (Colorado, Indiana, and Nebraska) had available some form of small claims court to which consumers could bring suits against merchants for maximum amounts ranging from $200 to $1,500 depending on the state. Fees for initiating such an action range from $2 to $15 (recoverable if the consumer wins).[9] Proceedings except in four states are informal; both sides state their case in plain language, rules of evidence are quite relaxed, and lawyers are not required. Trials are scheduled quickly and decisions usually rendered on the spot.

In the past, small claims courts have served primarily as collection agencies for sellers. However, when consumers do bring action, the odds of success seem to favor them. In a 1971 study Consumers Union found that only 14% of the 153 cases it reviewed were actually decided against the consumer, and two out of three of those responding to CU's mail questionnaire said that the suit, whether settled in or out of court, had turned out in their favor.[10] There are apparently additional psychological and educational benefits for some litigants. As one obviously middle-class respondent put it: "People should take the trouble to sue in small claims court. I found it a very educational experience. It gave me an opportunity to actually use my government. . . . Since I had to initiate and prepare the case myself, I now know the necessary procedures if the need should arise again." [11] The typical finding from several studies is that involvement in small claims courts is a satisfying process.[12]

Despite this apparent ease and simplicity, there are a number of defects in small claims court processes which may make the outcome less desirable from the disadvantaged consumer's standpoint:

1. In all but six states the seller or finance company can bring its lawyer into court if it wishes to. It is often the case that disadvantaged consumers feel themselves at a distinct disadvantage when facing a lawyer, a problem that would be less likely to bother a more educated and sophisticated consumer.
2. In all but six states the seller or finance company can appeal a judgment against it to a higher court, where additional time is involved for the consumer and where the proceedings are *not* informal and being without a lawyer is a serious disadvantage.
3. In 27 states the maximum allowable claim is $300 or less. This often precludes many of the claims of the disadvantaged (e.g., in automobile sales, one of the two largest sources of deception as noted in Table 9-3) or requires them to scale their claims down to meet the courts' maximums.

4. Securing a judgment does not always mean that the consumer can collect. In 62 of the cases Consumers Union studied where the consumer prevailed, 13, or about one in five, judgments were uncollectable. As CU put it: "The court machinery for enforcing a judgment —usually a writ of execution against the defendant's property, his bank account or his wages—is not always effective. It probably won't help if the firm you've sued is bankrupt or if a tradesman leaves town or conceals his assets." [13]
5. In some states it is often very inconvenient to use small claims courts; they are often located only in the county seat and often are not open nights or weekends. Thus a disadvantaged consumer must not only risk the filing fee in the hope of winning, he often must also risk a half or whole day's wages. And the latter are not typically recoverable in the event he wins.

In sum, the small claims court is potentially a very useful vehicle for the disadvantaged consumer, and in some areas, such as Harlem, it actually is. In the main, however, the conclusion most observers have drawn is that "by and large the small claims court has not given poor people the ability to use the law and the courts affirmatively." [14]

Typically, there are several barriers the disadvantaged consumer faces. There are the knowledge barriers—not knowing of the existence of the court or of the procedures for filing suit. There are the monetary barriers of fees and lost wages. But, perhaps most importantly for the disadvantaged, there are the almost overwhelming psychological barriers:

1. There is the need to fill out forms. Although clerks of the court can be of assistance, one wonders how many of the disadvantaged have been deterred by knowing they must fill out a legal document on their own. Having learned from television and from others' troubles with financial agreements, leases, and the like that the *wording* of documents is very important, they may simply feel overwhelmed at the prospect of filing a complaint.
2. There is the need usually to go downtown to the courthouse. Most of the disadvantaged undoubtedly have strong negative feelings about appearing in court. As noted earlier, the disadvantaged are more likely than the nondisadvantaged to have been to court before in less favorable circumstances—as a defendant, as a witness, or merely to support a friend or relative. They may even have been to small claims court before as a defendant in a default suit brought by a seller. Even if they don't already have negative feelings, the formal, imposing surroundings of the courthouse may be sufficiently intimidating, even if the small claims hearing itself is described to them as "informal."
3. If they can conceive of themselves at least getting into the courtroom, disadvantaged consumers must imagine themselves pleading their own cases, possibly against a lawyer for the seller. Again the

prospect must be quite intimidating for those who have little education or have difficulty with the language. And even for those who do not have such problems, many of the disadvantaged must feel they will have to perform like a Perry Mason or an Owen Marshall in order to win or, even worse, feel they will *face* a Perry Mason or an Owen Marshall in their courtroom encounter. And the latter are lawyers who always win by cleverly tripping up confused witnesses such as the disadvantaged see themselves to be. And, of course, Mason and Marshall never lose a case.

4. Then there are the psychological barriers of facing an accusing creditor, a problem the disadvantaged would face even in other courts than small claims and even if they had their own legal counsel. How many of the disadvantaged feel they might really be better off not attacking a creditor? How many feel that doing so would cut off their supply of credit (forever?), that it would bring down upon them all sorts of imagined extra penalties (repossession of household goods, loss of job, garnishment of wages, and/or public humiliation), and that the court, which has often seemed to be the seller's agent in other encounters, will support the creditor in these punitive actions?
5. Finally, many of the disadvantaged will feel, apparently contrary to fact, that no matter how well they present their case, the odds of winning are definitely against *people like them*.

For all these economic and psychological reasons, it is not surprising that Caplovitz found that only 3% of his public housing residents said they would go to the small claims court if they were being cheated by a merchant.[15]

USE OF A LAWYER. If a disadvantaged consumer is unwilling, as seems likely, to try to press his own case or if, on the other hand, he finds himself a defendant in an action brought by a seller or a finance company, whether in small claims court or not, he may consider turning to a lawyer for help. Three sources of legal advice are available in most disadvantaged areas: private attorneys, legal aid societies, and neighborhood legal service projects such as those of the Office of Economic Opportunity. The major difficulty in using private attorneys is, of course, their cost. Bar association minimum fees for civil cases are on the order of $25 an hour for preparing a brief, $50 for a pretrial conference, and $200 for each day in court. This is not to say that such fees, or even any fees, are always charged. More and more major law firms are willing to free a significant percentage of the time of their junior partners and articling lawyers to offer no-fee or low-fee legal counseling to the poor.[16] However, the extent to which bright young law school graduates are demanding such opportunities for outside social involvement seems to ebb and flow with the job market and other external influences.

An alternative system for providing free legal services to the poor through private lawyers is the Judicare system now being tested in upper Wisconsin and northwestern Montana.[17] Under Judicare, a poor consumer eligible for the program merely contacts a private lawyer of his choice, who, if he takes the case, is paid by public funds at a rate between 50% and 75% of minimum state bar fees. Initial evaluation of the program by poor clients has been quite favorable, apparently principally because it offers poor consumers a *choice* of lawyers who are usually *from the local community* and who appear to be quite *experienced*.[18] There is, however, considerable present public opposition to Judicare from those who prefer the staffed office model such as that of OEO Legal Services.

In cases where the disadvantaged turn to private counsel, it is not always the case that a fee *need* be charged. If the buyer's needs are relatively simple —e.g., to get his refrigerator repaired or replaced or to get a default action dropped—a lawyer may settle the matter for little or no fee by merely contacting the seller or his lawyer directly. As Ray Narral, a lawyer working for New York City's Mobilization for Youth Legal Services Unit, notes with respect to default cases:

> When the plaintiff learns that the buyer intends to defend the case against him, in 95% of our cases he offers to settle for much less than the contract price. A seller or a finance company depends on being able to move against defendants and obtain default judgments and immediate income execution without opposition. Plaintiffs will settle in the face of even slight pressure, because it is cheaper than prosecuting in court.[19]

As an alternative to private attorneys, Legal Aid is not particularly helpful if the disadvantaged consumer wishes to sue the seller. In the past, Legal Aid offices were funded primarily by broad-based charities such as the United Fund. As a consequence they were usually reluctant to take plaintiff cases, although some would do so if as many as three complaints had been brought to them about the same merchant. On the other hand, Legal Aid *would* defend consumers brought to court by the seller or finance company in consumer matters. Now that some Legal Aid programs have been brought under OEO, one might expect more plaintiff actions. However, a major problem with Legal Aid is still that it typically has very limited staff and budgets. A secondary problem is that it imposes an income ceiling on clients, although when Legal Aid offices have staff, some will remove the income ceiling when the amounts involved in the case are clearly exceeded by legal fees.

Barring the use of private attorneys or Legal Aid, the final alternative available to many disadvantaged consumers is the neighborhood Legal Services Program of the Office of Economic Opportunity. Begun with a modest budget of $4 million in 1964, the OEO Legal Services Program (LSP) in 1971 was operating at a level of over $75 million, handling over 1.19 million new cases annually out of 616 offices.[20]

The OEO program is based on the concept of central offices staffed by full-time lawyers to whom consumers can bring their problems. Staff lawyers are paid on a salary rather than a fee basis and so theoretically can spend as much time on each case as it needs. The salaried staff concept was planned to attract lawyers who were more committed to the poor and their problems (than, say, private lawyers under the Judicare program) and who might also be able to establish better rapport with the poor and thereby have more effect. They also would be more likely to bring so-called impact cases that could make major changes in the social system engulfing and stifling the disadvantaged. Finally, the staff office system could provide legal services at a much lower per case cost to the public than, say, Judicare.

Unfortunately, LSP has had a very checkered career and has had difficulty meeting these goals. Despite its large budget and despite its very considerable growth in output, LSP offices can nowhere meet the demand for their services. Thus cases usually do not get adequate attention and the poor often feel frustrated by delays and apparent neglect of their problems. Further, having "committed" lawyers usually means having young lawyers, and as Brakel notes, ". . . clients often view staff lawyers as something less than 'real lawyers.' "[21] On the other hand, its "impact program," which really makes LSP more of an agency for social change than lawyers for the indigent (as is the emphasis under Judicare), has had more success. LSP impact offices have induced major reforms in both landlord–tenant and welfare law. Unfortunately, it is just this social activism that has put the program in hot water with state and local politicians who were often the targets of impact litigation. Pressure from state politicians has always made annual congressional hearings on OEO operations very difficult for OEO, which always fought back until 1972, when pressures were exerted to bring LSP offices under local control. Whether the program concept will survive at its present level of aggressiveness, or indeed survive at all, is thus now problematic. While highly effective despite limited funding, the program has proved too aggressive for the current federal administration, and at the time of writing the Legal Services Program is in great danger of being dismantled.

This is a most distressing prospect in that a major problem with private litigation as a means of consumer protection has been poor people's ignorance and fear of what the legal system could do for them (or *to* them). More often the *victims* of the legal system, especially in consumer matters, they are reluctant to believe the system can work for them, a belief that is reinforced by their general sense of powerlessness. As Ray Narral states:

> But the most important impact a legal services unit can make on the community is to convince the poor that the law is not always on the side of the rich. When a client is extricated from an unfair and unjust sales agreement or garnishment he and his neighbors feel a greater respect for our legal system, for themselves and for the larger society of which they are a part.[22]

Without OEO and without rapid expansion of Judicare, it would appear that private litigation is very unlikely to prove a significant avenue for controlling exploitative merchants. The only remaining major proposal now being discussed that offers some hope for reversing this situation is widespread class action legislation that would allow consumers with similar complaints to bind themselves together for purposes of bringing an action. This proposal will be discussed in some detail later in this chapter.

STATE AND LOCAL PROSECUTORIAL AGENCIES

Even if the consumer acts on his own behalf, this does not assure that the offending practice will be stopped or that the seller or finance company will be punished. To achieve this end, the next logical step would be to turn to the government, which government depending on the nature of the complaint and whether the seller's business was or was not in interstate commerce. At the state and local level, the consumer's first reaction might be to seek out a district attorney's office. In many states, he will soon discover that the office gives consumer complaints very low priority. Many district attorneys simply do not see consumer problems as very serious, taking the view that they only have limited resources to deal with much more serious crimes such as murder, armed robbery, and the like.[23]

Should the district attorney choose not to prosecute (although like the private lawyer he may try to help by contacting the merchant in question), in some states the defrauded consumer can force the matter, although he will face a time-consuming process. He must first file a criminal complaint with a justice of the peace. If the justice believes the case has merit, the consumer will have to pay for a private warrant and appear for a preliminary hearing before a justice of the peace. There will next be a grand jury hearing, and then, if the action proceeds, the district attorney will have to take over the prosecution and the consumer will have to appear as witness. It goes without saying that the fearlessness, sophistication, money, and time required to take these steps are possessed by very few individuals, disadvantaged or not.

STATE CONSUMER PROTECTION AGENCIES

A growing number of states, and some cities, have recognized the fact that local district attorneys will not have the time, resources, or inclination to try to cope with the problem of merchant exploitation and have established consumer protection agencies, sometimes within the state attorney general's office. The first of these state agencies to have been formed, and now one of the more effective, is the New York State Bureau of Consumer

Frauds and Protection, founded by State Attorney General Louis Lefkowitz in 1959. This agency, which has been a prototype for many others, takes informal action to remedy consumer complaints and brings court actions under various New York State consumer statutes in serious cases or where complaints are frequent. In addition to such direct actions, state agencies can:

1. Hold conferences with industries about the industries' efforts to combat deceptive advertising and selling practices.
2. Work jointly with industries in drafting codes of ethics.
3. Serve as a clearinghouse for information on consumer fraud, collecting data on local frauds from local agencies and making such information available statewide through bulletins so as to trap deceiving sellers who switch counties just as prosecution is imminent.
4. Counsel county district attorneys and private attorneys as to "legal theories and approaches that may be used in dealing with business firms which have improper business practices." [24]
5. Train local law enforcement officers in the detection and prosecution of defrauding merchants.
6. Assist in developing and carrying out consumer education.
7. Propose and lobby for needed state legislation in the consumer protection area.
8. Advise the governor on consumer protection matters generally.

The problem with state consumer agencies is that while they significantly increase consumer access to advice and prosecutorial assistance, this fact itself and the state's willingness to publicize it have meant that requests for assistance consistently outrun the agency's quantity of staff and funding. For example, the New Jersey Office of Consumer Protection between 1968 and mid-1971 had received a total of 36,500 complaints yet at the end of the period still had a current backlog of 7,120 complaints. According to a recent study, the New Jersey office had other serious problems, which are probably not atypical of consumer protection agencies:

1. *Deterrence*: The formal actions initiated by the Office have been infrequent and unpredictable, despite abundant evidence of deception and fraud. [Between 1967 and mid-1971 the office held fewer than 100 administrative hearings and brought only 53 court actions despite over 36,000 complaints.] The chances are slight that a merchant who practices deception will be prosecuted by the Office.
2. *Restitution*: When the Office believes a consumer has been deceived by a merchant and deserves restitution, it may attempt to persuade the merchant to restore money to the consumer voluntarily, or it may seek a restitution order from Superior Court. Both approaches have proved to be unsatisfactory. Negotiating with merchants rarely results in voluntary restitution if the merchant is engaged in widespread deception or if

> the amount of money involved is large. . . . The other alternative, Supreme Court action is rarely sought by the Office. On these few occasions it has proved to be exceedingly time-consuming. . . .
>
> 3. *Consumer Education*: . . . [This] responsibility is one the Office is capable of executing well.
>
> In sum, New Jersey consumers have been short-changed by state government. They have not been served well by the legislature, which has repeatedly rejected tough new measures. . . . At the same time, it has denied the executive branch adequate funds to enforce the consumer laws now on the books. . . . These failures are particularly dismaying because consumers have no other place to go for protection.[25]

In some areas, state and local protection agencies have been very vigorous. For example, New York City's Department of Consumer Affairs has been exceedingly active and in recent months has caused passage of municipal laws mandating unit pricing of food and price posting of the 150 best-selling prescription drugs in pharmacies.[26] However, not all areas are covered by consumer protection agencies of any kind, and most of those agencies that do exist are badly understaffed. A 1973 study by the National Association of Attorneys General showed that only 40 states plus the Virgin Islands had consumer protection agencies under their attorneys general. And of these agencies, only 14 had more than *five* full-time lawyers or investigators.

Besides funding and staffing problems, there is a further question of whether these agencies, usually centered in state capitals, can be truly effective in reaching consumers in disadvantaged areas of urban centers. Do the disadvantaged know such agencies exist, and if so, do they believe that the agencies can be effective in helping them? Given the New Jersey experience and the disadvantaged consumer's general distrust of governmental agencies, it is entirely possible that in most states the answer to both questions is likely to be no.

Finally, there is the question of whether a state or local consumer protection agency even with very vigorous leadership and imaginative investigators and prosecutorial strategies can outwit the system and the merchants who can use it so well. A case in point is the New York City Department of Consumer Affairs under Philip Schrag. After 15 months of trying very creatively to implement a consumer statute that he wrote, Schrag concluded in disappointment that "we were having little discernible impact on the level of consumer fraud in New York." [27] Despite impressive convictions and growing abilities to use undercover investigative methods, raw political and social pressure and related techniques to achieve desired ends outside the courtroom, Schrag felt he was handicapped in four distinct ways:

1. New York City consumers, especially the disadvantaged, did not know when they were deceived; cases often came up just by chance or by referral from other agencies.

2. Consumers who knew they had problems didn't complain to the department. Again the problem was most serious with the disadvantaged: ". . . whether out of lack of information about the Department, cynicism about its effectiveness, or preoccupation with other types of problems, minority group victims rarely brought us their grievances." [28]
3. The time and manpower necessary to resolve each case was considerably more than expected; typically these problems were the result of bureaucratic squabbles *within* the city government as well as a function of the skills in delaying and frustrating normal court procedures employed by defendants and their counsel. As Schrag notes ironically, "Only when we avoided going to court were we able to achieve results before the complainants forgot that they had complained." [29]
4. Merchants were never intimidated by the threat of litigation; they expected the court procedure to be long and costly to the prosecuting agency; they expected to rarely have to pay prosecuting costs or refund much to consumers; and they often had lawyers on full-time retainer to keep their own costs of litigation down.

On a cost/benefit basis, Schrag concludes that governmental prosecutorial agencies should concentrate only on the most serious frauds. In addition to advocating increased educational programs to forewarn consumers and licensing and business self-regulation to prevent specific practices, Schrag suggests that improvement in the consumer's lot on a broad scale is most likely to come from extended class action legislation (discussed below) and "neighborhood tribunals." The latter idea, not unlike the Swedish system utilizing a Public Complaints Board,[30] envisions a local arbitration system where consumers could bring suits on modest claims using simplified informal legal procedures. In this sense the proposal is for a local consumer small claims courts, and thus one must watch out for the problems of inaccessibility, excessive formality, and the like found in existing small claims court systems.

FEDERAL, STATE, AND LOCAL REGULATORY AGENCIES

There are a great many federal, state, and local agencies which have regulatory responsibility for specific products or services, specific sets of practices, or specific industries and which can accomplish a good deal to protect disadvantaged consumers. Such agencies would include state and local licensing agencies, state and federal departments of agriculture, state banking and insurance commissions, and agencies regulating public utilities, airlines, common carrriers, sales of stocks and bonds, and the like. The difficulty here is that with the existence of these agencies and the procedures for bringing their powers to bear on consumer problems are known only to a very few of the most sophisticated consumers. They are certainly not very accessible to the disadvantaged consumer. Perhaps one major exception is the Federal Trade Commission.[31]

THE FEDERAL TRADE COMMISSION. The Federal Trade Commission is the *federal* agency most consumers think of turning to for protection against exploitation. The FTC has perhaps the broadest mandate of any agency in the country to deal with market exploitation. This mandate is contained in the key phrase of the Federal Trade Commission Act of 1914 (as amended in 1938 by the Wheeler–Lea amendment), contained in Section 5, which states that "unfair methods of competition in commerce, and unfair or deceptive acts or practices in commerce are hereby declared unlawful."

The strength of the act as amended is that it does not require the Commission to prove either *intent* on the part of the perpetrator of some deceptive act or *injury to competition* before it can bring action to stop the exploitative practice. The FTC need not bother with intent or injury (although it can) and need only show that some statement, advertisement, or other marketing tactic has the tendency to be unfair or could deceive some consumers. A final advantage is that the act does not proscribe specific practices (e.g., bait and switch or referral sales) as is the case in many state statutes, but leaves the Commission to determine for itself what is unfair and deceptive, a strong feature for legislation in areas where offenders are noted for the speed with which they change tactics.

Given such a broad mandate, one would expect the FTC to be in the vanguard of efforts to protect disadvantaged consumers. That some members of the Commission have felt that it does have such a responsibility is indicated in the remarks of FTC Commissioner Mary Gardiner Jones:

> Surely, no other responsibility of the Federal Trade Commission in the field of deception has any greater importance or public interest than that of ferreting out those deceptions practiced by the quacks and swindlers who specialize in every conceivable device to induce the poor to their doors, to coerce them into making unwanted purchases and to sign them up to long-term credit arrangements which leave them forever at the mercy of their debtors with little hope of ever extricating themselves from the pyramiding tentacles of debt in which they find themselves.[32]

Again, she has said:

> . . . the Federal Trade Commission is perhaps the sole agency which has the stature, the power and the expertise to study in depth all of the various facets of the purchasing problems affecting the low-income consumer and to come up with a comprehensive program which must be undertaken in order to win, on a lasting basis, this aspect of the Nation's war against poverty.[33]

Despite this obvious potential, the FTC has been a considerable disappointment to consumer activists in combating problems in disadvantaged areas. To understand why this is so requires a brief accounting of recent FTC history.

Until 1969 the FTC was an agency subject to the ills of most federal regulatory agencies. As detailed in damning reports by associates of Ralph Nader[34] and the American Bar Association[35] in 1969, the FTC:

Was weak on priority setting and long-range planning.

Catered to influences from those it regulated (often by default—consumers did not participate) and Congress.

Was overly influenced by its mailbag, which tended to have a distinctly middle-class bias.

Was slow and ponderous in processing complaints and taking action.

Only succeeded in halting practices (often long after they had been withdrawn in the normal course of competitive dynamics) without really restoring competition to where it was before the deceptions.

As a direct result of these two reports, major changes in the leadership and performance of the FTC were instituted beginning in 1970. First, after a brief interim period of organizational restructuring under Caspar Wienberger, the chairmanship was given to Miles Kirkpatrick, the director of the highly critical ABA study. Under Chairman Kirkpatrick a number of reforms were initiated:

Organizational changes were made and procedures established to try to undertake long-range planning and priority setting within the agency.

Proceedings were made more open to public participation and review.

Imaginative new stratagems were developed to restore competitive conditions after deception, including the corrective-advertising program, which required firms to devote a specific percentages of future advertising to correcting deceptive statements made in the past.[36]

The agency moved more aggressively into areas which could have profound effects on basic market performance:

1. A program was developed to require advertisers to substantiate questionable advertising claims to the FTC.
2. Rules were proposed and cases brought to hearing in a number of new areas attacking practices injurious to consumers, including door-to-door selling, "holder in due course," negative option plans,[37] debt collection agencies, vocational schools, gasoline octane ratings, and advertising of specials.

Despite this great change in emphasis at the Commission, it remains true that its impact on ghetto consumer problems is minimal. As noted in the ABA report, there are two basic reasons for this, both inherent in the basic powers of the agency:

First, there is the problem of inherent tactical limitations. The basic objective of the FTC's day-to-day administrative actions has traditionally been to *stop* unfair and deceptive trade practices. To achieve this end, Commission officers have five basic approaches ranging from relatively little to relatively great coercion:

1. Securing informal assurances of voluntary compliance from specific firms
2. Issuing advisory opinions on *proposed* marketing practices of specific firms
3. Issuing industry guidelines outlining acceptable and unacceptable practices in particular industries
4. Issuing trade regulation rules
5. Issuing cease-and-desist orders to specific firms for specific wrongdoing

The difficulty here is one already noted: that those businesses that prey most upon the disadvantaged consumer are small and fly-by-night. They do not belong to industry groups, and they are not intimidated by the threat of cease-and-desist orders.

Second, there has been a jurisdictional problem. Most perpetrators of ghetto fraud and deception are *local* businesses. The FTC has interpreted the language of Section 5 of the FTC Act as applying only to unfair or deceptive acts and practices in interstate commerce. Thus it has believed it was effectively barred from involving itself in issues better left to local and state governments. This barrier, however, now appears to have been effectively removed with passage of the Magnuson-Moss Warranty–Federal Trade Commission Improvement Act in late 1974, which allows the Commission to attack unfair practices *affecting commerce* not just *in commerce.*

The FTC has made one major effort to try to assist disadvantaged consumers locally. At the prodding of Senator Magnuson, Chairman of the Senate Commerce Committee, the FTC in late 1965 established a Consumer Protection Program in the District of Columbia, where it *did* have local jurisdiction, as a "model program for policing those unfair and deceptive practices to which the poor are particularly susceptible." [38] Significantly, as a report on the study in June 1968 noted, the lawyers setting up the program realized that "major reliance on . . . usual law detection methods would not be adequate" in securing corrective action.[39] To provide more direct contact with Washington's disadvantaged and to stimulate a heavier flow of complaints, the Commission did the following:

1. It opened an office specifically to receive consumer complaints both in person and by telephone.
2. It developed working relations with OEO and its neighborhood planning organizations and Neighborhood Legal Services programs in the District.
3. It had attorneys attend neighborhood block meetings (five attorneys on the average were assigned to the entire project).

4. It had an attorney participate in a consumer credit education program sponsored by the Federal Bureau of Credit Unions;
5. It reviewed garnishment records in the clerks' offices in the Civil Division of the Court of General Sessions and the District of Columbia Small Claims Court to identify merchants making the most use of garnishment proceedings and the employees most often affected. A "substantial number" of affected consumers were then interviewed as sources of possible violations.

As of June 1968, 98 investigations had been conducted and 27 formal complaints issued. Complaints in the remaining cases were either filed for possible future action, turned over to other federal agencies such as the Corporation Counsel's Office, the Post Office Department, or Neighborhood Legal Services, or turned back to the complainant suggesting that he contact a private attorney or Legal Aid. As the result of the 27 formal complaints, 19 cease-and-desist orders were issued. Only one case was dismissed outright. Ten District of Columbia companies involved in the FTC investigations went out of business after, although not necessarily because of, these investigations. The District program also resulted in the FTC publishing guides relating to retail installment credit transactions. It also provided important data that contributed to the passage of truth-in-lending legislation as well as the study of District of Columbia credit sellers reported in Chapter 9.

Despite the considerable success of the program given its small staff, the program's scope has diminished considerably, and there have been no attempts to extend it to other cities. A report on the program concludes once again:

> . . . the resources and jurisdictional limitations of the Commission do not permit extension of this program to such other cities. Although the impact of such practices is vast, most of them are local in character and can be dealt with most effectively by vigorous investigative, prosecutorial and educational effort at the local level.[40]

As a result of this conclusion, the agency has determined that a major contribution it can make to disadvantaged consumers' problems can be to improve its contribution to state and local enforcement. Responsibilities for this effort have been given to its Office of Federal–State Cooperation, which carries on the following activities:

1. Maintains an up-to-date manual of state trade regulation laws and enforcement programs.
2. Maintains a reference system of state-level complaints and actions taken.
3. Receives state requests for federal action.
4. Maintains central records, accumulating information on deceptive

companies and/or practices moving from state to state and providing it to states on request.

5. Participates in conferences related to trade regulations.
6. Develops training programs for state officials in "techniques applied in antitrust, antideceptive practices, and consumer protection, [and] law enforcement at federal and state levels."
7. Provides legislative assistance in drafting of new or revised state laws.[41]

Beyond these efforts, the FTC has, as already noted, been seeking to promulgate rules in subject areas of great concern to the disadvantaged, affecting the use of holder-in-due-course, door-to-door selling practices, creditors' remedies, and so on. It has developed projects to provide better information to Spanish-speaking consumers. It has developed proposals and begun experimentation through its regional offices in direct cooperation with local agencies in detecting and prosecuting local frauds. Finally, under the 1974 Warranty–Federal Trade Commission Improvement Act it has been given the power not only to attack local unfair trade practices but also to sue sellers for retribution for deceived customers. The success of these efforts in helping the disadvantaged, however, seems highly problematic given the agency's apparent belief that its resources could be better used elsewhere.

Legislative and Administrative Reform

In the future, greater consumer protection from exploitation can be achieved in three basic ways: (1) through passage of stronger laws at the federal, state, and local levels, (2) through the strengthening of both governmental and nongovernmental agencies administering consumer protection programs, and (3) through extension of opportunities for private legal action. The following sections note several proposals that have been made in each of these areas, giving special attention to their particular impact on disadvantaged consumers.

NEW CONSUMER LEGISLATION

Recommendations about new consumer legislation fall into the broad categories of laws (or rulings in the case of the FTC) *proscribing* specific practices sellers should stop, laws (or rulings) *prescribing* specific practices sellers should adopt, and *model statutes* that incorporate several of the proscribing and prescribing recommendations but give a major redirection to state and federal law. Obviously, the laws that will most benefit disadvantaged consumers are those outlawing the practices discussed in Chapter 9, those regulating consumer credit practices, and, in general, those laws that have their greatest impact at the local level.

LEGAL PROSCRIPTIONS. There have been a broad range of suggestions as to revisions in consumer law, principally state codes, that would ensure that practices now barred or circumscribed in some states are barred in all. Among the revisions proposed that have the most relevance to disadvantaged consumers are the following:

1. Laws eliminating the contract clauses discussed in Chapter 9 that increase the consumer's chance of default or eliminate his rights to due process if he does default. Among such clauses are:

Balloon payment clauses that greatly increase the chance the poor consumer will default after having paid a substantial portion of his debt (and perhaps after having afforded the seller a substantial profit).

Cross-collateral clauses that tie the consumer's past purchases to his latest purchase, increasing the chance he will lose everything for a modest default and reducing his opportunities for building his asset position along the way.

Confession-of-judgment and *waiver-of-defense* clauses that allow the creditor to plead the consumer guilty in the event of default, depriving him of any opportunity to defend himself in court or any opportunity to introduce into evidence any mitigating exploitative practices on the part of the seller.

Clauses permitting *repossession of goods* or *garnishment of wages without a court judgment* that would represent seizure of a person's property without due process.

2. Laws that would eliminate deficiency claims (claims for remaining debts after merchandise has been repossessed and sold) unless the original default amount (i.e., the unpaid balance) exceeded $2,000. Laws such as this that put market pressures on the creditor are necessary, it is argued, because at present deficiency judgments are very seldom reviewed by the court for unconscionability, making exploitation relatively easy. Suggested laws would still permit deficiency judgments where the amount unpaid is substantial and the goods may have depreciated substantially in a short period of time, as in early defaults on auto sales.

3. Laws eliminating referral sales schemes, where poor consumers are duped into purchases with the expectation they will recover the purchase price through future commissions, commissions that seldom materialize.

4. Laws that make it impossible for the creditor to bring suit against a debtor in a place (venue) that is inconvenient for the debtor, for example, in a court where the creditor firm's head office is located.

5. Laws prohibiting a debt collector from using the following tactics:

Pretending to be a lawyer when he is not
Using threats or coercion
Harassing or abusing debtor
Informing employers of a debtor's default
In general, using fraudulent, deceptive, or misleading representations

6. Laws prohibiting negative purchase option contract schemes such as are frequently used by record and book companies. These schemes require that once a member has joined (i.e., signed the basic contract), merchandise will be sent to him unless he says he does *not* want it. Schemes like this are quite onerous for the disadvantaged in that they require *them* to keep records to prove they did *not* order something. The seller can say the item was ordered *when it heard nothing.* If, for example, the seller throws a negative response out or merely loses it, the lack of any record would tend to favor the seller unless the *buyer* can prove otherwise. If the seller tries to take him to court, the buyer must present evidence that he returned the notice; the seller need present *no evidence.* This, in effect, means the buyer is responsible unless he can prove otherwise.

Since the disadvantaged are generally very poor record keepers, laws that force the record-keeping burden onto the seller, as in normal sales, are sought as being particularly beneficial to the disadvantaged. A *prescription* in this regard for grocery merchants is discussed below.

7. A final practice that a great many would like to see outlawed is the holder-in-due-course protection afforded to banks and finance companies that buy consumer paper from exploitative sellers. A number of agencies, individuals, and study groups, including the FTC, the American Bar Association Commission to Study the Federal Trade Commission, the National Consumer Law Center, and others, have recommended abolition of holder status. As the FTC notes:

> Application of the holder in due course doctrine to consumer instruments has led to many abuses. It is simply unfair to permit a vendor to sell shoddy or defective goods, which sometimes are not even delivered, coax, wheedle or coerce the buyer into signing a negotiable instrument, disappear or dissipate the funds, and, by assigning the instrument, prevent the deceived or defrauded consumer from asserting his legitimate defenses in an action on the note. Legislation . . . providing that commercial paper must be labelled as such and is not negotiable, and that the holder of such a note takes subject to all contract defenses and to all rights that the buyer would have under the state's consumer fraud law, is both reasonable and necessary.[42]

Because the holder issue is symbolic of many of the problems and potentials in the area of legal reform, this issue will be treated at somewhat greater length.

ABOLISHING HOLDER IN DUE COURSE. It will be recalled that the holder-in-due-course (HIDC) doctrine places a particular burden on the disadvantaged consumer, since it frees the "arm's length" purchaser of a credit contract from claims against the original seller. The doctrine forces a poor consumer to continue paying for merchandise even if it was not as ordered, undelivered, or defective or if otherwise the purchase involved serious merchant exploitation. Instead of being able to withhold payment until an exploitative situation is corrected, the disadvantaged consumer must bring the merchant to court to achieve this end. Altogether this is an onerous financial and psychological burden, a much more severe burden for the disadvantaged than for those of us who can afford the temporary outflow of funds and who have the knowledge and confidence to make use of small claims or other courts.

As noted above, there has been a growing outcry against the holder doctrine and a number of states have outlawed the practice in some or all transactions. According to a report prepared by the National Consumer Law Center, on June 1, 1973, HIDC had the following standing in the 52 U.S. jurisdictions:

A total of 37 jurisdictions including Puerto Rico and the District of Columbia have placed some restrictions on the holder doctrine; 25 jurisdictions have not.

Of the 37 jurisdictions, 21 have made "sweeping bans" against HIDC in credit transactions for all goods and services.

An additional 10 states (and some of the above) have banned HIDC for such transactions as sales of consumer goods only, sales that are solicited in the home, home repairs, sales of goods and services except sales of motor vehicles, and sales of motor vehicles.

Six additional states (and two of the above) have eliminated HIDC protection only for a limited period of time, for example, for 90 days after the sale.

In addition to the above, some states that have not restricted HIDC by specific legislation have done so through the accumulation of case-by-case-decisions.[43] There are in fact a number of relationships between the finance company and the seller which have been introduced to remove holder-in-due-course status. Thus HIDC status may be denied if one or another of the following is found:

1. The finance company recommends the type of sales contract and credit obligation to be used in all sales of the seller.
2. The finance company supplies blank forms on which its name is prominent.
3. An arrangement (contract) is made for the finance company to buy all the seller's paper at a specified discount.

4. The finance company requires that the contract state that the buyer has defenses *only* against the seller and payment *must* be made to the finance company.
5. The finance company requires that a certain kind of credit check be run on all customers or does this check itself.
6. The finance company personally checks to see whether the product is delivered and whether the consumer is satisfied at that time.
7. The finance company and seller have managers or directors or major stockholders in common.
8. The finance company and seller use the same or contiguous office space.
9. The paper is discounted significantly, implying that the finance company is aware of the risk due to deception—for example, in a case where the attorney general or Better Business Bureau has already informed the finance company directly of the seller's practices. In one example, a finance company paid only $831 for a $1,079 note due in *three days* (25%), knowing the sale involved a referral scheme and that the seller had changed his name three times in the last year. The finance company, the court said, "was bound to inquire further into the operation of the seller of these notes, and having made no inquiry, it is held [responsible] as though it had knowledge of all that inquiry would have revealed." [44]

Courts considering these arguments sometimes also use the concept of *agency* to rule that the seller is merely an agent for the finance company which is the principal party securing the credit contract. Logic and law argue that the principal always is assumed to have knowledge (notice) of what its agent is doing and so cannot be held an innocent holder. A related but distinct argument is that the finance company is in fact an *original party* to the transaction and therefore knows of its nature.

The basic argument for *total* abolition of HIDC is that the burden of suffering in the event of exploitation should not rest on consumers, but should be shifted back to sellers and finance companies. Barring total abolition, states should at least (1) make finance companies undertake reasonable inquiry into sellers and their paper and (2) give buyers at least 30 days to notify the finance company of impending defenses before allowing holder status. In effect, the states should adopt a policy of encouraging financial agents to deal only with nonfraudulent companies—or take the consequences. Legitimate sellers should not be affected at all. On the other hand, companies with a history, for example, of skipping town should be made to have trouble getting their paper discounted at all.

A problem for those proposing abolition of "holder" is that it is not known what consequences will follow from the abolition. If finance companies must share some of the risk in the event a seller defrauds a consumer, then one should expect that either the cost of discounting contracts for disreputable sellers will increase in the short run in direct proportion to their disreputability or their sources of financing will dry up.

In the first instance, either some lower-cost finance companies will stop financing disreputable sellers and be replaced by higher-cost and less choosy companies or existing companies will simply pay less on existing contracts or require some form of escrow account from the seller proportional to the expected rate of consumer complaints. It is possible that in such circumstances some sellers will respond to the increased costs by giving up their unsavory ways. Presumably, most would try to pass the cost on to their customers and only if they couldn't do this might the effect be to reduce exploitation. If they *can* pass the cost on, the effect will be to spread the losses of those who are defrauded across all customers of the same firm (and, if some oligopoly pricing exists, across the customers of all credit sellers in inner city markets). While some customers may see this added cost as an acceptable insurance premium permitting them to stop payment in the event of deception or fraud even if a contract is taken over by a finance company, others may feel they can adequately protect themselves.

In the case of the other alternative outcome—the drying up of sources of financing for merchants in disadvantaged communities after removal of HIDC protection—the benefits to the disadvantaged would be mixed. It is possible that they would no longer have to pay the very high interest charges that sellers must charge on contracts sold to finance companies (See Table 9-1). Thus the average rate of interest paid by the disadvantaged might decline. On the other hand, they might also find less credit available to them under these new circumstances.

The critical factors, then, for this key policy decision are (1) how price elastic disadvantaged consumers are with respect to credit costs and (2) what the response of finance companies and exploitative merchants will be to the new circumstances. Unfortunately we here enter two areas—the credit behavior of the disadvantaged and business dynamics in the inner city —where, as noted throughout this volume, the present state of knowledge is very weak. The only available evidence as to the likely effects of the abolition of HIDC is the following passing remark in the report of the National Commission on Consumer Finance:

> There is . . . some indication that the abolition of holder in due course defenses and waiver of defenses tend to result in *lower* finance rates to the customer. Although this result appears to be somewhat contradictory, it is possible that finance companies impose more stringent quality standards and charge less when such creditors' remedies are abolished. This explanation is reinforced by the fact that rate ceilings in some states prevent any substantial increases in rates when such creditors' remedies are abolished.[45]

Whether this result is desirable depends, in part, upon what happens to the supply of credit, a piece of data not given by the NCCF, which also does not offer empirical support for the conclusion it does reach.

Legal prescriptions. Prescriptive laws are intended to force sellers to give consumers more information than the least reputable seller might give in the normal course of business, as well as to give consumers opportunities to escape undesirable contracts under certain circumstances. Among the information now required in consumer credit contracts in most states is the following:

1. The contract must be entirely filled out before the buyer signs it.
2. The buyer must receive a copy of the contract at the time of purchase.
3. The following information must be clearly set forth:
    a. Cash price of goods
    b. Amount of down payment
    c. Unpaid cash balance—difference between (*a*) and (*b*)
    d. Amount of insurance and other benefits if a separate charge is made
    e. Amount of official fees
    f. Total principal balance—(*c*) plus (*d*) plus (*e*)
    g. Amount of time price differential, i.e., total finance charges
    h. True annual rate of interest on principle
    i. Amount of final balance—(*f*) plus (*g*)
    j. Time sales price—(*b*) plus (*i*)
4. Above the space for the buyer's signature the following must appear in at least 10 point bold type:

   NOTICE TO RETAIL BUYER:

   Do not sign this contract in blank. You are entitled to a copy of the contract at the time you sign. Keep it to protect your legal rights.

Additional prescriptions currently being suggested include:

1. A requirement that in areas with significant foreign language–speaking populations (particularly Spanish) the seller must offer the buyer the option of having his contract written in his own language.
2. A requirement that large-type contracts be available to the poorly sighted and the elderly.
3. A requirement that the most important clauses of a consumer contract (e.g., those on costs, payment schedules, penalties in the case of default) be communicated to the buyer both in writing and orally (in the language of the contract).
4. A requirement that buyers be given 48 to 72 hours after the signing of a contract to repudiate the contract. As noted above such a cooling-off period is now required by an FTC ruling for door-to-door sales, a ruling that is particularly beneficial to disadvantaged consumers because of their much higher contact with, and reliance on, peddlers and other in-home salesmen. Cooling-off periods may also be desirable in store sales where buyers receive the following inducements:

(*a*) the price is alleged to be "the lowest in town," and/or (*b*) free goods are offered with the purchase of the product.

Chapter 10 noted a number of additional prescriptive laws currently being discussed that would give consumers valuable information about product and service alternatives at the point of sale, including unit pricing, open dating, and nutrient labeling.

MODEL STATUTES. A broader approach to consumer protection problems at the state level that would incorporate many of the above proscriptive and prescriptive laws is the promulgation and enactment of model statutes. These statutes, which are designed by the National Conference of Commissioners on Uniform State Laws (NCCUSL) or by other interested legal and consumer groups, are intended to strengthen existing state laws and to make the laws uniform across states. One such law designed to incorporate many of the suggestions enumerated above is the Uniform Consumer Credit Code (UCCC) written by the NCCUSL. The UCCC has now been adopted in some form in seven Midwestern and Western states (Colorado, Idaho, Indiana, Kansas, Oklahoma, Utah, and Wyoming). The most recent sixth and final draft of the statute eliminates many deficiencies of earlier versions, particularly permission of holder status when funds were loaned specifically to finance a sale. This is a major concession to consumer interests and a reflection of the effect of the National Commission on Consumer Finance study cited earlier on the Commissioners. Still, the UCCC:

1. Permits higher interest rate ceilings than many states allow, and, as George Gordin of the National Consumer Law Center argues, these may quickly become the norm.[46]
2. Does not eliminate deficiency judgments in sales over $1,750, which includes many home furnishings and automobile sales. These, as noted elsewhere in this volume, are a particular source of difficulty for the disadvantaged.

Many critics argue that even with its strengths, the UCCC too much reflects its early sponsorship in the lending industry. An alternative statute which more strongly reflects the consumer advocate position is the Wisconsin Consumer Act.[47] The passage of the Wisconsin act in many ways signifies an important milestone in the advancement of the consumer movement because of the exceedingly great consumer impact on its drafting.[48] However, probably the strongest comprehensive model legislation drafted to date supporting the consumer advocate position is the Model Consumer Credit Act (called the National Consumer Act in an earlier draft) promulgated by the National Consumer Law Center.[49] This act incorporates virtually all the suggestions made in these paragraphs. The early form of this act has been adopted in the state of Oregon.

Another model act which has received serious attention for different reasons is the Uniform Unfair Trade Practice and Consumer Protection

Law prepared by the Federal Trade Commission. This statute is popularly known as the "little FTC Act" since it is intended to give state attorneys general the same very broad powers for attacking unfair and deceptive acts as the FTC has. While private actions in such cases are possible in most states, this act would explicitly allow the attorney general to bring action in the public interest and, among other things, seek injunctive relief. Some states permit this relief, for instance through state departments of consumer protection; however, a uniform law would extend coverage to all states. At the end of fiscal 1971 the FTC reported that 36 states had adopted "little FTC Acts."[50]

The "little FTC Act" if widely adopted would be *potentially* very useful to disadvantaged consumers. We have already seen that these consumers, through ignorance, apathy, or fear, are particularly unlikely to seek court action at the state level in their own behalf. And we have also seen that state district attorneys are now very reluctant to tackle consumer cases. While this is partly the result of their sense of priorities (i.e., they believe crimes such as murder and robbery are more important than consumer deception), it is also a product of their difficulty in winning consumer cases under existing statutes, which often require that they prove either *intent* to defraud or *injury* to competition. Since neither proof would be required under a "little FTC Act," (i.e., one need only prove that a practice has the *potential to deceive* some consumers), the way is made clear for the state to take on more responsibility for the protection of disadvantaged consumers. However, it must also be made clear that passage of laws does not of itself mean that protection of disadvantaged consumers will *in fact* increase. This is a matter of increased will and resources of the state and local consumer protection agencies themselves.

Stronger Administration

With the specific exceptions noted above, it has been argued that much of the legislation to effectively protect disadvantaged consumers already exists, that all that is needed is stronger, more imaginative enforcement. A major target of such criticism is the FTC.

RECOMMENDATIONS FOR THE FTC

A number of recommendations have been and can be suggested for making the FTC more effective in helping poor consumers:

1. Revise priorities. In choosing among cases to prosecute, complaints to investigate, business practices to study, the FTC must give major weight to the effects on the most disadvantaged consumers. In its *1971 Annual*

Report the Commission suggested the following criteria for choosing among consumer protection problems:

The relative importance of products in terms of the proportion of consumer spending involved
The numbers of consumers affected
Advertising intensity relative to total sales of the product
The prevalence of consumer complaints both inside and outside the agency
The existence of health and safety factors[51]

A principal argument of the present volume is that the first two of these criteria ought to be revised to explicitly consider the relative importance of products in the consumer spending *of the disadvantaged* and the number of *disadvantaged* consumers likely to be affected by disputed practices. On economic grounds disadvantaged consumers ought to be given heavy weight because dollar losses from exploitation mean much more to them. And on social grounds they ought to be given explicit consideration because they are less likely than other consumers to complain directly to the FTC or to seek other remedies (e.g., private litigation).

2. REVISE PRIORITY-SETTING PROCEDURES. To meet the above goal, less emphasis must be given to complaints and to likely success of prosecution in choosing among cases on which to take action. To give priority to these works to the disadvantage of poor and minority consumers. Particularly, in the case of "mailbag" priorities, disadvantaged consumers are less likely to write, as are competitors in disadvantaged communities. Thus, the FTC must itself assume the watchdog function, substituting its own active investigations in disadvantaged areas for the more passive role of waiting for disadvantaged consumers to complain themselves.

3. EXTEND JURISDICTION. With the passage of the Warranty–Federal Trade Commission Improvement Act, the problem for the agency is again one of allocating resources. The jurisdictional problem apparently has masked a reluctance by the FTC to become involved in what it believes are issues involving firms not responsive to the agency's sanctions. If local agencies become more vigorous, this judgment may represent a sensible division of labor. However, in the absence of local vigor the FTC, with its broad powers, ought well to rethink this implicit resource allocation decision in light of the greater vulnerability of the disadvantaged, their apparent inability or unwillingness to use standard remedies, and the greater injury any fraud or deception, no matter how trivial, works upon them.

At minimum, as the ABA argues, the FTC has a responsibility under its legislative mandate to *study* local frauds and to recommend needed changes in legislation to the Congress.[52]

4. ESTABLISH MORE LOCAL OFFICES WITH LOCAL ENFORCEMENT RESPONSIBILITIES. This recommendation would be designed to decentralize FTC operations to emphasize local action (a move now under way) and to facilitate contact by disadvantaged consumers with the FTC. The ABA suggests such expansion, although only on a pilot basis: staffing each office with about 10 lawyers plus other professional and clerical staff, with responsibilities varying depending upon the strength of local consumer protection agencies. The ABA study notes that "there seems to be no serious problem of resistance to federal activity; almost all state attorneys general seem to welcome federal law enforcement efforts in the consumer fraud area." [53] The ABA argues that a major function of these offices should be to cooperate with and train local officials so that they might eventually take full responsibility in this area. A pilot cooperative effort with other local consumer protection agencies as part of a so-called Consumer Clearinghouse is now under way in Buffalo, New York.

5. EXTEND MONITORING ACTIVITIES. Since disadvantaged consumers may not always know when they are being defrauded, it is important for the FTC to move beyond its national advertising monitoring to monitoring marketing practices at the local level, including both local ads and local court records.

6. STRENGTHEN FEDERAL-STATE COOPERATION. Here the FTC has responsibilities not only to be more often present on the local scene and to consult, cooperate with, and train local authorities but also to help establish a national data bank on frauds and their perpetrators and to encourage the passage of state laws such as those discussed in the previous section. The FTC's current efforts to establish consumer protection coordinating committees in metropolitan areas and consumer protection specialists in regional offices are important steps in this direction.

7. PERMIT PRIVATE SUITS BASED ON FTC DECISIONS. This would be particularly beneficial to disadvantaged consumers in that it would minimize initial outlays for private litigation and encourage the disadvantaged to think that private litigation might work.

8. SPEED PROSECUTION. Delays in prosecution are particularly harmful to the FTC's credibility among the disadvantaged, whose need for relief is immediate. One must ask how, for example, the elderly feel about the federal system when it takes years to force a company like Geritol to discontinue its extensive "patent medicine" propaganda.[54]

9. INCREASE FTC MUSCLE. This means increases in dollars and manpower to extend FTC activities and in willingness to exact substantial penalties on more offenders rather than rely extensively on voluntary cooperation by FTC "friends" in business.

As noted earlier, the FTC has made considerable progress in the last five years (i.e., since the ABA and Nader reports). The agency's vigor and aggressiveness has grown considerably. It has begun systematically attacking larger industries; it has begun requiring written justification of ad claims and affirmative disclosures of necessary information on packages and in ads, and it has been forcing deceptive advertisers to include corrective messages in ads for a period of time following an agency judgment or a consent agreement. However, it is also true that with the exception of a trade regulation rule permitting a cooling-off period for door-to-door sales and abolition of HIDC in certain cases, the Commission has not significantly increased its impact on the particular problems of the disadvantaged consumer.

BUSINESS SELF-REGULATION

As already noted, business self-regulation has expanded considerably in recent years. Many companies have established consumer affairs departments to try to improve their abilities to solve consumer complaints[55] and have improved their own production and sales processes, sometimes at some cost to profits.[56] Companies in some industries have bound together to provide a "court of last resort" in unresolved disputes between customers and sellers, like the various consumer action panels. Unfortunately, all these efforts rely primarily on consumer-initiated complaints on which the companies, or associations, can act, a procedure that makes the system more helpful to middle-class than to disadvantaged consumers. These efforts are, however, a step forward, and if information about them can be more effectively communicated in disadvantaged areas, they may prove much more effective than the more highly touted Better Business Bureau.

THE BETTER BUSINESS BUREAU. Major criticisms of the Better Business Bureau have already been discussed, and note has been taken of the Bureau's efforts at reforms. To keep these reforms in perspective, indication of what is needed has been spelled out by Congressman Rosenthal:[57]

1. Local BBBs should be more standardized in policies, practices, and procedures.
2. Membership receipts should be pooled and allocated by the BBB Central Council. This would remove local BBBs' reliance on (and possibly their fear of prosecuting) local business firms and permit funds to be allocated according to need rather than according to collection abilities.
3. BBBs should reduce emphasis on monitoring advertising (which is being covered to some extent by the FTC) and strengthen their ability to handle specific consumer complaints and to provide better prepurchase reports on companies.
4. A firm's ratings should be based less on its cooperation with the Bureau and more on its actual business practices.

5. BBB staffs should include a lawyer who would screen complaints for possible legal violations. Such findings could be passed on to federal or state agencies or back to the consumer for possible private action.
6. Consumers should be given better representation on BBB boards and committees.
7. Bureaus should publish a monthly list of abuses and distribute them as widely as possible.
8. BBBs should more actively support proposals for new consumer legislation and support rigorous federal and local enforcement of existing laws.
9. BBBs should require members to agree to binding arbitration by BBB arbitrators in the case of "controversial disputes."
10. BBBs should establish part- or full-time offices in low-income areas, to be staffed by people residing in those areas.
11. BBB managers should be given more independence from their boards of directors.
12. Customers should be allowed to submit complaints by telephone as well as by filling out a written form.

The BBB has great potential in protecting disadvantaged consumers. Still, its present lack of specific binding sanctions against its generally pro-business members and its unwillingness to make its services directly available in poor and minority areas, combined with the fact that some of the worst offenders in disadvantaged areas do not belong to the Bureau, make one pessimistic about the Bureau's present abilities to contribute to solutions of disadvantaged consumer problems. Succinctly, is it really likely that local business firms will put up more money for or join an organization that will align itself much more often on the consumer's side and may indeed encourage increased "harassment" of "legitimate" business? This seems only likely if the BBBs get much more imaginative and aggressive leadership at the national and local level and/or more small businessmen turn from their traditional position that stronger self-regulation is not really in their own interests.

There is, of course, a major barrier to stronger self-regulation contained in the various antitrust statutes, particularly the Sherman Act. These laws discourage strong sanctions by groups of businesses in the name of self-regulation because legislators have feared that such powers would ultimately be used to drive out competitors and thus limit competition. Some ardent antitrusters like Donald Turner believe that *most* kinds of collusion among competitors would not be in the consumer's interest. Citing an antitrust case involving American Gas Association standards, Turner noted two dangers:

1. Due to diverse manufacturer interests, the standards procedure might be used by a dominant group of manufacturers to handicap or exclude competitors for any one of several wholly unacceptable reasons —that the competitor is a price cutter or that he has developed a new

product which threatens a serious invasion of established producer markets; and

2. Due either to diverse manufacturer interests or conflict of interest between manufacturers and consumers, the standards might cut off from the ultimate consumer product options that a substantial number of them would very much like to have.[58]

Louis L. Stern, on the other hand, feels that such regulation *can* be in the consumer's interest and all that is needed is amendments to the Sherman Act by Congress or the courts to permit "meritorious restraints of trade," specifically in the form of boycotts against offending merchants. Stern would leave the determination of which restraints are meritorious to the FTC and the courts. As he notes:

> If, after open hearings, the FTC cannot distinguish between meritorious (from the public's point of view) restraints of trade and self-serving restraints of trade, then surely the restraints are not of much consequence to begin with. If a half-open door policy toward restraints of trade complicates the enforcement task and increases court loads, so be it. That is the price for freeing private energies on behalf of consumer interests. Self-regulation cannot be fully effective without enforcement power.[59]

MEDIA REGULATION. One form of informal regulation that holds particular promise for assisting disadvantaged consumers is the issuance and policing of advertising guidelines by local newspapers and radio and television stations. Such guidelines are needed despite the fact that most state and federal laws absolve carriers from responsibility for deceptive advertising. One should not be optimistic, however, about the likelihood of extensive media regulation of advertising, since, for example, only 60% of commercial AM and FM radio stations and 35% of commercial television stations support the already-existing code of the National Association of Broadcasters.[60]

Another promising means by which media can assist consumers at the local level is through consumer action columns, both in newspapers and on TV. Such columns seek to intervene in consumer disputes and apparently can use the threat of publicity as an effective tool in securing settlements. However, although no study has been made of the effects of these columns, it is likely that they operate with only limited staffs, and like the Better Business Bureau are probably most successful with cases involving "misunderstandings."

Private Remedies

As discussions in earlier sections of this book have suggested, the problem of encouraging the disadvantaged to use private litigation as a means of protecting themselves and others from exploitation has three major components:

1. The disadvantaged must be made *aware* of the opportunities for and/or the need of private action.
2. They must be *motivated* to take such action.
3. The *hindrances* to such action should be *minimized.*

AWARENESS

Earlier sections noted the potential benefits of increased consumer education in making disadvantaged consumers better aware of their legal rights. Suggestions were also made as to how these consumers could be better informed of their rights in the contracts themselves. The availability of more consumer organizations in their communities would further serve this end.

One major problem in creating awareness of consumer rights is that the disadvantaged often do not receive adequate notice of impending actions against them. Many disadvantaged consumers only realize they needed a lawyer at the point where goods are repossessed and/or wages are garnisheed. A major contributor to this problem is the practice of "sewer service"—process servers throwing summonses away and swearing they were delivered, in the expectation that the poor and minority consumers upon whom the practice is most often used will not know enough or be motivated enough to complain.[61] Several approaches have been suggested to eliminate, or at least minimize, this practice:

1. Permitting service by low-cost certified mail, return receipt requested, with personal service only as backup when persons cannot be located
2. Making process servers salaried appointees of the court (as are marshals already and process servers in 20 states and in federal civil cases)
3. Licensing servers
4. Making lawyers responsible for the actions of servers they hire

But some of these approaches will meet opposition from process servers as well as the legal community, and perhaps a more direct approach would be to change the summonses themselves. If summonses were made clearer, defendants would be more likely to realize they had in fact been issued one. Summonses could also contain some information that would constitute the means of beginning a search for legal help, which would serve also to further emphasize the seriousness of the situation. For example, telephone numbers of legal aid societies, bar association referral services, and OEO Neighborhood Legal Services where they exist could be included with all summonses.

MOTIVATION

Even when disadvantaged consumers become aware of the fact that they ought to initiate a legal action or defend themselves in one, they often lack the motivation to do so. This lack of motivation is the result of both distrust and fear. Distrust stems from disadvantaged people's deep-rooted sense that in confrontations with "the system," they have a decided handicap. They often feel that "big business" or "the man" will always win. This basic fear is that they will be worse off going to court than not going, that:

They will lose their credit standing by attacking a seller.
They will lose salary or possibly even their jobs by taking time out to go to court.
They might somehow incur extra costs or worse penalties in the process.

All these fears make them less likely to fight an action and also make them more willing to settle out of court when they needn't do so.

The solution to the first two fears may well be (1) to explicitly prohibit changes in credit status as the result of involvement in a court case where the consumer *wins*, (2) to require that when a consumer whose earnings are below some poverty criterion wins a case, the judgment include payment as part of court costs for the consumer's lost time in pursuing the case, and (3) to prohibit employers from changing a consumer's job status as the result of his involvement in a consumer court case.

Motivating the buyer to go to court when he fears that the settlement will make him worse off is more difficult to overcome, since, in rare cases, he may indeed be worse off. One suggestion for coping with this problem was that of Attorney Ray Narral:

> We are investigating the possibility of inducing public spirited local businesses to offer to reimburse buyers for any losses they sustain because they have chosen to defend in Court in order to challenge unethical sales practices. For example, if the buyer refuses a $50 settlement offer and then loses his suit with judgment entered against him for $170, the private sponsor would pay $120 of the judgment.[62]

A further suggestion made in several quarters to motivate the disadvantaged consumer to bring action against exploitative merchants is to increase the possibility (and amount) of punitive damages awarded to the consumer. As argued in Walker v. Sheldon, a case of a company publishing books of unsuspecting authors for the fees they would pay never intending to follow up on promises of extensive promotion and distribution, punitive damages would also have a deterrent effect on the seller:

> In the calculation of his expected profits, the wrongdoer is likely to allow for a certain amount of money which will have to be returned to those victims

who object too vigorously, and he will be perfectly content to bear the additional cost of litigation as the price for continuing his illicit business. It stands to reason that the chances of deterring him are materially increased by subjecting him to the payment of punitive damages.[63]

REMOVING HINDRANCES

Hindrances for the aware *and* motivated disadvantaged consumer stem from the inaccessibility of small claims courts and the difficulty of getting legal assistance. In the case of small claims courts, several suggestions can be made to greatly increase their value to the disadvantaged:

1. The maximum allowable claim should be raised to $1,000, and there should be an automatic cost-of-living escalation every five years.
2. Hours of operation should be extended to evenings and weekends.
3. Judges should consider taking the court to disadvantaged communities on a regular basis. This would not only make it more convenient for the disadvantaged to present (or defend) claims but also make the consumer's appearance in court seem more informal and less awe-inspiring. (An alternative here would be Schrag's suggestion of neighborhood tribunals.)[64]
4. Barring periodic court hearings in disadvantaged areas, court clerks could be sent out to strategically located neighborhoood centers in disadvantaged areas on a regular basis to help the disadvantaged file claims, to explain court procedures, and generally to make the use of small claims courts seem less intimidating. Clerks, whether "downtown" or in the neighborhood, should be trained in paralegal skills to help the disadvantaged strengthen their claims and prepare evidence. Some clerks in areas with major foreign language concentrations should, of course, have fluency in those languages. Many small claims clerks in major metropolitan areas should, of course, be black.
5. In states where lawyers are permissible in small claims courts, the disadvantaged consumer who is a defendant in a case involving, say, $100 or more and who cannot afford legal help should be afforded counsel by a public defender, or the creditor should be barred from using his lawyer. (This recommendation would also be valid for higher courts.)

With respect to private legal assistance, efforts should be strengthened to increase the availability of low-cost legal help to the poor. Again, several courses, in addition to the provision of public defenders already suggested, are open:

1. If the OEO Legal Services Program is dismantled at the federal level, states and cities should be urged to allocate substantial portions of

their revenue-sharing funds to keep it alive, or, barring this, major foundations ought to step in to fill the breach and keep the program afloat as a nongovernmental undertaking.

2. Further experimentation with Judicare should be undertaken with a view to making it complimentary to, but not a substitute for, OEO Legal Services.
3. More and more legal firms should be encouraged to free a given percentage of the time of their staffs to provide free legal services in poor and minority areas.
4. Programs should be established through law schools or state bar associations to train paralegal personnel to work in poverty agencies and the like in order to provide the disadvantaged with information on their legal rights and opportunities, helping them fill out claims, interceding with merchants on their behalf, etc.
5. Recruitment of minority people into law schools and the legal profession should be accelerated.

It seems unlikely that over the near term any of the above suggestions will make very much of a dent in the consumer problems of the disadvantaged. Even if the number of legal aids available to the disadvantaged were to be doubled immediately, much of the time of the increased staff would be involved in non-consumer protection matters, marital problems, criminal complaints, real estate transactions, and the like. (About 10% of OEO and Judicare cases involve consumer issues.)[65] Given this, it seems that the only remaining means of providing a substantial amount of low-cost legal help to the disadvantaged is through legislation that would permit consumers with similar complaints to join their complaints together in a single *class action* against an offending seller.

CLASS ACTIONS

The essence of class action is a needed procedural court reform which would permit unlimited numbers of individual plaintiffs with essentially the same claims to be joined together in one action. Typically the claim would be carried forward by one plaintiff and one legal team in behalf of other members of the class.

The advantages of class action are several and obvious:

1. Consumers who cannot afford court costs on small claims could now afford to go to court.
2. Class action cases could be large enough that most lawyers would take them on a contingency fee basis, thus giving protection to the small consumer, who might not otherwise have access to any court procedure at all.
3. Because of the amounts involved, a better case could be presented;

better lawyers might take the case, expert witnesses could be hired, professional studies done, and the like. As described earlier, in many consumer suits the quality of the defendant's (merchant's) legal staff puts the consumer at a considerable disadvantage.

4. Court efficiency would be greatly enhanced, since for the original case only one judge would be involved, one jury, one set of expert witnesses, one transcript, and so forth. Further, only one set of appeals would be involved. The alternative is any number of essentially identical proceedings in diverse courts. The savings would be to the litigants as well as the court system.
5. Finally, the *deterrent* effect on exploitative merchants who otherwise would feel they could escape litigation if only they kept the amount of the exploitation small enough should be substantial.

The arguments against class action are that it will (1) overburden the courts, (2) stimulate a great number of unnecessary and harassing suits, and (3) take too long. It should be noted that opponents of class action fall into basically two groups, those who wouldn't oppose it at the state level but don't want it at the federal level (as was the position of the Nixon administration) and those who don't want it at all.

1. Overburdening of courts. Prof. Milton Handler of the Columbia University Law School testified before the Consumer Subcommittee of the Senate Commerce Committee on the class action issue that "a large consumer class action could put a Federal court out of action for years and disqualify it from performing its other important duties." [66] This argument seems to stem from three assumptions about class actions: first, because of the stakes involved, the quality of counsel for both sides, and the complexity of the issue involved, trials will take a long time; second, determination of membership in a large class will take a long time; and third, determination of damages ought to involve separate hearings for each member of the class (coplaintiffs), and in each case the defendant (merchant supplier) has a constitutional right to insist on a trial by jury and/or a chance to cross-examine, making the courts, in essence, small claims courts. Supporters of class action grant the first assumption, although providing counterarguments (see below) as to its desirability. They directly argue with the remaining two.

a. With respect to determination of class membership as well as damages, the courts have considerable power to restrict cases to manageable sizes. One method of such control might be to restrict members of a class to those whose injury and right to damages are identical with those of the plaintiff actually carrying through the action. Such membership may be established by possession of some attribute, e.g., ownership of some item, or patronage of some outlet over a specific time.

b. In federal cases, determination of class membership may be delegated to a master upon motion of litigants or the judge himself under Rule 53 of the Federal Rules of Procedure.

c. Defendants may not want to bear the cost of litigating all the damage claims. The insurance industry frequently does not. Hearings on the Consumer Protection Act of 1970 report a case where a defendant agreed that the lawsuit of the estate of 1 person among 40 killed in a bus accident would be tried and total damages would be 40 times those awarded in the case.[67]

2. HARASSING AND UNNECESSARY SUITS. The potential for large recovery in class actions, it is argued, will occasion a great many harassing class action suits which will be brought largely to encourage merchant defendants to settle out of court for substantial amounts. It is also argued that it will encourage many trivial actions which won't bring much to *each* consumer but will bring a high fee to the lawyer. An example to support the latter contention cited in hearings before the Senate Judiciary Committee was an action against the Playboy Clubs in which each plaintiff was awarded about $8 in credit chits while the lawyer received a $275,000 fee.

Counterarguments are as follows:

a. Enabling legislation for class action cases typically gives the judge in a possible class action suit many grounds to rule out trivial, harassing, or unmanageable cases. The plaintiff, for example, must show that a common question of law exists and that the class action is superior to other types of proceedings in terms of judicial efficiency. Federal law allows the court broad powers to ensure that no great delay and unnecessary costs are incurred and that the class suit can in no way harm the interests of the court or the defendant. The judge can consolidate or stay related suits and impose conditions upon the suit itself before he will allow class action. To quash possible harassing suits, a judge can require the plaintiff to show a substantial possibility that he will prevail on the merits. Finally, to prevent quick out-of-court settlements benefiting lawyers, federal law forbids such settlements without court approval.

b. Other controls can be specified in enabling legislation; for example, it can be required that the amounts involved for each plaintiff be at least $10.

c. Finally, it may be noted that in the Playboy example cited above, while the individual awards were small, the *total* award was $3.8 million, well justifying the action as well as the lawyer's fee.

As to the general question of overburdening the courts both with many and long class action cases, proponents of class action argue that:

a. Class action is now very commonly used in stockholder's derivative suits, antitrust actions, and civil rights suits.

b. Courts at the federal and state level are already overburdened because of too many trivial civil suits. Class action would consolidate many of these.

3. INCREASED LENGTH OF TIME IN LITIGATION. In actions in small claims courts, results in terms of recovery come within a few weeks or months, in other state courts in a not greatly longer time. Richard McLaren, feels, therefore, that it would be "a cruel joke on the plaintiffs, to give them a class action that supposedly is going to be effective and really what it amounts to is that it bogs down in 5 years of legal proceedings." [68] But:

a. As noted above, judges may bar a class action if it unnecessarily delays prosecution.
b. Length of time is not necessarily bad if this means that justice is more likely to be served. Brevity of litigation does not necessarily equate with fairness.
c. Most important, for a consumer who cannot afford an action, a lengthy action is obviously better than none.

PRESENT STATUS. At the federal level, class actions were first permitted when the U.S. Supreme Court, which has power to set rules for federal courts, revised Rule 23 of the Federal Rules of Procedure as of July 1, 1966. Rule 23 permits class action *even if* one of the other requirements for federal venue, i.e., involvement of a federal law or diversity of citizenship of one or both parties, is not met. Rule 23 requires that (1) a common question of law or fact must exist, (2) the basis for defense must be reasonably similar to all members of the class, (3) the plaintiff must be a member of the class and must adequately represent all members of the class, and (4) claims must equal or exceed $10,000. A subsequent ruling by the Supreme Court, in *Snyder v. Harris*,[69] stated that individual claims cannot be aggregated toward the $10,000 minimum and must each be at least $10,000. A more recent ruling stated that initiators of class actions at their own expense must make reasonable efforts to notify all members of the class before going to court. Both judicial restrictions will require new law making to again make class actions useful to consumers at the federal level.

A number of states have used Rule 23 (either its 1966 or its earlier 1938 version) or similar codes to establish state precedents for class actions. However, a survey by the National Consumer Law Center in 1970 was quite pessimistic about their usefulness:

> On the whole, optimism for the future of consumer class actions at the state level is not justified. In 7 states virtually no class action is possible, in 2 states it is doubtful and in 27 states only limited class actions for equitable relief seem likely. That makes 36 states where consumer class actions for damages are extremely unlikely and for equitable relief variable and limited. In the remaining 14 states class actions for most types of equitable relief seem

assured, but class actions for damages are still uncertain and restricted to certain types of cases. Actions that are based on fraud apparently will gain only limited success.

70% of the 14 states placed in the category of those allowing consumer class actions broadly are there on the assumption that as their law is based on the 1966 Federal Rule of Civil Procedure, Rule 23 that they will therefore permit such suits as readily as the federal courts—an uncertain assumption at best. It is probable that consumer class actions will not become a meaningful and viable way of enforcing consumer rights in the marketplace until a federal consumer class action statute has been enacted.[70]

NEED FOR ACTION. Thus, critically important legislation needed to help the disadvantaged consumer is federal and state legislation permitting class actions even where the individual dollar amounts involved are small. The recent Warranty–Federal Trade Commission Improvement Act does appear to permit the agency to bring what are in effect class action suits in behalf of consumers defrauded by specific practices of specific sellers. Whether this will be applied to cases involving local merchants in disadvantaged areas is, as noted above, problematical. In general, federal government enthusiasm for stronger federal class action has been minimal. As Robert McLaren has put it, ". . . we think the preferred course is to develop and improve State and Local consumer remedies and procedures rather than, in effect, to preempt the field by Federal Legislation." [71]

Despite this argument there is still need for stronger federal legislation. However, while there is a good case for such legislation—the interstate character of many marketing organizations, the superior qualifications of federal judges to handle complicated class action cases, etc.—major benefits will come to poor consumers only when enabling legislation for class action is passed at the *state level*. McLaren seems to be optimistic that this will come about: "If the State court does not provide [a remedy], then this would be an incentive to [the consumer] to get out to work and get his State Legislature to get him a bill." [72] Unfortunately, as noted throughout this book, the disadvantaged person's awareness of a lack of remedy is likely only to reinforce his sense of hopelessness, frustration, disillusionment, and even anger with the judicial system, not to spur him to action. Whether others will take up the cause on his behalf is a central issue we shall turn to in the next, concluding chapter.

Notes

1. New York Times, *Standards of Advertising Acceptability*.
2. David Caplovitz, *The Poor Pay More* (New York: The Free Press, 1967), p. 175.

3. "The Better Business Bureau," *National Better Business Bureau Bulletin*, July 1943.
4. Caplovitz, *op. cit.*, p. xxiii.
5. Hon. Benjamin S. Rosenthal, "Report on the Better Business Bureaus," *Congressional Record*, Dec. 17, 1971, p. E13764.
6. *Ibid.*, p. E13764.
7. Will Lisner, "Arbitrators Aid Consumers Here," *New York Times*, Aug. 25, 1974, p. 50.
8. See *Staff Studies Prepared for the National Institute for Consumer Justice on Arbitration* (Washington: National Institute for Consumer Justice, 1973).
9. "How to Use Small Claims Courts," *Consumer Reports*, vol. 36, no. 10, October 1971, pp. 624–31.
10. *Ibid.*
11. *Ibid.*, p. 626.
12. See, for example, Robin Bunker et al., "A Report on the Small Claims Courts of Boston and Roxbury, Massachusetts," and "Ann Arbor Small Claims Court Study: Cases Involving Consumers," *Staff Studies Prepared for the National Institute for Consumer Justice on Small Claims Courts* (Washington: National Institute for Consumer Justice, 1973).
13. "How to Use Small Claims Courts," p. 627.
14. *Staff Studies Prepared for the National Institute for Consumer Justice on Small Claims Courts*, 1973, p. 273.
15. Caplovitz, *op. cit.*, p. 175.
16. Philip Lochner, "Distribution of No-Fee and Low Fee Legal Services by Private Attorneys," paper given at Conference on the Delivery and Distribution of Legal Services, State University of New York at Buffalo, Oct. 12, 1973.
17. Samuel J. Brakel, "Free Legal Services for the Poor—Staffed Office versus Judicare: The Client's Evaluation," *Wisconsin Law Review*, vol. 1973, no. 2, pp. 532–53.
18. *Ibid.*
19. "Counsel for the Poor Consumer: The Storefront Perspective," in Carol Hecht Katz (ed.), *The Law and the Low Income Consumer* (New York: Project on Social Welfare Law, New York University School of Law, 1968), p. 333.
20. National Legal Aid and Defenders Association, *1971 Statistics of Legal Assistance Work in the United States and Canada* (Chicago: National Legal Aid and Defenders Association, 1972); includes Puerto Rico.
21. Brakel, *op. cit.*, p. 540.
22. "Counsel for the Poor Consumer: The Storefront Perspective," p. 338.
23. "Translating Sympathy for Deceived Consumers into Effective Programs for Protection," *University of Pennsylvania Law Review*, vol. 114, no. 3, January 1966, pp. 395–450.

24. *Ibid.*, p. 432, quoting a letter from Maurice E. Hunt, Field Representative, Consumer Protection, Antitrust and Public Service Division, State of Michigan.
25. Robert S. Powell, Jr., Murray Gendzel, and Allan Zask, *The New Jersey Office of Consumer Protection: A Promise Unfulfilled* (Princeton, N.J.: Center for Analysis of Public Issues, 1970), pp. 54–55.
26. Nathaniel Sheppard, Jr., "Few Prescription-Drug Prices Posted Here, despite New Law," *New York Times*, Sept. 23, 1973, p. 53.
27. Philip G. Schrag, *Counsel for the Deceived* (New York: Pantheon Books, 1972), p. 185.
28. *Ibid.*, p. 186.
29. *Ibid.*, p. 187.
30. Donald B. King, *Consumer Protection Experiments in Sweden* (South Hackensack, N.J.: Fred B. Rothman and Company, 1974).
31. A second exception may be the Food and Drug Administration.
32. Mary Gardiner Jones, "Deception in the Marketplace of the Poor: The Role of the Federal Trade Commission," in Frederick D. Sturdivant (ed.), *The Ghetto Marketplace* (New York: The Free Press, 1969), p. 248.
33. Quoted in Daniel Jay Baum, "The Federal Trade Commission and the War on Poverty," *UCLA Law Review*, vol. 14, no. 4, May 1967, pp. 1087–1088.
34. Edward F. Cox, Robert C. Fellmeth, and John E. Schultz, *The Nader Report on the Federal Trade Commission* (New York: Grove Press, Inc., 1969).
35. *Report of the ABA Commission to Study the Federal Trade Commission* (New York: American Bar Association, 1969).
36. "Profile Bread's Well-buttered Correction," *Consumer Reports*, February 1972, pp. 64–5.
37. A negative option plan is where the consumer must take an action (e.g., mail in a card) only if he *doesn't* want the product or service.
38. Federal Trade Commission, *Report on District of Columbia Consumer Protection Program* (Washington: Government Printing Office, June 1968), pp. 1–2.
39. *Ibid.*, p. 3.
40. *Ibid.*, p. 16.
41. Baum, *op. cit.*, pp. 1081–2, quoting a letter to Senator Harrison Williams from Chairman Paul Rand Dixon of the FTC.
42. Federal Trade Commission, *op. cit.*, pp. 17–8.
43. National Consumer Law Center, "Statutory Limitations on the HIDC Doctrine," unpublished paper from the National Consumer Law Center, Boston, September 1972.
44. "Translating Sympathy for Deceived Consumers into Effective Programs for Protection," p. 416. For a general comment on defenses to HIDC, see Neil O. Littlefield, "Good Faith Purchase of Consumer Paper: The Failure

of the Subjective Test," *Southern California Law Review*, vol. 39, no. 1, 1966, pp. 63–4.

45. National Commission on Consumer Finance, *Consumer Credit in the United States* (Washington: Government Printing Office, December 1972), p. 126.
46. George Gordin, Jr., "Statement of George Gordin, Jr., to the Law Revision Commission Hearings on the Uniform Consumer Credit Code," New York, Jan. 12, 1972, unpublished paper, National Consumer Law Center, 1972.
47. Wisconsin Statute 421.101–427.105 (1971).
48. Jeffrey Davis, "Legislative Restriction of Creditor Powers and Remedies: A Case Study of the Negotiation and Drafting of the Wisconsin Consumer Act," *Michigan Law Review*, vol. 72, no. 1, November 1973, pp. 1–83.
49. National Consumer Law Center, *National Consumer Act*, final first draft, official text with comments, January 1970.
50. Federal Trade Commission, *1971 Annual Report* (Washington: Government Printing Office, 1972).
51. *Ibid.*
52. *Report of the ABA Commission to Study the Federal Trade Commission*, *op. cit.*, p. 53.
53. *Ibid.*, p. 58.
54. Cox, Fellmeth, and Schultz, *op. cit.*, pp. 65–67.
55. *Company Leadership in Consumer Affairs: Fulfilling Consumers Rights* (Washington: Chamber of Commerce of the United States, 1972).
56. John A. Prestbo, "Seller Beware: Consumer Proposals Bring about Changes in American Business," *Wall Street Journal*, June 21, 1971.
57. Rosenthal, *op. cit.*
58. Donald F. Turner, "Consumer Protection by Private Joint Action," in Ralph M. Gaedeke and Warren W. Etcheson (eds.), *Consumerism: Viewpoints from Business, Government and the Public Interest* (San Francisco: Canfield Press, 1972), p. 313.
59. Louis L. Stern, "Consumer Protection via Self-Regulation," *Journal of Marketing*, vol. 35, July 1971, pp. 49–50.
60. *Ibid.*
61. "Abuse of Process: Sewer Service," *Columbia Journal of Law and Social Problems*, vol. 3, June 1967, p. 25.
62. "Counsel for the Poor Consumer: The Storefront Perspective," p. 334.
63. *Walker v. Sheldon*, 10 N.Y. 2d 401, 223 N.Y.S. 2d 488 (1961).
64. Schrag, *op. cit.*, p. 199.
65. Brakel, *op. cit.*, p. 535.
66. Hearings before the Consumer Subcommittee of the Senate Committee on Commerce, 91st Congress, 2d Session, Mar. 18, 1970, pp. 285–301.
67. *Consumer Protection Act of 1970*, Hearings before the Committee on the Judiciary, United States Senate, 91st Congress, 2d Session (Washington: Government Printing Office, 1970), p. 74.

68. *Ibid.*, p. 37.
69. *Snyder v. Harris*, 394 U.S. 322, 89 S.Ct. 1053, 22 L. Ed. 2d, 319 (1969), rehearing denied 394 U.S. 1025, 89 S.Ct. 1162, 23 L. Ed. 2d 50 (1969).
70. George Gordin, Jr., "Tentative Summary of Center Survey of the Status as of January 1, 1970, of Consumer Class Actions in the 50 States," unpublished paper from the National Consumer Law Center, Boston, April 23, 1971, pp. 2–3.
71. *Consumer Protection Act of 1970*, Hearings before the Committee on the Judiciary.
72. *Ibid.*, p. 59.

13. Some Concluding Observations

THE PRECEDING CHAPTERS have described in graphic detail an often neglected but very serious problem facing our society's most disadvantaged members. The chapters have shown that the disadvantaged, because of who they are, where they shop, and what some marketers are willing to do to them, constantly obtain much less value for their bitterly fought-for incomes in the urban marketplace than does the rest of society. More formally, these chapters have sought to establish three major theses:

1. That there are important groups of individuals who, because of their income, age, race, or language difficulties, are disadvantaged in the urban marketplace
2. That this disadvantage stems from three interacting causes—the disadvantaged consumer's own characteristics, the inefficient and depressed market structure he must patronize, and, finally, the exploitative marketing practices of merchants who operate businesses in disadvantaged areas
3. That because of the interacting character of these causes, improvement in the market position of the disadvantaged consumer requires improvement in the three causal areas simultaneously

The preceding chapters have presented most of the available evidence supporting these assertions. The present chapter attempts to draw together some of the major threads of this material by first returning to the major issues raised in the opening chapter and then considering the difficult but unavoidable questions of what it all means and what it implies for future action.

Major Themes

This volume began by noting that the present interest in the disadvantaged consumer grows largely out of the middle-class public's growing involvement in consumerism. And, indeed, largely as a result of that involvement there have been a number of significant developments that have in greater or lesser degree benefited the disadvantaged:

New laws have been passed in various parts of the country mandating unit pricing, eliminating holder-in-due-course protection, mandating interest rate disclosures, etc.

New studies have been conducted by federal agencies (e.g., the FTC study of District of Columbia retail installment practices), private interest groups (e.g., the ABA study of the FTC), and academics (e.g., the various food-pricing studies reported in Chapter 8)

New agencies have been formed to help protect the consumer's interests, as in the formation of the Consumer Product Safety Commission and of several new state consumer protection agencies (such as that in New Jersey)

New powers have been given to, or taken by, existing agencies, as in the passage of "little FTC" state laws giving new powers to states' attorneys general and in the FTC's new willingness to require corrective advertising in serious cases of deception

Chapter 1 also raised the question of whether the fact that consumerism has caught the fancy of the middle class is really in the long-run interest of disadvantaged consumers. While it is obviously difficult to predict the future course of any movement as young as the present wave of consumerism or, indeed, to characterize its present status,[1] there appear to me to be a number of serious *potential dangers* for the disadvantaged in this "relocation" of the movement. Five such dangers seem paramount:

A danger of misunderstanding
A danger of haste
A danger of excessive reliance on consumer protection legislation
A danger of excessive antibusiness sentiment
A danger of overprotectiveness

THE DANGER OF MISUNDERSTANDING

One of the most serious potential dangers for the disadvantaged inherent in the relocation of the consumerism movement is that middle-class consumers may well see the problems of the disadvantaged as different from their own only in *degree* and not in *kind*. It is, of course, true that disadvantaged consumers' problems *are* in many respects different only in degree: they have less income, less education, larger families, and so on. It has been a major theme of this analysis, however, that the problems of the disadvantaged are often significantly different in kind. Among the more important examples of such differences noted earlier are the following:

1. Unstable incomes. The poor lack a critical piece of planning information available to the nonpoor, namely how great their incomes will be over the near term and how steadily those incomes will flow in. The lack of such information, it was suggested, seems to be a major contributor to, among other things, excessive indebtedness on the part of some disadvantaged consumers. Unstable incomes also affect the disadvantaged by affording them credit ratings that drive them into the hands of high-cost exploitative merchants and lenders. This fact and the unstable incomes themselves lead them more often to default on their debts and incur the trauma and penalties this process entails.

2. Racial discrimination. Minority racial status has serious direct and indirect effects on black consumers even when income is controlled. Middle-class blacks are just as likely as poor blacks to be charged higher interest rates, to be subjected to exploitation, and to meet with harassment when they are delinquent on their debts. Many blacks, both poor and nonpoor, feel they will not be treated politely by white merchants, that they will be suspected of shoplifting or of being "easy marks." These feelings, in turn, seem to sharply restrict their mobility and thus their access to outlets with wider assortments, lower prices, and the like. Their allocations to product categories seem to be affected by racial discrimination; some categories they can't or won't spend in, others they overspend in, possibly as a reaction to the psychological scarring of race.

3. Inner city residence. A major consequence of race, and of poverty for poor whites, is that it forces the disadvantaged to live in areas where the outlets they can patronize are small, run down, understocked, overpriced, and badly managed and where the transportation system makes it difficult to escape. Many of these areas are declining economically at a pace that frightens off the mass merchandisers and well-managed outlets the disadvantaged so desperately need. The resulting lack of competition, along with disadvantaged people's lower mobility, creates ideal conditions for merchant exploitation.

4. Different shopping goals. Finally, disadvantaged status apparently leads to different shopping goals. Many of the poor seem quite willing—even anxious—to patronize small, local high-cost neighborhood outlets and door-to-door peddlers partly because of the important social gratifications it brings. Also, blacks, and Spanish–Americans, often choose local outlets because of their interest in supporting minority enterprise, because of their different tastes and preferences, because of differences in languages, and so on.

These qualitative differences set the disadvantaged consumer apart in important ways from the rest of society. And when these differences are considered along with major quantitative differences—lower incomes and education, smaller homes, larger families, fewer automobiles—one is tempted to speculate on whether there exists what might be called a distinctive *disadvantaged consumer subculture*. While this speculation wrenches a major assumption of the anthropological concept of culture (that is, the concern here is essentially with only *one* set of behaviors of members of the culture), it does seem useful in emphasizing the self-contained, symbiotic relationships among the principal participants of the disadvantaged market system—the consumers, the merchants, the financial institutions, and the courts. These relationships are highly self-reinforcing and circular, as the following four examples from our analyses indicate:

1. The powerlessness of the disadvantaged encourages some merchants and finance companies to exploit them and to use the courts to enforce their frequently deceptive contracts. This behavior, in turn, only makes the disadvantaged feel *more* powerless.
2. Merchants in declining disadvantaged areas cut back their assortments and raise their prices in order to improve their profits, which only drives more consumers away and increases the remaining consumers' frustration with the system, which in turn only accelerates the merchants' loss of profits and aggravation so that they further cut their assortments, postpone repairs and other capital improvements, raise prices, and so on.
3. The consumers' unstable job histories force them to patronize high-cost, less ethical merchants and lenders, who often draw up contractual relationships that lead the consumers eventually to default, garnishment, and bankruptcy, which, to complete the cycle, only worsens their job instability.
4. The reluctance of the disadvantaged to appear in court stems in part from their feelings that they cannot win. This then encourages process servers to practice "sewer service." When the disadvantaged do not appear in court, the judge may take this as expected behavior and not inquire into the nature of service. This further encourages the sewer server. And when a consumer receives notice of judgment from a court proceeding of which he was never aware, he becomes even more convinced that the courts connive with the merchants and the finance companies to defeat him.

And so it goes.

If this conception of a disadvantaged consumer subculture has validity, there are two immediate implications for public policy. First, the conception suggests that the *main* problem for external change agents who wish to improve the disadvantaged consumer's lot is to somehow intervene to break the convoluted cycles that bind the system together to the disadvantaged consumer's disadvantage. We shall return to this point later.

Second, the conception suggests that there is a serious danger that those who are not members of the self-reinforcing, largely separate subculture will frequently misunderstand the behavior and problems of the subculture's members. Evidence of the very real nature of this danger was noted in Chapter 3 in the work of Louise Richards.[2] As noted there, Ms. Richards, in her analysis of the consumption problems of the poor, concluded that they did not follow "the recommended rules of financial management." Yet it has been suggested throughout this volume that much of the consumption behavior of the disadvantaged does, on the contrary, follow the best rules possible, *given their circumstances.* Thus those applying middle class standards may be seriously misunderstanding the true nature of the disadvantaged consumer's problems and may be seriously disqualifying themselves from offering and/or implementing effective solutions. That the consumer movement is moving toward an understanding of the special character of the problems of disadvantaged consumers is indicated in this 1973 policy resolution of the Consumer Federation of America:

> Low income consumers have *special problems* and directly suffer when their problems are not considered by consumer groups and consumer protection councils. They have *special economic problems* and special health and nutritional needs. We urge all consumer groups to solicit membership among the poor and to develop programs to alleviate their problems. We also urge all public agencies involved in consumer protection and services to insure meaningful participation of low income consumers in policy and program development and to include representatives of the poor on all citizen advisory groups. *We further urge that low income consumers be involved in CFA efforts to expand consumer organizations and that special funds be made available by CFA affiliates*—particularly labor, credit unions and cooperatives —*to organize low income consumers* [emphasis added].[3]

THE DANGER OF HASTE

If action must follow understanding, then it is important to assess how much it is we really know with enough certainty to be reasonably confident of the success of our public policy recommendations. To act in haste without a substantial degree of certainty would do the disadvantaged a serious disservice and might well widen the gap between the subculture and the rest of society. Certainly, there is the risk that undue haste would create its own self-reinforcing cycle: the disadvantaged consumer mistrusts and is reluctant to communicate with external change agents (consumerists, academics, politicians); the latter act too fast on imperfect understanding; the job is botched; the disadvantaged consumer is further convinced he was right not to trust "the man," "the establishment," whatever; future communication is hindered; misunderstanding becomes worse; and so on. The analysis here has shown that there are a number of critical areas in which our present understanding is very weak. Some of these are the following:

1. Despite our more or less confident speculations in earlier sections about the extent to which disadvantaged consumers try to maximize the value of their consumer dollars the issue is far from well documented. Yet the true state of affairs has important implications for policy recommendations in this area. If, as speculated here, the disadvantaged try to be as rational as they can given their circumstances (low and unstable incomes, racial discrimination, atomistic local marketplaces, and so on), then the problem essentially is one of *changing those circumstances*. If, on the other hand, the disadvantaged in the main really make little effort to be rational—to plan or to make decisions carefully even when they have little information—because of apathy, impulsive personal traits, and so on, or if they fail to carry through their plans for these reasons or because of unrealistic fears and trepidations about their marketplace encounters, then the answer would lie more in the direction of trying to make them *as individuals* more planful and self-confident.

2. Despite some evidence reported by the National Commission on Consumer Finance,[4] it is not altogether clear what would happen to the behavior of customers, retailers, or financial institutions if holder-in-due-course protection were to be eliminated. Certainly the benefits in protecting some disadvantaged from burdensome costs when they are exploited are substantial. On the other hand, there is no empirical evidence as to what will happen to the *supply* and *cost* of retail credit and consumer loans to *all* disadvantaged consumers in the event of "holder's" elimination. Surely, those advocating the abolition of HIDC should at least consider whether their course would be best for disadvantaged consumers if the supply of credit dwindled and/or its cost went up and whether either or both of these would in fact eventuate.

3. The analysis here has also noted at length the considerable present ignorance about the consequences of alternative income supplement programs for the disadvantaged as consumers. Certainly, based on Chapter 10, the consequences in general are likely to be quite favorable to the disadvantaged consumer, particularly in the long-run. As will be suggested below, income supplement programs may well be the *best* long-run strategy in this area. Unfortunately, however, it is not known specifically what the consequences will be in the *short run* and, in particular, whether the programs need to be accompanied by other policy actions such as increased consumer education, accelerated business development in disadvantaged areas, or greater control of exploitation. At least one can conclude that to assume that income supplements will cure all disadvantaged consumer problems in the short run both ignores the tripartite nature of those problems and severely overstates our present level of knowledge.

4. As noted in the introductory remarks of Chapter 1, almost all the data presently available on disadvantaged consumers refer to the *urban* disadvantaged consumer. Clearly, if effective and just national policies are to be developed, say with respect to holder in due course or small claims courts,

one must first ask whether such policies will also meet the needs and problems of those disadvantaged people who reside in small towns and rural areas. For example, it must be asked whether more extensive use of small claims courts in rural areas would help consumers or in fact would simply make it considerably easier for rural sellers to use the courts as debt collection agencies as effectively as did the District of Columbia low-income area retailers described in Chapter 9. Until more is known about whether the patterns and problems described in this volume also apply to those residing outside the urban setting, policy choices run the risk of being overly hasty and of making some consumers worse, not better, off.

THE DANGER OF EXCESSIVE RELIANCE ON LEGISLATION

There is, in this writer's judgment, a serious danger that the consumer movement will place undue reliance on the power of central government consumer protection legislation to improve the disadvantaged consumer's position where it can. This approach, if emphasized, would fly directly in the face of perhaps the single most important conceptual contribution of this volume, namely that *the consumer problems of the disadvantaged stem from three interacting sources and solutions therefore must proceed along three fronts simultaneously*. In some respects, as will be noted below, direct legal control of merchant exploitation may *not* be the most important of these fronts.

There are several natural reasons why a movement populated primarily by part-time activists (full-time housewives, scientists, academicians, and so on), is likely to focus heavily on the passage of consumer protection legislation:

1. Passage of specific legislation represents an easily defined goal; what you wish to achieve can be easily described. In contrast, it is much harder to establish a clear comprehensive definition of goals with respect to, say, disadvantaged consumer education or inner city market development.

2. The human target of the consumerists' activity is definable, manageable, and accessible. There is a specific set of committees, staff members, and legislators that must be influenced if certain legislation is to be passed. On the other hand, it is often difficult to determine to whom one directs efforts at consumer education or at developing a credit union or consumer cooperative.

3. There is a measurable point of success; the legislation is passed without compromise, passed with compromise, or not passed. There is a point at which a consumerist can feel he or she has been successful. On the other hand, how does one *really* know if a consumer education program works or if a strengthened Better Business Bureau is having real impact?

4. There is a limited time horizon. It is much easier to become "psyched

up" to fight for some improvement in the disadvantaged consumer's lot if one knows that one's efforts must have an outcome before the end of a given legislative term. It may be much harder for part-time activists to face the problems of starting a consumer co-op or trying to entice a discount house back into the ghetto, since these can seem like undertakings with endless futures.

5. The individual's contributions can be made from time to time, often at his convenience. With legislative initiatives what is involved is attendance at meetings from time to time, periodic letter-writing campaigns, perhaps phone calls or visits to assemblymen or senators, and the like. Again by contrast, efforts at breaking into the circular patterns in the disadvantaged consumer subculture frequently require full-time involvement. For example, developing consumer education programs or monitoring a consumer protection agency must be seen by the prospective consumer activist as a full-time job.

While consumer groups have broadened their tactics and their legislative focuses lately, it is still fair to say that consumer protection legislation is their major interest. This means that many sets of programs attacking the central sources of difficulty for disadvantaged consumers are outside the ordinary range of interests of most consumer groups. As has been pointed out here, disadvantaged consumers' problems are at least as much the result of their income and job situations, racial discrimination, and scarcity of minority entrepreneurs as they are the result of exploitation. If consumerists are to be truly effective with respect to the full range of disadvantaged consumer problems, they must *balance* their interest in consumer protection legislation with interests in programs that would seek to:

Supplement the incomes of the poor.
Increase their employment stability.
End racial segregation in housing.
Rapidly extend black business ownership.

The 1973 policy resolutions of the Consumer Federation of America do in fact contain a recommendation supporting "a guaranteed annual income equal to the modest but adequate family income budget" but they ignore the other three issues.[5]

THE DANGER OF EXCESSIVE ANTIBUSINESS SENTIMENT

Many spokesmen for the consumer movement identify their principal targets as "the corporation," a perfidious evil that has swallowed up the individual, gained control of much of government, and diverted our national priorities. As Ralph Nader has described the growth of the movement:

> The consumer movement, which is now acknowledged as one of the most significant social movements in this century, was deceptively modest in its origins. It began on many fronts, but always concerned itself with the manifestations of corporate power which daily touched people's lives: unsafe automobiles, dangerously adulterated and filthy food, overpriced drugs, hidden credit charges and the reckless use of pesticides. These issues, taken separately, were not generally perceived to be a concerted attack against a common opponent, the nearly limitless power of big business. Even so, it was a novel approach. The previous targets of consumer protectors had been the "bad apples in the barrel," the fly-by-nights, the few who polluted the honest business atmosphere and spoiled it for legitimate businessmen. This was a myth that business, through such organizations as the Better Business Bureau, cultivated assiduously. It was, therefore, a monumental shock to the business guardians of this myth when they were exposed as the rottenest apples of all.[6]

Statements such as this have two very serious consequences. First, they have a major influence on how others view, and relate to, the consumer movement. Second, they have a major influence on movement *participants*, how they view themselves and their goals and how they relate to other groups which might help them to achieve these goals.

In the first instance, the antibusiness rhetoric tends to cause others to view the movement as *merely* antibusiness. A good example of such a view is the 1973 effort of Hustad and Pessemier to describe "the *real* consumer activist," in which they *defined* the real activist as someone holding antibusiness views.[7] Such a definition contributes significantly to the paranoia of the business community that leads to the kinds of responses noted in Chapter 1—suggestions, for example, that consumerism is a communist plot to destroy the free enterprise system. As long as businessmen hold this view they are likely to be very reluctant to debate responsibly with movement activists, to engage in what Bauer and Greyser call "the dialogue that never happens." [8] Nor are they likely to cooperate enthusiastically with the movement in achieving goals on which the two groups may well substantially agree.

In the same fashion, antibusiness rhetoric is likely to harden the movement's feelings toward business and therefore its willingness to actively seek out the cooperation of business in its programs. To some extent the movement's antibusiness feelings are related to its emphasis on consumer protection, since by definition this usually (but not always) means "protection from business." If, however, the goals of the movement are broadened beyond protection as suggested here and as in many respects is now being done, then it becomes clear that there are a number of key consumer objectives which business can be brought to share and in the accomplishment of which its cooperation is essential. With respect to the disadvantaged consumer, such goals would include:

1. Extending greater credit availability to the disadvantaged.

2. Moderating (or reducing the impact of) antiblack prejudices existing among white retail employees.
3. Providing training opportunities for prospective minority businessmen.
4. Providing purchase contracts, turn-key divestiture arrangements, management assistance, and other support to nascent minority businesses.
5. Reintroducing, where feasible, mass merchandise outlets to disadvantaged areas.
6. Assisting in consumer education programs in disadvantaged areas.

The present antibusiness mood of many in the consumer movement, therefore, constitutes a serious danger to the future consumer welfare of the disadvantaged. The middle class may feel it does not "need" business help, but as indicated throughout this volume, the disadvantaged certainly do.

THE DANGER OF OVERPROTECTIVENESS

There is a very serious danger that taking the consumer problem out of the ghetto will mean that the white middle-class leaders of the consumerism movement will *completely* dominate efforts to improve the lot of the disadvantaged. This, of course, is exactly what happened with the war on poverty. As Moynihan has noted: "The war on poverty was not declared at the behest of the poor: it was declared in their interest by persons confident of their own judgment in such matters." [9] Such an approach has a great potential weakness:

> . . . the forces . . . set in motion would operate primarily within the Negro slums of the nation's large cities. . . . However the various planning groups were made up exclusively of middle-class whites. At no time did any Negro have any role of any consequence in the drafting of the poverty program. . . . Yet it was the Negro community that was to be primarily affected. Whether Negro involvement—participation—in *this* planning process would have produced the same formula cannot be said. But it is clear to the degree that risks were involved, whites were taking them for blacks.[10]

It would be a not unexpected course of events for the white middle class to dominate efforts to improve the lot of disadvantaged consumers. On the one hand, middle-class people are more sophisticated politically, better educated, and more articulate and more often hold leadership roles outside the movement. They are also very often highly motivated to *do something* for the disadvantaged (as opposed to helping the disadvantaged do something for themselves). On the other hand, as seen in Chapters 2 and 4, the disadvantaged tend to be apathetic, alienated, suspicious of institutions, lacking in self-esteem, and without the education, articulateness, and life experiences to make their presence felt in organizations which might meet their community's needs. It would be a common scenario for them to acquiesce to middle-class domination of efforts to help them.

To let the middle class dominate these efforts would, I believe, be a serious mistake for several of the reasons enunciated by Bloomberg and Rosenstock:

1. There is "a crude correlation between the degree of participation on the part of any given segment of a community in politically relevant associations and in community decision-making roles and the extent to which the private and public agencies of the community serve the interests and meet the perceived needs of that segment."
2. ". . . effective participation by the poor on behalf of what they believe to be their own interests and needs is seen as an antidote to the derogatory view of the poor as either undeserving or self-defeating held by a majority of Americans, a view which either relieves the rest of the community of responsibility for poverty or provides a rationale for emphasizing and reinforcing the dependency of the poor."
3. ". . . the experience of power through relevant association and participation in decision-making and the concomitant development of relevant organizational and political skills have been proposed as a necessary 'therapy' for the alleged alienation of the poor, which is said to be derived from their powerlessness and in turn reinforces it in a continuing vicious circle of causation." [11] This experiencing of power may assure that in the long run the poor will be able to take over complete responsibility for their own consumer assistance initiatives.

Given the further dangers of misunderstanding, haste, excessive emphasis on consumer protection legislation, and an antibusiness stance inherent in white middle-class domination of the movement cited earlier, it would seem essential that the disadvantaged obtain maximum feasible participation in the consumerism movement if the movement is to have lasting effects on their problems. That the consumer movement has not yet been successful in obtaining such participation is implicit in the policy statement of the Consumer Federation of America cited earlier: "We further urge that low income consumers be involved in CFA efforts to expand consumer organizations and that special funds be made available by CFA affiliates . . . to organize low income consumers." [12]

Conclusions and Recommendations

If there are serious dangers inherent in the middle class taking over the major thrust of efforts to improve the disadvantaged consumer's lot, then where should this major responsibility lie? And further, what should be the major objectives and principal action strategies of these efforts over the near term? These are the questions to which we turn in this concluding section.

OBJECTIVES

Stating an objective for action programs that incorporates the principal findings of the present analysis is relatively straightforward. The goal is *to significantly increase over the long run the value the disadvantaged consumer believes he gets from his total consumption expenditures.*

"Significantly increase" defines a pragmatic orientation that recognizes that ideal states are unlikely to be achieved and that in this specific case it is not really known in detail what the ideal state would look like.

"Over the long run" defines an approach that seeks *permanent* change, that is willing to underemphasize "bandaid" programs that correct relatively unimportant, short-run symptoms, willing to undertake programs that may be painful in the short run but beneficial in the long run, and willing to risk bureaucratization for the benefit of longevity.

"Value" defines the totality of benefits the consumer derives, which, as has been seen, includes not just goods and services but safety, absence of racial prejudice, pleasant social contacts, minority ownership, etc.

"The disadvantaged consumer believes he gets" defines *whose* benefits are to be increased—not what a bureaucrat or middle-class consumer believes the disadvantaged *ought* to want, but what he really *does* want.[13]

"Total consumption expenditures" defines the costs the return from which is to be significantly improved as including not just the consumer's after-tax income but also his dissaving and not just the direct costs of goods and services but also attendant costs such as those involved in subsequent litigation.[14]

STRATEGIES

There are three basic strategies that may be adopted to achieve this objective; strategies that are labeled here the *free market strategy*, the *incentives strategy*, and the *penalties strategy*. Each has its particular role and its particular strengths and weaknesses.

THE FREE MARKET STRATEGY. This strategy essentially seeks to *remove constraints* that inhibit the disadvantaged consumer's exchanges with merchants and lenders in existing marketplaces. Included here would be tactics removing constraints on interest rates and loan policies of various financial institutions, eliminating holder-in-due-course protection, and providing greater incomes and income stability to the disadvantaged. Also included would be tactics to eliminate racial segregation in housing, to eliminate social pressures on merchants to hold down prices in poor areas, and to eliminate pressures from black development groups to keep white retail businesses out of ghetto markets.

There are a number of advantages to this strategy:

1. It does not require judgments about disadvantaged consumers' goals. It merely seeks to give them the widest possible latitude to express those goals through their market expenditures. With free mobility of consumer dollars and free entry and exit of business, this wider latitude of choice should result in a market structure and a set of merchant, lender, and court practices that would better meet disadvantaged consumers' needs whatever they might be.
2. It does not require judgments about which merchant and lender behaviors are desirable or undesirable, since freer consumers will make such choices themselves.
3. The steps needed to implement the major part of such a strategy are straightforward, since they involve obtaining necessary federal or state enabling legislation; consumers and businessmen will do the rest.
4. The results ought to be relatively rapid and require limited monitoring.
5. Except for the guaranteed income program, the cost to the various governments ought to be relatively small.

These advantages are in addition to the free market approach's philosophical appeal to a broad spectrum of the population. In practice, however, there are a number of serious stumbling blocks:

1. One keystone of the free market strategy, the income supplement program, is, as recent legislative battles have shown, not at all an easy program to introduce at the federal or state level. It will be exceedingly costly in the short run (although perhaps less costly in the long run), and its concept of doling out to the disadvantaged money for which they have not worked runs *counter* to the strategy's conservative economic appeal. While it can be argued that the concept is much more compatible with a free market ideology than, say, categorical welfare grants, it is not clear that this argument (and the costs of the program) can be "sold" to the American public and its legislative representatives for some years to come if at all.
2. Even if the income supplement program can be sold, there are a

number of groups, such as the elderly, the uneducated, the over-indebted, and the apathetic, that may not benefit as consumers from the program and indeed, as suggested in Chapter 10, may be *worse* off.

3. Black and Spanish–American minorities also may not benefit significantly from the free market strategy for another reason, namely that the major sources of their disadvantage, housing segregation and racial prejudice, are not really subject to easy manipulation, for example by legislative fiat.

Thus in sum it would appear that while an underlying long-run strategy for consumer change agents ought to be to try to free up the market for the disadvantaged and while some aspects of such a strategy can be implemented in the short run, it must be recognized that in its major dimensions the strategy may well be a very long time in paying off and so other strategies will be needed in the short run, and that it may not benefit all disadvantaged consumers (i.e., it may just benefit those who are *only* economically disadvantaged), whose problems must therefore be dealt with in some other fashion.

The incentives strategy. The two alternatives to simply freeing up the market structure involve directly meddling in market transactions. One approach is to change the incentive structure to reward desirable behavior, and the other is to impose new penalties to discourage undesirable behavior. Each approach is capable of correcting a specific subset of the problems left largely untouched in the short run by the free market strategy.

Some behaviors that might result from changes in the incentives structure are the following:

1. Consumers might be encouraged to sign up for consumer education courses by the promise of increased credit at local department stores.
2. White mass merchandisers might be lured back to disadvantaged areas by land grants, tax breaks on property or profits, low-cost insurance, and the like.
3. Merchants might be encouraged to train minority businessmen if training grants were available.
4. Lenders might more readily loan to disadvantaged consumers and businessmen if loan guarantees were available.
5. Minority businessmen might be encouraged to enter business and develop appropriate managerial skills if the proper incentives were available.
6. Merchants might be encouraged to put contracts in Spanish or in large type if they could be convinced significant increases in patronage would result.
7. Consumers might well start up more food co-ops if overheads were covered and advice given by outside agencies.

The incentives approach is central to Theodore Cross's recommendations about black capitalism,[15] and it has value in a number of other areas. Further, it is based upon a positivist view of mankind, that people will respond in socially desirable ways if it is at least marginally profitable to do so. Since the strategy envisions a more or less permanent change in the reward structure, its effects ought to be relatively permanent and ought in theory to require relatively little monitoring. On the other hand, the approach has three major difficulties:

First, at least in the short run, it will require substantial direct annual expenditures of what are usually public funds, expenditures that would not be required in carrying out much of the free market strategy (except for income supplement programs) and that would be much lower in programs involving a penalties strategy. It will therefore be difficult to get incentive strategy programs past legislatures pressed for funds for other purposes and facing the present rapidly rising inflation. Even if passed, year-to-year variations in funding levels can seriously diminish the programs' incentive value. And finally, if passed, the funding *in practice* is likely to involve a substantial amount of bureaucratic control, which, again, may or may not seriously diminish the intended value of the programs.

A second problem, mentioned earlier, is that incentive programs require judgments about what the disadvantaged want and what behaviors are desirable. These judgments require in many cases better research data than we possess at present. And even if it were known what changes were desirable, it is not often altogether clear what form and level of incentives will lead to the desired results.

A third difficulty is that not all behaviors nor all businessmen respond to incentives, again running the risk of leaving some consumers either no better off or worse off because of the programs.

THE PENALTIES STRATEGY. Some behaviors that cannot be eliminated by freer markets or by restructured incentives may respond to new and/or stronger penalties. Such penalties could include both stronger legal sanctions, e.g., stricter laws and tougher fines, and much more rigorous enforcement by the public and private agencies involved, as well as the kind of organized consumer pressure that threatens, and if necessary carries out, boycotts against merchants behaving in undesirable ways.

The key to the success of the penalties strategy, as has already been seen, is *enforcement*, which means convincing public agencies as well as private groups such as the Better Business Bureau that laws and regulations are not self-enforcing. This is particularly the case for disadvantaged areas, where neither consumers nor competitors can be counted on to generate the complaints that could make a penalties strategy involving limited enforcement work. The enforcement agencies must be of sufficient scope to take on a substantial monitoring and complaint-generating function themselves. This of course significantly increases the cost of this strategy. And it should be pointed out that even with substantial enforcement only limited results should be expected from a penalties strategy, since it would be focused primarily on exploitative merchants and lenders in disadvantaged areas, a group which, given no change in the underlying incentives to exploit, can be expected to keep several steps ahead of most regulations and most regulators.

LEADERSHIP, COORDINATION, AND PERMANENCE

How, then, is the combination of strategies to be implemented? The answer lies in part in what the relative emphasis will be among the strategies. It has been suggested above that:

1. The major components of the free market strategy, income supplements and an end to residential segregation, in all likelihood will be a long time in coming. Also, securing their implementation is not primarily a consumer problem, although consumer groups have an important supporting role to play in pointing out the consequences of these important social policies for consumption behavior as well as for the more typically mentioned goals of increased employment, education, racial harmony, and the like.
2. The secondary components of the free market strategy—eliminating HIDC, removing loan restrictions, and so on—require further investigation, possibly some experimentation, and careful monitoring once they are implemented, since it is not now clear what their effects will be.
3. The free market and incentives strategies must be coordinated to minimize the former's potential negative consequences and to implement changes, such as changes in market structure, that the free market strategy is unlikely to achieve in the short run.
4. The penalties strategy may have relatively little effect if its programs do not contain very substantial increases in agency monitoring activities.

This summary in turn suggests that implementation of long-term programs to permanently restructure the disadvantaged consumer's relationships with his marketplace must (1) involve substantial coordination among the three complementary strategies but (2) rely heavily on an incentives strategy and (3) involve significant research, experimentation, and monitoring activities.

With respect to implementation, I am reluctant to adopt the social scientist's favorite remedy in social policy areas, the "let's create another government agency" recommendation. However, the present analysis leads inexorably to this conclusion. An *agency* must be established for the following reasons:

1. If change is to be permanent, it must be institutionalized.
2. If change is to be effective, it must be coordinated.
3. If an incentives strategy is the key to change, this necessarily will involve the accumulation, distribution, and monitoring of substantial amounts of incentive funds.
4. If an incentives strategy is to work, it must involve a significant research and experimentation component.

A *government* agency is preferable because:

1. Much of the coordination will have to be with existing government agencies.
2. A government agency is more likely (although, of course, not certain) to be able to enlist the cooperation of such diverse groups involved in solutions in this area as consumerists, the majority business establishment, minority economic developers, and legal aid specialists.
3. The often criticized longevity of government agencies and their vaunted abilities to protect their budgets and their bureaucracies in the midst of the worst political storms *can* engender the kind of long-term perspective that is necessary if one is serious about permanently breaking up something as deep-seated and tenacious as an entire subculture. (Suggestions will be offered below about coping with the dangers of lethargy and unimaginativeness that bureaucratic longevity *also* brings.)

If it is agreed that a government agency is the appropriate vehicle for achieving the goals set forth in this chapter, the remaining question is whether this government agency ought to be at the federal or state level. There is, of course, a natural tendency among social scientists and consumer activists in matters of broad social policy change to turn for solutions automatically to the sometimes more foresighted and innovative leadership available at the federal level. Indeed, it has been a major goal of the consumer movement and its legislative champions for some 10 years to establish a high-level federal agency, preferably at the Cabinet level, that would give consumers "muscle" equal to that of labor, business, and farmers in federal deliberations. Supporters of this position point out that 33 of the 35 principal agencies of the federal government are now concerned with consumer issues. The existing Office of Consumer Affairs in the White House—previously headed by Esther Peterson and Betty Furness and now by Virginia Knauer—has only advisory and some relatively weak coordinating responsibilities with respect to these agencies. What Congressman Rosenthal and others would like is "a new central consumer agency, by statute, with real powers and far-reaching responsibilities." [16]

While these consumerist proposals are laudable, they have in recent years come to focus, as the movement often does, on the limited problem of consumer protection. As the 1973 policy resolutions of the Consumer Federation of America recommend:

> We endorse creation of an independent consumer protection agency with full powers of advocacy and capable of representing consumers before all government agencies and the courts. The new agency must have full powers of investigation, subpoena and intervention in formal and informal proceedings. It must have full access to judicial review and maximum independence from the Executive Branch.[17]

And while intervention of the consumerist view in governmental policy making and day-to-day decision making—frequently in opposition to the view of government or business—is an important component of the proposal outlined in this chapter, it misses the central point. What is needed is not a *voice* in the deliberations of various existing governmental agencies, but new, coordinated programs that will *fundamentally restructure* the pattern of relationships between disadvantaged consumers and the marketplace. An agency is needed that can control resources rather than discuss them, that can get businessmen's cooperation rather than argue with them, that can directly bring about changes in the priorities and modes of operation of government consumer protection agencies and the courts rather than merely represent consumers in *existing* operations.

Not only should the type of agency be different, so should its governmental level. It is this writer's judgment that several of the major conclusions of the present analysis point most strongly to lodging the new agency at the *state* level:

1. Most of the free market tactics that can be implemented immediately—eliminating HIDC, changing loaning regulations, and expanding Judicare—are state-level matters.
2. Most of the major elements of the penalties strategy involve the control of local behaviors of *intra*state firms, behaviors over which most federal agencies believe they lack jurisdiction.
3. Many parts of the incentives strategy—consumer education in the schools, business taxation policy in inner city areas, and insurance and banking regulations—are also state matters.
4. Many of the business groups—department stores, Better Business Bureaus, food chains—which must be involved in carrying out the various strategies are also state (or at most regionally) based, as are many of the interested consumer groups.
5. Where programs that must be coordinated are at different levels, it is more likely that the federal government would give up some control of its programs to the state than vice versa.
6. The institutional and legal structure that must be coordinated at the state level varies so greatly between states that it would be very difficult to coordinate these very different structures in some central location.

7. More generally, the mood of the public and its legislative representatives at the present time seems to be swinging toward pushing funding and control of major programs back to the state level; certainly one could expect that the public and federal legislators will now be very reluctant to undertake another major federal incentives program in an area so closely related to the less-than-successful recent war on poverty.[18]
8. The more local the agency, the easier it should be to involve the substantial numbers of disadvantaged consumers in the program planning and implementation that are necessary if (*a*) the programs are to be based on a full understanding of and sympathy with the disadvantaged consumers' own goals and values and (*b*) disadvantaged consumers are to begin to rebuild confidence in their abilities to control their own destinies.
9. Focus at the state level would permit the consumerist groups that will have principal responsibility for lobbying for the present proposals (*a*) to concentrate their limited resources on very specific small targets, (*b*) to concentrate these resources on the more innovative and consumer-minded states where adoption is most likely, such states then to serve as demonstration projects for the remaining, more reluctant states; and (*c*) to discuss these proposals on their merits without having to spend inordinant amounts of time countering criticisms of "massive governmental spending."
10. Positioning programs at the state level would permit the variety of experimentation in program structure and content that it has been said is essential in an area where present comprehension of precise causes and effects is, at times, very weak.

THE STATE MARKET DEVELOPMENT AGENCY

It is beyond the scope of this work to specify in any detail what the proposed agency should look like. In my judgment, the agency's "clients" should be restricted to disadvantaged consumers, since it may from time to time be necessary to ask for special powers which would only be acceptable if the agency had such a special responsibility. The agency's basic mandate should be that it take whatever steps are necessary to remove the handicapping effects of (1) disadvantaged consumer characteristics, (2) atomistic, depressed, and inefficient market structures in disadvantaged areas, and (3) the practices of exploitative merchants and lenders in those areas. Because of the broad character of this mandate and its emphasis, not on consumer protection, but on a fundamental restructuring of the disadvantaged consumer's relationship with his marketplace, it is suggested that the proposed agency be called something like the *State Market Development Agency*.

At minimum, the agency would be given the following permanent responsibilities:

1. To recommend legislation that will benefit disadvantaged consumers both to the governor and to the legislature
2. To intervene in the deliberations of other agencies on behalf of disadvantaged consumers (conceivably, this could be broadened to include *all* consumers as suggested in the CFA proposal)
3. To make recommendations to other agencies as to how they might better serve disadvantaged consumers' interests
4. To conduct research on basic disadvantaged consumer problems and on proposed solutions either on its own or through outside contracting agencies
5. In cooperation with affected agencies, to conduct experiments on programs that give promise of substantially benefiting disadvantaged consumers

As noted earlier, the agency should be required to include in its deliberations representatives of the disadvantaged, minority economic developers, the majority business community, and other groups whose welfare will be affected by, or whose cooperation is needed in, the carrying out of the agency's programs.

Whether the agency ought to take on full-time operating responsibility for the programs it initiates and whether it ought to take over any existing operating responsibilities from other agencies are problematic. While the resolution of this issue will inevitably vary by states, the fact that the agency's clientele will be only one part of that served by existing agencies suggests that attempts to secure such operating responsibilities may create serious jurisdictional problems and possibly substantial intragovernmental resistance to the agency's establishment in the first place.

If the agency will not have many operating responsibilities, it ought then to conceive of itself as a *change agent*, to see its responsibilities as advising, goading, demonstrating, and proving ways in which the disadvantaged consumer's lot can be improved by existing agencies. Such a stance should not only minimize inter-agency conflict but also help to maximize the agency's imaginativeness and flexibility and increase its ability to attract creative and dedicated staff.

RESEARCH ALTERNATIVES

Finally, it should be noted that not all responsibilities for restructuring the disadvantaged consumer's market relationships need fall to the state level. One such responsibility that might be centralized is the basic research function. Many questions have been raised in this volume whose answers are critical to policy alternatives in *every* state. It would seem desirable, therefore, to establish what might be called a National Consumer Policy Research Center, say at some major university, to investigate some of these questions. Several of the more pressing issues unresolved by the present analysis are the following:

1. How rational are disadvantaged consumers? Who among them seem to be more rational, and what leads to this difference? Why are those who are less planful and seem less diligent about trying to achieve their goals this way? Indeed, what *is* a workable definition of rationality in this context?
2. Why do the poor use credit? Do they know they will pay extra costs, both in higher cash prices and higher interest rates? What is the role of hope in the use of credit? More basically, what is the role of income instability on credit use, and how does it enter the decision-making process?
3. What explains the very high credit use of higher-income blacks and those who have moved out of disadvantaged areas? How is this behavior related to conspicuous or compensatory consumption? Is this behavior at all related to blacks' use of name brands?
4. Under what, if any, circumstances is it appropriate to suggest that blacks seek to emulate whites in their consumption behavior? Is it valid or useful to consider this a distortion of behavior? Is black emulation of whites changing in response to the growth of black pride? If so, how?
5. What is the relative influence of the ignorance, constraints, and preference hypotheses proposed to explain disadvantaged consumers' price-minimizing behavior in Chapter 3?
6. How do businesses make decisions to enter or leave a disadvantaged market, and how can these decisions best be influenced?
7. What is the distribution of disadvantaged areas across the three stages of market development outlined in the market dynamics model of Chapter 6?
8. How do the prejudices of white employees of retail and financial firms affect the way they treat disadvantaged consumers, and how can this be changed?
9. What are the *cost* justifications of higher interest rates charged to the poor and to blacks? To what extent are these higher rates a function of higher costs and to what extent a function of disadvantaged consumers' presumed more inelastic demand for credit?

Conclusion

Structures and plans for institutions are, of course, still not enough. To make a significant and permanent change in the market plight of America's disadvantaged consumers, the nation also needs vigorous leadership and a quantum increase in the public's willingness to tackle these very serious problems. This willingness is, in turn, a function of the public's awareness of the seriousness and complexity of the issues. The present volume is designed to heighten this awareness of seriousness and to give order to some of the complexity. But also, because of the programmatic alternatives it suggests, the volume more importantly is intended to move the society materially forward in its search for effective and lasting solutions to this all too frequently neglected major social problem.

Notes

1. I shall beg the question of trying to define "consumerist." One operational definition might be "anyone affiliated with a group belonging to the Consumer Federation of America." Nadel, however, points out that there are in fact several different kinds of consumerists with different kinds of functions. See Mark V. Nadel, *The Politics of Consumer Protection* (Indianapolis: The Bobbs-Merrill Co., Inc., 1971).
2. Louise C. Richards, "Consumer Practices of the Poor," in Lola M. Irelan (ed.), *Low-Income Life Styles* (Washington: U.S. Department of Health, Education, and Welfare, 1966), p. 82.
3. *Policy Resolutions* (Washington: Consumer Federation of America, July 21, 1973), p. 8. These resolutions represent the most comprehensive position of the largest consumer movement group. There are other groups and individuals that differ with CFA's position on specific issues.
4. National Commission on Consumer Finance, *Consumer Credit in the United States* (Washington: Government Printing Office, 1972), p. 126.
5. *Policy Resolutions.*
6. Ralph Nader (ed.), *The Consumer and Corporate Accountability* (New York: Harcourt Brace Jovanovich, Inc., 1973), p. 2.
7. Thomas P. Hustad and Edgar A. Pessemier, "Will the Real Consumer Activist Please Stand Up: An Examination of Consumers' Opinions about Marketing Practices," *Journal of Marketing Research*, vol. 10, Aug. 1973, pp. 319–34.
8. Raymond A. Bauer and Stephen A. Greyser, "The Dialogue That Never Happens," *Harvard Business Review*, vol. 45, Nov.–Dec. 1967, pp. 2 ff.
9. Daniel P. Moynihan, *Maximum Feasible Misunderstanding* (New York: The Free Press, 1969), p. 25.
10. *Ibid.*, pp. 98–9.
11. Warner Bloomberg, Jr., and Florence W. Rosenstock, "Who Can Activate the Poor: One Assessment of 'Maximum Feasible Participation,'" paper prepared for American Sociological Association Meetings, San Francisco, Aug. 29, 1967, pp. 4–5.

12. *Policy Resolutions.*
13. It is recognized that "success" might be achieved by manipulating disadvantaged consumers' wants rather than changing their environmental circumstances. It is assumed that change agents would not take this approach. The point, however, emphasizes the fact that a lack of real change may be masked by inadvertent (and undesirable) change in consumer wants.
14. In more elaborate analyses such costs would undoubtedly include opportunity costs such as those involved in the use of potential work time for court appearances.
15. Theodore L. Cross, *Black Capitalism: Strategy for Business in the Ghetto* (New York: Atheneum Publishers, 1969).
16. Hon. Benjamin S. Rosenthal, "Consumer Protection," *Congressional Record,* Nov. 4, 1969, p. E9332.
17. *Policy Resolutions.*
18. See, for example, Daniel P. Moynihan, *op. cit.*

INDEXES

Name Index

Subject Index